THE LETTERS OF THE THIRD
VISCOUNT PALMERSTON
TO LAURENCE AND
ELIZABETH SULIVAN
1804–1863

THE LETTERS OF THE THIRD VISCOUNT PALMERSTON TO LAURENCE AND ELIZABETH SULIVAN 1804–1863

edited by

KENNETH BOURNE

CAMDEN FOURTH SERIES
Volume 23

LONDON
OFFICES OF THE ROYAL HISTORICAL SOCIETY
UNIVERSITY COLLEGE LONDON,
GOWER STREET, WC 1
1979

ISBN: 0 901050 55 5

Printed in Great Britain by Butler & Tanner Ltd
Frome and London

CONTENTS

PREFACE

THE provenance of the Palmerston Letters printed in this volume is described in the Introduction, p. 27, and in the Note on Sources. In the list of Abbreviations will be found brief descriptions of the other principal sources consulted. I owe most to Laurence Sulivan's descendants, who so generously gave me permission to reproduce the large majority of the Palmerston Letters. A few others are printed by the kind permission of the Broadlands Trustees. I am grateful also, for the use made of other materials, to the Duke of Devonshire and the Chatsworth Trustees, the late Earl of Powis, the late Earl Spencer, the Earl of Harewood, the Earl of Malmesbury and the History of Parliament Trust, Lord Hatherton, Lord Lambton, Major J. C. Blackett-Ord, Mr George Howard, Capt. R. Neall, M.B.E., and the Trustees of the Goodwood Estate and of the National Library of Scotland. I must also acknowledge the gracious permission of Her Majesty the Queen to make use of material from the Royal Archives. Finally I must thank Dr Ian Roy, Assistant Literary Director, for his great care and kindness in the preparation of this volume, and the London School of Economics for the generous support it has provided.

December 1978   KENNETH BOURNE

ABBREVIATIONS

Unless otherwise stated the place of publication is London

Add. MSS.	Additional Manuscripts in the British Library
Airlie	*Lady Palmerston and Her Times*, by Mabell, Countess of Airlie, 2 vols., 1922
Alumni Cantab.	*Alumni Cantabrigienses*, ed. J. A. Venn, Part II, 6 vols., Cambridge, 1940–54
Arbuthnot Journal	*The Journal of Mrs Arbuthnot 1820–1832*, ed. F. Bamford and the Duke of Wellington, 2 vols., 1950
Ashley	*The Life of Henry John Temple, Viscount Palmerston*, by E. Ashley, 2 vols., 1879
B.P.	Broadlands Papers: the political papers of the 3rd Viscount Palmerston temporarily deposited in the National Register of Archives, Quality Court, Chancery Lane, London
B.P.W.	Broadlands Papers, Winchester: the Palmerston family and estate papers deposited in the Hampshire County Record Office in Winchester
Brougham Papers	The papers of Henry Brougham in the D. M. S. Watson Library, University College, London
Broughton	*Recollections of a Long Life by Lord Broughton (John Cam Hobhouse) with additional extracts from his private diaries*, ed. Lady Dorchester, 6 vols., 1909–11
Broughton Papers	The papers of John Cam Hobhouse, Baron Broughton, in Add. MSS.
Bulwer & Ashley, i & ii	*The Life of Henry John Temple, Viscount Palmerston: with Selections from his Diaries and Correspondence*, by H. L. Bulwer, 2 vols., 1870
Bulwer & Ashley, iii	*The Life of Henry John Temple, Viscount Palmerston: with Selections from his Correspondence*, vol. iii, by H. L. Bulwer (Lord Dalling), ed. E. Ashley, 1874

Bulwer & Ashley, iv & v   *The Life of Henry John Temple, Viscount Palmerston: 1846–1865. With Selections from his Speeches and Correspondence*, by E. Ashley, 2 vols., 1876

Chatsworth Papers   The papers of the 6th Duke of Devonshire at Chatsworth

C.H.P.   The papers of the Earls of Carlisle at Castle Howard

Connell   *Portrait of a Whig Peer compiled from the papers of the Second Viscount Palmerston 1739–1802*, by B. Connell, 1957

Creevey Papers   *The Creevey Papers. A Selection from the Correspondence & Diaries of the Late Thomas Creevey, M.P. Born 1768—Died 1838*, ed. Sir H. Maxwell, 2 vols., 1904

Ellice Papers   The papers of Edward Ellice the Elder in the National Library of Scotland

Fitzherbert Papers   The Papers of Sir William Fitzherbert, 3rd Bart of Tissington, in the Derbyshire County Record Office, Matlock

George IV   *The Letters of King George IV 1812–1830*, ed. A. Aspinall, 3 vols., Cambridge, 1938

Glenbervie Diaries   *The Diaries of Sylvester Douglas (Lord Glenbervie)*, ed. F. Bickley, 2 vols., 1928

Goderich   *'Prosperity' Robinson. The Life of Viscount Goderich 1782–1859*, by W. D. Jones, 1967

Goodwood Papers   The papers of the 5th Duke of Richmond in the West Sussex County Record Office, Chichester

Greville Memoirs   *The Greville Memoirs 1814–1860*, ed. L. Strachey and R. Fulford, 8 vols., 1938

Grey Papers   The papers of the 2nd and 3rd Earls Grey in the Department of Palaeography, University of Durham

Guedalla   *Palmerston*, by P. Guedalla, 1926

Hardwicke Papers   The papers of the Earls of Hardwicke and the Yorke family in Add. MSS.

Hatherton Papers   The papers of E. J. Littleton, Baron Hatherton, in the Staffordshire County Record Office, Stafford

Herries   *Memoir of John Charles Herries*, by E. Herries, 2 vols., 1880

Liverpool Papers	The papers of the 2nd Earl of Liverpool in Add. MSS.
Lorne	*Viscount Palmerston, K.G.*, by the Marquess of Lorne, 2nd ed., 1892
Lowry Cole Papers	The Papers of the Lowry Cole family in the Public Record Office, London
Malmesbury Diaries	*Diaries and Correspondence of James Harris, First Earl of Malmesbury*, ed. the 3rd Earl of Malmesbury, 4 vols., 1844
Malmesbury Papers	Transcripts made by the late Professor A. Aspinall from the papers of the 1st Earl of Malmesbury, now in the possession of the History of Parliament Trust
Minto Papers	The papers of the 1st Earl of Minto in the National Library of Scotland
Namier & Brooke	*The History of Parliament. The House of Commons 1754–1790*, by L. B. Namier and J. Brooke, 3 vols., 1964
Palmerston's Journals	*Selections from Private Journals of Tours in France in 1815 and 1818*, by Viscount Palmerston, 1871
P.O.W.	*The Correspondence of George, Prince of Wales 1770–1812*, ed. A. Aspinall, 8 vols., 1963–71
Pryme	*Autobiographic Recollections of George Pryme, Esq. M.A.*, ed. by his daughter, Cambridge, 1870
RA	Royal Archives, Windsor
Ripon	*Life of the First Marquess of Ripon*, by L. Wolf, 2 vols., 1921
Sedgwick	*The Life and Letters of the Reverend Adam Sedgwick*, ed. J. W. Clark and T. McK. Hughes, 2 vols., Cambridge, 1890
Shee Papers	The papers of Sir George Shee, 2nd Bart, formerly in the National Register of Archives and now in the British Library
Smith Letters	*The Letters of Sydney Smith*, ed. N. C. Smith, 2 vols., Oxford, 1953
S.P.	The Sulivan family papers remaining in private hands
Spencer Papers	The papers of the 3rd Earl Spencer at Althorp, Northampton

Stratford Canning	*Life of Stratford Canning, Lord Stratford de Redcliffe*, by S. Lane-Poole, 2 vols., 1888
Teignmouth	*Reminiscences of Many Years*, by Lord Teignmouth, 2 vols., Edinburgh, 1878
W.N.D.	*Despatches, Correspondence and Memoranda of Field Marshal Arthur Duke of Wellington*, ed. by his son, 8 vols., 1867–80
Wright	*Alma Mater: or, Seven Years at the University of Cambridge*, by a Trinity-Man [John Martin Frederick Wright], 2 vols., 1827

INTRODUCTION

T HE career of Henry John Temple, third and last Viscount Palmerston (1784–1865), is almost unrivalled in English politics. He was a member of Parliament for nearly sixty years and a minister of the Crown for almost fifty; only two British statesmen in the nineteenth and twentieth centuries, Gladstone and Churchill, have sat longer in the Commons, and none has been minister so long. Palmerston's bold hand and lucid style are justly famous; yet, apart from the many semi-official letters he wrote to diplomats abroad, we have very little of a private nature from his pen in the first half of his ministerial career. Consequently the details of his early political life and the development of his character and beliefs remain obscure; and we lack much shrewd commentary from a high vantage-point in an important period of British history.

For this deficiency accident and design must share the responsibility. In his boyhood Harry Temple wrote frequent, and detailed, letters to his parents from school and college. But his father died in 1802 and his mother in 1805, only as his political career was beginning; and few of his letters to his principal guardian, the first Earl of Malmesbury, have so far come to light. His relations with his two surviving sisters, Frances ('Fanny': 1786–1838) and Elizabeth ('Lilly': 1790–1837),[1] were very affectionate but their correspondence has comparatively little political interest. On the other hand, his brother William (1788–1856) was abroad on diplomatic service during most of his adult life and Palmerston's letters to him are therefore more numerous and informative.[2] But while they figure quite prominently in the material used by the official biographers, Bulwer and Ashley, there is about them a somewhat formal and distinctly cautious tone. In this respect they do not compare with those written by Palmerston's mistress to her brother, who was also in the diplomatic service. Lady Cowper's letters to Fred Lamb (1782–1853: Baron Beauvale from 1839 and third, and last, Viscount Melbourne from 1848) more than make up for lack of dates and punctuation with racy political gossip and court scandal.[3] By contrast, the substantial

---

[1] Another sister, Mary, born 15 Jan. 1789, did not survive infancy, succumbing to the after effects of inoculation against smallpox on 17 May 1791. The second Viscount's first wife had died on 1 June 1769, a few days after giving birth to a stillborn child. (Connell, pp. 94, 165, 195, 206 and 213.) It is extraordinary that, over fifty years later, Debrett should have been permitted to go on recording Elizabeth as this child, 'born 16 May 1769'.

[2] B.P., G.C./TE nos. 137–372. There are also a few detached items in B.P.W.

[3] Many of the more interesting passages in those letters have been omitted from *The*

number of Palmerston's letters to her that survive among the Broadlands Papers in Winchester are for the most part very dull indeed. Only the half dozen or so deriving from the period before their marriage in December 1839 are really interesting. Since their intimate friendship seems to have begun as early as 1808 or 1809,[4] there may perhaps be rather more of the same period among the inaccessible Lamb Papers in the British Library. But these too can hardly be very informative about politics. For shortly before they married Lady Cowper is supposed to have asked Palmerston how it happened that he was for so long a time in a comparatively minor official position.[5]

Palmerston's response to this inquiry was the famous 'Autobiographical Sketch' printed in full and with only a couple of changes by Bulwer.[6] Covering the period down to November 1830, this is an important and often cited sketch. But it lacks immediacy and, naturally enough, is not entirely reliable, though probably as much so as Palmerston's memory and prejudices allowed. His surviving pocket diaries and journals are also very disappointing. Of the former there is nearly a complete run from 1847 to 1864: those for 1850 and 1856 alone are missing. But for the earlier period there are only those for 1818, 1819, 1829, 1833 (from June only), 1835 and 1836.[7] These, moreover, contain mainly notes about appointments and assignations and have very few political or other comments. Palmerston tended to be more discursive only when covering trips abroad, such as in Ireland in 1841 and Germany in 1844.[8] There are also rather more extensive journals of his European travels in 1815, 1816 and 1818 than have appeared in print. They seem to have been discovered among his papers only after the first volume of his official biography had been printed. Bulwer was strongly opposed to their being published, arguing that their anti-French bias would do Palmerston no credit. The essayist Abraham Hayward, who had known Palmerston well in the latter part of his life and published a stylish notice of him,[9] argued against this that people would easily appreciate how a generation of

---

Letters of Lady Palmerston, edited by T. Lever, 1957, and from *In Whig Society 1775–1818*, 1921, and *Lady Palmerston and Her Times*, 1922, edited by Mabell, Countess of Airlie. The dates in both cases are also unreliable. The originals in B.P.W. are now freely accessible; others, in the Lamb Papers in the British Library (Add. MSS. 45546–56 and 45911), will remain closed until 1980.

[4] Sir George Leveson Gower and I. Palmer, eds., *Hary-O. The Letters of Lady Harriet Cavendish, 1796–1809*, 1940, p. 307.

[5] Ashley, i. 10, n. 1.

[6] Bulwer & Ashley, i. 367–83; *cf.* B.P./D no. 26.

[7] B.P./D nos. 3–24.

[8] B.P.W. nos. 1989 and 1988. There are also a notebook of memoranda concerning his visit to Ireland in 1826 (B.P./D no. 25) and two very dull journals of a journey from London to Edinburgh in the autumn of 1800 and a tour of the Highlands in the early summer of 1803 (B.P.W. nos. 1943 and 1945).

[9] *Fraser's Magazine*, lxxvii, Nov. 1865.

war had influenced the writer and suggested that Bulwer was merely jealous of anything being produced which he had overlooked in the biography.[10] So, with a few editorial amendments and omissions and rather more mistakes, there appeared in 1871 *Selections from Private Journals of Tours in France in 1815 and 1818*. The journal for 1816, however, remained unnoticed and unprinted.[11]

Of political journals there are only two, each covering a disappointingly brief period.[12] The first extends only from June to December 1806 and contains very perfunctory and jejune remarks about the major political and martial events of the day. Characteristically Palmerston in 1812 appended the following note: 'The opinions and remarks contained in this volume are the exact expressions of my feelings at the moment when they were written. Upon many points, however, relative both to persons and things, cooler reflection, and a few more years' observation and experience, have, as is natural, very much altered my sentiments.'[13] The second political journal, covering the period 9 March 1828–24 January 1829, for the first two months of which Palmerston was in the Cabinet, is much less cautious and therefore far from dull or uniformative.

Both the political diaries were made available to Bulwer, who printed virtually the whole of them as well as the autobiographical sketch complete in the *Life*. Yet, as he complained to Palmerston's family,[14] they fill only short stretches of time in the large gaps made by the relative paucity of Palmerston's letters covering his early political career. One feels all the more surprised, therefore, that neither he nor his successor, Ashley, made more use than they did of Palmerston's correspondence with his friend and brother-in-law, Laurence Sulivan.

Although Palmerston in later years would fondly recollect his happy days at Harrow (1795–1800) and Edinburgh (1800–3), it was at Cambridge that he made his only really lifelong friends among men. When he was travelling with his parents in Italy he had made friends of the youngest Bessborough children, Caroline Ponsonby (who married William Lamb) and William Francis Ponsonby (afterwards first Baron de Mauley), and he continued his friendship with William and his elder brother Frederick in the same house at Harrow. An ancient Harrovian informed Bulwer in 1870 that Palmerston had also 'messed together' with Althorp, afterwards third Earl Spencer,

[10] Undated correspondence, *c.* 1870, between Henry Bulwer, Abraham Hayward and Palmerston's heir, William Cowper-Temple, B.P.W.
[11] 'Journal of Tour in France Italy & Swizzerland in 1816', B.P.W.
[12] 'Journal Historical and Political Commenced June 1806', B.P./D no. 1; 'Journal from Mar. 1828', B.P./D no. 2.
[13] Bulwer & Ashley, i. 24 note.
[14] Undated correspondence, *c.* 1870, B.P.W.

and Duncannon, the eldest Ponsonby boy and afterwards fourth Earl of Bessborough.[15] But neither they nor Lord Burghersh (afterwards eleventh Earl of Westmorland), whom Palmerston himself later mentioned as a friend at Harrow,[16] figures much in Palmerston's letters home. In them, rather, one finds—in addition to a passing report of Lord Haddo, his rival, the future Earl of Aberdeen[17]—Lord Royston (the Earl of Hardwicke's heir), William Bruère (the son of an Indian official of the same name), John Madocks (the son of a noted amateur actor who committed suicide on the failure of Watier's in 1806), Philip Sydney Pierrepont (the fourth and youngest son of Viscount Newark, afterwards first Earl Manvers) and the two young Ponsonby boys. Royston preceded Palmerston to Cambridge but died soon after; Bruère turned up both in Edinburgh and in Cambridge but disappeared thereafter. Madocks, perhaps, became too good a friend of Byron's, for Byron reputedly hated Palmerston. But there is no trace in the Broadlands Papers of any lasting friendship even with the closest of Palmerston's old Harrovian friends. Both Ponsonbys seem to have drifted away, the elder into the army and the younger into a quiet and prosperous married life. Pierrepont joined Harry Temple in Edinburgh in the winter of 1801 and in Cambridge in 1803; but he too soon passed out of sight.

After Henry Temple had passed his first and probably rather lonely few months in Edinburgh he was joined in January 1801 by the son of a blue-stocking friend of his mother's, Francis Cholmeley of Brandsby near York, who as a Catholic would have little future at an English university. The following winter there also arrived three old Harrovians he knew, Pierrepont, Thomas Orde-Powlett and Charles Henry Rich. Rich was also the eldest son of a Hampshire neighbour of the Palmerstons, Sir Charles Bostock Rich, first Baronet of Shirley House; but Harry did not like him much. On the other hand, Powlett, who was the younger son of Lord Bolton and a contemporary of William Temple's at Harrow, he thought 'one of the greatest quizzes' he had ever seen. Powlett lived in Edinburgh as one of the pupils of the witty Sydney Smith and there was some notion that he would be joined there by an even earlier acquaintance of Henry Temple's, Francis George Hare (1786–1842).[18] Henry Temple had met Francis

[15] Bulwer & Ashley, i. p. x.
[16] Palmerston to 12th Earl of Westmorland, 18 Oct. 1859, Westmorland Papers, Perkins Library, Duke University.
[17] Henry Temple to the 2nd Viscount Palmerston, 13 June 1800, B.P.W.
[18] Bulwer's informant may possibly have been correct in identifying one of Palmerston's fags at Harrow as a son of Earl Poulett (Bulwer & Ashley, i. p. x); but it was certainly Lord Bolton's son in Edinburgh. Curiously neither Orde-Powlett nor Hare is mentioned by Sydney Smith's biographers though the facts are clearly stated in Henry Temple's letters to his father of 22 Mar. and 6 Nov. 1801, B.P.W. See also *Smith Letters*, i. 67, n. 2.

Hare, the youngest of four brothers who were all to become famous for their learning, at the age of four or five and this unlikely pair are supposed to have kept up their friendship until Hare's death in 1842. Hare spent most of his later life in Italy and had only occasional meetings with Palmerston. But it is fascinating to think what might have been their influence upon each other had Hare been able to find room with Sydney Smith instead of proceeding as he did to Aberdeen.

Palmerston did make several new and interesting acquaintances in Edinburgh, but most of them, like Lord Henry Petty (afterwards third Marquess of Lansdowne), Henry Brougham and Sydney Smith himself, were politically antipathetic to him.[19] So was Gilbert Elliot (afterwards second Earl of Minto), the eldest son of his parents' closest friends. Gilbert was two years older than Henry and although they saw a good deal of each other, it was only during the years of Melbourne's premiership that politics made close allies of them. In Edinburgh, moreover, Henry Temple lived at the opposite end of the town from the Mintos, with Professor Dugald Stewart. There, he just missed John William Ward (future Earl of Dudley and also Foreign Secretary), and found instead as fellow-student and lodger Richard Barré Dunning, second Baron Ashburton (1782–1823). Ashburton was the only surviving child of the famous politician, John Dunning, who had died in 1783 when his son was still a baby and had left the boy to be sadly smothered by his mother's care. But young Ashburton eventually broke free at last by marrying his professor's niece. The Stewarts by no means approved and the affair seems also to have put a strain on Palmerston's patience (nos. 13, 48). But in any case, although they kept on reasonably good terms, Ashburton was not the sort of man who could ever have made a close friend of Palmerston. For he was as eccentric in mind as he was unprepossessing in person and at eighteen was already displaying many of the signs of the madness which overtook and killed him as early as 1823.

When Palmerston went up to Cambridge in October 1803 he was, therefore, at the age of twenty, still without any really close friends. But at St John's, which he had chosen in part because of the large number of Harrovians who went there, he found 'remarkably good society at present ... the best in the University', he thought. Among them he picked out: Lord Henry Seymour Moore (1774–1825: younger son of the first Marquess of Drogheda and father of the third); Lord John FitzRoy (1785–1856: youngest son of the third Duke of Grafton); the Hon. Edward Clive (1785–1848: grandson of Clive of India;

[19] At a 'hoppin' to celebrate the birthday of his first daughter, Sydney Smith revealed to Palmerston why, in the search to give her a less commonplace name than Mary or Sarah, he had called her 'Saba' from a reference in Psalm 72: it brought to mind, Smith said, 'Arabian valleys, and cinnamon groves, and palm trees'. (Palmerston to Frances Temple, 2 Feb. 1803, B.P.W.; cf. Smith Letters, i. 61.)

succeeded his father as second Earl of Powis in 1839); and two Percys, Hugh (1784–1856: third son of the first Earl of Beverley and afterwards Bishop of Carlisle), and his cousin, Hugh, Lord Percy (1785–1847: succeeded his father as third Duke of Northumberland in 1817).[20] According to the diarist, Thomas Raikes, Lord Henry Moore, though possessing 'a certain irascibility of temper', was 'extremely fascinating when he pleased' and 'one of the most amiable and agreeable companions ... his manners ... the very type of a high-bred gentleman'.[21] But he took his degree in 1804 and is not known to have had any particular contact with Palmerston thereafter.

Lord John FitzRoy, the only Harrovian in the group, moved across the road to Trinity soon after Palmerston arrived at St John's. Palmerston, however, formed some sort of friendship with another old Harrovian, Thomas Knox (1788–1872: grandson of Viscount Northland; succeeded his father as second Earl of Ranfurly in 1840), and later in his first term was joined at St John's by two more, Pierrepont and Edward Berens Blackburn. Pierrepont, now grown rather fat, was a migrant from Christ Church, Oxford;[22] Blackburn (c. 1784–1839) was the fourth and youngest son of John Blackburn of Bush-Hill, Middlesex. It was Blackburn who addressed a sort of official farewell to Palmerston in March 1806, probably as President of the Harrow Club.[23] But Palmerston's particular friends were to be found rather in a small Saturday club at St John's. It met every Saturday in one of the members' rooms to dine at four and spend the rest of the evening together. When Palmerston reported its establishment, early in his second year at Cambridge, he remarked that they had some thought of following the example of the Beefsteak in London and limiting each person to two bottles of wine, though on 'extraordinary occasions a little excess' might be permitted. The founder members included, besides Palmerston, only one Harrovian, Knox (though Pierrepont may have been admitted later). The others were Clive, the two Percys and three fellow-commoners, Cludde, Shee and Sulivan.[24]

Edward Cludde (ob. 1840) was the son of a Shropshire squire from Orleton, near Clive's English house, Walcot. George Shee (1784–1870) had been born in India, the eldest son of an Irishman of the same name. George Shee the elder (1754–1825) had followed a profit-

[20] Palmerston to his mother, 26 Oct. 1803, B.P.W. He also mentioned Lord Altamont (1788–1845: succeeded Palmerston's neighbour in Ireland as 2nd Marquess of Sligo in 1809). But Altamont was a student of Jesus and unless he made an unrecorded migration must merely have been visiting St John's when Palmerston arrived.
[21] *A Portion of the Journal Kept by Thomas Raikes, Esq. from 1831 to 1847*, 1856–7, ii. 115 (but Raikes confuses the family relationships).
[22] Palmerston to Elizabeth Temple, 11 Feb. 1804, B.P.W.
[23] Blackburn to Palmerston, 13 Mar. 1806, B.P.W.; *Reminiscences of Henry Angelo*, 1830, ii. 162.
[24] Palmerston to Frances Temple, 10 Nov. 1804, B.P.W.

able career in India, where he was a friend of William Hickey, with another career in the public service in Ireland, where he became an intimate of the Irish Secretary, Thomas Pelham, afterwards second Earl of Chichester and one of Palmerston's guardians. He was created a baronet in 1794 and further rewarded for voting for the Act of Union in 1801 by being made Receiver-General of Customs and a Privy Councillor.[25] In 1800–3 he was also undersecretary to Pelham at the Home Office and in 1806–7 to Windham at the Colonial Office. He was described in 1803 as 'a vulgar-looking and most superlative dull fellow',[26] but he had money enough, however much he grudged it,[27] to enter his son as a fellow-commoner at St John's.

Laurence Sulivan (1783–1866) had a very similar background and was, at first sight, hardly less surprising as an intimate friend of a most fastidious viscount. His grandfather, also named Laurence (1713–86), had made a fortune in India and was said to be one of the East India Company's ablest rulers. But the elder Laurence lost a good part of his fortune after his return to England in 1753 in his speculations and battles (principally with Robert Clive) as a Director (Chairman in 1758–9, 1760–2 and 1781–2) and as a parliamentary candidate for Ashburton. In 1778 he sent his son Stephen (1742–1821) to recoup the family fortunes in India. Stephen, having begun as Persian Secretary, was prevented by his father's enemies from exploiting his appointment as Resident at Tanjore. But Warren Hastings rescued Laurence Sulivan with a gift of £10,000 and made his son Judge-Advocate General in Bengal and his own acting private

---

[25] M. MacDonagh, *The Viceroy's Post-Bag. Correspondence Hitherto Unpublished of the Earl of Hardwicke First Lord Lieutenant of Ireland after the Union*, 1904, pp. 49 and 203–6.

[26] C. K. Sharpe to his sister, 11 Feb. 1803, A. Allardyce, ed., *Letters from and to Charles Kirkpatrick Sharpe, Esq.*, 1838, i. 158 (Sir George Shee the elder is confused with his son in the footnote).

[27] The correspondence of George Shee, jnr, with his father makes it clear there were frequent disagreements about money. In a letter of 6 Feb. 1803 he explained: 'My acquaintance is not very extensive I admit, but then my intimacies are comparatively numerous, & of them a great majority are remarkable either for *rank* or *abilities*.' His 'nominal' income was, at £300 per annum, at least £50, and in two cases as much as £100, less than his colleagues'. He also insisted that while their expenses might be £100 more than those of pensioners, fellow-commoners did not study any less hard. Their expensively bought privileges, on the other hand, he had complained in another letter of 25 Mar. 1802, were sometimes under attack. One privilege had been that of not being obliged to attend college chapel more than four times a week. But two or three years earlier the number had been increased to five at a poorly attended meeting of the fellows and more recently 'a newly appointed Dean [Daniel Bayley], a man most notorious and disliked in the College (even among the Fellows) from officiousness & desire of innovations' had obtained an increase to seven for fellow-commoners and four for noblemen. Since there was no change for pensioners this meant a comparative, as well as an absolute reduction in the privileges of others and the noblemen had successfully resisted the change. The best the fellow-commoners could secure, however, was a short postponement and afterwards an unofficial understanding that absences would be excused more frequently than in the past. (Shee Papers; *cf.* G. H. Francis, ed., *Opinions and Policy of the Right Honourable Viscount Palmerston*, 1852, p. 264.)

secretary. While in India Stephen married Elizabeth Davis, the widow of a reputed slave-trading sea captain named Forde, and his only surviving child, Laurence, was born in Calcutta on 7 January 1783. Stephen Sulivan seems then to have returned to England, his son Laurence attending school in Hackney and eventually living with Dugald Stewart in Edinburgh. Laurence left Edinburgh before Palmerston arrived, but Ashburton had known him and dubbed him 'Lazy Laurence'. He was admitted as a pensioner at St John's on 4 July 1800 and as a fellow-commoner on 2 October 1801.[28]

At the formation of the Saturday Club Palmerston had promised himself that it would be 'a very pleasant thing, ... very agreeable while at College, and ... an additional tye between us afterwards'.[29] Cludde, Knox and even Pierrepont were before many years had passed to have, if anything, only a tenuous connection with Palmerston. In several cases, however, that 'tye' even formed a marriage knot. In 1811 Sulivan married Palmerston's younger sister, Elizabeth; in 1817 Lord Percy married Clive's younger sister. Clive himself married outside the circle but his fourth son married Cludde's only child.

The Sulivans, Percys and Clives seem to have maintained long-lasting friendships among themselves and with other Johnian connections. In his early years in particular Palmerston was also often to be found among them, visiting Powis and Walcot or Alnwick and Kielder (nos. 11, 12, 28, 30). He also patently enjoyed frequent visits to his old college, for the Commencement Ball in June (nos. 27, 28, 54) and the Feast of St John's between Christmas and New Year (nos. 92, 98, 125, 148, 198). He was inordinately fond of dancing (no. 5) and probably as fond of the common-room nuts and turkey-pie as he charged Sulivan with being (no. 98). But these Cambridge visits had a great deal to do with politics, and politics severely tested his closer friendships. Among the Johnians only Sulivan, Shee and to a creditable extent Clive survived the test.

Palmerston's life at Cambridge had been touched by politics from the very first. There were fewer radicals or even liberals at St John's than at Trinity and, probably, that had been one of the reasons for his family's choice. But he certainly did not avoid controversy. Instead the first club he seems to have joined in November 1803 was a debating society. Having, for reasons that are not known, been denied participation in the famous Speculative at Edinburgh and restricted

[28] L. S. Sutherland, *The East India Company in Eighteenth-Century Politics*, Oxford, 1952, *passim*, and especially pp. 50, 58–63, 192, 284 and 349; Namier & Brooke, iii. 508–11; *Alumni Cantab.*; Lady Minto to Minto, 30 Mar. 1812, Minto Papers IE/41; Laurence Sulivan, jnr, to Sir Henry Fitzherbert, 10 May 1844, Fitzherbert Papers; Dugald Stewart to [Stephen Sulivan], 9 Dec. 1799, S.P.; Ashburton to Palmerston, 10 Nov. 1803, B.P.W.

[29] Palmerston to Elizabeth Temple, 11 Feb. 1804, B.P.W.

instead to the puerile domestic imitations arranged by Professor Stewart in his own house, Palmerston was delighted to find a debating club already in existence at Cambridge. It was 'quite private', possibly even a 'secret' society, since the university authorities disapproved of political discussion among the students in war-time.[30] Palmerston usually refers to it in his letters as the Fusty. The meaning of the term is unknown but it may have had some connection with a story told by Palmerston's father about the House of Commons once having been adjourned, in May 1792, on account of the smoke produced from a pair of 'fustian breeches' which had caught fire.[31] If so, it was probably a private nickname, since from the many coincidences of names of members and subjects of debate, it seems to have been that more commonly known, in emulation of its model in Edinburgh, as the Speculative.

A year or two before Palmerston's time in Cambridge, two future politicians from Magdalene, Charles Grant (later Baron Glenelg) and his brother Robert, had been leading members of the Speculative. And a couple of years after Palmerston had gone down there were also one or two King's men, Stratford Canning and, probably, his friend Thomas Rennell.[32] But in Palmerston's time the membership seems to have been drawn exclusively from St John's and Trinity. Who the members were in his first year is not known. Professor Pryme talked of there being twenty members meeting once a week in term-time in his 'early days' at Cambridge. Pryme took his degree in 1803 but for a few years afterwards he led an undecided existence between Cambridge scholarship and London law and the others he names—all Trinity men like himself save one, who was from King's— belong to a later period.[33]

Whatever the desired number of members, at the beginning of Palmerston's second year it was 'rather diminished'; there were only six in addition to himself. One, called Brown, is not precisely identified and there was no-one likely of that name among the noblemen and fellow-commoners to whom membership seems to have been restricted.[34] The other Johnians were Shee, Sulivan and Palmerston's 'cousin Raikes'.[35] There was then a fellow of the college, Richard

[30] Palmerston to his mother, 15 Nov. 1803, B.P.W.   [31] Connell, pp. 258–9.
[32] The diary of J. C. Hobhouse, 26 Jan. 1832, Broughton Papers, Add. MS. 56556; Stratford Canning, i. 25 and 27–8.   [33] Pryme, p. 117.
[34] Dominick Browne (afterwards 1st Baron Oranmore and Browne: 1787–1860) in a letter to Palmerston on 16 May 1855 (B.P., G.C./OR no. 1) recalled his student days in such a manner as strongly to suggest that he was not only a member of Palmerston's 'set' but probably also of the Fusty. However he was not admitted a fellow-commoner at St John's until July 1806 and he talks distinctly in his letter of being an undergraduate there when Palmerston was a graduate. He was really a contemporary of William Temple whom he recollects as a member along with Palmerston, the 1st Earl of Ellenborough and Michael Bruce.
[35] Palmerston to his mother, 1 Nov. 1804, B.P.W.

Raikes (1743–1823) who was married to Lady Palmerston's aunt or cousin, Ann Mee; but Palmerston's expression refers rather to Richard Raikes's nephew Henry (1782–1854), the younger brother of the diarist. After leaving Cambridge Henry Raikes travelled in Greece with Aberdeen, who had also been at St John's but is never mentioned by Palmerston since he had left the college before his old enemy from Harrow went up. 'Facetious Raikes', as Palmerston called his cousin on his return from Greece (no. 28), later wrote some rather tedious books, but gained an entry in the *D.N.B.* as a divine. The two Trinity men were Henry Goulburn (1784–1856), who became Peel's friend and Chancellor of the Exchequer, and Gerard Thomas Noel (1782–1851), whose elder brother was afterwards created Earl of Gainsborough. In their early years in Parliament, Goulburn and Palmerston mixed a good deal together and were both members of a small and select group of enthusiastic young Tories.[36] Eventually, however, their political courses diverged and all the intimacy between them utterly disappeared. Noel became Palmerston's vicar at Romsey from 1840 until his death in 1851. He devoted much of his time in Romsey to 'restoring' the Abbey Church. Palmerston tried to keep him on the right lines, telling him he was not sure that all the proposed work would be a genuine improvement and refusing to subscribe for any more 'embellishments' until the very considerable church rates were applied to putting the building in a proper state of repair (nos. 316, 317). It is clear, indeed, that he found his vicar rather tiresome.

In the course of 1805 two new names made fleeting appearances in Palmerston's reports about the Fusty. But 'Frazer', whoever he was, is mentioned only once and William Douglas never seems to have taken up his place at Trinity. This was a pity since Douglas, and possibly Frazer as well, had been in the Speculative at Edinburgh (nos. 7, 9).[37] In May, however, there were three new recruits from Trinity: J. C. Hobhouse (1786–1869), who became Lord Broughton;

---

[36] For the 'Alfred Set', see *Goderich*, pp. 30–3. But the identification of the Marquess Wellesley as a member is surely an error. The Marquess belonged to the wrong House of Parliament and the wrong generation. Goulburn's unpublished autobiography (Goulburn Papers, Surrey County Record Office, Kingston-upon-Thames) seems rather to say 'Mr Wellesley'. The Marquess's eldest, illegitimate son, Richard Wellesley (c. 1787–1831) was returned M.P. for Queenborough on 1 June 1810. Sir George Shee, 1st Bart, was 'co-manager' of the Alfred (Lord Hertford to Shee, May 1811, Shee Papers).

[37] Sulivan to Palmerston, 20 Feb. 1805, S.P. William Douglas, the son of James Douglas of Orchardton, Kirkcudbrightshire, was admitted to the Edinburgh Speculative on 28 Feb. 1804 and to Trinity on 12 Oct. 1804. But it is doubted that he ever resided at Cambridge. He was admitted to Lincoln's Inn on 20 June 1806 and later became a member of the Scottish Faculty of Advocates. (*Alumni Cantab.*; *History of the Speculative Society of Edinburgh from its Institution in MDCCLXIV*, Edinburgh, 1845, p. 235.)

Henry Pepys (1783–1860), who became Bishop of Worcester; and J. F. Pollock (1783–1870), who became Peel's Attorney-General and a baronet (no. 9).

Perhaps in the debating society, as in so many other things, Trinity was already overtaking St John's. For Sulivan and Shee both left Cambridge in the summer of 1805 and though they came back from time to time for meetings and debates, Palmerston had to rely in the following session on Clive as his faithful lieutenant ('Achates').[38] However, he soon recruited at least one new Johnian in the person of Michael Bruce (1787–1861), the Etonian son of an East Indian banker, but 'a staunch Foxite' (no. 14). Soon Palmerston was immersed again in a fierce debate on the 'Revolution of 1788' (*sic*); 'I was a furious Jacobite', he reported.[39] No wonder that others should have tried to find out what was going on. In the Broadlands Papers there is an item addressed to Bruce and endorsed by Palmerston: 'Latin lines by W. Bankes [of Trinity] at Cambridge upon his being caught listening at the door of the Speculative Society 1805.'[40]

Evidently, and in spite of the strength of Trinity's representation, Palmerston had become the dominating figure, perhaps even 'President', as was in 1807 another Johnian, Edward Law (afterwards first Earl of Ellenborough).[41] According to Hobhouse's recollection, the Fusty met in Palmerston's rooms, usually on a Wednesday.[42] As at Edinburgh, the subjects for debate were usually written up beforehand by the principal 'speaker' and read out aloud at the meeting. Palmerston himself prepared five such essays, each of them preserved along with his Edinburgh pieces among the family papers and under their author's cautionary endorsement: 'N.B. These Essays were written to set off to the best advantage a given argument or a particular side of a debatable question. They are therefore to be considered as Exercises in Composition and not as Records of decided opinions. P.'[43]

[38] Palmerston to Malmesbury, 19 Nov. 1805, Malmesbury Papers.
[39] Palmerston to Frances Temple, 7 Nov. 1805, B.P.W.
[40] B.P.W.
[41] *Stratford Canning*, i. 28. The other members mentioned are Pollock and Charles James Blomfield, afterwards Bishop of London.
[42] Hobhouse's Diary, 29 May 1847, Broughton Papers, Add. MS. 43750.
[43] 'Edinburgh 1800. H. Temple. Essays on various Subjects Historical & Political written between the years 1800 & 1806 at Edinr & Cambridge & read in debating Societies', B.P.W. The titles and dates, amplified where possible from Palmerston's family correspondence, are:

In Edinburgh:
A Vindication of Mary Queen of Scotland, [19] Dec. 1800
On the Comparative Advantages and Happiness of a Savage and Civilized Life, Jan. 1801
On Public and Private Education, Jan. 1801
On Gowry's Conspiracy, 14 Mar. 1801
On the Advantages derived from the invention of Printing, Mar. 1801

Palmerston made his formal farewell to Cambridge on 13 March 1806.[44] But William Temple, who succeeded to his brother's place with Dugald Stewart and to his rooms in St John's, became a member of both the Edinburgh and the Cambridge Speculatives, and Palmerston himself seems occasionally to have returned to Cambridge to take part in the club's debates. Palmerston was also proud to recall that the Fusty had been amalgamated with two other clubs in 1816 to form the Cambridge University Union (no. 159).[45] He might possibly have claimed the Oxford Union too. It is said that Augustus Hare founded a debating club at Oxford in 1810 in emulation of what he called the 'Cambridge University Political Society'. Francis Hare seems to have been his brother's close adviser and it may be significant that in the interval between Aberdeen and Oxford Francis had attended a private tutor just outside Cambridge and visited St John's just when Palmerston was transforming his essay on the East India Company into his required declamation in Chapel.[46] It is not known what Palmerston thought when his old college tutor, since become Master of St John's and Vice-Chancellor, ordered the dissolution of the Union as an undesirable political society in 1817.[47] His references to James Wood, as also to his private tutor Edmund Outram, had usually been rather condescending; but by the time he left college he, and most of his friends, were already involved in other political affairs at Cambridge that were far too serious to risk a clash with the University establishment for so frivolous a cause.

Palmerston afterwards said that Outram had 'more than once' suggested that his performance in the college examinations and the 'general regularity' of his conduct might justify his standing for one of the two university seats whenever a vacancy occurred.[48] Outram was not an entirely unbiased adviser, since he was seeking support in his candidacy for the Regius Chair of History and had probably given similar encouragement to other old tutees like Lord Royston. However, when Pitt died in January 1806, Palmerston rushed off to

In Cambridge:
   On the Probability of Europe Relapsing into Barbarism, [22] Feb. 1804
   On the Policy of opening the East Indian Trade, [31] Oct. 1804
   On the Policy of Transferring the Portugueze Government to the Brazils, [1 or 8] May 1805
   On the Political Character of Cardinal Fleury, Oct. 1805
   On the Disadvantages Resulting to Great Britain from the loss of her North American Colonies, Mar. 1806

[44] Blackburn to Palmerston, 13 Mar. 1806, B.P.W.

[45] According to Teignmouth, i. 47, one of the others also had a nickname, 'the Anticarnalist', because one member had been expelled for 'a flagrant act of immorality'.

[46] A. J. C. Hare, *Memorials of a Quiet Life*, 1870, i. 148–9 and 168–71; Palmerston to his mother, 16, 23 and 28 Nov. 1804, B.P.W.

[47] Wright, i. 203–4, claims to have denounced the Union to Wood.

[48] Bulwer & Ashley, i. 367–8.

Cambridge (no. 18). So began an involvement with the parliamentary elections there that lasted until 1831. At first he was unsuccessful, in the by-election of February 1806 largely because of the Saints' doubts about his stand on the abolition of the slave trade (nos. 19–26), and in the General Election of May 1807 because of the intrusion of another, and more senior, ministerial candidate (nos. 38–46). Malmesbury, still his mentor, was consequently obliged to look elsewhere, and after his protégé had been unseated upon a double return at Horsham in November 1806 (no. 37), and disappointed of an accusation of corruption securing a vacancy for him in Great Yarmouth in February 1807, he closed for the purchase of a seat in Newport, Isle of Wight, as soon as he learned of Palmerston's second defeat in Cambridge.[49]

In the meantime the Ministry of All the Talents had collapsed and Malmesbury had secured for Palmerston minor office under Portland as a Junior Lord of the Admiralty from 6 April 1807. A little more than two years later, on 1 November 1809, Palmerston, having already refused the Exchequer, kissed hands as Perceval's Secretary at War and began his eighteen and a half years of hard labour at the War Office. But Palmerston maintained his interest in the University of Cambridge and received one of its seats at last in a by-election in March 1811 (no. 76). Upon the dissolutions of September 1812, June 1818 and February 1820 he was also returned unopposed (nos. 84, 118), even though he had publicly announced his conversion to the cause of Catholic relief in 1812 and, more definitely, in 1813.[50]

The decisive victory of a 'Protestant', however, in a by-election for the other seat in 1822, suggested that anti-Catholic feeling was mounting among the University voters and cast doubt on the 'Catholic' Palmerston's chances at the next General Election (nos. 124, 126). Thus encouraged, two more anti-Catholics joined him and his new colleague in a scramble for the two seats, and Palmerston found himself, to his dismay, involved in a contest with his own colleagues in Government, and in a canvass six months ahead of the General Election scheduled for June 1826 (nos. 156–8). He was still more disgusted when he found that his opponents were being favoured, not only by the active support of the Duke of York, who was a leading anti-Catholic and had clashed with Palmerston rather personally as Commander-in-Chief (nos. 102, 128–32, 176, 219), but also by the 'neutrality' of the Prime Minister, Liverpool, and some of his senior colleagues (no. 159).

In the event Palmerston held his seat quite comfortably, largely because of the support he received from 'Catholics' and, in the absence

[49] Bulwer & Ashley, i. 367–70; Malmesbury Papers.
[50] 1 *Hansard*, xxiii. 707 (22 June 1812), and xxiv. 971–6 (1 Mar. 1813).

of an opposition candidate, from Whigs (nos. 161–2, 164–5). But the experience was one of the most decisive in his political development, comparable with his declaration in favour of Catholic Emancipation in 1813. Henceforth he fiercely disassociated himself from what he now called 'the stupid old Tory party'.[51] He did not, however, move over to his new supporters, the Whigs. Instead he survived the rapid succession of prime ministers in 1827–8, and his political fortunes frequently promised to revive. He was promoted to the Cabinet and twice again nearly became Chancellor of the Exchequer (nos. 175, 179–80, 183–92). He survived Canning's death, Goderich's dithering and, for a time, even Wellington's displeasure. Nor was he by any means written off after he seceded from the Government with Huskisson, Grant, Dudley and William Lamb in May 1828. Instead he was approached on several sides, apparently by the Lansdowne Whigs, certainly by the High Tories (no. 231), and more than once by Wellington's associates.

Almost the last of these approaches from Wellington was made through Clive. Although the highest positions Clive ever reached were as Lord Lieutenant of Montgomeryshire and High Steward of the University of Cambridge, he was not an insignificant political figure among the Tories. For a long period he shared with his younger brother (also a Johnian) the parliamentary representation of Ludlow and by 1817 he had become, according to Lady Holland, 'quite a Treasury runner & jobber'.[52] He played some part in helping Palmerston's Cambridge elections, even in 1826,[53] and Palmerston was certainly dragged into some of Clive's affairs in Ludlow. Another local family in Shropshire, the Charltons, shared with the Clives the patronage of Ludlow and in spite of all attempted compromise they seem to have quarrelled frequently over the spoils. Palmerston intervened, perhaps even to avert a duel, in June 1823, with a draft of settlement in six foolscap pages of ambiguous compromise. When trouble threatened again in May 1829 Palmerston similarly drafted a careful letter of rebuttal from Clive and in the election of the following summer was the formal channel of communication between them.[54] Soon afterwards Clive was performing a similar task for Palmerston. By early middle age, if not sooner, Clive was very hard of hearing and while Sir Walter Scott might still consider him 'intelligent and good-humoured', Mrs Arbuthnot in 1830 dubbed him 'deaf as a post and not

---

[51] Bulwer & Ashley, i. 171.
[52] Lady Holland to Grey, 10 Jan. 1817, Grey Papers.
[53] Mrs Sulivan to William Temple, 16 June 1826, B.P.W.
[54] 'Minute of a Conversation between Lord Palmerston on the part of Lord Clive, & the Hon. H. G. Bennet on the part of Mr Charlton at Lord P.'s house in Stanhope Street on Sunday, 29 June 1823' and draft of Clive to Charlton, 3 May 1829, B.P.W. The bitter rivalry, however, persisted: see T. H. Duncombe, *The Life and Correspondence of Thomas Slingsby Duncombe*, 1868, i. 368–70.

very bright'. Her friend Wellington would probably have agreed, having known Clive's father in India as 'old Puzzlestick', if he had not had such good personal reasons to deny the equation of deafness with stupidity or the son with the father. However, since Clive was, as even Mrs Arbuthnot admitted, 'a very honest man & a gentleman & quite a person we can trust', he was employed in an attempt to reconcile Palmerston with the Duke's Government in October 1830 (no. 242). He was not successful, though the combined diffidence, caution and pride of the two principals may have contributed as much to that as any obtuseness of his own.[55] This failure left Clive and Palmerston politically apart for the rest of their lives. But they kept up a desultory correspondence and a social contact until Clive, who succeeded as Earl of Powis in 1839, was accidentally shot by his son in 1848 (no. 322).

Political differences seem to have ended rather more abruptly Palmerston's friendship with Lord Percy, though the Duke of Northumberland was probably more to blame than his son. In his first attempt at Cambridge in early 1806 Palmerston evidently received support from Percy's cousins, Lord Lovaine (the Earl of Beverley's heir and another Johnian) and his younger brother Hugh Percy. But the Duke had already been approached by Carlton House and his son actively canvassed in St John's for Lord Henry Petty (nos. 20, 23). At the General Election later in the same year, Percy threatened to emerge as an active candidate for the seat and though Palmerston had decided not to stand lest he suffer a more un-dignified defeat he very much resented Percy's intrusion (no. 33). Percy soon withdrew, but Palmerston never got any answer to the letter of remonstrance he had addressed to Percy and their friendship seems permanently to have been strained (no. 224).

Palmerston's friendship with Michael Bruce, by contrast, survived many years of strain. Bruce was evidently a romantic and a hothead, his early life as misadventurous as his father's later business affairs. He had canvassed actively for Palmerston in May 1807 but left im-mediately afterwards for an extended tour of northern Europe (no. 48). Possibly he needed a break and a rest—his second year at St John's had evidently also been interrupted by illness (no. 37)—but he missed the beginning of the next academic year and after a mere two terms in Cambridge was off again, to Portugal, in November 1808. His second, sudden and unexplained, departure disappointed his friends' expectations of the highest academic honours and upset his father bitterly. Worse, however, was to come. Abroad he soon became entangled with Lady Hester Stanhope and Mme Ney, the latter

---

[55] *The Journal of Sir Walter Scott*, Edinburgh, 1891, ii. 181; *Arbuthnot Journal*, ii. 389; E. Longford, *Wellington. Pillar of State*, 1972, p. 223 (though she confuses Clive with his father).

involving him also in the escape of some Bonapartists from Paris; an adventure which earned him a short period in jail and the nickname 'Lavallette Bruce'.

At home and abroad his character and his politics were too volatile for Palmerston. In his few surviving letters, however, Palmerston always signed himself 'Yours affectionately', and he seems to have helped his friend whenever he could. After his father's bank had crashed, Bruce settled down in England to the comparative dullness of marriage, belatedly took his degree and tried his hand at the bar and politics. For some reason his father did not approve of his marriage to the widow of Captain Sir Peter Parker, but Palmerston, who had always believed that while Bruce had shown much 'want of judgement & discretion . . . in his public conduct', he nevertheless had 'a good heart', acted as best man. He could not conceive why the father disapproved, he wrote in August 1818, for Lady Parker was 'a pleasing & amiable person & really sensible enough to be of some use to him who is so deficient in ballast'. Indeed, time worked to bring Palmerston and Bruce a little more together in politics. In 1826 Bruce was again serving on Palmerston's election committee in Cambridge and in 1831 Palmerston found him a profitable appointment as commissioner of claims. But a few years later their friendship was finally in ruins, probably because Bruce discovered Palmerston had played a part in stopping Lady Hester Stanhope's pension from the crown.[56]

Some of Palmerston's other Johnian friends also appear to have benefited from his patronage. It was evidently with the help of Palmerston, among other Cambridge friends, that Blackburn, after some years at the English bar, was appointed Chief Justice of Mauritius in 1824 (nos. 133, 134). So far as Palmerston was concerned the favour was probably as much for Mrs Blackburn's sake as her husband's. Eliza Madocks was the sister of his contemporary at Harrow and the granddaughter of Lady Craven, Princess Berkeley of Anspach. She married Blackburn in 1816 and by 1819 was already having an affair with Palmerston.[57] In Mauritius Blackburn laid the foundations of a minor reputation as naturalist, but his wife became entangled with his private secretary, the private secretary ran off with his daughter and Blackburn himself finally wrecked his legal career by a clash with the public prosecutor, John Jeremie.

Jeremie was a fierce abolitionist who felt that his efforts against the local planters were not sufficiently supported. When, in August 1833, he found himself faced with prosecution for false imprisonment he

[56] Palmerston to W. Temple, 4 and 21 Aug. 1818, B.P., G.C./TE nos. 160 and 161; Mrs Sulivan to W. Temple, 16 June 1826, B.P.W. See also I. Bruce, *The Nun of Lebanon. The Love Affair of Lady Hester Stanhope and Michael Bruce*, 1951, and *Lavallette Bruce, His Adventures and Intrigues Before and After Waterloo*, 1953.
[57] Palmerston's diary, 16 Aug., 13–25 Sept. 1819, B.P./D no. 4.

denounced the bench for having a notorious vested interest in slavery. As the Governor had very little sympathy for him he was forced to resign, returning towards the end of 1833 to England. There he was joined by one of the four judges, John Reddie, who had also denounced his colleagues and been recalled for 'unbecoming conduct'. In all this Blackburn seems to have been the particular object of accusations that extended beyond collusion to fraud, being charged in particular with having conspired to transfer slave property illegally to friends. The Colonial Secretary, Aberdeen, determined to recall him as well, but lost office before his wish could be carried out. The Melbourne Government must also have decided that Blackburn could not continue on the bench and he was induced to leave quietly by the promise made through his wife's uncle, the Earl of Sefton, of a place worth £400 a year on the Judicial Committee of the Privy Council. Unfortunately the place belonged to Sir Alexander Johnston who would not make way and Blackburn returned home a widower in 1836 to find himself in the middle of a major row. In the end, while Reddie and Jeremie both got new appointments, Blackburn had to rest content with being made commissioner on the estates of his old friend the Duke of Northumberland.[58] He died at Alnwick on 7 August 1839. Palmerston had, however, already found a place in the Foreign Office for his eldest son (nos. 261, 262).

Palmerston's other Johnian friends fared much better. Shee and Sulivan not only outlived him but profited more from his goodwill. Both went down from Cambridge before their noble friend, and began to study for the Bar, Shee at Gray's Inn and Sulivan at Lincoln's Inn. This turned out very well for Palmerston's Cambridge elections, as his friends could then make up committees to canvass the voters among the London lawyers while others served in Cambridge. Neither Shee nor Sulivan, however, stuck very long to the law. Shee in fact had told his father in 1803 that he doubted his fitness for the law and that he preferred to try his luck in India.[59] His father refused to provide the necessary funds, but in February 1808 he was married for the first time, much against his parents' wishes, and having soon become tired of his wife's ill-health sought the distraction of alternative employment (nos. 48, 49, 53). In October 1810 Palmerston, exercising his authority as Secretary at War, seized the opportunity of a chance vacancy and made him Agent-General of Militia. That office was wound up soon after the war ended. But when Palmerston

---

[58] P. J. Barnwell, *Visits and Despatches (Mauritius, 1598–1948)*, Port Louis, 1948, pp. 241–3; *Greville Memoirs*, iii. 75 (26 Aug. 1834); John Reddie to Brougham, 21 Feb. 1834, 28 April 1835 and 21 Jan. and 5 and 16 Mar. 1836, Melbourne to Brougham, 6 and 23 Jan. 1836, and Sefton to Brougham, 2 and 11 Sept. and 6 Nov. 1836, Brougham Papers; J. Jeremie, *Recent Events at Mauritius*, 1835.

[59] Shee to his father, 15 Feb. 1803, Shee Papers.

became Foreign Secretary for the first time in November 1830 Shee was made his undersecretary after Lord Ashley had refused.

Shee lasted only four years in the Foreign Office and his subsequent career in the diplomatic service was rather fitful and limited to a decade. In the Foreign Office he was reputedly given the special task of handling the press and gained no credit by it either in the Government or out of it. In October 1834 Palmerston decided he must move Shee out of the office and nominate him minister to Berlin. 'Tout le monde sera surpris,' said Talleyrand, 'y compris Sir George Shee.'[60] Talleyrand may have had a personal grudge against Shee as well as against Palmerston. For Shee's father, who had died in 1825, had played a most discreditable part in India many years before in the seduction of a young married woman who later became Talleyrand's wife.[61] But Shee's appointment was greeted with disgust on all sides and when Wellington succeeded Palmerston shortly afterwards he cancelled it (no. 263). Palmerston found Shee another legation, in Stuttgart, as soon as he could after his return to office in 1835. But Shee ruined his career, apparently by marrying his mistress, and in October 1844 he was recalled, never to be employed again (nos. 310, 312, 313). He seems, for a while, to have stayed on in Stuttgart as a private citizen, but to have returned in 1845 when he found it all too uncomfortable there. 'I think he is right,' wrote Palmerston, 'for at all events if he makes up his mind to leave his wife at home he may himself enjoy the society of his friends.'[62] For two more decades of their lives Palmerston's diaries and letters record sporadic visits by Shee to Broadlands, alone and unaccompanied.

Sulivan, by contrast, made a most satisfactory marriage and kept the official place his friend had found him until old age forced him to retire. It is not known whether Sulivan had also expressed some dissatisfaction with the law, but in October 1809 Palmerston raised with him the possibility of his becoming his private secretary should Perceval in the end make Palmerston Secretary at War (nos. 64–5). Fourteen months later, in January 1811, Sulivan was promoted on a chance vacancy to one of the senior positions in the War Office as the third Superintendent of Military Accounts. Then, after a nominal change from Superintendent to Chief Examiner in 1824, he succeeded as Deputy Secretary in September 1826.

Sulivan must have been reasonably competent, since after Palmerston's resignation from the War Office in May 1828 his Deputy survived a succession of twelve different ministers before his retirement

[60] Viscountess Enfield, ed., *Leaves from the Diary of Henry Greville*, [1st series], 1883, p. 23.

[61] J. Parkes and H. Merivale, *Memoirs of Sir Philip Francis*, 1867, ii. 137–50, and A. Spencer, ed., *Memoirs of William Hickey*, n.d., ii. 159.

[62] Palmerston to William Temple, 15 Nov. 1845, B.P., G.C./TE no. 310.

at the age of sixty-eight in July 1851; he was then made a Privy
Councillor and an honorary Governor of the Royal Military Asylum.
He was perhaps a little self-important and from time to time complained to his old friend that several of Palmerston's successors and
in particular Hardinge, who was Secretary at War in 1828–30 and
again in 1841–4, was attempting to circumscribe his authority and
degrade his position in the Office. But when Hardinge retired in
1830 he certainly put on record his appreciation of Sulivan's 'very
able superintendence' (nos. 253, 255, 301–2). Hobhouse, as an old
friend in the Fusty, naturally recorded his appreciation still more
warmly during his brief tenure of the office.[63]

Yet Sulivan was resented a good deal both by the military at the
Horse Guards and among his colleagues in the War Office. Palmerston
had become Secretary at War at a time of very serious parliamentary
and official criticism of the War Office, which was viewed as a
notorious example of the eighteenth-century system of government,
clinging to its venal privileges and perquisites even as it proved itself
ever more incompetent to cope with the increasing business generated
by the long-drawn-out war with France. The Department of Military
Accounts was one of the major innovations designed to deal with the
vast amount of arrears in the War Office's principal function, the
checking and clearing of regimental accounts. That department was
not invented by Palmerston and Sulivan was not among its three
original Superintendents. But Palmerston had the job of instituting
and improving it and Sulivan, surviving all his colleagues, made it
the springboard of his official career. Sulivan, however, liked to think
that all the major proposals for reform had originated with him, and
he even nursed a resentment—which surfaced, or came near to sur-
facing, on the eve of his retirement—that Palmerston had got all the
public credit while he, Sulivan, had incurred all the private resentment in the strained and straitened office without ever being
rewarded, as Deputy Secretary, with the proper salary for his post.[64]

[63] Hobhouse's diary, 4 Jan. 1833, Broughton Papers, Add. MS. 56557.
[64] There is in Add. MSS. 59782–3 a small exercise book endorsed 'Account by
Laurence Sulivan of his public service in the War Office written in 1857 or 1851'. In
fact it is dated 17 Jan. 1851 and was evidently a draft or copy of a narrative he had
enclosed with a letter to his chief, Fox Maule, intimating that he wished to retire. In it he
claims that from the time of his appointment as Junior Superintendent in 1811 his 'most
zealous endeavours were from that moment exerted to sift the whole system to the
bottom. I very soon became convinced that it was calculated to perpetuate every
mischief which it professed to remedy.' Palmerston resisted, 'strongly deprecating any
present change'. However, having gained by his new position 'a thorough insight' of
how bad things really were and being better placed therefore to combat 'the inveterate
prejudices of those who had been brought up in a vicious school', he eventually prevailed upon Palmerston to give the matter his 'deliberate attention' and in 1813 finally
to put a stop to the practice of the three superintendents acting as a virtually independent board. Thenceforth, Sulivan claimed, it was he who put *all* suggestions for
improvements to Palmerston and kept a close watch over their application after his

He was not entirely fair in this. Palmerston certainly made public as well as private testimony to his Deputy's able assistance. As for the Deputy's salary, Palmerston had always striven to temper, for the sake of justice and efficiency, the economising onslaughts of both Parliament and Treasury. Sulivan's official salary rose very substantially in any case. As Superintendent he had a salary of £1,000 per annum; as Chief Examiner he received £1,200; and as Deputy Secretary £2,000.

Sulivan's reputation, however, did suffer both in and out of the office by his association with Palmerston. Inevitably his name was linked with Palmerston's famous clashes with the Horse Guards and when Hobhouse also tried his hand at bringing the Army to heel, Sulivan was seen behind him too (no. 252). He was a meddler, it was said in official circles, who if not restrained 'would drive the Army half mad, & make his principal so unpopular as no exertion of his own would undo'.[65] Sulivan also suffered special odium in the office as the personal favourite of his chief. The Senior Superintendent, Michael Foveaux, was particularly venomous. He was hardly in a position to complain about favouritism since both he and his father had in earlier days profited from the support of a previous Secretary at War.[66] But he evidently resented Sulivan's promotion to Superintendent in 1811 and still more his juniors taking over from him the supervision of the current accounts later that summer. Perhaps he sensed that he might be compulsorily retired when his own work on the arrears eventually came to an end. Quite possibly it was he, therefore, who fed the Opposition newspapers with War Office dirt with which to smear both Palmerston and Sulivan (no. 98). Certainly, when he found he was to be pensioned off in 1821, Foveaux's bitterness overflowed and, but for the intervention of his wife, might have threatened his pension as well as his job. Others in the office also complained of Palmerston and Sulivan (no. 302). They may have included Sulivan's predecessor

brother-in-law had gone, though incurring in the process a good deal of 'unfair opposition' while others claimed the credit.

[65] Quoted by R. E. Morse, 'Money or Merit? The Early Development of a Modern Officer Promotion Process in the British Army, 1815–1830', unpublished University of London Ph.D. thesis, 1978, p. 239.

[66] Michael Foveaux (1762–1832) had entered the War Office in 1783 when Gen. Fitzpatrick (1747–1813) was Secretary at War for the first time; Joseph Foveaux senr (*ob.* 1 Jan. 1814) in 1806 when Fitzpatrick was again Secretary at War, even though he was too old and ill to perform his duties of office-keeper and paid a substitute out of the considerable perquisites. Lt Col. Joseph Foveaux jnr (1765–1846), the controversial Lt-Governor of Norfolk Island, was evidently the younger son. The *Australian Dictionary of Biography* (i. 407–9) records that he was reputedly the son of a French cook employed in the household of the Earl of Upper Ossory and suggests that his very rapid promotion as a soldier in New South Wales must have been due to the influence of a powerful patron in England. Fitzpatrick was the Earl's younger brother. Possibly Michael and Joseph jnr were the natural children of the Earl or his brother who were both great philanderers.

being 'too violent & bullying' with the Peruvian Government.[80] Two
years later, on 11 August 1857, a man broke into Stephen Sulivan's
house and fired a blunderbuss point blank into his stomach. Within
two days Palmerston's nephew was dead (nos. 362–6).

The accounts of what had happened were extremely confused.
Some said that Sulivan was dining alone; others that he had two
companions with him. One account had it that the assassin never said
a word; another that he exclaimed 'I am revenged' or something of
the sort in Spanish. All were agreed that there were several accom-
plices—at least six or possibly fifteen—in the courtyard or the street
outside; two of them, a Frenchman and a negro, were subsequently
arrested. The motive was an even bigger mystery. The victim himself
could offer no explanation. The Peruvian Government's opinion was
that from the number of men involved it must have been political
and something to do with the rebellion of General Vivanco. The
initial suggestion was that it concerned two former rebel ships, the
Loa and the *Tombes*. One or both of them had attacked and plundered
a British steamer and, after the Royal Navy had seized one of them
in retaliation, Sulivan had agreed to hand it over to the Government.
Later it was suggested that the Vivanco party's hatred had been
aroused instead by Sulivan's negotiation of a convention that upset
their plan for a great guano swindle. Subsequently the Frenchman's
role was also changed from that of an unimportant accomplice to that
of principal assassin, and punished with a maximum sentence of
fifteen years in the chain gang.

The British, both Government and family in London as well as the
remnants of the consulate in Lima, readily accepted the notion that
it was a political murder. But there were always rumours it was something much more personal. The *Panama Herald and Star* reported as
early as 12 August that an intrigue with a woman was the cause, and
soon afterwards it was rumoured that the brother of the deserted Mrs
Sulivan had lately been seen in Chile or Peru, bent no doubt on a
'horrible vendetta'. These suggestions were indignantly denied by
Sulivan's secretary John Cheesman. He explained them away as
prompted by American jealousy of the influence Sulivan had secured
in Lima. Cheesman was the principal witness, but the consular staff
in Lima seem to have been strangely reticent about the dinner party
which had been so tragically interrupted. They may not, perhaps,
have been responsible for the initial version that said Sulivan was
dining alone. But when Cheesman corrected that version and reported he had been dining with Sulivan he neglected to mention that
there was also another guest. The reports of the vice-consul and of
the captain of the *Retribution* stationed in the harbour also referred

[80] Palmerston to William Temple, 12 June 1855, B.P., G.C./TE no. 358.

merely to a third 'person'. Only in a subsequent statement on oath did Cheesman reveal that it was a certain Doña Nicida Vidal. The following year Palmerston received a begging letter that conveyed a gratuitous and second-hand account from Lima. Stephen Sulivan, it went, had left his wife in Chile and soon after arriving in Lima had been 'ensnared by one of the *most beautiful* and ... most diabolical women in Peru'. She had two handsome sisters, one of whom was kept by 'a wealthy English merchant' and the other lived with the British vice-consul as his 'housekeeper etc.'. But Sulivan's was the villain of the three. Of his several predecessors, two had already met with violent deaths 'when she had had all she wanted out of them and wished for a change'. Sulivan in turn had made property over to her and further provided for her in his will; while she had already selected his successor before his death. Palmerston recognised blackmail when he saw it. He endorsed the letter with a note of his reply: 'Cannot assist him. The causes were quite of another nature.' Stephen Sulivan's will, of which Cheesman was executor, ordered his private correspondence to be burned and divided his money between his wife Margherita and his 'best friend', Doña Nicida Vidal.[81]

Whatever Laurence Sulivan may have thought about the circumstances of the murder of his elder son, his sympathy reached out once more towards his deserted daughter-in-law. When she was tracked down in Italy in 1862, it was found that she had remarried in the year following Stephen's death. But she professed still to be in desperate straits and Laurence Sulivan sent her substantial periodic payments totalling nearly £1,500.[82]

Although these may have been Margherita's portion from his son's estate, Laurence Sulivan was undoubtedly a kindly man. Even his Army critics acknowledged he was 'an excellent father and husband' (no. 252). One of his daughters, as well as both his sons, was probably a disappointment to him. For when the second of his girls, born on 8 February 1820 and christened Mary Catherine Henrietta, married as his second wife the local vicar, the Rev. Robert George Baker of Fulham was seventy-seven and she was forty-five. She nevertheless predeceased him and died childless on 20 October 1871. The eldest daughter, Elizabeth Mary, born on 26 April 1814, married in 1851 Henry Hippisley of Lamborne Place in Berkshire. Hippisley was also a widower and already had a large family. The marriage seems to have been very happy and Elizabeth Hippisley took loving care of her unmarried stepdaughters. But her own elder son was a ne'er do well who, after a brief career in the Navy, died unmarried and in disgrace

abroad. Elizabeth Hippisley died in 1886. She was survived only by
her youngest sister, born on 14 April 1823 or 1824. Charlotte Antonia
Sulivan had some talent as a painter, but she never married and it
was to her that Laurence Sulivan left his papers and his house in
Fulham. At Charlotte's death in 1911 Broom House was sold to the
Hurlingham Club, and its contents were dispersed, by the curious
provisions of her will, room by room among the descendants of her
sister Elizabeth. Among those contents were Palmerston's letters to his
friend Laurence Sulivan.[83]

The collection of letters was subsequently broken up. Most of the
three hundred and eighty letters printed below were divided among
two of Elizabeth Hippisley's descendants. A third portion is evidently
the remnant of a group of letters loaned to Palmerston's official
biographers and not subsequently returned. Bulwer and Ashley, however, made only very limited use of the Sulivan papers and so far as
is known very few outside the family have seen them since. Lord
Lorne (afterwards ninth Duke of Argyll) and Mabell, Countess of
Airlie, printed a few of them, not very accurately, in their respective
volumes on Palmerston and Lady Palmerston, and Lord David Cecil
is understood to have read some of them for his study of Melbourne.
But for the most part they have remained neglected. The interest and
importance of the earlier letters, with their wealth of comment on
national affairs, parliamentary elections and the War Office, need no
underlining here. There are obvious gaps in the surviving correspondence, though the letters addressed to Mrs Sulivan, usually when
Palmerston was abroad, have also been included.[84] Probably the gaps
are not as large as might appear, for Palmerston was considered an
unreliable correspondent by his friends. Shee once chided him:
'Counsellor Sulivan ... says that he is *sure* I have quite as good a
chance of an answer to my letter as of the first prize in a lottery.'[85]
But after Palmerston's departure from the War Office, and still more
after his younger sister's death in 1837, the letters declined very much
in quality as well as quantity. Nevertheless they serve as the record
of Palmerston's principal adult friendship with a man, and in major
political crises continued to the end to provide interesting comment
and details.

[83] Other portions of the family papers, notably those concerning the Sulivans' Indian
interests in the eighteenth century, have found their way by private transfer or public
auction into the Bodleian, the India Office Library or private collections. Much of
the nineteenth-century material seems to have been long ago destroyed, but an appreci-
able quantity, including a few scraps derived from Palmerston's elder sister and her
husband, was retained as an autograph collection.

[84] There is also a considerable correspondence, preserved in B.P.W., with both his
sisters during their earlier, unmarried years.

[85] Shee to Palmerston, 3 July 1809, B.P., G.C./SH no. 81.

NOTE ON SOURCES AND EDITING OF
THE LETTERS

M OST of the letters printed below were copied from the originals in the possession of two of Elizabeth Hippisley's descendants. Subsequently one of these descendants has transferred most of her portion to the British Library where they will now be found in Add. MSS. 59782–3. Since they still await final arrangement these are headed simply Add. MSS. A few other letters are to be found in the Broadlands Papers and are therefore headed B.P. or B.P.W. A small number of the originals has not been traced and the versions printed have therefore been taken from typescript copies made early in this century and remaining in the possession of the family. Previously printed letters have usually not been reproduced but summarised. Wherever the original survives, however, any significant corrections and additions have been made. These calendar entries, and all other editorial matter, are printed in italics.

Unless otherwise stated, all the letters are addressed to Laurence Sulivan. They usually begin 'My dear Sulivan' and end, in the early years, 'Adieu My dear Sulivan', often with some such addition as 'pray remember me to Mr and Mrs S. & believe me yours affectionately', or, in later years, simply 'Yrs affly Palmerston'. With a few exceptions, these formalities have been omitted, and the styles of dates and places of writing have been standardised. In all other respects the effort has been made to preserve the original. Abbreviations and variations of spelling in particular have been retained. Editorial insertions in the text are italicised and placed within square brackets. These include addresses and dates supplied, from internal or other evidence, by the editor. Palmerston's punctuation, however, defies exact reproduction. Since there appears to be no significance whatever in his famous but random resort to capital letters, these have not usually been retained. When combined with his equally random use of commas, colons and dashes, they also make it very difficult to discern when the end of a sentence or a paragraph is intended. The punctuation has therefore been adapted, where necessary, to render the text more intelligible.

PALMERSTON'S LETTERS TO
LAURENCE AND ELIZABETH SULIVAN

1. *Broadlands. 5 Sept. 1804.*

Many thanks for your very kind letter of the 24th which I received on my return from the music meeting. I am very glad to find that our tour has answered to you as well as it has to me, and I am almost tempted to pay you the same compliment I did to Cholmely to whom I observed on our return from the Highlands, how glad I was that he went, as had he not been able to have gone, I could not have got any other companion.[1] But however a real travelling *companion* is by no means easily found, and many are the pieces of live lumber who will fill one side of a chaise or curricle without the least pretensions to that appellation.

My mother has been going on very well since you left us.[2] Her spirits are generally very good, and she has had better nights, and been more free from pain than ever when in London. She goes out whenever the weather will permit her, and it has of late been remarkably favourable. She has now got a kind of garden chair, which being very easy will enable her to be driven all over the grounds, & I think the air is of much benefit to her.

The Salisbury Music Meeting was remarkably well attended, we had a concert each of the 3 evenings, balls on Wednesday and Friday and music in the cathedral on Thursday and Friday mornings. The balls were so crowded that dancing was quite impossible and the heat so great on the last night that a gentleman, his sister and cousin fainted one after the other. The Messiah was well performed on Friday morning. It is a very fine piece of music but rather too long. Mrs Billington sang very well, but connoisseurs say that she is scarcely equal to Mara in that kind of music.[3] We were on the whole extremely well amused. The party at Wilton consisted of Lord & Lady Bruce, Count & Countess Woronzow, and Mrs Robinson.[4] Lord Pembroke

[1] Cholmeley had been Palmerston's companion on his Highland tour of 1803; Sulivan (not William Temple, as stated by Guedalla, p. 47) had just returned with Palmerston from a tour of Wales.

[2] Lady Palmerston was dying of cancer, but her son had been told only that she was ill and encouraged to take his holiday in Wales (Minto to Lady Minto, 13 June 1804, Minto Papers IE/15).

[3] Elizabeth Billington (1768–1818) was 'the greatest singer England has ever produced', according to the *D.N.B.*, and a great rival of the German Mara who nearly twenty years earlier had been hired to sing at the celebration of Palmerston's first birthday (The Countess of Minto, ed., *Life and Letters of Sir Gilbert Elliot, First Earl of Minto*, 1874, i. 98).

[4] Lord Bruce was the son of the Earl of Ailesbury; Count Simon Woronzow (1744–1832) was Russian Ambassador in London from 1785 to 1806; and the widowed Mrs Robinson was the sister of the 1st Earl of Malmesbury and aunt of Palmerston's future colleague, Frederick Robinson, afterwards Viscount Goderich and Earl of Ripon.

would have been happy to have seen you but he expected the Duke of Cumberland for whom and his suite seven rooms were kept, & Ld & Ly Bath were also to have been there but were detained by visitors at home. Ly Bruce & Miss Hill are sisters of Ld Berwick; the latter remarkable only for her taciturnity, which is equal to that of her brother without the same cause for it. I heard from Ashburton & Mrs Stewart[5] a few days ago. The former is bathing at Leith, that being the only possible place in the island where according to him it is possible to get good bathing. He will remain there till October. Poor Mrs S. has had another though not dangerous return of her complaint, but is making use of the warm bath, and finds it does her good. I hope you see that your friend Cobbet [sic] & consequently the Windhams & Grenvillites, have espoused the cause of that persecuted martyr Sr F. Burdett. I presume for the sake of *consistency* you will now begin to find out with Cobbett, that it is foolish to rake up old quarrels & revive former animosities, by recurring to the conduct of public characters during the last war, and maintain that people are not to be judged by their past actions, but present promises. This last measure of the Emperor of Austria seems to be a pretty strong proof that the revolutionising spirit has not yet subsided in Europe.[6] It will now be quite a low thing to be an Emperor, they will soon be as cheap as our peerages. I should vote for making our King Emperor of Hanover, or Grand Autocrate of the Isle of Man. I have been tolerably successful in the sporting way. I killed three brace on the first and one brace on the third. We have not been out since, but when William's Manton [gun] comes, we shall make a most dreadful havoc in the country. I am now very busily employed in taking some lessons from Mr Heaphy so that in any future tour I shall be able to dirty a whole quire of paper.[7]

2. *Broadlands. 30 Sept. 1804.*

I will not aggravate my fault by any attempt at justification, but immediately confessing that I am much to blame and have behaved extremely ill to you, throw myself intirely on your mercy and generosity for forgiveness. It sounds very like an *ex post facto lye*, but, really & truly I was just setting down to write to you when I received your letter, and as you construed a long delayed answer into a hint for silence on your part, I hope this quick riposte will receive a contrary interpretation. It will I am sure give you great pleasure to hear that my mother has, since I last wrote, gone on as well as we had any

[5] The wife of Professor Dugald Stewart.
[6] On 11 Aug. Francis II had assumed the title of hereditary Emperor of Austria.
[7] There is a sketch-book of Palmerston's in B.P.W. (no. 1946) apparently dating from a tour he made in the following summer.

reason to expect; she has gained in strength and spirits, and I really think she is better than she was before she left town. The air and quiet of this place has been of great service to her; and this unexpected prolongation of summer has enabled her to enjoy all the advantages which the country could afford. She has had a garden chair made in which we wheel her about the grounds, and even when the weather becomes too cold and damp to admit of her sitting out, this will, I think, enable her to take a little air, whenever a fine day presents itself. Hitherto she has lived chiefly out of doors; she is carried out after breakfast & has generally dined out. This is fortunately the very thing she used to prefer when well. The weather has however now, I fear, thoroughly changed, and from the appearance of the sky, I am afraid that the rain which has begun this morning is the forerunner of much bad weather. I am very sorry to hear that Shee's illness has been of so serious a nature. Pray remember me to him, and beg him not to hurt his health by attacking my essay.[1] You do not mention which side you mean to espouse. *Shee* I am certain falls foul of ye Company, as the little consideration I have given the subject induces *me* to support them. Mr Henchman[2] did not throw much light upon the subject, and I am at present, in a state of profound ignorance not having been able to procure any history of India. As to St John's I really cannot say when I shall be there; my return depends so entirely upon my mother that I can scarcely fix any particular day. You may naturally conceive that I am desirous of remaining with her as long as possible, and I had, in case of her continuing well, some ideas of leaving this about the twentieth, but that arrangement will not suit well with the Green Street meeting.[3] I am much obliged to you for your kind wishes with respect to Ponsborne,[4] and though it is impossible this season, I do not despair of being able to admire your beauties, before those vile anti-picturesque loppings and inclosures have taken place. I condole with you upon the ignoble termination of the Hertford meeting; it must I should think have proceeded from mismanagement in the conductors.[5] I find your Grenvillite zeal has been fermenting a good deal since your return to Ponsborne. I am glad to hear that party did *not* support Burdett. I had supposed that

---

[1] 'On the Policy of Opening the East Indian Trade', read to the Fusty on 31 Oct. 1804.

[2] *Observations on the reports of the Directors of the East India Company respecting the Trade between India and Europe*, by Thomas Henchman, 1801.

[3] According to *Pryme*, pp. 117–18, meetings of the Union were afterwards held in a former dissenters' chapel in Green St.

[4] The Sulivans' house at Waltham Cross, bought by Laurence Sulivan in 1761 (Namier & Brooke, iii. 509).

[5] Sulivan had written on the 27th (B.P., G.C./SU no. 4) that the 'beau monde' had been driven from a music festival and ball at Hertford by 'an inundation of *townfolk* ... who ... thought that the price of admission was a sufficient title to be present'.

they went with Windham. I differ with you with respect to the pilot you allude to [*Pitt*], whose vessel seems I think going on very prosperously. If some of his crew, deceived by the appearance of a fat old whale floating on the surface, perversely trusted themselves on his back, and have been carried down by it the fault surely is not in the pilot, who could not prevent them. I really feel great compassion for the suicidical churchwardens and were I poetically turned would write an elegy upon the subject—it would afford a great deal of pathos. Were you not delighted with the King of Sweden's note,[6] it is very severe and spirited, and will mortify Buonaparte beyond measure, it forms a good contrast with the meanness of the German Emperor. The papers seem de[*termined*] to persuade us we are going to war with Spain. Ministers however I hear are not particularly anxious for it unless it should be necessary, as it would furnish France with a great addition to her navy and a number of good ports to sail from. The Spanish Monarchy if the account of the insurrections are true, seems on the eve of its dissolution and perhaps we may soon see Emperor Louis or Loison[7] at Madrid. The intercepted correspondence contains some interesting letters, that of Ld Grenville & Mr Wellesley in particular.[8] I think all that relate to the negociations in May 1803 between Addington & Pitt, place the conduct of the latter towards Ld Grenville in a very advantageous point of view, and add therefore to the shabbiness of Ld G.'s subsequent behaviour towards him. The King is now perfectly well and has received very great benefit from his residence at Weymouth. The Prince's behaviour to him in the negociation which took place between them previous to his going down, was worse than one could have conceived even him capable of. The only conditions for which the King stipulated at their projected interview was that no mention or allusion should be made to anything that had passed, than which after the usage he had received from the Prince, nothing could be more generous. The P. suffered him to go down to Windsor on the appointed day to wait two hours and then sent word he could not come, a resolution he had made the day before. I have not been much more successful than you in sporting having only killed 7 brace, the ground has been too hard & the birds wild.

3. *Broadlands. 19 Oct. 1804.*

I am sorry to find from your last letter that Shee continues so unwell, but I hope I shall see him next week much benefited by the

[6] Of 7 Sept., breaking off relations with France.
[7] Presumably Gen. Louis Henri Loison (1771–1816).
[8] *The Times* of 29 Sept. had reprinted extracts from some private correspondence captured at sea earlier that year and published by the French Government.

regularity of St John's. You tell me that you have disabled one of your right hand fingers, but do not mention how. I hope however that as it has not prevented your writing, the accident is not a bad one. I was certain that it never could so happen, that I should support the same side of an argument, as you and Shee had adopted, and so it has turned out; for though at first I was inclined to take the part of the Company, upon reading for the subject, I am determined to attack them tooth and nail. I confess however that I am not so secure in my new post, as not to feel some alarm at the effect of the batteries you and Shee have been preparing though I think on the whole my position is the most tenable of the two. In your former letter you said that we met on the 21st which must be a mistake as I am very sure, that not the eloquence of a Demosthenes, or *even* that of your humble servant would induce some part of our house to meet that day. I conclude however you meant the ensuing Wednesday, the 24th. I am afraid that I must beg you to exert your influence with the members to grant me a respite of a few days, as I shall most likely not be at Cambridge till Thursday. My mother has been rather low and not quite so well lately, today however she is better, and Mackie[1] is to call again on Sunday when I hope he will be able to give a favourable report. Her lowness proceeded from several accidental circumstances (among others the death of poor Cave's wife)[2] and she seems today to be getting rid of it. I shall however wish to stay till Mackie's next visit, and shall then if she continues well, set off for St John's. I shall be detained one or two days in town, in my way so that it will most probably be Thursday before I reach Cambridge.

I wrote to Clonmell to offer him the curricle and horses, having promised to let him know whenever we intended parting with them, and I thought that as he is just married he might like the little blacks for his young Venus.[3] I offered them to him for what we gave him, but I vote for asking more of anyone else, 120, for horses, & 100, for carriage. It is not impossible that should he not want them we might find a purchaser in the neighbourhood, as there are several gay West Indians near Southampton, & the equipage has had many admirers. Poor young Robins[4] has been all but dead since I last wrote. He was seized with a fit of palsy combined with apoplexy, he was insensible for several days, and was for an hour supposed to be dead, his pulse having entirely ceased. He has however almost entirely recovered; it is really a most miraculous cure. I see you must always have a sly

---

[1] John Mackie (1748–1831), physician.

[2] Cave had been butler to the 2nd Viscount.

[3] Thomas, 2nd Earl of Clonmell, seems to have celebrated his marriage twice, in Oct. 1804 and again on 9 Feb. 1805.

[4] Perhaps Thomas William Robbins (*ob.* 1864), who is recorded as having been admitted to Trinity and then to Lincoln's Inn in 1802.

cut at the present ministers. As to Ld Melville's crackers, as you will call them, I hear from good authority, that those who planned and those who executed the scheme are perfectly satisfied with the success of their *experiment* (for it was nothing more) and the silence of the French papers on the subject shews at least that they do not consider it as a *feu de joie*, although they may call it a *feu d'artifice*.[5] What do you say to the capture of these Spanish Frigates, it must one would think be decisive with respect to our situation with Spain. What lucky fellows those four captains are. Ministers I am told are adverse to the blockading system and wished Admiral Cornwallis to give it up. He said he should if they insisted upon it, but, that he must in that case also resign his command as he is persuaded it is the only system that can effectually secure Ireland and our Colonies. It was stupid in me to put you into Essex, but it was a deliberate blunder for I consulted the map on the occasion and in my hurry mistook the boundary of the counties.[6] As to Ashburton, I believe he never will leave Scotland again, till he goes abroad. Poor Lady Ashburton [*his mother*] came over here in despair two days ago to enquire if we knew any thing about him. Pray remember me to Shee etc.

[*PS.*] Pray is it our Parke who has been acting as negociator in the duel that did *not take place* at Liverpool?[7]

4. *Broadlands. 25 Dec. 1804.*

Rich[1] and I left Cambridge at nine on Wednesday evening and from the sleepiness of the drivers and badness of our horses did not reach Ware till two in the morning. Having with some difficulty wakened an old greasy cook who acted as chambermaid she lit some fire for us in the kitchen and we amused ourselves for an hour and a half with making and eating Welsh rabbits. After satisfying the cravings of an appetite rendered by the frost quite *Sullivanian*, we went to bed but both sheets and bed were so wet we were obliged to lay in our clothes on the outside. Poor Rich was prevented by the cold from shutting his eyes, I, who as you know am a tolerable hand at a nap, slept very soundly till nine. We then set off again and by being

[5] Sulivan had written on 14 Oct.: 'What do you think of your friend Lord Melville's *fire-works*? He is polite in the extreme to provide *amusement* for the French, in their confinement. I am afraid his *crackers* cost more than Addington's large stones.' (B.P., G.C./SU no. 5.)

[6] Palmerston had addressed his last letter to Essex but Ponsborne was in Hertfordshire.

[7] James Parke, afterwards Baron Wensleydale (1782–1868), a Cambridge contemporary, came from the vicinity of Liverpool.

[1] George Rich, Sir Charles's second son, had probably been visiting his uncle, Dr Humphrey Sumner, the Provost of King's.

obliged to wait an hour at Enfield and then being carried round the whole of the city by a driver who did not know his way into town, we did not reach Hanover Square till past two. I found Campbell in town and on the point of setting out to look at a curacy at Shrewsbury (how your heart jumped up into your mouth when you read that word). If it suits him he will marry directly.[2] Poor Colonel Whitworth I found very unwell. He has a confirmed black jaundice and they think his liver a little affected; he is rubbing mercury into his side. He will however I hope with proper care recover his health, but his cure will be a slow one.[3] We went in the evening to Drury Lane, were disappointed of seeing the Roscius, but were in momentary expectation of seeing another little Roscius produced by Mrs Jordan, who although in the last stage of pregnancy acted Mrs Sullen in the *Beaux Stratagem*—it was really disgusting—she looked very old and ugly. We left London on Friday morning and reached this by nine in the evening. I found my mother looking as well or even better than I expected. She certainly is rather thinner than when I saw her last, and had not about a fortnight ago been quite so well. She has however within these few days been much better, has had some good nights and has received benefit from having lived better. She has lately been a good deal annoyed by spasms in her stomach proceeding from indigestion. The lowness of her diet, her want of exercise, and the coldness of the weather had weakened her stomach a good deal and she was advised occasionally to eat some meat and drink two spoonfuls of madeira, which as she had no fever whatever, has been of service to her. This cold weather however does not agree with her, as indeed always was the case. Today the thermometer gives us some hopes of a thaw by rising to 36°; but from the rawness of the air, I fear it is only a prelude to a fall of snow, which I abhor. I went out shooting yesterday and fired twice at woodcocks with no greater effect than frightening them. We have a few but they are not abundant this season. William was to be at Minto the day before yesterday to spend his holidays there. They last but ten days. I wish they were long enough to admit of his coming down here. Clive may congratulate himself upon this frost, as it has most probably saved him a broken neck. He was to have been mounted upon one of Lord FitzWilliam's horses, and

[2] The Rev. Henry Campbell (*c.* 1774–1846) was the natural son of the 2nd Viscount Palmerston. After graduating from Christ Church he had obtained the living of St John's, Antigua, but had returned to collect an inheritance of £10,000 after his father's death in 1802. He obtained the promise of a curacy at Bicton in Shropshire early in 1805 and on the strength of it married in May of that year Anne, daughter of Thomas Rose of Chipping Wycombe. In spite of Palmerston's support he received only very modest preferment thereafter. He was subsequently curate at Nailsworth in Gloucestershire and, from 1839, at Cowley in Surrey.

[3] Sir Francis Whitworth died 16 Jan. 1805. Whitworth, his elder brother Lord Whitworth and their sisters were close friends of Palmerston's parents.

talked of leading the field the second time he went out. You will see that old Knox has not been getting up at six for nothing; he has got up amazingly on the boards. Clive and I with all our whipping and spurring have been near thrown out. I rather expected it as I had lost so much time from coming up late, and spouting in Chapel. Wood's letter amused me, it was pithy and concise. 'I give you a copy of the first class without comment, and am etc.' Just like Jemmy.[4] I would lay anything he will lay it to the charge of the poor Saturday picnic.[5] You see the puissant Doctor[6] or sapient Doctor is joining Pitt, what a mighty assistance! I saw Ash in town; he is going down to Bath for six weeks. He is looking just as when I left him. He never alters, and he began his puns where he left off just as you would resume an interrupted conversation.

5. Broadlands. 10 Jan. 1805.

I am much obliged to you for your wish to have prepared Rich and myself for our Hampshire Gaieties by a good night on the road, but I fear that we should have been but unwelcome visitors to a *regular* family at the hour of two in the morning and as we should necessarily have been off long before you had finished your last nap *on the floor* in the morning, we should have lost the inducement which a sight of your honour's face would have afforded.

Upon consideration and due reflection, as we cannot sell our equipage till spring and it is possible that in the summer I may want to make a little excursion for which it will be very useful, I shall propose myself to you as a purchaser, and shall be much obliged to you if waving the Jewish expectations we entertained of cent pr cent profit, you will allow me as original partner in the firm to take the goods at prime cost. As I did not know the name of your banker in town I have enclosed the amount, and have no doubt that under protection of Ashburton's *parole* it will reach you in safety. We have been excessively gay in this neighbourhood and have had nothing but balls. There have been three since I came down, and tonight we are

---

[4] 'All the big-wigs who happen to be liked by the students, are generally honoured with some familiar appellation, such as ... *Jemmy Wood*.' (Wright, i. 52.)

[5] Palmerston was always placed among the first class in the college examinations at St John's. But in Dec. 1805 he was ranked only tenth out of thirteen in that class. Palmerston attributed his relative failure to the disproportionate time he had given to converting his Fustian 'essay' on the East India Company into the declamation in Latin that every undergraduate was required to give in Chapel. He spent nearly a week translating it and learning it by heart and twenty minutes instead of the usual ten on the actual performance. (Palmerston to his mother, 23 Nov., 28 Nov. and 16 Dec. 1804, B.P.W.)

[6] Addington.

going to a magnificent assembly in the celebrated town of Romsey.
The rooms to be sure are not the most splendid in the outward
appearance. They are at one of the inns, and upon entering the house
you descend into a kitchen from which having mounted a ladder the
rooms open full on your view, and I can assure you that if the blaze
of beauty displayed by the apothecary's daughter and attorney's wife
etc., or the still more dazzling lustre of six tallow candles stuck in tin
chandeliers, did not at first overpower one's imagination, it would not
be difficult to conceive oneself in Elysium, to which deception the
harmonious scrapings of the rheumatic fidler (who by the by is barber
and hairdresser) and the ambrosial exhalation of gin punch and
tobacco would much contribute.

My mother has been better within these few days than she had been
since I came down, has had better nights and spirits, and has not
been annoyed by a recurrence of her spasms in her stomach. Adieu
my dear Sulivan I have not time to add more. The hurry in which I
have written this will apologise for the nonsense. '*Exquouse 'aste and
badd speeling.*'

6. *Broadlands. 31 Jan. 1805.*

> *Bulwer & Ashley, i. 12–13; MS. not found.*

Palmerston acknowledges Sulivan's condolences on the death of Lady Palmerston on 20 January.

7. *Hanover Square. 5 Mar. 1805.*

Many thanks my dear Sulivan for your very affectionate letter, and
believe me I feel truly grateful for the kindness and feeling contained
in it, indeed severely as I have been afflicted by the loss of those who
were most dear to me I have been most uncommonly fortunate in
experiencing unceasing and invariable kindness from my friends, at
periods when their attentions were most wanted. We left Broadlands
on Thursday last, and having spent two days with my sisters at the
Lavender House, my uncle, William and I came to town on Sunday
evening.[1] William sets off in the mail on Thursday for Edinburgh. I
shall be detained here some days longer by business, but I shall be
at St John's the latter end of this week or the beginning of the next.
The exact day I cannot at present determine.

[1] Lavender House was the place near Henley-on-Thames of William Culverden, the
brother-in-law and former partner of Andreas Grote. Culverden had married Lady
Palmerston's elder sister, Sarah, on 14 May 1767.

My aunt had for some time previous to her leaving Broadlands been annoyed by a return of some of her old bilious symptoms, not however in a sufficient degree to be at all alarming, although troublesome to her. She was better when we left her and we had a favourable account this morning. Fanny and Elizabeth we left as well as we could have expected. I am very sorry to hear that Clive has been alarmed about his knee; I shall send to enquire whether he is still in town and if he is will call upon him. Ashburton I saw this morning, he looked very well, and says he still perseveres in a strict neutrality, attends the debates but withdraws before the division. Cholmeley is in town, but goes to York on Thursday to be upon the Grand Jury, a mark of distinction I fancy seldom conferred upon Catholics. I saw poor Miss Whitworth yesterday, she is looking very ill but on the whole as well as I expected. She is on the point of removing to a house in Park Lane the gaiety of which will I trust be of great service to her. I always hear with pleasure any accession of strength to our Society and am in hopes that an élève of the Speculative may prove a real acquisition.[2]

I cannot give you a word of news not having indeed seen any one from whom I could collect any. William desires to be kindly remembered to you, pray do as much for me to our Johnian friends.

8. *Lavender House. 11 April 1805.*

As you said you should be in town today and are a man of your word I enclose this to Ashburton whom you will probably see tomorrow as early as the postman. You will I conclude have found London in an uproar about Ld Melville and are of course like all Grenvillites for having him hung, drawn and quartered. I own that though I think the vote of the House of Commons on Monday did them great honor, and should have given fifty votes, if I had had them, against the previous question, I am exceedingly sorry for the whole business, and wish it had never come on, as I fear it must in the end lead to the admission into office of Fox and all his Jacobine set. We shall have a second edition of the Peace of Amiens, and Sr Francis Burdett will be sent to compliment Buonaparte upon his new dignities, and perhaps the installation may be put off till a new vacancy offers for a Corsican knight. *Dio meliora piis*;[1] Anglice G—d D—n the *Saints* for deserting their friend Pitt. Unless they come round again with the weathercock, I do not know what we shall do. The

[2] In his letter of 20 Feb. Sulivan had announced the imminent accession of 'Douglas' to the Fusty (S.P.).

[1] Virgil, *Georgics*, 3, 513.

Opposition however had better take care how they attack Pitt for participating in Ld Melville's peculations or they may find that they are only knocking their heads against a stone wall, and if they merely blame him for having applied navy money to secret services, Ld Grenville who had the foreign department & Windham who very probably sunk some of it in Quiberon Bay should be the last to find fault with that, as it was all replaced.

I found all here well. Lilly whose face has been swelled to a most preternatural size has nearly recovered her usual appearance and they think she has by this swelling escaped a severe bilious attack. My aunt is quite well excepting a cold for which this treacherous weather easily accounts. Today the warmth is really very great although I daresay the night will be as cold. The vegetation has not made much progress, and but a few flowers have ventured out; a short continuance of this sunshine will doubtless inspire them with greater confidence. I suppose you have seen Clive who I hope has recovered [*from*] the fatigues of the long debate in the House. He however was not so persevering as Ash and I, but went away before the division. The debate though very long and important in its result was not in itself interesting. Petty spoke remarkably well, but Pitt and Fox made much better speeches three days before upon Francis's motion, indeed their speeches on that evening though short were (particularly Pitt's) extremely fine. I suppose you left Shee preparing a set of violent Philippics for the three next meetings, and you of course will give us an hour and a half upon Charles. I went by the way, to hear Sidney on Saturday last, and was disappointed; he seemed to have exhausted his collection of jokes and was reduced to the necessity of having recourse to the stale one of a Scotchman being surprised with the taste of ripe fruit upon his first arrival in England, which struck me as rather infra dig for a moral philosopher.[2]

9. *Cambridge. 19 May 1805.*

I know not whether I am most angry or obliged for the dreadful piece of folly, of which Clive informs me you were guilty the other day, in giving me your bedroom, and mounting up into a garret where if you had wished it, you could not have swung a cat. Really such an exertion of civility from a man of your party, and a *B.A.* into the bargain I should not have expected; I am sadly afraid Lord Chesterfield has corrupted you. You may however say of your civility *sic itur ad astra* with as much truth as Ld Jersey (I think) has affixed

[2] Sydney Smith gave his first course of lectures on Moral Philosophy at the Royal Institution from Nov. 1804 to May 1805.

it as a motto to his crest, a stag's head. You have I conclude of course
seen Ashburton since his return from Ware. I really had a remarkably
pleasant drive and dinner with him. I delivered your message to Shee
who seems to have quite recovered from the bad effects of his London
expedition and is relapsed into his old Cambridge habits just as comfortably as if nothing had happened, only wondering occasionally at
the inconsistency of *some folks*, who go to town with the sober intention
of keeping a law term, and then discover that it is equally necessary to
go dancing about with all the girls for a fortnight afterwards. I hope
however that if your engagements permit it, you will honor us on
Friday evening, to which night, on account of its having been necessary from Frazer's absence to defer the debate on his essay till tomorrow, the merits of Charles and the Parliament will be discussed.
On that evening three new members, Pollock, a son of Hobhouse, and
a third Trinity man whose name I forget take their seats, and unless you
come to our aid with all that fund of knowledge which you have
extracted from Millar, I fear we shall not impress their minds with a
sufficient respect for the Society.[1] They will I fancy prove a considerable acquisition as well in talent as in number. Pollock you know.
Hobhouse, they say is brighter than his father, and possesses a good
turn for sarcasm, (we will match him with Shee), and the third is a
first class man. So it is to be hoped we shall begin to revive and shall
have no more quartets. You have I suppose heard of the little fracas
that took place a few nights ago in Hiron and Thrower's shop.
Sentence was pronounced on the delinquents yesterday: Sir Henry
Smith who had made a precipitate retreat to London but was brought
back by Beverley, has been expelled, and degraded from the rank of
M.A. Gascoigne and Bright have been rusticated the one *sine die* the
other for a year, and had not Grose of this college been fortunately
for himself too drunk to get as far as the shop he would probably have
shared their fate.[2] Pierrepont came down for the dinner (the Beefsteak
anniversary) but by good luck was not in the scrape, and returned the
next morning. The genius of the University has however not been
guided by Mars only, we have also had some poetical effusions since
you left us, and the *Suicide Prostitute* dedicated to Percy by Mr Gwyn
of our year, is already struggling between Litchfield and the fourth

[1] John Millar (1735–1801), Professor of Law and historian. For the other names see
above, pp. 10–11.
[2] Sir Henry Smyth, 6th and last Bart of Berechurch (1784–1852), a fellow-commoner
of Trinity, took his M.A. that same year; he was subsequently M.P. for Colchester.
Henry Bright (1784–1869) was a pensioner at Peterhouse; he took his M.A. in 1810
and was subsequently M.P. for Bristol. Thomas Charles Gascoigne (1786–1809) was
a fellow-commoner of Trinity; he did not return to Cambridge but was killed while
hunting. Edward Grose (1783–1815), a pensioner of St John's, took his B.A. in 1806
and was killed at Quatre Bras. John Beverley was senior Esquire Bedell.

court.[3] I think I have now told you all the Cambridge *news* worth
knowing. Will Wood's having absconded and his goods & chattels
being seized is I presume too common an occurrence to come under
that denomination.[4] In expectation therefore of an harangue two
hours long on Friday (for the deuce is in it if you do not make an
opening speech twice as long as a reply).

10. *Thomas's Hotel.*[1] *4 July 1805.*

I need not tell you that my journey on Saturday was as pleasant
as the humour I was in would allow. I required indeed an agreeable
companion to keep me tolerably dull, for in truth I scarcely recollect
ever leaving any place with such regret as I did St John's. The society
I have enjoyed there for the last two years has to me had something
so delightful in it, that I shall always consider the chance which
brought me to the same college with yourself and Shee, as one of the
most fortunate events of my life. Upon our arrival in town Sidney
Smith carried me with him to dine at the King of Clubs.[2] The party
was very pleasant and excepting Brougham all opposition men. Ld
Holland, Petty, Ward, a Mr William Smith a loquacious Irish
member and Horner were the most prominent characters: besides
these however there appeared to be two or three intruders like myself
who contrary to the old rule of giving conversation for food, seemed
by the activity of their teeth, and invincible repose of their tongue
determined to lose no time in regaling both mind and body. Clive is
still in town but goes to Powis Castle on Monday, on which day I also
leave town. I intended to have gone tomorrow but Miss Whitworth
who is going with me to Park Place,[3] chose the other day to make tea
in her shoe, and having forgot to take her foot out of it, the consequence of her frolic was a severe scald, which will prevent her
moving till Monday. I dined on Tuesday with Clive and went in the
evening with him to the opera, where I met a lady who enquired
very much after you, and if she was not lately married I would tell
you her name, as it is however I shall content myself with assuring
you she is very handsome. The only news I have heard since my arrival
in town was contained in a letter shewn me by Mrs Sulivan so that
it is not my fault if this letter contains none. The Committee of

[3] Probably Frederick Gwynne (*ob.* 1816) who had migrated from Christ's to St John's
in Oct. 1804 and was to move again to Jesus in 1806.
[4] William Wood (*ob.* 1821), a fellow of St John's until 1806, had been deprived of
the senior bursarship on account of financial irregularities as long ago as 1797.
[1] In Berkeley Square.
[2] See Lady Seymour, ed., *The 'Pope' of Holland House*, 1906, pp. 333–40.
[3] Lord Malmesbury's place near Henley-on-Thames.

Impeachment are to deliver in their articles of charge against Lord Melville to day and Petty seemed to think that if the Lords have not much important business before them next session the trial will probably not last longer than a month and may be concluded in a week. London is woefully empty. I never saw it look so forlorn as it did last Sunday. If I had not luckily fallen in with Clive, I believe I should have followed the example of the man who jumped out of the two pair of stairs windows though probably not with the same catlike impunity. The West Indians look very glum. I saw Grant two days ago with a face as long as my arm, so I turned in to see the great horse and escaped him.[4] I was a good deal entertained last night at Sadlers Wells with an exhibition in the anti-Horatian style. I allude to the line *Nec coram populo natos Medea trucidet.*[5] The story is taken from Johnson's Tour into the Hebrides, and in the last act they actually drown two people on the stage in Fingal's Cave; they let in a great quantity of water from the New River, and a boat with two men in it is made fairly to sink. In the first part a lady jumps out of a boat and swims to shore: really whatever faults our dramas possess they are accurate and lively representations.[6] By the way as I make you hear all my prose puns I do not see why you should escape those which are hitched into a rhyme, and the following nonsense may as well serve to fill up the corner of a letter as it did part of a very wet walk to my dear friend Mr White yesterday, where I bought a horse; it occurred to me as I was trudging to new model & enlarge the punning epigram of Haggit's on Miss Tenant, and accordingly *auctior non emendatior* it stands thus:

> Though it oft has been asked if by *Tenants* at will
> Or by lease yr estates it be wisest to fill,
> I'd eject every farmer I freely confess
> *At my will* such a Tenant as this to possess
> And from those pouting lips should consider it bliss,
> To receive for my heart but a song *and a Kiss.*

You see mine is not quite so platonic a pun as I insist on a *Kiss* as well as a song.[7]

[4] The French fleet had eluded Nelson and attacked the British West Indies. Alexander Cray Grant (1782–1854), a former fellow-commoner at St John's and afterwards 8th Bart, was a prominent spokesman for the West Indian interest.

[5] *Cf.* Horace, *Ars Poetica*, 1. 185.

[6] Sadlers Wells had advertised in *The Times* of 1 July an 'Aquatic Theatre' programme concluding with 'a grand Caledonian Melo-Dramatic Romance' by Charles Dibdin and entitled 'An Bratach, or The Water Spectre'.

[7] Wright, a Trinity man, wrote (i. 42): 'The Johnians, who are sometimes called Pigs, sometimes Hogs (the Trinity are named Bull-dogs, mind ye) have, from time immemorial, been famed for *bad* puns.' There were several Haggits in Cambridge about this time, but neither the Haggit mentioned here nor Miss Tenant can be specifically identified.

11. *Park Place. 22 July 1805.*

Your letter arrived by the post yesterday morning certainly sooner, though not (if he is like his brother) safer than by William, he having made his appearance in the evening. I am very glad to hear that your oracular consultation with the learned judge has terminated so favourably, and really considering the binding you have bestowed on him more so than you had a right to expect. I have written to Percy to enquire what his plan of operations is respecting the moors, and I think it would be best for us to be at Alnwick time enough to see his lions before we take up arms; he mentioned when we were in town, the 20th of August as the day for commencing hostilities, as on that day both the red and black game are in motion, and I should think he will probably adhere to that arrangement. In that case I had intended to bestow my tediousness upon you about the 12th or thirteenth of August, so that after having eat you out of house and home, we might reach Alnwick about the 19th or twentieth; but if we lionize before we shoot, which, if equally convenient to you would be more so to me, we had better be at Percy's sooner than that, & I will in that case come to Ponsborne earlier. William tells me that you really expect to get a new gun from Manton in sufficient time to employ it against the Northumbrian grouse. I only wish you success, but would recommend two strings to your bow, or rather two guns to your shoulder, that in case Mr Manton should prove perfidious you may be otherwise provided. William remains here till Sunday next and perhaps longer, as Ashburton is not one of the quickest dispatchers of business. They seem as yet a good deal undetermined in their plans respecting the tour, but talk of Aberystwith as their Ultima Thule, which would be missing some of the best parts of the country. What think you of the Doctor. He certainly sent Sheridan to the Prince three days before he resigned to let him know he was no longer in office. The choice of the messenger pretty plainly pointed out the object of the communication, & yet this is the *honest upright wellmeaning man*, whose purity made amends for his folly! It is not much expected I believe that Nelson will overtake the combined fleets but even if he does not, it is a great deal to have driven them away from the West Indies. Talleyrand it is said is gone to prepare Buonaparte's apartments below; he will be a great loss to him, and a good riddance for us. *Leo* goes on swimmingly though I do not expect quite to get through him before I see you.[1] I do not know what you advert to in the last few lines of your letter but sure I am that I defy your scandal, but could relate some unpleasant truths concerning you if necessary.

[1] William Roscoe's *Life and Pontificate of Leo the Tenth* was first published in 1805.

12. *Park Place. 28 July 1805.*

As Percy begins his shooting so much sooner than he originally intended it would undoubtedly be expedient for us proportionally to hasten our departure. I shall therefore with your permission be at Ponsborne on the fourth instead of the thirteenth, and I think we shall be able to contrive to reach Alnwick by the last mentioned day, which will allow us time to recover the fatigues of the journey before we go to the moors, and *you* will then also have so compleatly fallen a victim to the charms of *the* Lady Percy, that if I go out with you, as is probable, you will be too much occupied by thinking of her to attend to the game and I shall get all the shots. William remains here certainly till Wednesday and I should not much wonder if I left him still waiting for his companion. I have no conception of Ashburton's getting through business quicker than a spoon through a shoulder of mutton. This being likewise a letter of business I shall take the hint conveyed in yours and not exceed the legal limits. I know not a word of news of any sort or kind but that it is supposed the King will soon leave Weymouth where as he is not allowed to sail or go about as formerly he cannot find much amusement.

13. *Lavender House. 9 Oct. 1805.*

I just got to Ottershaw[1] in the very nick of time as my party were to leave it on Sunday morning. I was neither robbed nor murdered, and arrived in rather less than two hours and three quarters. I found them all quite well. We came through Windsor on Sunday and I saw the Castle. It is certainly a very magnificent residence. The King *ought* to live there. The alterations are far from compleated, what has been done is in admirable taste, and excessively handsome. The entrance hall is so good an imitation of the old style that it might deceive any one. The rooms contain some good pictures though not a very large collection. I have been terribly scolded for not writing, my letter from Brandsby did not follow Fanny to Ottershaw and was found lying here, so that they were in compleat ignorance of our motions, till I explained them myself. I hope you found Mr and Mrs S. quite well at Margate, and ye latter deriving benefit from the sea bathing. Your company is not I suppose very select as you must be annoyed by the *Hoy Polloi* although these latter often keep their heads above water by their close connection with *piers*. I found a letter here from Mrs Stewart full as you may suppose of surprize

[1] Then the home in Chertsey of Edmund Boehm (*ob.* 28 Aug. 1822).

and indignation at Ashburton's marriage.[2] She says 'who will believe that I was deceived by his solemn assurances ten thousand times repeated'—'Mr S. and I have taken our resolution from which nothing shall ever induce us to depart; we shall never behold either Ld A. or his wife. The total break thus made between my sister and me is indeed heavy heavy on my heart, but I am not to blame in it.' I am truly sorry that all this has happened, but I think the Stewarts are right. How Ashburton will be able to live without seeing them, particularly if he takes a house in Edinh next winter I cannot conceive. I had a note from S. Smith this morning; he says 'I am glad Ash has not married the one eyed chambermaid at Dorants to whom I understand he was engaged'.

I heard this morning from Percy who tells me he has settled with a breaker about the Brinkburn mare. I hope she will turn out better than my other attempts in horseflesh. The bay which I left here with a cold I found in *statu quo* and apprehending something like glanders sent him back to White yesterday morning, so that I am again in expectation.

Palmer Percy tells me has exchanged his tour to Constantinople for a good living for which I think he is much better qualified.[3] I should much doubt whether in a strange country he could muster up resolution enough to ask his way. Adieu my dear Sulivan, I should not perhaps have peppered your head so soon if I had not feared the possibility of my losing one of your productions by its being directed to Ottershaw.

14. *Cambridge. 15 Nov. 1805.*

I was very sorry that I was prevented from taking a peep at Ponsborne on my way hither, but, having reached London on the Sunday and being detained in town with William till Tuesday night, I had only time to make the best of my way to reach this early

[2] Ashburton had married Mrs Stewart's niece, Anne Cunninghame, on 17 Sept. He had announced his intention to her mother only on the day of the marriage and to the Stewarts less than a week before. He stated to Palmerston that, though he had proposed in 1805, he had resolved upon the marriage as early as May 1803 (Ashburton to Palmerston, 12 and 24 Sept. 1805, B.P.W.). But in Nov. 1803 he was making up to Fanny Temple (Lilly Temple to Palmerston, 27 Nov. 1803, S.P.). It was presumably this latter courtship that inspired the famous passage of words between John Ward (Dudley) and Lady Glenbervie about Mary, Lady Palmerston: '"I detested that woman. She was so fawning and mean. There was no sort of bassesse she was not guilty of in order to get that monster Ashburton to marry her ugly daughter." "Upon my word," said Lady Glenbervie, "you have a very long and a very sharp scythe. You have just mown down three at one stroke."' (*Glenbervie Diaries*, ii. 93.)

[3] Probably Francis Palmer (*ob.* 1842), a fellow-commoner of Trinity Hall, who became Rector of Combepyne, Devon, in 1805.

enough to satisfy the calls of hunger (which *you* know are imperious) before the meeting of the Fusty.[1] I was the more sorry for this as you have resolved not to quit Westminster Hall before Christmas. If however you are good and will agree to the proposition I am going to make, I shall submit patiently to your studiousness. Ld Malmesbury desired me to make use of all my eloquence, to prevail upon you and Clive to spend all or part of your Christmas at Park Place. I have great hopes of Clive, and I do not despair, notwithstanding the powerful attractions that Hertfordshire possesses, in the lively Emma,[2] of your acceding to the confederacy; pray think of this, and as I do not want an immediate decision you ought to let it be favourable. Your excursion from Margate must have been entertaining. I had no idea that the works on the coast had been so compleat as you represent them to be. So my poor friends the smuglers are knocked up, I thought that since you had learnt in the North that it was only fair trading you would not have been so hard hearted towards them. You ask for particulars respecting Cambridge. I believe St John's does occupy the same place it did, but, that is almost the only circumstance in which it is unaltered. It is indeed much changed.[3] Your room has not fared so well as you imagined; it is occupied by *Hundsfoot! Quam dispari dominare Domino.* He is fitting it up *à l'Egyptienne* with Sphynxes Pyramids Mummies and Catercombs. He himself may personate the Enigma, at least he must have been fully as mysterious before Lord Bandon not to have been discovered. Old Bernard has fitted up the rooms little P. used to inhabit. His flirtation is going on swimmingly and Middleton's report though premature will probably turn out prophetic.[4] The Young Bear is much the same, but fortunately I see nothing of him. We have two gentlemanlike fellow commoners besides Swinburn. Willis a goodnatured sportsman, and Bruce, an Etonian who seems to possess some talent, he is a staunch

[1] They debated the Revolution of 1688 on 6 Nov.

[2] Amelia Elizabeth Godfrey had been brought up virtually as a member of the family by Palmerston's mother. She was the sister of Peter and Thomas Godfrey of Old Hall in East Bergholt, and the daughter of William Godfrey (formerly Mackenzie) of Woodford. William Godfrey had evidently been a childhood friend of Mary Mee and her brother Ben. After the death of his wife, Godfrey had wished to make Mary his children's stepmother, but she had refused him. As Lady Palmerston, however, she or her sister eventually took in Emma Godfrey. After his mother's death, Palmerston made Emma Godfrey a substantial allowance until her death, unmarried, on 18 April 1840. (B.P.W.)

[3] 'You have no idea', Palmerston wrote to Fanny Temple on 7 Nov., 'how melancholy it is to look up to the windows of Sulivan, Shee and Percy.' (B.P.W.)

[4] From what follows (and from no. 27) the Houndsfoot (a scoundrel, *O.E.D.*) would appear to have been private tutor to the two eldest sons of the Earl of Bandon who had been admitted at St John's on 4 June 1804. Viscount Bernard eventually married a niece of the 4th Viscount Midleton, but this was not until 1809 and 'Middleton' was almost certainly William Fowle Middleton (*ob.* 1860), afterwards 2nd Bart, a fellow-commoner of St John's. 'Little P.' was the Hon. Hugh Percy (1784–1856), who had recently gone down.

Foxite. There is a cousin of Fitz, Knight Gally come to Trinity Hall whose first appearance I like very much.[5] The Fusty is at present rather drooping; it has not recovered the loss it sustained last term and Pollock has obtained leave of absence till after Xmas to enable him to beat Walter.[6] Pepys is come up, but we have no new members yet. Clive will soon be a match for you and Shee; he is attending Christian's lectures which I tell him is time thrown away.[7] He is as bad as ever. It was with the utmost difficulty that I restrained him last night at the concert from attacking Mrs Panton ci devant Miss Gubbins;[8] in short excepting that I believe he is always in bed of a morning and does not go out to breakfast with an old friend, as some people whom I know, are apt to do, he is a match even for you. Holworthy is come up to Caius to take orders and Miss Jones.[9]

I am not engaged in Newton, but am quietly endeavouring to dig through Thucidides which I hope to accomplish before Easter. Adieu my dear Sulivan I must defer the many sapient and sagacious observations I intended upon the state of affairs or the post will be gone.

[*PS.*] My Northumbrian purchase proves as I thought *rising* 3, and must therefore remain there till spring.

15. *Park Place. 27 Dec. 1805.*

Ld Malmesbury desires me to say that he shall be happy to see you whenever you please to come and the sooner the better. Indeed I believe you had better come as soon as you can, for on the 9th of January they expect some dozens of Auklands & Edens, and on the fourteenth they go to town to be present at the Birth day;[1] I have written to Clive to beg him to expedite himself, if it is possible to leave the Shropshire woodcocks. To you I should have made no such proviso, as you would of course long before this *have killed all*, & have

[5] 'The Young Bear' has not been identified. Edward Swinburne (1788–1855), eldest son of Sir John Swinburne, 6th Bart, and uncle of the poet, was admitted from Harrow as a fellow-commoner at St John's on 31 May 1805 and Richard Willis (1787–1858) was admitted fellow-commoner on 10 May 1805. But Michael Bruce was a pensioner. The mother of Henry Gally Knight (1786–1846) was an aunt of Sir Henry Fitzherbert, 3rd Bart of Tissington (1783–1858). Fitzherbert had been admitted a fellow-commoner at St John's in 1801 and was already one of Sulivan's 'set'.

[6] Pollock did win the contest, issuing senior wrangler and first Smith's prizeman from the Senate House examinations of 1806. Henry Walter (1785–1859), a pensioner at St John's, was second wrangler and junior prizeman.

[7] Edward Christian (*ob.* 1823) was Downing Professor of Law at Cambridge.

[8] Thomas Panton (1731–1808), a wealthy sportsman, had recently married Mary, second daughter of Joseph Gubbins of Kilrush.

[9] Matthew Holworthy (1783–1836) was admitted a fellow-commoner at Caius on 23 Sept. 1805.

[1] The Queen's Birthday was celebrated on 18 Jan. 1806.

had none to leave. The party here now consists of the Park Place family, my sisters & self, and a Mr & Mrs St Leger, of whom I beg you would not make *light*, for they are very pleasant people and their name is pronounced *Selinger*.

I direct this to Hertfordshire where I think you expected about this time to be, as I take it for granted that you have not accompanied Shee in his iniquitous expedition to Cambridge. Ashburton was still in town a few days ago. Upon my word his remaining so long absent from his dear Anne so soon after matrimony is not like the ardour of a young husband. If I was her I should be jealous; I hope however he performs his quarantine with greater strictness than he did last summer. I fear that the Elbe is frozen and that it may in that case be sometime before we receive further intelligence from Moravia; as to the French account of an armistice it is highly improbable, and Woronzow at the time the first accounts of the battle of the 3d & 4th arrived received from the Russian Minister at Hamburgh an account nearly similar to that which appeared in our papers, so that there can be little doubt of its correctness and truth. Indeed had the French gained any real advantage we should long before this time have had the news through the *Moniteur*, or sent in a bulletin from Boulogne. How extremely indelicate it was to publish poor Ld Nelson's will, surely everything should be done to conceal his weaknesses instead of dragging them before the eyes of the world. It is not unlikely that Lady Hamilton published it, but she surely did not hope that Ld Nelson's encomium upon her piety and virtue would convince the world that she was another much injured Lucretia Borgia. Pray is this Miss Thompson[2] any relation to the Miss Thompson that Fitz and Shee were seen walking with one day in Cambridge? I wonder that the Court suffered the evidence in Calder's trial to be published before the whole could come before the publick.[3] What has come out is not much in his favour. How uncommonly surprized he would be if he was sentenced to be shot after having sent home his title and desired remainders for his nephews. Adieu my dear Sulivan let me know when we may expect you.

16. *Park Place. 31 Dec. 1805.*

Not having heard any thing of you since I wrote last week I presume you may still be in town, and not have gone to Pondsborne to which I directed. My object in writing besides the disinterested view of *entertaining* you, was to benefit myself by expressing a wish of Lord Malmesbury's that you would come here as soon as you can.

[2] Not identified.
[3] The court martial of Vice-Adm. Sir Robert Calder had opened on 23 Dec.

They expect a whole house full of Auklands and Edens on the ninth
or tenth of Jany and on the 14th they remove to London to be present
at the Queen's birth day, so that you see if you think of putting into
execution your intention of coming here expedition would be advisable. Pray let me know if you can by return of post when we may
expect you (we had rather you would bring your answer yourself).
What shocking news from the Continent.[1] I fear the game is up.

17. *Park Place. 3 Jan.* [*1806*].

We shall be happy to see you on Monday, and are only sorry you
cannot come sooner. Though it is imprudent to tell you so, the dinner
hour is *five*, but you had better proceed upon the supposition of its
being four and then you will be in *time*. So this confounded armistice
is too true. The Emperor Francis must be either the greatest fool or
the most complete knave that ever existed. I fear a mixture of the two
in his character.

[*PS.*] Happy New Year. I wish you had been able to figure at ye
Henley ball tonight.

18. [*St John's, Cambridge. 24 Jan. 1806.*]

Both Wood and Outram encourage me to stand.[1] I can take my
degree on Monday.[2] No Johnian candidate has yet offered so that I
shall get this college, any votes you can pick up will be thankfully
received. You have of course told Shee every thing, which I shd have
done had I seen him after FitzHarris[3] spoke to me.

19. *St John's. Friday, 25 Jan.* [*24 Jan. 1806*].

I have been canvassing the whole of this morning. I am sure of all
St John's not even (I believe) excepting Jackson.[1] I met with only two
refusals to day in eight colleges, though but few gave me any distinct

---

[1] After Napoleon's victory at Austerlitz both Austria and Prussia had come to terms
with France.
[1] Pitt had died at 4.30 a.m. on 23 Jan., and Palmerston, who had been at a ball
in London till 4, left that same day to test the ground in Cambridge. He knew that
Petty and Althorp, who were both Trinity men, intended to stand and had heard that
Royston, a Johnian, might do so too. (Palmerston to Frances Temple, 23 Jan. 1806,
B.P.W.) Wood became 'manager' of Palmerston's canvass in Cambridge (Althorp to
Spencer, 4 Feb., Spencer Papers).
[2] The candidates had to be M.A.s of the University.
[3] Malmesbury's son and heir.
[1] Presumably Jeremiah Jackson (1775–1857), a former fellow of St John's.

promise; the greatest number refuse to give any decisive answer to a first application, but that, as I am rather late, is in my favour. I cannot find out any body in town to whom you can apply but the Primroses, Ld Henry Moore (if in town), FitzHerbert, & Hugh Percy.[2] If Fitz would say a good word for me to his uncle Ld St Helens it might be useful.[3] I fancy Ld Althorpe & Petty are playing into each other's hands, & the former will ultimately make over his interest to the latter. I should think however that many would support the one who might not like the party with which the other is connected. I shall take my degree on Monday. Adieu. I do not write to Shee because I consider writing to you as the same thing.

[*PS.*] I sent you a line by this morning's coach to say I shd certainly stand.

20. *St John's. Saturday* [*25 Jan. 1806*].

Many thanks for your kind letters and exertions. I have been trotting over all the University but Trinity, which, as little is to be hoped from it, I left for the last. I am much obliged to you for Christian's hint of which I shall if possible avail myself.[1] Royston is not to be named even for the next vacancy, and from what Marsh and Outram can collect from Ly Hardwicke, there is every reason to be sure that Charles Yorke does not intend to stand.[2] Their interest will go with me, since Ld Hardwicke means to be a candidate for the High Stewardship and will want Johnian votes. This circumstance may render the Duke of Rutland doubtful. He is mentioned as a competitor of Ld H. and may in consequence make some arrangement with Petty & Althorpe. The maneuvre you suggest is I fear impossible; Petty & Althorpe

[2] Fearing that Palmerston would suffer by any unnecessary delay Sulivan, with Shee's help, had already opened a canvass for him in London, in particular among the Inns of Court. Lord Dalmeny (afterwards 4th Earl of Rosebery) and his brother Francis Ward Primrose had both been at Pembroke. Dalmeny was now an M.P. and his brother was reading for the bar. On 28 Jan. Sulivan reported that Frank Primrose supported Petty (B.P., G.C./SU no. 9).

[3] Fitzherbert was also studying for the bar; his uncle was a distinguished diplomat and courtier.

[1] John Christian, a Johnian who was at Lincoln's Inn with Sulivan, had suggested that a University regulation requiring graduates who had allowed their voting rights to lapse to undergo a further month's residence before resuming them would be quite unenforceable (Sulivan to Palmerston, 24 Jan. 1806, B.P., G.C./SU no. 8).

[2] Lord Hardwicke was Lord Lieutenant in Ireland and Royston was with him. Since he feared that there might be rather severe competition to be High Steward of the University, he rather regretted that in his absence his wife had committed him to the contest. His half brother, Charles Yorke, was M.P. for Cambridgeshire, but there was some suggestion that he might come forward as the Johnian candidate for the University seat. Herbert Marsh (1757–1839) was then a fellow of St John's and a particular opponent of the evangelicals led by Charles Simeon (1759–1836).

understand each other perfectly and were seen breakfasting and writing their letters in the same room yesterday morning.[3] Marsh and Jackson have been particularly kind. Headley,[4] who by the way had I not started had some intention of proposing himself, assured me that all *his* friends were *mine* also; I conclude he means the Wilberforcians; I can assure you I have no qualms about the religious tenets of my voters, & if they will but support me care not whether they are Simeonites or Atheists, or, what may happen, both. I have written to the Bishop of Ely.

[*PS.*] Dr Clarke is at Ibbetson's Hotel. I do not believe much is to be expected from him but it might be as well to try.[5] I have written to Percy. I am aware he will feel some awkwardness in answering me but I thought it was as well.[6]

21. *St John's. Sunday* [*26 Jan. 1806*].

I will not take up your time by thanking you for your kind & friendly zeal, you know me too well not to guess what I feel. I enclose you a *long* list[1] at which you will doubtless 'turn pale with affright'. It contains the names of all the non resident Masters of Arts who are in London. Of course my only object in sending it you was that, if there should be among them any to whom you can get easy access, you might apply. They will all have a circular letter in the end, so that unless you happen to know any, or their friends, do not plague yourself about them. Young Cust of St John's promised to write to his brothers.[2] Hodgson of St George's has interest as well as a vote.[3] Those names to which a cross is affixed I have sent to Ld Malmesbury also, in case he might know anything of them. The Saints & Sinners are I am sorry to say united, & I hear that Wilberforce supports Petty manfully. This is unfortunate & unexpected; I thought Headley had known his politics. However I am still in hopes of having

---

[3] Sulivan had suggested an arrangement with one of Palmerston's opponents.

[4] According to Petty a handful of Pittites at Trinity had decided to run one of their fellow-students, the 2nd Baron Headley (1784–1840), against Althorp and himself (Petty to Creevey, Jan. 1806, *Creevey Papers*, i. 76).

[5] Edward Daniel Clarke (1769–1822), a fellow of Jesus, was promised to Petty (Shee to Palmerston, 27 Jan. 1806, B.P., G.C./SH no. 72).

[6] Lord Lovaine and Hugh Percy both supported Palmerston, but the Duke of Northumberland and his son supported Petty (Petty to Creevey, 28 Jan. 1806, *Creevey Papers*, i. 76).

[1] Lacking.

[2] William Cust (1787–1845) was a younger son of the 1st Baron Brownlow; his elder brothers Henry Cockayne and John (afterwards 1st Earl of Brownlow) were also Cambridge graduates.

[3] Robert Hodgson (*ob.* 1844), formerly of Peterhouse.

a few of his sect. Some of the small colleges have luckily thought that it would [*be*] dangerous to the balance of power in ye University if both members were returned by Trinity. I never felt more partial to the balance of power. Some zealous churchmen too have taken alarm at Petty's approving the Catholic emancipation. I heard today that Milner of Queens had catechized him on the subject. Charles Yorke does not come down but some of his friends hang back till his determination is publickly known. The loss of the Duke of Rutland & the Saints is certainly great, but still I do not despair, provided the Bishop of Lincoln, & Charles Yorke would come forward.

22. *St John's. 28 Jan. 1806.*
    Bulwer & Ashley, i. 14–15; MS. not found.

Palmerston reports that his canvass is going on 'very well', especially among the college heads. He also has in his favour that the small colleges resent Trinity's attempts to monopolise the university offices and that Lord Hardwicke will lose support among the Johnians if his brother also stands for the parliamentary seat. However, Hardwicke's uncle, the Bishop of Ely, is proving difficult and Palmerston's friend, Thomas Knox, has promised himself to Althorp.[1] On the other hand, James Gill (afterwards Varenne), a fellow of St John's and Junior Dean, is well pleased to follow the example of Lord Grantham, the nephew of Mrs Robinson, who had promised his support to Palmerston.[2] So, provided Althorp does not give way to Petty, Palmerston entertains 'strong hopes of success'.

23. *St John's. Wednesday [29 Jan. 1806].*

I confess I rather expected that the bulk of the law would go with Petty; he has lived much with them and has many friends in that profession, besides that, saving your presence, the gentlemen of the gown have been very apt to be am I to say oppositionists or ministerialists? but favourers of Foxe's principles. I fear that unless the opposite party have recourse to it, Christian's manœuvre would not be advisable, it would give incalculable offence to all the old dons, who would consider me as a most profligate fellow were I to attempt to infringe the sanctity of a University Grace; indeed it seems the opinion of those whom I have consulted that it had better not be attempted, it would produce endless confusions in the University as there would be no limit to the possible number of voters. Petty I find

---

[1] Sulivan to Palmerston, n.d., B.P., G.C./SU no. 7.
[2] Malmesbury to Palmerston, n.d., B.P.W.

has committees every where and we have thought his example not to be despised. Would you and Shee with any other of your friends form a sort of committee at any place most convenient to you it might be of great service.[1] Tatham has written to a Mr or Dr Remmet & desired him to call upon Shee for the purpose of arranging matters.[2] The first thing to be done is to engage as many places as can be procured in all the publick conveyances from London here on Monday, Tuesday and Wednesday next, for those voters who may come from or through town and if you will let me know where your committee sit, we will let the voters know where to apply to.[3] The Bishop of Ely I am sorry to say goes against me, but in favour of Althorpe which is better than Petty, still however I have hopes of neutralising him. Charles Yorke supports me, I had a promised vote this morning in consequence of an application from him. Marsh has I think mismanaged the Yorke interest *entre nous*. If you should meet with any Althorpites it may not be amiss to canvass them for a second vote in case Althorpe should resign which may still notwithstanding Ld Spencer's declaration take place shd it suit ministerial arrangements.[4] Adieu. Percy is here, but as I supposed [?*wishes*] to be neutral; he cannot support because the Duke will not allow him, Petty having written to him on the *Wednesday* the day before Pitt died, but he will not oppose.

24. *St John's. 3 Feb. 1806.*

We will after the receipt of tomorrow's post make out and send you a list of all the *certain* voters, not according to Petty's interpretation, those who are *certainly* adverse, as in the case of Mr Remmet; but those who are propitious. I fear Althorpe will certainly stand the poll as he has said so himself. I begin to be convinced that his resignation in favour of Petty would be advantageous to us, for though it might

[1] It was established at Gray's Inn Coffee House (Sulivan to Palmerston, n.d., B.P., G.C./SU no. 10).

[2] Thomas Tatham was a contemporary at St John's; his elder brother Ralph was a fellow. Robert Remmet was also a fellow of St John's and a member of the Inner Temple.

[3] The travelling arrangements were made for Palmerston by Shee in London and Wood in Cambridge. The bills for horses and carriages etc., from Mr Mills of the Sun Inn in Trumpington Street, Cambridge, and from James Warner of the Falcon Inn in Waltham Cross, totalled £341. 5s. 9d. (B.P.W.; see also Shee to Palmerston, n.d., B.P., G.C./SH no. 76.) Althorp complained to his father that Wood 'began by complaining of both of us [Petty and Althorp] separately to each other for stopping up the road and then was the first to take all the carriages himself'. (4 Feb., Spencer Papers.)

[4] Spencer, who had joined Fox with the Grenvilles and was destined for the Home Office, had refused to allow his son to make any arrangement with Petty for the weaker candidate to withdraw and instead made a similar but unsuccessful approach through Malmesbury to Palmerston (Malmesbury to Palmerston, 29 Jan. and n.d. 1806, B.P.W.).

unite Trinity, it would throw a large part of Althorpe's supporters into our scale, and wd excite great indignation in the University, Masters of Arts not liking to be turned over like Fen sheep from one hand to another. That hundsfoot Simeon will not vote at all. He told me today that if either Althorpe or I stood alone against Petty he would vote for us but that having a great respect for Ld Spencer he would not oppose Althorpe & therefore should not vote, though were he obliged to vote it would have been in my favour. Perhaps he does not wish to appear much in publick after the unfortunate mistake made the other day by one of his parishioners who would come into his wife's room while Simeon's curate was proving to her in a most zealous manner his partiality for *works* as well as for faith. Have you had the day of election inserted in all the papers, if not pray do immediately, and it might be as well to have it put in by *authority*, as it would take away any doubt that the distant voters might have about it. The election will begin at twelve o'clock.

I am sure the delay in delivering the writ was a trick of Petty's friends. As it did not come time enough to be proclaimed on Saturday the Vice Chancellor could appoint the election only on Friday, Saturday or Monday. Blackburn has secured you and Shee rooms at Flack's. I could not any how get you a room in College unless you would take a bed in my apartment, as every room is secured for Fellows who are coming. Rocky Smith[1] will certainly attend. I wrote to Shee yesterday about the reports you mention, of which I know nothing, and even had they been circulated they would probably not have been less founded or intended to do more mischief than that relative to the slave trade. Besides I wonder at Petty's friends thinking it so injurious to him that he should be represented as supported by *Foxites*.[2]

[*PS.*] I forgot to ask Shee yesterday whether he received a blank draught from me three days ago. If he did not I wish you would mention to Forster[3] that I sent it, that he may intercept it, it was a check upon Hankey to George Shee. Percy would have written but

[1] Not identified.

[2] Palmerston had sent Malmesbury a paragraph for the London papers that included a reference to Petty 'depending upon the friends of Mr Fox'. Malmesbury had deleted it as being 'neither quite fair nor sound policy'. (Malmesbury to Palmerston, 29 Jan., B.P.W.) But the accusation had nonetheless got about Cambridge. Petty wrote to Creevey on 1 Feb.: 'What with reports circulated by enemies & the indiscretions of some friends, I am afraid an impression has gone abroad, that I am standing on mere party grounds & some of Pitt's friends, who had given me hopes, are gone off upon the idea that they might have given their vote personally to me, but to *Mr Fox's candidate* no.' (Microfilm of Creevey Papers in the D. M. Watson Library, University College London.) Meanwhile the rumour had been spread, probably by Brougham, that Palmerston was unsound on the slavery question.

[3] Palmerston's solicitor in London.

that you are coming so soon. D$_0$ to Fitz. He has got a bed for Fitz at Samson's.

25. *St John's. Tuesday [4 Feb. 1806].*
   Add. MSS.

Inman[1] has written to Remmet to say that we or rather *they* have sent to all the Inns [*of Court*] to say that all who declare in writing that they are coming down to vote with us may have horses. We found it quite impossible to make out any thing like an accurate list of those who were coming through town, and thought the above-mentioned arrangement most likely to answer. Mr Chas Woollaston[2] & a friend are coming down to vote & have been desired to apply to you at the committee, as they were afraid of not being able to get conveyed. Our numbers are increasing rapidly, out-voting Johnians are dropping in incessantly. Blackall of Emanuel is come; he is a valuable man.[3] Milner still wavers though I think we shall have him at last.[4] Dr Procter of Cath. Hall is gone in residence to Norwich.[5] I tried today to ascertain the point respecting Mr Worsley but could not. Indeed the only way is by application to the Master, as they will tell a Johnian nothing. Inman attempted it, but we will try again by more roundabout means. I should hardly think Tavil capable of such a trick.[6] Adieu my dear Sul. Have you written to the wretch; I write by tonight's post but you may more certainly hit him.

26. *St John's. Wednesday evening [?5 Feb. 1806].*
   From typescript; MS. not found.

Remmet does not return tonight as he thinks it would not be of much use. I just send you a line to inform you of it in case he should not have written. Our voters are dropping in from all quarters. Cambridge will be as full as it can hold. Adieu I have not time to say more as I have new comers to take the first shot at every moment. Mrs Hopper is in despair about my Lord Clive, her tender heart is distressed at his non arrival.

[1] James Inman (1776–1859), astronomer and fellow of St John's.
[2] Charles Hyde Wollaston (1772–1850).
[3] Samuel Blackall (*ob.* 1842) was a fellow of Emanuel.
[4] Isaac Milner was wavering on account of the rumours about Palmerston and the slave trade; but he finally came round.
[5] Joseph Procter was Master of St Catherine's.
[6] Ralph Worsley (1764–1848) had found his name removed from the boards at Trinity and suspected it was a trick (Malmesbury to Palmerston, 3 Feb., B.P.W.). George Frederick Tavel was a tutor at Trinity and a supporter of Petty.

[*PS.*] I wish you & Shee would think over the propriety of my standing again in credulity in case of Petty's vacating his seat after
success.[1]

27. *St John's. 26 June 1806.*

The ball is on Monday and not on Tuesday as I thought it would
have been.[1] I hope this will not prevent you from coming down. I
have delivered your note to Sampson so that every preparation will
no doubt be made for your receipion. With respect to letters I can
assure you that though I am sometimes guilty of indulging myself by
keeping them, yet whenever the writer gives directions to have them
destroyed, they are most scrupulously consigned to the flames, so that
I beg that no fears on that score may ever cramp your fingers when a
pen is in them. I am very glad to hear that *one* difficulty is removed,
and need not say what sincere pleasure it will afford me to hear that
all the rest are surmounted of which I own I have stronger hopes than
you appear to entertain.[2] Clive arrived here the night before last,
looking much better than when he left town; he takes his degree on
Monday. The Bernards have got another tutor to supply the place of
Price, he is a Dr Hickey of Dublin College, & seems an inoffensive
pompous little man, quite delightful compared with the other.[3] I am
very sorry for the latter part of your news, I cannot conceive anything
much worse than Ld St Vincent's returning to the head of the
Admiralty, & I should think it would be an impolitic measure in the
new ministry who would render themselves very unpopular by such
an appointment, to a very large part of the nation. Ld Howick would
probably make a very good Governor General, if the heat of the
climate would not produce a perpetual effervescence in his fretful disposition. It looks very much as if Fox was actually broaching a
negotiation with Talleyrand. Peace will always & under any circumstances find a certain number of advocates in a commercial & heavily

[1] Petty would have had to seek re-election if his appointment as Chancellor of the
Exchequer had been deemed to be of a subsequent date. Malmesbury thought it 'a
nice legal question', but in any case was inclined to think Palmerston would gain no
credit if he made a contest out of any new election. The poll, which gave Petty an
easy victory, did not take place until 7 Feb.; but a new election was avoided on the
rather controversial grounds that although the poll had been completed before his
patent of office was sealed, that patent had already been signed and Petty had kissed
hands. (Malmesbury to Palmerston, 6, 7 and 8 Feb. 1806, B.P.W.; Croker to Peel,
19 Mar. 1828, Peel Papers, Add. MS. 40320.)
   [1] There was usually a ball following Commencement Sunday.
   [2] Sulivan seems to have been disappointed in a courtship, perhaps of Elizabeth
Temple.
   [3] Ambrose Hickey (1750–1826).

taxed country but I should think that no reflecting man could approve
of it at this moment, since whatever terms we obtained it could only
be regarded as a suspension of arms under which name nobody would
venture to recommend it. But Fox probably is ambitious of entering
with Talleyrand into the lists of negociation, and of building his
reputation upon an advantageous Treaty. What will the Grenvilles
say to it, or how will Windham slip his neck out of the noose.

[*PS.*] I consider Petty's coming down as a great compliment.[4]

28. *Park Place. 16 July 1806.*

You are really as good as your word, and better than my expectation, for notwithstanding my knowledge of your epistolary diligence,
I scarcely expected that among the various occupations of Chancery
Courts, packing up portmanteaux etc. previously to your leaving
London, you would have found leizure to fulfill your promise of
writing by sending me such a well filled letter. It had but one bad
effect and that was spoiling Ly Malmy's breakfast, the envy she felt at
the sight of it having taken away her appetite. I must however scold
you for one part of it, & that is the sort of apology you make for mentioning yourself & your own affairs, as if whatever nearly concerned
you, did not also in consequence excite a lively interest me. I therefore beg leave to put in a protest against such nonsense in future & in the
Hornbuckle style 'I gies ye to know that (though not a senior fellow)
I wont bear it'.[1] I am not surprized at your spirits being affected and
I think you have judged very well in resolving to remain quiet at
Pondsborne for the present.[2] But I own I should strongly recommend
you not to stay there any great length of time, but to employ some
part of the summer in a touring excursion. The sort of retired uniform
life which a person usually leads at home, is to a quiet mind as pleasant
as any other, but when anything presses upon the spirits nothing is so
good as change of scene, which by a rapid succession of objects affords
the only amusement of which perhaps the mind is capable, and
prevents it from preying upon itself and increasing its own disorder.
I know that in such cases the *vis inertiae* is very strong, but one is
always repaid for the exertion of overcoming it. I really regret that my

---

[4] Palmerston and Petty both regarded Commencement as a time to canvass for future
parliamentary elections.

[1] Thomas Waldron Hornbuckle (1775–1848), a fellow of St John's, figures as 'Horny'
in Wright's list of popular 'big-wigs'. Wright also mentions (i. 52) that he was 'famous
for a habit he had acquired of pulling up his inexpressibles'. Hornbuckle was Bruce's
tutor.

[2] Sulivan's letter is not in the Broadlands Papers and its contents are therefore
unknown.

engagements this summer prevent me from offering myself to you as a
tourist, which I certainly would otherwise have done, but I should, if
I were you, look out for a companion, and put travelling shoes upon
my Hanoverian steed. Having thus discharged my volley of advice,
for which I can conceive you desiring his Sable Majesty to thank me,
I will endeavour to communicate to you all the foreknowledge I
myself possess of our future motions. We intended to have set out in
our peregrinations about this time, but as the Sheen business will be
settled sooner than I expected it will be better for me to stay a few
days longer in order to sign a certain number of deeds, etc., which
cannot so well be sent after me. The man who bought the house has
agreed to take the furniture also and is to have immediate possession.
I get 6950£ for the whole concern, and though it falls a little short of
the valuation, to have sold it by auction would have been so much
more troublesome that I am very well satisfied with the arrangement.[3]
We shall probably set out about Wednesday or Thursday next and
mean to make the best of our way down to Minto, as Ld Minto's
intention of bringing his family to town with him in the beginning of
September preparatory to his sailing in October, will of course oblige
us to remove towards the latter end of August.[4] From Minto we mean
to go to Bothwell for a day or two; and thence to return by Carlisle
to the Lakes. They will I fancy occupy us about ten days, and from
them we descend through Cheshire to the Powis's. I am not sure
whether they will be at Powis Castle or Walcot; we are to get there
about the 12th or 14th of Septr and after a decent visit of a week or
ten days, return here. Whether after that we shall remain here any
time or go soon to Broadlands I am not certain. I fulfilled your orders
& fabricated divers & various lies for Lady Malmy assuring her that
your cruel parents insisted upon your remaining some time at home to
make up all the lee way in your legal studies which had been produced by the tide of dissipation in which you have been plunged.
She has however I find written to you herself, as she accuses me of
inventing lies to keep you away till I return. Fitzharris is still at
Broadlands which I believe he soon leaves for Heron Court.[5] Ld
Malmesy comes here on Saturday from Hampshire. Fox has been
declared by Vaughan to be out of immediate danger, but I should

[3] Temple Grove, the Palmerstons' old family mansion in Sheen, had been let since
the 2nd Viscount's death and had brought in hardly more than £300 a year in rent.
But, fortunately for Palmerston, the 1806 sale seems to have fallen through. For two
years later William Temple reported that it had been sold by Peter Coxe, the auctioneer,
for no less than £12,065 (to Elizabeth Temple, 23 July 1808, B.P.W.). It subsequently
became a preparatory boarding school and was pulled down after the school moved
from Sheen.
[4] Minto had just been appointed Governor General of India.
[5] Palmerston had loaned Broadlands to Fitzharris for his honeymoon. Heron Court
was another house of the Malmesburys near Christchurch, Hampshire.

think it impossible he could ever be able to apply to business with safety. I trust he is not on the eve of making peace, as in that case my wish would certainly be father to my thought. With respect to Cambridge politics, I believe things remain nearly *in statu quo*, though I fancy Petty has certainly lost ground since he has been in office. He wrote a foolish letter to Trinity about the beer tax against which the College remonstrated, & offered to allow them the same exemptions as were to be enjoyed by schoolmasters, viz. a deduction of 5s. for each person in the House. I did not canvass when I was there excepting two or three new Masters of Arts whom I thought favourable, [*such*] as Maud, Starkie etc. but merely contented myself with calling upon all my resident voters. Baines of Christ's however (the Cambridge Skeffington) gave me his vote in the *ball room*, of course unasked.[6] I think in general Outram and Wood seem to consider things as going on well, but as probably no dissolution will take place this year nothing further can be done; except (what I should at all events have done) going up with William in October. Petty I understand was a good deal annoyed at my being Steward.[7] I wonder at ministers opposing the votes of thanks to the volunteers, it will render them more unpopular in the Country than any thing they could have done, & is really wrong, for if the volunteers deserved thanks for merely coming forward in the time of alarm much more do they now for three years unremitted exertion [*by*] which the Country has certainly been saved. Sheridan will not thank Petty for styling his motion factious & dictated by party spirit; he must have been asleep when he first rose & have supposed himself speaking upon Sr H. Mildmay's motion.[8] I should like very much to have the pumping of *Facetious Raikes* after his return from Greece, & envy him his tour much.[9]

[*PS.*] Strange to say I have just read Park's Travels for the *first* time. I have been most uncommonly entertained. What a capital fellow Inman would be for such a journey. Though he would not find the

[6] Thomas Starkie (1782–1849) was a student at St John's; Robert William Henry Maude (1784–1861) of Trinity. There were three Baines's from Christ's, but this was probably James Johnson Baines (1778–1854). Sir Lumley Skeffington (1771–1850) was a well-known playwright and fop.
[7] Noblemen traditionally took their degrees on the Monday of Commencement Week, one of them being elected by the ladies to be steward of the ball that evening. Admission was by invitation only, but the men paid only one guinea each and the ladies nothing at all. Consequently the steward 'generally found himself out of pocket'. (Henry Gunning, *Reminiscences of the University, Town, and County of Cambridge, from the year 1780*, 2 vols., 1854, i. 26–8.) There survives in B.P.W. a bundle of bills for the expenses Palmerston incurred as steward. It includes large amounts for fruit—including fifty-eight plates of strawberries and fifty-nine of cherries.
[8] Sir Henry Mildmay had proposed on 11 July a vote of thanks to the Volunteers (1 *Hansard*, vii. 1105–6).
[9] Henry Raikes had spent the greater part of 1805–6 travelling in south-east Europe and the Mediterranean area, part of the time with Aberdeen.

Moors quite so quiet as the Botany Bay negroes, who, he says only grinned when in an awkward attempt to shave them he cut large slices out of their faces.

29. *Minto. 8 Aug. 1806.*

I conclude you have long before you get this returned to the shades of Ponsborne to which place I shall direct. We have been here since Tuesday week, having by our usual rapid method of travelling spent only four days and a bit on the road. We found William in patient expectation, and not only looking well but wonderful to say actually grown *fat*, though in Scotland. Gilbert we have seen scarcely at all, he has been employed in saying soft things to Miss Brydone at *Coldstream*, the neighbourhood of which does not appear to have *damped* the ardour of his flame.[1] We have not yet seen the future Mrs Gilbert and it is probable shall not while we stay here as they are so proper as to think it wrong for her to come to Minto until she has been executed. You must admit that considering our *curiosity*, it is a very tantalizing situation to be so near without seeing her. All the rest of this family are well, and *Watty* in high health, but he has been so much employed in taking the pointers out, that we have not yet had *Eh! losh tis a fish!!* Watty since we saw him has commenced a new character, and is turned fox-hunter. One day last year instead of running after the hounds as he used to do with his terrier under his arm, he was put upon a horse and soon distanced the whole field. They say he was an excellent figure. In his little shooting jacket, without boots, his stockings hanging about his heels, his shins all bloody from having come in contact with half a dozen pairs of spurs as he tore past the other riders, his face exhibiting successively the extremes of enjoyment and fear, at one time making much of the mane, at another screaming out, *Eh Dinna stope me!* he made Gilbert almost die of laughing. He said afterwards that he had been *sae frichted he never thought he wad ha lived to see the end ot*. Miss Mary Anne is I fear rather fickle and has taken to William in preference to me, having discovered his great abilities in eating toast and butter—its well for her poor tender heart that you did not stay longer at Mount Teviot, you would certainly have made a deep impression on her.[2] So we are certainly to have peace if we have it not already. A peace negotiated by Fox, and concluded by Ld Lauderdale cannot fail of being a *chef d'œuvre*. I am most heartily sorry for it, it is a wretched thing and I cannot help thinking

[1] Gilbert Elliot, afterwards 2nd Earl of Minto, married Mary Brydone in Sept. 1806.
[2] Marianne Elliot (1730–1811) was Lord Minto's maiden aunt. Mount Teviot was the home of her brother, Adm. John Elliot (*ob.* 1809).

the majority of the sensible part at least of the Country will be of the same opinion. We must of course give up the poor King of Naples, which after his de[*sertion*] to us, is infamous: indeed I cannot see how at present peace can bring us any thing but dishonour and defeat. The ministerial plea I understand is that our finances will not admit of a continuance of the war. If they find that to be the case they deserve to be turned out for incapacity. How did Pitt make the finances of this Country carry it through a period of difficulty and distress, compared with which the present is certainly a *bed of roses*. I wonder how Lord Grenville could be induced to consent to a measure so contrary to all his former language and principles. But political consistency seems long since to have been banished to Utopia, or to be laid up among the collection of things lost to this earth that are to be found in the lunar repository. But though adverse to peace I own I envy Stewart having been able to go to Paris, though I should not much like the company of Lord Lauderdale.[3] As proof of Buonaparte's pacific disposition, while he is signing Peace with us with one hand, with the other he is signing the dispatches to his General in Dalmatia, who is to subvert the Ottoman Empire.

[*PS.*] We stay here till the 21st or 22nd and then go to Ld Douglas's Bothwell, Glasgow.

30. *Minto-Hamilton. 17–25 Aug. 1806.*

Many thanks for your long and entertaining letter which considering the *assiduity* of your studies I wonder you could find time to write. Nothing certainly but your want of piety could have given you the leizure, even your excessive *early* rising would have been insufficient. We have been nearly as quiet here, though not quite so diligent, as you describe yourself at Ponsborne. The only considerable variety that has lately occurred was produced by the most violent storm I ever witnessed, which on Saturday week almost demolished the whole of this place. For three hours it thundered and lightened with as much violence as it had done the morning I met you in London and the rain fell not in drops but in actual streams. The damage done is quite inconceivable; the water that fell upon the ground immediately above the house poured in torrents through the lower storey, carrying before it tables, chairs, dinner etc., formed a cascade down the bank and very soon converted the green grass slope from the house to the pond, into a perpendicular scar. In short its violence was such that had the storm continued two hours longer in all probability part of the house

[3] Dugald Stewart accompanied Lauderdale on his abortive peace mission to Paris.

would have been carried away. The glen and the bridges over it suffered dreadfully. The trees etc. which lined the former are in a great measure carried away & the latter almost impassable. The pond too before the house is in one part nearly filled up with the rubbish torn away from the bank. In short the place will never recover its former beauty, and will not for a long time be tolerable in that part which has suffered. You may conceive the violence of the rain which in about four hours raised the Teviot nine or ten feet. Luckily no person was mort any where about the country though much damage has been done to the bridges, cattle etc. Watty Sharpe is now obliged to be *idle*, as he calls it, in other words to work hard at his masonry and repair all the bridges about the place. His despair was quite diverting. The thing took place three days before the moorfowl shooting began, and he was of course unable to go to the moors. It was very hard he said, after having been employed in preparing powder, shot etc. just to have sick a thing happen to prevent his going, for upon enquiry he told Ly Minto that he did not think it wad be *judecious* for him to gang, as the masons said they could not *want* him & they wad na work if he did na stay wi them. He used always to maintain that there were no foxes on the rocks, and it was always the stotes & polecats (*foumarts*) that took other people's fowls etc. but the other day these ungrateful vermin carried off all his hens etc. Gilbert met him the next day and asked him about the foxes. He replied with great candour and a long face 'Deed Sir they are unco bad indeed, I cannot *justify* them to you Sir; ye ken it as weel as I due; I justify them to every body else but it is no use. I tell them it's the foumarts, but hoot Sir they winna believe me. Deed Sir I'm thinking there are o'er many o' them.' He does not however object to them elsewhere than near his own yard, for having been sent as a guide with a surveyor who was looking for coal, he said he had seen the *grandest* place in the world over the hills, 'deed it was *a' full of foxes*, and sic a number of banes & rabbits' heads, that *no yearthly man* could count them, eh! it was a *grand place!*'

William and I went for two days to the moors. Gilbert was gone with Ld Minto on a visit to his Dulcinea near Coldstream and did not get to the moors till the third day. I killed 7 brace of moorfowl and a brace of hares, & William 6 brace of moor game. The great rain had made them wild and as we had neither Watty or Gilbert with us we did not know exactly which way to look for the birds. Besides however the birds we bagged, we wounded many according to the opinion of the herd who held our horses, who upon being asked whether a bird was not struck said, Ah! he maun certainly be wounded, he *fleed awa sic quick*. The Mintos are canvassing away as hard as they can but I fear Gilbert has a bad chance if Parliament is dissolved this year, as many of his votes are new and have not been a year upon the rolls. Next year he would be strong, unless the Duke of Buccleugh makes new votes, which he is not likely to do. The Minto interest is certainly increasing in the County and the Governorship General has done Gilbert no harm. I have not heard any thing for certain about a dissolution but the general opinion of those who are likely to know is against it. I am very glad to hear that you have thought of becoming a *Parliament Man*, but can give you very little information about the terms of such agreements.[1] Proprietors of boroughs I believe *never* will make any provision against a dissolution, that being a chance of which they reserve to themselves the full benefit. The only way of obviating the difficulty is if possible to persuade him to take an annuity instead of a sum paid down at once, and even this is not always to be done, but by giving annually a little more than the seventh part of the sum proposed, it might be so arranged that both parties might find their advantage in the agreement. The price of boroughs of course varies but I believe something about four thousand pounds to be the common sum. Some people I know ask as much as *five*. I had not yet made any actual agreements when I left Park Place, and have not yet heard from Ld Malmesbury upon the subject. He has undertaken to manage it, and understands that sort of thing very well. The two seats he is treating for are in the borough of Horsham in Sussex belonging to Ly Irwin, from whom they go to Ly Hertford. He wants to get them both if he can as annuity seats, but Fitzharris's certainly as there is a double risk in the life of the King & of Ld M. himself. These are certainly transactions in which one can be neither too cautious or too explicit with the other party, as the whole affair is strictly speaking illegal and one rests entirely upon his honour. You may of course depend upon my secrecy and I need not add that what I write to you on this subject need not be mentioned. I see you are become a strong advocate for peace; your reasoning is certainly plausible and ingenious but I cannot add convincing. The hands we are in are certainly new (for one cannot deny that this is a Foxite Government; Ld Lauderdale's appointment is alone a proof) and I hope they will not prove *Young* ones.[2] I certainly do not approve of peace at this moment & shrewdly suspect that such an opinion does not prove me to be a partizan of opposition, but that I might find even some of the ministerial party of the same way of thinking. In fact the question is not, 'Shall we wage war with France

[1] Sulivan had written on 11 Aug. to say that there was some thought of his being put forward as a parliamentary candidate and asking for details of Palmerston's negotiations. Malmesbury had been looking out for a pocket borough in case Palmerston's informal canvass in Cambridge seemed unpromising.

[2] Perhaps a reference to Sir William Young (1749–1815), who had deserted Pitt for Grenville in 1801.

eternally'. Buonaparte has decided that for us in the affirmative, for it is evident and may be assumed upon the ground of notoriety that his enmity to this country is implacable. With former sovereigns of France when one war was terminated we remained upon friendly terms till some new quarrel arose from circumstances unconnected with the old one; but Buonaparte is pursuing one uniform course of policy, one great object in which is the annihilation of England as a free country, and to that end will be unremittingly employed his subtle perfidy in peace as well as his open violence in war. We are the grand obstacle between him and that naval empire which would extend his dominion to every quarter of the globe. Europe is much too confined a sphere for his ambition, and we alone prevent him from reducing India, America, and Africa under his power. A legiti-mate hereditary monarch sits down quietly satisfied with the territory that devolves to him, but the ambition of an usurper never can be satiated. The question then is, how we can best defend ourselves, and whether we should at this moment suffer most from his attacks in open hostility or under the cover of pacific intercourse, and I think the latter is most to be dreaded. We have him now at arms' length but peace once signed we could not keep up our navy and by reducing it we should give him the only advantage he does not possess. I cannot con-ceive that this is any thing but a question of *expediency* for no one has yet asserted that peace is *necessary* for us, or that our resources are unequal to the prosecution of the war. In fact our commerce is nearly as flourishing in war as it would be in peace, since the French manu-factures and colonies suffer by war, and the same demand existing for the produce of both, the supply must be afforded by us, nor can Buonaparte prevent it. In peace indeed by reestablishing his own commerce he might perhaps exclude ours. That peace could not be secure you admit; indeed from the hatred Buonaparte bears us and his total want of faith that is evident. If then we disarm we throw ourselves bound into the lion's grasp. *We* dismantle our fleet from necessity; *he will not* destroy or surrender his flotilla, but gets back his seamen. If in this state we venture to remonstrate at any injury or insult offered to us or to Europe, our mouths will be immediately stopped by a threat of invasion, and should we begin to arm in defence, before our army is on the war establishment, our militia *enlisted*, our volunteers organized, and six sail of the line ready to oppose him, the flotilla will have safely deposited a French army on our coast, with which we shall have to contend under every disadvan-tage of hurry & confusion. We should remember the great difference between the state of France *now* and at the beginning of the war. Had Buonaparte *then* possessed the means of invasion, *now* in his hands, we might have had a practical solution of the problem about the possibility of his landing. If to avoid these dangers we were (which is impossible) to keep up a large military and naval establishment, the difference of expence would be too trifling to compensate for the disadvantage sustained, & peace would be in fact a *truce*, which no one would I think recommend. But do you think that we could obtain an honourable peace, at this moment? As to the terms for instance; Buonaparte has always told us we should have the *Peace of Amiens*, & *nothing* but the Peace of Amiens. Fox, or at least his organ, in the *State of the Nation* says we are in a much worse situation than we were when that peace was made, and have no right to expect such *good terms*. Do these two circumstances combined lead us to form any high expectations? and is it probable that Ld Grenville who appears to have been overruled in the question of peace, will be able to influence with any effect the terms of the treaty? But even granting (which is highly improbable) that we were allowed to retain Malta, The Cape, and Pondicherry, and get back Hanover, what could *honor* have to do with a peace which so immediately sanctions the establishment of two of Buonaparte's brothers as independent sovereigns, which abandons a faithful ally the King of Naples, whose misfortunes have originated solely in his attachment to us, and which is negociated and perhaps concluded during the prosecution of the boldest scheme of aggrandizement, the most flagrant subversion of ancient establishments, the most violent stride towards universal empire, that has hitherto marked the career of the usurper and I must confess that I differ with you in thinking the present moment the *best* for pacific overtures. To treat with a conqueror flushed with success, immediately after the failure of our grand scheme for the liberation of Europe, somewhat resembles submission, and a peace made so soon after that of Presburgh would appear too much a part and sequel of it, to be very glorious to England. We surely ought not to make Peace while there is a *chance* of any resistance to Buonaparte's innovations in Germany, and indeed the very presence of an English negociator in Paris while such things are going on is a little falling off from our old pride. I do not quite see the necessity of that change in our ideas to which you allude, as far at least as regards *us*, and nothing but imperious necessity can reconcile one to it. I have endeavoured to shew that peace is not necessary and can be neither safe or honourable at the present moment. With respect to the regard Fox may feel for our interests, I do not place the confidence in him which you appear to do. Not that he would deliberately betray his country but there is a danger that from his eagerness to obtain peace, and from his opinion of Buonaparte's sincerity he might be much more easily satisfied than either you or I should be. The extract from the *Moniteur* upon the subject of ye negociations is curious, and indirectly charges Ld Grenville with being what I strongly suspect he is, adverse to Fox's pacific system. I am happy to find that Bruce though a zealous Foxite agrees with me upon this subject, & says that this attempt at peace is creditable neither to the understanding or patriotism of Fox. I am surprized at the account you give me of Ashburton's letter, for I have just received a very long one in which he expresses a perfect concurrence in *my sentiments* about peace, saying Buonaparte's plan is to exhaust by peace our resources of men and money, and then *kick us to the devil at once*, but he differs with me in thinking that our ministry will be *fools enough to make peace*. 'Fox doubtless would do so' but he hopes Ld Grenville will prevent him, and he adds that he hopes the latter will serve as *a bridle upon the unsound & hurtful political opinions of the former*. He likewise thinks Fox may live a year or two but doubts whether to do good according to Ld G.'s suggestion or *evil* according to *his own*. He must be a compleat hypo. to write such contradictory letters. You will see in the date of this that it was begun sometime ago but I have not had an opportunity of finishing it till today and though I hate to send a stale letter yet as it was written I thought it might even go. We left Minto on Thursday, spent Friday in Edinr. running about from shop to shop, & turning over all sorts of pebbles etc. and arrived here yesterday. We shall remain here a few days, and then after spending a day at Buchanan move downwards by the lakes to Clive's where we shall arrive about the 14th or 15th of Septr. If you have any inclination to write before that time direct to Penrith. Pray what the devil induced the Duke to put Percy into a close borough belonging to Ld Buckingham?[3] The *auri sacra fames* must be strong indeed upon him. I hope it is only a temporary arrangement. Even if he has bought it he should have put somebody else in it, and at least let Percy have had the credit of sitting for one of his own. This looks very much as if there would be no dissolution this autumn. Were you not amused with the duel between Jeffrys and Anacreon Moore, loading their pistols with pellets of paper was an excellent idea.[4] So Brougham is gone out envoy to Portugal. I am glad he is getting on, his talents are certainly very great if he contrives to keep himself out of a strait waistcoat.[5] The following are some conundrums I made at Minto one evening that we had a grand punning match.

1.   Why if Ld Cranley were to lose the use of his hands would it cripple one of his servts?[6]

[3] Lord Percy had been returned for Buckingham on 1 Aug.

[4] The duel between Tom Moore and Francis Jeffrey had been prevented by the police. The story of the pellets is corrected in Lord John Russell, ed., *Memoirs, Journal, and Correspondence of Thomas Moore*, 1853–6, i. 208.

[5] Henry Brougham accompanied Lords Rosslyn and St Vincent on their special mission to Lisbon.

[6] Cranley (afterwards 2nd Earl of Onslow) was a buffoon and a reprobate, with a passion for driving.

2.   Who would be most likely to make the lady he married go bare-headed?

3.   Why would it be better to tumble half way down Greenwich hill than have Sheridan's nose?

4.   Why should Ld Nelson have been fond of a consumptive stag?

5.   Why if Mrs Culverden were to get upon my shoulders, when the cook came upstairs after dressing the dinner would the latter be like Augustus?

6.   What piece of furniture is most like a flea on the devil's back after he has got a good beating?

7.   Why is a six feet wall surrounding a field like Ld MacDonald when dressed?

The solutions are on the other side of the paper. Adieu my dear Sulivan pray remember me most kindly to Mr & Mrs S. and to Shee who I conclude is with you.

[*PS.*] Write any nonsense to Ly Malmesbury, she will like it all the better.

1.   Because it would ruin his *coachman's hip!*

2.   Mr Hatsell because he would make *her hat-sell.*

3.   Because half a *roll* is better than *nob-read.*

4.   Because a *hero* ought to love a *lean dear.*

5.   Because she would beat *aunt on I in grease* (Anthony in Greece).

6.   A *can'd De'els tick.*[7]

31. *Spring Gardens.*[1] *Wednesday, 15 Oct.* [*1806*].

William and I are on our way to St John's, and intend to make an attack upon you the day after tomorrow. Seriously if you can receive us we will dine and sleep with you on Friday. If you cannot just let me have a line at Waltham Cross to say so and we shall with *disappointment* continue our journey. We are going à la curricle. I told Ly *My* I should probably see you. Her curiosity is raised to a high pitch.

32. *Spring Gardens. Thursday, 17 Oct. 1806* [*16 Oct. 1806*].

There is certainly to be an immediate dissolution of Parliament.[1] I shall consequently go down to Cambridge without loss of time to

---

[7] The response to 7 is lacking.
[1] The Malmesburys had a house in Spring Gardens, Whitehall.
[1] Fox had died on 13 Sept.; Parliament was dissolved on 24 Oct.

see how the land lies. I am rather of opinion myself that it would be better for me to lie quiet at present and make the grand push at ye Duke of Grafton's death but I shall be guided by the opinion of my friends at Cambridge.[2] Do not expect us tomorrow as I shall proceed strait to Cambridge.

33. Sun Inn [Cambridge]. 19 Oct. 1806.

I have only time to write you two lines to say that I do not mean to stand at present.[1] It is the result of much enquiry & deliberation and I think you will acquiesce in the propriety of my determination. Petty is still too strong to be assailable, though sunk in the opinion of some individuals since ye last election. He is backed by the *undivided* strength of a government, which appears pretty *energetic* in election cases, and which at the last here, had not assumed a shape sufficiently solid to enable it to do him much good except from the hopes to which it gave rise. Euston is supported by a large number of friends whom in the course of four elections he cannot fail to have made and you may be sure Petty would support him tooth and nail in preference to me. There appears therefore a very bare chance of success, for the accession of strength I may have made since last winter though something is not to be reckoned upon. Now I cannot think that it would do me any good in any way to be defeated a second time, and I think & most of the most sensible here coincide in the opinion that by making a sort of merit of not disturbing at present the tranquillity of the University I may claim their support at the Duke of Grafton's death with a better prospect of success. Some sort of public address or circular letter will be necessary & will answer the purpose of keeping up that sort of uniform claim to which you allude fully as well as standing.[2] I have no fear of any other candidate occupying my ground as

---

[2] Grafton's death would translate Petty's Cambridge colleague, Lord Euston, to the Lords and so force a by-election.

[1] As soon as Malmesbury had confirmation that there was to be an imminent dissolution he wrote to Lord Pembroke, who was acting for Lady Irwin, to complete a bargain for her two seats at Horsham. Palmerston and Fitzharris were each to pay £4,000 (or, if necessary, 4,000 guineas) 'on condition you & James are brought in with all re-elections *gratis* on *all* vacancies in the ensuing parliament during Lady Irwin's life'. The particular object, so far as Palmerston was concerned, was to allow him to vacate Horsham if another opportunity occurred to stand at a by-election in Cambridge with a guarantee of a free re-election in Horsham if he failed in the University. But so far as the General Election was concerned, Malmesbury was convinced Palmerston had no chance in Cambridge. (Malmesbury to Palmerston, 17 Oct. 1806, B.P.W.)

[2] Malmesbury had advised such a precaution. Palmerston's draft is B.P.W. no. 398. The particular danger they had in mind was Lord Percy's coming forward. When Sheridan offered himself to the electors of Westminster the Duke of Northumberland withdrew his son from that unequal contest and sent him westwards on another search.

the same reasons that influence me must operate upon any other person at all acquainted with the University. I am very sorry we hap-

But Percy stopped en route in Cambridge, with a view to the General Election according to his father, but with an eye to the seat Lord Euston would one day vacate, Palmerston rather feared. Percy arrived in Cambridge on 24 Oct., just as Palmerston was leaving. There followed some sort of public 'scene' between them and an apparently inconclusive promise from Percy to consult his father again. (Northumberland to Col. McMahon, 24 Oct., *P.O.W.*, v. 501–2; F. Horner to J. A. Murray, 15 Nov. 1806, Horner Papers, British Library of Political and Economic Science.) So after Percy had left for the west, Palmerston took the precaution of sending a long letter to Alnwick to await his return:

London. 30 Oct. 1806.

My dear Percy,

As you did not appear when last I saw you to have come to any final determination respecting your future plan of conduct relative to Cambridge I avail myself of the privilege given me by the habits of intimacy in which we have hitherto lived to submit to you certain considerations, to which in the decision you are about to make, I should wish now to direct your attention.

In the first place then I am anxious to have it clearly understood that from the connexion I have already formed with the University it *is impossible* for me to retire in favor of any other candidate. The support which I received at the last election, and that which was promised me at the present had not motives of delicacy prevented me from availing myself of it, was of a nature so respectable in itself and so flattering to me, that I should consider myself as in some degree deserting my friends, and certainly doing an injustice to myself, were I to omit seizing the first fair opportunity of again urging my claims to the representation of the University. If then you should determine to stand there must be a contest between us; an event which I can assure you independently of all interested motives, I should from the regard I feel for you most sincerely lament. But let us consider what the probable result would be. No man can entertain any rational hopes of success at Cambridge unless he be heartily supported by his own College, and consequently unless you should have the majority of the Johnians to form the basis of your strength you could never expect a successful combat with a Trinity candidate. But the ground upon which you must begin to open your trenches, I have already preoccupied, and from the number of actual promises which I have received from our common friends at St John's, I am convinced that the majority of the College would be *against* you. Moreover, not to mention that it is an unpleasant thing for a candidate to be opposed by the members of his own College, I do not conceive that you would be able to make up the deficiency by your success in the smaller colleges in which I apprehend that I have perhaps more the start of you than in St John's. Should you therefore find the resolve to attack me, it may in my opinion safely be predicted, that although you might so far undermine me as to prevent my success, you would not be able to preserve yourself from a complete overthrow, and your only consolation would be, that although a third candidate carried off the prize, you had involved me in your fall.—Such being the state of the case it remains for you to consider, whether as the son of the Duke of Northumberland commanding many borough seats, & able if willing to sit for either of the two great counties of Middlesex and Northumberland, you would chuse to expose yourself to the certainty of a defeat in such a voluntary contest. With respect then to the mere arithmetic of the case, you see the balance is against you, and the rules of common policy should induce you to decline. So far I have argued upon the plain and broad basis of facts, upon a comparison of physical strength, in which there can be no deception, since the refutation is easy & simple. But there is another consideration of a nature less substantial though not less important, and the decision of which must lie chiefly within your own breast. I mean the point of delicacy between us. This is a subject upon which I feel the most extreme reluctance to enter, and where I am very diffident of expressing an opinion. I am aware that from the circumstances of my situation my feelings are too liable to the imputation of being influenced by my interests to allow me to deduce from them a rule of conduct for the guidance

pened to take the Epping road by which we missed seeing you. I thought it the most expeditious in point *of time* though a little longer in distance. I shall be glad to pass by Ponsborne in my way to town but you will hear from me before that. I shall remain here some days longer. I am sure of Horsham for 4000£. What has been the result of the negociation to which you alluded? Are we likely to have another Fustyarian in the Senate or not?[3] Pray remember me to Mr and Mrs S. the latter of whom I hope to hear a good account of.

34. *Broadlands. 20 Nov. 1806.*

As I understand you have taken the law into your own hands & indulged in a round of abuse of me for my silence I shall suppress all the pretty apologies which I was going to have made and which, if your patience had lasted a little longer or my information been less accurate you would have had the pleasure of reading.

In fact however now that I can frank there is no inducement for me to write; when I could make my friends pay for a thumping double letter there was some fun in corresponding.[1] I had however intended on my return from Horsham to have sent you a long account of our proceedings there had I not been prevented by being obliged to trot down here immediately for our Winchester business. *Sic Io servavit Apollo.* Our double return will be productive I fancy of no other bad consequence than putting several guineas into the pockets of some

of others. But I most earnestly entreat that before you finally make up your mind upon the subject under consideration, you would upon this point consult some of your friends who have your *real* interests at heart. Might not the world if they saw you attack a friend with whom you are known to have lived at college in the habits of the closest intimacy, and who had by priority of occupancy established a sort of claim upon the University, might they not I say indulge their propensity to view men's actions in their worst light, and attribute to you motives and sentiments which I am persuaded it is the furthest from your nature and character to entertain. I am sure that your candor will lead you to understand what I have here said in the sense in which it is meant, and to believe me when I assure you that nothing but the regard I feel for you would have induced me this strongly to call your attention to a point, in the decision of which I am convinced your interests no less than mine are closely involved.

Ever yrs affly
Palmerston

[*The draft is endorsed*:]
This letter never was answered but at the General Election which took place upon the change of administration in the following spring Ld Percy turned Ld Howick out for Northumberland having assured Sulivan as soon as the dissolution took place that he did not mean to oppose me at Cambridge. (B.P.W.)

[3] Sulivan's parliamentary ambitions presumably evaporated.
[1] Palmerston and Fitzharris had received only a minority of the votes for Horsham on 3 Nov., but when they challenged the result the returning officers declared all four candidates elected and left it to the House of Commons to decide between them (W. Albery, *A Parliamentary History of the Ancient Borough of Horsham*, 1927, pp. 197–229).

of your brother lawyers, a misfortune to which, as they will not come
out of my pocket, I submit with Christian fortitude.[2] The case from
all I can hear is a very clear one, & unless the Committee chuse to
legislate for themselves upon a new plan they must shove our competi-
tors out of the seats into which they have intruded themselves. It is
fortunate in the meantime that Members of the Commons are not
restricted to the same limited seat as the peeresses in Westminster Hall,
for in a crowded debate eighteen inches would be a narrow allowance
for two Members. Our Hampshire contest you see has terminated as
might have been expected in failure on our side, but we mustered
a very respectable number, and had almost all the independant &
landed interest on our side. The Winchester nigri were violently on
our side, Ld Temple was hissed and hooted on the hustings on the
first day, and they would not suffer the successful candidates to be
chaired although they had two magnificent cars prepared for them.
I really think that if Sir Wm Heathcote had stood at first or even if
Sir H. Mildmay had made up his mind immediately we should have
carried the thing but as *we* know, delay in elections is ruin, and the
opposite party had nearly a fortnight's start in their canvass. Mildmay had published a very good advertisement, which will of course
be in the papers. The expense incurred by all parties is immense; I
daresay it will cost the government candidates between forty & fifty
thousand pounds at least.[3] The Westminster affair seems to have been
continued longer than is usual; one feels awkwardly respecting it. To

[2] Palmerston seems to have been a little too complacent about the financial consequences of the Horsham affair, though they remain obscure. Malmesbury assured
him again and again that he and Fitzharris had no liability beyond the £4,000 since
their bargain with Lord William Gordon (Lady Irwin's son-in-law), he wrote, specifically stated that 'should the Duke of N[orfolk] create any trouble at the Election of
course no payment will be expected until they are securely seated'. They would have
to guarantee the legal expenses of the hearing before the House of Commons Committee, but that was merely 'a matter of form' and made them 'liable to nothing'.
But Lady Irwin's agent, William Troward, did demand some money in advance. Malmesbury was deeply suspicious of Troward but, relying on Lord William's honour,
expected any money to be returned or deducted from the purchase price. Many years
later, however, Palmerston related in his 'Autobiography' that he and Fitzharris 'paid
about £1,500 each'. He may have exaggerated the figure, as he did that of the price
of the seats themselves, but it is unlikely that his memory would have been so much
at fault as to overlook being repaid all his expenses. (Malmesbury to Palmerson, 11
and 28 Dec. 1806, B.P.W.; Malmesbury to Fitzharris, 8, 9 and 11 Jan. 1807, Malmesbury Papers; Bulwer & Ashley, i. 368–9.)

[3] There had been a furious contest for Hampshire, as Palmerston explained in his
journal. Both the old members, Sir William Heathcote and William John Chute, were
followers of Pitt, but neither had taken much part in Parliament. In the previous session,
however, Chute had voted against the Government occasionally, while Heathcote had
not attended the House at all. So Temple, the son of the Marquess of Buckingham
who had estates in Hampshire, went to Heathcote and told him that while the Grenvilles and their friends were determined to oust Chute, they would not set up an opposition to Heathcote if he would declare himself in favour of the Government. This Heathcote indignantly refused to do; Palmerston thought he ought to have ordered his servants to show Temple to the door. Instead, when he found there were two government

wish for Paul's success after his conduct in Parliament & elsewhere, & his unconditional adoption of Burdett's principles is impossible, & it is equally out of one's power to feel any sort of interest in such a blackguard as Sheridan. As to his constitutional doctrines which you mention, he is such a political *charlatan* that one knows they are put on with his cockade, and his character is so mean and degraded that I never can give him credit for his affected principles & patriotism. What can be more pitiful than the tricks and artifices by which he has on this occasion tried to court popularity, what would Fox have said to have seen the man who sets up as his representative coaxing *Mother Butter* from the hustings at Convent Garden and publicly thanking all the *whores of both theatres* for their assistance and support! I most truly rejoice that the Foxites have cut Burdett, but if they come to a comparison of *principles* with him, it will be found that *he* has been consistent while they have suited *theirs* to *existing circumstances*. One cannot help smiling to hear Sheridan, Whitbread & Byng expressing such abhorrence of Burdett's *present* doctrines, when in fact the only addition or alteration which he has made to those sentiments & principles to which 2 years ago they gave their most unqualified assent is, that his old friends the *new* whigs are very different people *in place* from what they were *in opposition*, & that after all their bawling about independance liberty and patriotism, they are to the full as arbitrary and corrupt as any of their predecessors, a discovery certainly ill calculated to please those who are the subjects of it, but which it did not require much sagacity to anticipate. So at last after 13 weeks *seasoning* in stinking transports our unfortunate expedition has sailed just in time to fall in with the tremendous hurricane that roared all last night. I hope that it may escape it, but should it as is most probable be nearly destroyed what excuse will those who *mis*managed the business invent. Fine weather cannot indeed be contracted for, but troops need not be kept two months & more to be sent out as soon as the winter sets in, but I suppose they were too busy with electioneering to think of anything so unimportant as our colonies & troops.[4]

This place & country are looking as well as falling leaves and bare

candidates—William Herbert, a younger son of Lord Carnarvon, and Thomas Thistlethwayte, a local squire—Heathcote took fright and withdrew. His place was taken by Sir Henry St John-Mildmay, but only after such hesitation as to give the Government plenty of time to organise the dockyard vote. (Bulwer & Ashley, i. 56–8.) Mildmay consequently came last and felt obliged to concoct an apology, a printed copy of which he sent Palmerston (18 Nov., B.P.W.). Palmerston had been advised by Malmesbury that since he had contracted to lay out £4,000 on his own seat, he should not feel obliged to make any financial contribution in Hampshire (19 Oct., B.P.W.). But Palmerston campaigned very actively for Mildmay and Chute: there is in B.P.W. 'A New Song called the Modern Whigs in place addressed to the Loyal & Independent Freeholders of Hampshire', copied in Palmerston's hand and marked that it was printed in Lymington.

[4] Gen. Craufurd's expedition had at last set sail for South America on 12 Nov.

twigs will permit. I have got far advanced in what will be an amazing improvement in comfort, which is turning the footpath that went through the park. It is to be carried quite on the outside of it, and though an expensive job at first this alteration will double the enjoyment of the place. How long I shall stay here I do not know as it depends upon the proceedings of Parliament. At any rate we shall be at Park Place at Christmas.

35. *Broadlands. 16 Dec. 1806.*

Without contending at length for the truth of the assertion with which I began my last letter I shall merely give you my authority: I heard the circumstance at secondhand from a young lady who was a party concerned and whose veracity is unquestionable. I shall not bore you with any more details about the Horsham election as I sent Shee an account in full of all I knew about it and I think that statement in my view of it very satisfactory. Our counsel are Lens and Dallas two very able men I am told, and at any rate whether equal or not to their antagonists, quite able to make the most of our case.[1] The reports you mention of a change in the ministry seem to be at present groundless. Indeed the circumstances attending the dissolution indicate a determination on the part of Lord Grenville to retain for the present at least his Foxite friends. The ensuing session will probably be a little stormy if the list of subjects to be discussed be as I have heard: a provision for the Irish Catholic priests, a revision of the Scotch Union in order to make the peers elected for life, the payment (no. *3*) of the Prince's debts, and a provisional Regency Bill. The two latter will cause some debates. I cannot conceive on what grounds they can call upon the Country now to pay the Prince's debts, since when last they were discharged it was solely upon the ground that his income of 120,000£ would be set free and he might then resume that splendour which his rank required. Since that time however he has never increased his establishment or altered his mode of life, and has not even paid his wife and daughter the allowances which it was stipulated they should receive. As to a Regency Bill, I think it would be very indelicate and perhaps dangerous to agitate the question at the present moment. By the bye you are the best twister and perverter of a clear assertion, I ever met with, and have displayed your legal ingenuity with great effect upon what I said about Paul & Burdett. So far from a preference of Paull I distinctly stated that his adoption of Burdett's principles prevented one from giving him my good wishes, although from other reasons I could feel no interest for Sheridan. As

[1] John Lens (1756–1825) and Robert Dallas (1756–1824).

to my edging round to Burdett, if the adoption of two principles disgusted me with *Paul a fortiori* they were an insurmountable objection to *himself*. I never, moreover, expressed any *admiration* of Burdett's consistency, but only of the impudence of Byng & Whitbread who thought they could persuade the world that they left him, because he was inconsistent in his principles, whereas it is apparent that his principles now are not more objectionable or treasonable than they were, when they all supported him, and the only difference in his language is that he accuses his quondam cronies of being as corrupt when in office, as they had ever accused their predecessors of being. I am just as glad as you can be that they have left him, but think they would have done just as well to have quitted him quietly, since their manifesto is precisely the counterpart of the King of Prussia's. 'Your principles are abominable, and subversive of good order, we assisted you in them as long as you only attacked *others*, but if you are so ungrateful a dog as to turn them against *us* we will have nothing more to say to you' is the pith and abstract of each. I am glad to find the situation of continental affairs begin to look a little less gloomy: the King of Prussia had collected 30,000 men at Graudentz and the first Russian army of 120,000 had nearly all joined him when Burrell[2] came through the country. All Russian Poland too was perfectly quiet although the Prussian part was turbulent. The arrangement with the Porte also sets free the left arm of the Russian force; and if any troops in the world except ours can beat the French they are the Russians, who have a high national character, great obstinacy and perfect courage, and have inspired the French with a considerable fear of them. The Austrian army amounts to 200,000 in every respect better appointed than at any former period and though she has a difficult game to play, yet if she does it well, she has some good cards in her hand. The Woronzows and Matthew Stewart[3] are here, & we expect Ld Malmesbury today for a few days. I have been jabbering French like any monkey and shall very soon be expert enough at it to be minister plenipotentiary. Woronzow is remarkably pleasant and has as little stiffness about him as a foreign *diplomatique* can; he is full of anecdote, and being a staunch & enthusiastic Pittite it is very diverting to see him attack Matthew. The Scotch have I see established their national character, for ministerial obsequiousness. Ld Melville's enemies will of course rejoice to see the decline of his influence but in a public view it seems mighty immaterial with regard to the freedom & independance of Scotland whether it is governed by Melville or Lauderdale, and notwithstanding Matt's encomiums

[2] Peter Robert Burrell, afterwards 2nd Baron Gwydyr, a former fellow-commoner at St John's.
[3] Dugald Stewart's son.

upon the meekness & forbearance of Lauderdale's disposition, I should imagine he would make as tyrannical a ruler as his predecessor could have been. One regrets that a better order of things cannot be established and that the only question is who shall be the governor of the country. We shall remain here about ten days or a fortnight longer and then remove to Park Place whence I shall probably be called to town to attend the election affair. I hear we are to meet you at Park Place.

Ashburton is going on much better than I expected with Anne. She has completely subdued him and manages everything with great cleverness. They very soon came to a sort of rupture and he flew into a violent passion with her, & swore at her like a trooper. She felt much disposed to *cry*, but recollecting that if she gave way once she was lost for ever, she summoned up all her courage *took him by the collar* and gave him *a good shaking*, asking him how he *dared* use such language to her. By this timely exertion she has obtained a decided superiority and Ashburton is under *petticoat government!* All this of course *entre nous*. The last thing Matt heard of him was his being seen walking upon the sea sands of the Largs opposite his own door and close to the high road stark naked with a little stick in his hand to drive away the crabbs while bathing. Adieu my dear Sulivan pray remember me to Mr and Mrs S. the latter of whom I hope is better.

36. *Park Place. 28 Dec. 1806.*

Lady Malmesbury has, no doubt, written such full instructions relative to your coming here that it would be needless for me to say anything on that subject, and conclude that you will favor us with your company at no very distant day. Though indeed I ought not to say *us* as I shall most probably be in town when you arrive. Two circumstances neither of them of a very entertaining nature call me to London. The one is some legal business about our petition, the other an unlucky assault made upon my front teeth by my horse's head as I was hunting the other day. The consequence of the two parties coming into very close & sudden contact has been rather fatal to the former, two of which suffered the arithmetical process of *fractionizing*. This ejectment has not you may conceive, produced very happy effects upon the suavity of my countenance, or the distinctness of my articulation. The vacuity which it gives to the former, and the soft lisp imparted to the latter qualify me at present to shine in old women's parts on any boards and if the place of one of Macbeth's witches was luckily vacant I should certainly be preferred to any other candidate.

However I am in hopes that these inconveniences will be only temporary and that the skill of Mr Parkinson or Dumergue will very soon restore to my potatoe trap its usual complement of mutton grinders; and render my loss at least if not invisible to the naked eye, imperceptible by the *naked ear*. I am very glad to hear that Mrs S. has derived so much benefit from the bath waters. The consequences of a severe illness are often apt to be of long continuance but I trust that in this instance you may find the recovery more rapid than you imagine.— Linois must be an interesting character to know, I am glad to hear he was more *merciful* than *brave*. I never heard him celebrated for cleverness. Indeed he displayed neither talent nor enterprise in his Indian cruize. He has however shewn a more useful quality, good sense, in not following Villeneuve's example of returning to France.

I quite agree with you in your opinion of the French answer to the Prussian manifesto. It was able, severe and conclusive, as far as regards the former conduct of Prussia. There was great judgment in abstaining from any attempt at direct self-justification, and being satisfied with what alone was practicable a full retort upon Prussia. There never was a fairer opening, and it was a home thrust. The reports of victories obtained by the Russians are certainly premature but their force will soon be very considerable and will act with great advantage against the French at this time of year. They seem to have adopted the prudent plan of avoiding general actions and harassing the French by partial engagements. Those who oppose the French armies should never forget the maxim of Saxe or Turenne I forget which, 'that a bad general when he does not know what to do always gives a general battle'.

It is confidently reported in London that Petty & Tierney are to exchange places. It would be a very good arrangement for ministers who will otherwise be a good deal pushed in their financial business. Windham is said to have been the father of the State of the Negociation. It is not improbable; he is just the man to have instigated such a production.[1] Ld Howick when Nicolay[2] the chargé d'affaires remonstrated upon the subject, said government knew nothing of it & if they *knew the author would certainly prosecute him*. It might have occurred to *Lord Howick* who knows something about prosecutions for libels, that the *printer* was to be discovered though the author was not. The excuse was absurd and proves the connection which it denies. Sheridan they say is what you call *in for it*; he has *put his foot in* it completely. People in London talk of the pillory and Newgate, but it seems certain he will be turned out of his seat and in that case his creditors will

---

[1] *The State of the Negotiation; with details of its progress and causes of its termination in the recall of the Earl of Lauderdale*, 1806, was, however, by Charles James Fox.

[2] Baron Nicolay was secretary of the Russian Embassy.

take care of the rest. I shall be sorry for it, as we shall lose some entertaining speeches in Parliament, otherwise I shall feel great pleasure that he at length gets his desert.

The Prince they say is quite well again excepting that gentle languor which the tender passion has thrown over his features. His northern tour did not succeed much better than his western, at Doncaster he was hissed, & the people cried out No Harry Ye Eighth! No putter away of wives! At a dinner too given to him when he left the room somebody gave 'The Prince! & may he never know the loss of a father!' To those who merely look to the gratification of party spirit, and even just indignation at the injuries suffered by Ye Princess, this may all be very satisfactory, but to those who look forward to the event of his being King, and who consider the dangerous consequences in times like these of a general disaffection to the *person* of the sovereign cooperating with the latent sparks of Jacobinism still lurking in the country, it affords matter for very serious and painful reflections.

37. *Lavender House. 1 Feb. 1807.*

The decision of our Committee did not at all surprize me, as I was quite prepared for it, by what I had heard & seen of their proceedings; but I own, that though their unanimity precludes the supposition of their having acted from party motives, I do still think their decision wrong, and that they were bamboozled by Plomer.[1] The case turned, as you rightly conclude, entirely upon the existence of the general law, upon which my arguments here rested; and it did not appear to me, that it was satisfactorily disproved; & it is very strongly established indirectly, by an Act of Parliament. But however enough of this. I am much obliged to you for your communication about Colchester, of which however your friend does not give me a *very favourable* idea.[2]

Well, what does *old Croaker*[3] say of the present state of affairs? I hope the news from Poland & Petty's speech[4] have afforded some

[1] The committee had reported on 20 Jan. in favour of the Duke of Norfolk's candidates; Thomas Plumer (1753–1824) had presented their case.

[2] Having failed both in Horsham and in Cambridge, Palmerston was unwilling to rush into a third attempt About the end of the month he made provisional arrangements to contest one of the seats at Great Yarmouth in the event that a petition should unseat the members returned at the General Election. He therefore began with a merely informal canvass and insisted on keeping his candidacy 'as secret as possible'. (Palmerston to Frances Temple, 'Saturday ½ past 5' [28 Feb.], B.P.W.) There is no reference to it in his correspondence with Sulivan. The petition eventually failed and Palmerston was again left without a seat.

[3] Sulivan had admitted to being a pessimist.

[4] Petty had presented his financial proposals on 29 Jan. (1 *Hansard*, viii. 564–97).

relief to your gloomy apprehensions. Who was the true prophet about the issue of the contest between the French & Russians? & by the way, apropos of Petty's speech, allow me to bring to your recollection a certain correspondence, which took place between two persons of my acquaintance last summer, in which an assertion made by one party, that peace was not *necessary*, & that our commerce & finances were quite *adequate* to carrying on the war, till the aspect of affairs should change, was treated by the other with a considerable degree of contemptuous scepticism. Petty's plan & detail decide the question of fact pretty completely. By the way is it not curious, that people who a year ago complained so bitterly, that instead of being upon a bed of roses they had succeeded only to disappointed hopes & *dilapidated resources*, should now tell us, that not from any *recent or occasional causes*, but from the gradual *operation of firmer industry, wisdom, & foresight*, we can carry on the war for twenty years, not only without danger of ruin, but with a very slight increase of debt, & that in fact our present danger is not that we may sink under accumulated burthens, but that our debts may be *payed off too soon!* But however in good earnest, things are looking very well, & there appears every reason to believe that Buonaparte's star is on the wane. What a field for speculation would his complete defeat open. Joseph may find the two supporters of his crown (*2 syrens*) more appropriate & emblematical than he supposed.

So Buenos Ayres is gone. It is very unfortunate for poor Popham, as it will put him very much in the wrong with many people, who only estimate merit by success. But as ministers determined that his conduct should be tried by the abstract principle, independently of results, they ought not to consider this as any aggravation. Should it however appear that he did not send any dispatches from the 12th of August till the 6th of November, he certainly will deserve much blame on that account.

I suppose you saw William in his way to St John's; he was only in town one day. I shall be in London on Tuesday, the rest of the family will continue at grass for some time longer. There are sad complaints here of your having broken your promise. The Henley damsels expected to have seen you at their ball in your way to London, & *Mrs Higgins* was considerably disappointed. What ridiculous weather (to use Ld Minto's expression). Yesterday evening was as fine as spring, when all on a sudden it began to snow, without reason; I was going to say without *rhyme*, but it did *freeze*, which made it the more extraordinary. Bruce dined here the other day previous to going to Cambridge. He had adopted your fashion and mounted a wig, to the full as unlike the colour of his hair, as yours was. He looked much better than when we saw him & indeed his being allowed to return to St John's, though I think at any rate it would have been more prudent for him to have staid away, is a proof that they think him better. Has Ly Malmesbury pressed you into the service to attend her to *Mother Goose* on Thursday? I dare say she will & you had better join the party. Adieu; Fanny & Lilly having been *putting on their things*, almost during the whole time I have been writing this are at *length* ready, & I must go like a good boy & *take a walk*.

38. *9 o'clock, Saturday evening* [*25 April 1807*].

A dissolution will take place on Monday.[1] I am going instantly to Cambridge. Perceval does *not* stand, but Sr Vikery Gibbs is thought of. I do not know it however for certain.[2] Pray endeavour to form a committee as soon as you can, and commence a canvass immediately.[3] Have you any lists? There are plenty at Spring Gardens. I told Ld Malmy you would communicate with him upon ye subject. I think a paragraph should appear in *Tuesday's* papers simply stating that I have begun a canvass for the University.[4] I have not time to add more.

[*PS.*] What do you think best about P——cy.

39. *Cambridge. 28 April 1807.*

Outram is gone to town today & will probably call upon you in the course of tomorrow; at any rate if you do not he means to dine at Ye Gray's Inn Coffee House at five & if you are not engaged would be glad to meet you & Fitzherbert there. My canvass goes on very well hitherto. Pearce, Milner, Mansel, Ramsden, Douglas Master of Bennet, Clarke of Jesus, the Master of Emmanuel, Blackall of do.,

---

[1] The Duke of Portland had formed his government at the end of Mar. and Palmerston had accepted office as a junior Lord of the Admiralty at the beginning of April. The news that there was going to be a dissolution was communicated to 'the independent friends of Government' on the evening of 25 April. (*Malmesbury Diaries*, iv. 389 and 393.)

[2] Spencer Perceval, a Trinity man, had already assured Malmesbury that he would support Palmerston at Cambridge whether or not he was a candidate there himself. Sir Vicary Gibbs (1751–1820) was Attorney-General in the new government.

[3] The committee in London seems to have included Fitzherbert and Shee, as well as Sulivan, and was based at the Crown and Anchor in the Strand. That in Cambridge, again with Wood at the head, consisted of Ralph Tatham, Jackson, Blackall, Clarke, Thomas Sowerby of Queens' and William Cooke of King's.

[4] Sulivan suggested in reply that Palmerston strengthen his circular by adding a reference to his attachment to the 'excellent constitution in Church and State' ([27 April], S.P.).

Mortlock have declared in my favour. Turner & Barker of Christ's have all but decided.[1] I purposely avoided in my circular letter any unnecessary allusion to recent events, conscious that to those who were likely to concur with me a slight hint would be sufficient while to others a more explicit allusion would only afford an opportunity of abuse. I have however in consequence of your suggestion added '*in Church & State*' to the letter as it stood as that will I think answer your purpose to a certain extent & being a simple addition to the press did not cause any loss of time, which would have been produced had I changed the whole.

Gibbs is come down. I & all my friends here think his standing will be of advantage to me as it will prevent my second votes from being given to Euston, it being impossible to prevent some from giving a double vote however well inclined, & I do not imagine he will carry sufficient weight with himself to overpower me. At any rate he will neutralize some of Petty's votes & thus deduct from Euston. They make common cause & it will therefore be necessary for me perhaps to unite with Gibbs. Pray tell Shee in case I should not have time to write tonight it being already late that the note I sent him was entirely the result of thoughtlessness on my part, & which a moment's reflection would have pointed out the impropriety of—but the fact was I was so hurried the night I left town that I wrote away without consideration.[2] With regard to carriages Wood has agreed with Smyth on ye part of Petty & Tavel for Euston *not* to engage *any*.[3] This arrangement is I think much better for all parties. How long I shall stay here I know not but shd think that as the election will probably come on next week I ought to remain here till then.

40. *Cambridge. 30 April 1807.*

I fear the letter the committee sent up yesterday with regard to the separation of committees has created some confusion in your proceedings. I therefore take the first opportunity after the receipt of Outram's letter to explain the matter. *Here*, I must again say, a joint canvass is *impossible*, it could not have succeeded if originally adopted. Neither I nor Gibbs could have canvassed personally for each other, & the very idea that such a union was formed would have lost me

---

[1] William Pearce, William Lort Mansel, Philip Douglas, John Barker and Joseph Turner were the Masters respectively of Jesus, Trinity, Corpus Christi, Christ's and Pembroke. The Master of Emanuel was Robert Towerson Cory. Richard Ramsden was a fellow of Trinity and Thomas Mortlock a fellow of St John's.

[2] The allusion is not known.

[3] William Smyth, Regius Professor of Modern History, was chairman of Petty's committee. Tavel was Euston's chairman; he married Euston's half sister in 1811.

many second votes. But at any rate my canvass is now very nearly complete here, & therefore such a union out of the question. As to your operations *in London* the case is different, & as it appears you have already commenced a joint canvass do not interrupt it in consequence of what you have heard from us but act entirely as may appear best to you upon a view of the state of things. Gibbs carries up with him complete lists of all the voters so that it is unnecessary to detain the messenger to afford time to write them out. I have written to Ld Malmesbury about the writ which had better be managed by him than by the committee. We have secured between 70 & 80 of the resident members, I will send you their names tonight.

41. *Cambridge. 1 May 1807.*

The election is fixed for Friday ye 8th in next week. Wednesday was too early to allow the distant voters to come, Thursday was quite out of the question being Ascension Thursday, with two sermons in St Mary's, & Friday was the only remaining day, as you appeared to consider a delay till the week after next so prejudicial to our interests. Friday is not so near the Sunday but that those who live at a distance may by voting early & setting off immediately afterwards reach home in time.

The adverse party evidently appear alarmed. Smythe says Cambridge is nothing but a venal borough, & Ly Harwood told me today she thought Petty & I should certainly come in.[1] We have got some few more University votes. Ld Hinchinbroke is coming over from Huntingdon with 6 or 7. Ld Bayning has got six.

I sent Ld Malmesbury yesterday a list of actual promises but I will endeavour to make out tonight for you some more extensive calculations.[2] We have received scarcely any answers from the distant voters,—but if they go tolerably in our favour we need not be afraid. We shall I fear get few or no votes from the residents at King's as almost all their second votes go to Petty or Euston. This made us cautious of making actual promises to Gibbs, the general answer at St John's was they would give him all ye support they could consistently with my interest, & they will no doubt almost all vote for him if his friends are favourable to us. We have written applications to *all*, never mind there being duplicates as possibly the first letter may fail. I can assure you that nothing is done in the committee without the opinion of

[1] Yet Sir Busick Harwood, Professor of Medicine at Cambridge, wrote to Hardwicke on 4 May that his first vote would go to Petty and his second to Euston (Hardwicke Papers, Add. MS. 35658 ff. 118–19).
[2] Probably those following the end of this letter.

Jackson, Wood, Blackall, & Sowerby, who as well as Tatham & Cook are constantly here. Clarke of Jesus comes in occasionally.

I really do not agree with you in the impropriety of our arrangement about stages & horses; Smythe, Tavel, & Wood came to an agreement upon honor, not to hire any, & I should hardly think they would violate it. The only thing to be done, is to hire half a dozen chaises to carry away our distant voters who may be in a hurry to return, & that Wood has done with the concurrence of Smyth. I believe I must remain here till the day of election in order to catch any fellows who may be dropping in, unless there is any very particular object in my being in town.—Adieu I have nothing more to add.

[*PS.*] Can Ye Bishop of Ely be moved.[3]—

Davis,	St John's	Marquis of Bath
Cook,	Emmanuel	Archbishop
Revd Gilpin,	Hull	Bp of Durham
Beresford,	St John's	Ld Aylesford
Walmesley,	Cliffords Inn	Bp Rochester
Revd Toke,	Barnston, Dunmow, Essex	Col. Bullock
Champneys,	Canterbury	Archbishop
Hasted Revnd,	Bury St Edmonds	Ld Bristol
Revnd Parker,	Curate of Islington	Dr Rennell—for
		Dr Gaskin.[4]

I have not time to write to Ld M.

42. *Cambridge. 1 May 1807.*

I add a few lines to what I wrote by the express to say that we have this evening sent off almost all the letters announcing the day of election; so that the committee need only give themselves the trouble to send such notices to those from whom they have received promises in case our letters to these people might fail. The dinner on J.P.L. day[1] had better take place on Wednesday, & if it should be considered as very expedient for me to be in London on that day, I can go up to it, although perhaps as there may be perpetually people coming in to College it may be useful for me to be here to catch them. I sent a list [*of*] some interests in addition to those you already have.

---

[3] Malmesbury expected Hardwicke's uncle to vote against Palmerston in 1807 as he had in 1806 (Malmesbury to Palmerston, 1 May 1807, B.P.W.).

[4] Dr Gaskin was an Oxford man, but Parker married his daughter in 1807.

[1] The festival of the college's patron saint (*S. Johannes ante Portam Latinam*) was on 6 May. (I am grateful to the Librarian and Sub-Librarian of St John's for this explanation.)

[*PS*. It would be well to put the day of election into most of the papers.

Dr Herbert	Trinity	Duke of Rutland
Dr Parkinson	Kegworth	
The Revnd Thoroton	Trinity	do.
Thoroton	Peterhouse	
Kerrison	Pembroke Hall	Sr R. Kerrison, receiver-general Norwich
Lushington of Jesus		Duke of Portland
Manners	Trinity	Duke of Rutland
Sr Thos. Little[2]	Trinity	The Rt Honble T. Steele
J. Palmer	Trinity	J. Palmer M.P., Bath
Ainsley	Trinity	Sr Philip Ainsley
Lees	Triny	Sr John Lees, Dubline
Sutton	Triny	Arch Bp Canterbury
Alpe	Emml	Lord Wodehouse
Hallifax	Triny Hall	Dr Hallifax, M.D., London
Dr Jenner	Triny Hall	Jenner, King's Proctor, Drs Commons
Farmer	Emml	Duke of Rutland
Manners	Emml	Sr Wm Manners

Sr Wm Wynne, Master of Triny Hall, may fix Walker of his Coll. His own vote also to be applied for.

Revnd J. Bouverie at Honble E. Bouverie's through Ld Louvaine

---

43. *Cambridge. ½ past 12 o'clock, Friday night* [*1 May 1807*].

Outram arrived here about half an hour ago with your letter. I immediately pulled Wood & Blackall out of bed to consult them upon the point, & they perfectly concur with me in agreeing to a union of interests. Wood tells me he wrote to Dampier[1] a letter expressing a wish that there should be a cordial cooperation between the two parties; which letter he will receive tomorrow morning. I will certainly endeavour to assist Gibbs as far as I can, provided he will do the same for me, & I have no doubt that all those Johnians & many others of my friends who gave him an indecisive answer will vote for him. I fear however that he will not be able to procure me any second

[2] Sir Thomas Liddell, 6th Bart, was the grandson of Thomas Steele, a former Paymaster-General.

[1] Henry Dampier (1758–1816), afterwards a King's Bench judge, was a King's Scholar and a member of the Middle Temple.

votes among the resident King's men, but however after all the out votes are the most important from their numbers, and Gibbs will probably not get much fewer from my not joining him while it certainly appears that I may be a considerable gainer by the junction: I cannot of course take upon me to answer for my friends but in point of fact I know that a considerable number will exert themselves for Gibbs if they are assured *he* & his friends will do the same for me, & nothing kept them back but the doubt that by giving him decisive promises they might enable him to beat me with my own strength. I enclose a letter for you to shew Gibbs; the purport is as strongly *co-operative* as it is in my power to make it.[2] I am glad to hear from Outram that you have been going on so well with regard to promises; I really begin to entertain hopes. I am also glad to find by your letter that you still wish for an early election; indeed the writ having come down, I could not well have kept it back long enough to have prevented the precept from reaching the Vice Chancellor till Tuesday which would have been necessary in order to delay the election till Wednesday sennight.

44. *Cambridge.* ½ *past 12, Friday night* [*1 May 1807*].

I lose no time in answering your letter of this morning, which was given me an hour ago by Outram. The lateness of the hour has prevented me from consulting all my friends, but Blackall, Wood, Jackson & Tatham fully concur in my sentiments and as far as I have hitherto had an opportunity of ascertaining the disposition of the rest of my friends here, they are not averse to making common cause with Sr V. Gibbs, particularly were they assured that the same cordiality prevailed among his friends in & out of the University. With regard to myself I am quite willing to make it at once a matter of honour between Sr V. & myself that each shall use his best endeavours to promote the success of the other, and I think that if Sir V. recollects the general answer which he received at St John's he will be convinced that there at least, it will not be difficult to procure him support.

I am anxious not to detain the express longer than necessary that he may arrive early in town.

45. *Cambridge. 12 o'clock, Friday night, 8 May 1807.*
    Bulwer & Ashley, i. 22; MS. not found.[1]
Palmerston reports his defeat at the poll.

---

[2] No. 44.
[1] But see no. 46, n. 3.

46. *Cambridge. 11 May 1807.*

I certainly was very much mortified & disappointed at being a second time foiled in my attack upon the University,[1] & particularly as from my knowledge of my own strength, & the accounts of the state of ye poll circulated in the Senate House during the morning I did entertain strong hopes of success. In fact it was merely a maneuvre of Petty's that threw me out; finding himself beat, he made over to Euston a certain number of votes which he had kept back & thus brought him up.[2] We might have guarded against this by not polling so many early in the day; but as there were a certain number of waverers who would go with the strongest I thought it best to poll strong in the early part of the morning. In fact however it is a real victory, to have a majority of 45 over a man who a year ago beat me by upwards of two hundred; & I feel not the least doubt that I shall at the first vacancy come in to a certainty. Petty means however to stand again & his friends have had a meeting to keep up his interest. I had rather he opposed me than anyone else, for the sense of the University being so decidedly declared against him he is not likely to gain adherents. I am employed in calling upon all those who voted for me or were not decidedly adverse & in canvassing them for another occasion, & I shall as soon as possible write to all the absentees. I shall bring to town all the lists etc., to make out a register immediately. Gibbs before he went away expressed himself very sensible of how much he owed his election to the assistance of my friends & promised whenever I stood to assist me to the utmost. I shall nail if possible the King's men upon that plea. I shall probably be in town on Wednesday morning.

[*PS.*] I trust Remmett has played me fair & didn't keep back any plumpers; the polls when published will shew it. If he has he deserves to be exposed. I am not altogether without some suspicions of him because upon counting up certain votes the night before I had 288, Gibbs 283, & yet he beat me by 2, not 3, as I stated at first.[3] This

[1] Malmesbury, however, had already taken the precaution of securing a pocket borough for him at Newport, Isle of Wight. It cost £4,000. (Malmesbury to Palmerston, 2, 4 and 9 May, B.P.W.)

[2] This is confirmed by *Pryme*, p. 79, and by Petty to Lady Holland, [8 May 1807], Holland House Papers, Add. MS. 51689.

[3] In no. 45 Palmerston had reported that Gibbs had received 313 votes (instead of the correct figure of 312) and, presumably, that he had therefore been defeated by three, not four as Bulwer prints. It is further characteristic of Bulwer's editing that, either not having seen or not having noticed the correction Palmerston made in no. 46, he should have amended the margin of defeat Palmerston recorded in his Autobiographical Sketch to 'four votes' although the manuscript (B.P./D no. 26) clearly reads 'two'. Bulwer was no doubt further induced to do this because of the affair of the four would-be 'plumpers'. Calculating that neither could beat Euston, Palmerston and Gibbs had agreed the night before the poll to exchange their supporters' second votes

suspicion of course I have not hinted to anyone but you. Gibbs himself behaved most honourably. He made a man who was going to vote for him & *Euston* give a plumper to Petty, that he might [*not*] injure me by raising Euston.

47. *Admiralty. 14 Sept. 1807.*

Your letter of the 8th which I have just found lying for me here (it having followed me from Broadlands) has relieved me from the very considerable degree of uneasiness which your long silence occasioned. Our ingenuity has been quite exhausted in making conjectures to account for it, & the most plausible we could form was that you had taken ship for Italy in search of another *Corinne*, having expressed so much admiration of Mme de Stael's. However, joking apart, with whatever anticipatory sarcasms you may have treated the excuse, the fact really is, that I have for some time past been prevented from writing to you by not knowing where to direct my letter, & William has had one sealed & signed in his drawer I know not how long which he has not till now been able to send. But now we have *found you out* we will shew you no mercy. I am sorry to hear the cause which curtailed your tour, but trust that Mrs S. will soon find from the Buxton air & waters the benefit she desires. I do not wonder at your sketching mania having returned in all its former fury at the sight of Warwick Castle & I conclude there was not a boots, ostler, beggar, mangy dog etc. that escaped your pencil. Kenilworth I have never seen but have heard Culverden speak of it with great admiration. One of his nieces lives very near it, but he has hitherto contented himself with the eloquence of verbal description. I trust soon to have a more lively conception of its beauties from the powers of your masterly pencil. I am glad to hear your statement about the sale of negroes as it confirms all the grounds upon which I had formed my opinion upon the question. I certainly did not expect that you were to rejoice at our prospect of failure in Denmark, & for the best of all reasons,

---

in order that one of them should at least secure the second seat from Petty. Four of Palmerston's supporters still wanted to plump for him, but were at last persuaded to cast their second votes for Gibbs. However, according to his Sketch, Palmerston afterwards found that he had ended up with twelve plumpers to Gibbs's seven (Bulwer & Ashley, i. 369–70). Remmet, on the other hand, was not among them. Lady Malmesbury attributed Palmerston's defeat to Lord Camden's canvassing for Euston and Gibbs 'against all pressure and reason'. Camden was 'a block', she said, and completely under the influence of Hawkesbury and Castlereagh, who were jealous of Canning and anxious, presumably, to damage anyone connected with him, as Palmerston might have been considered to be through Malmesbury. (Journal of Lady Malmesbury, 12 May 1807, Lowry Cole Papers, P.R.O. 30/43/37.)

because to the naked eye at least no such prospect is visible. So far from it that I feel the most perfect confidence that we shall succeed fully in all the objects of the expedition. I agree with you in regretting the delay, but the only part of it that could have been avoided was that which intervened between the arrival of the forces and the commencement of ye operations. Gambier was in the Sound on ye 4th, but all the land troops were not assembled till some days afterwards and it was better not to make any attack till the whole was in readiness to act—as it was, eight or ten days were spent in negociation & the troops did not land till the 15th. How far this attempt to negociate was right, perhaps neither of us possess information enough to determine, but I will fairly own that to me it appears that we gave the Danes more time for consideration than was at all necessary or expedient & that it would have been much more consistent with the vigour that marked the conception of the plan, to have given the Danish Government but so many *hours* to determine upon our proposals, & if they refused them, to proceed immediately to ye attack. But although eight days were given them to consider, it was expressly told them, that if during that time the least preparation for resistance was made (& our Minister remained on shore to see fair play), it would be considered as a signal for attack. As to any secret understanding I believe none whatever existed, but that on the contrary our government knew pretty well that a secret understanding if not something more subsisted between the Danes & French. But depend upon it we did not wait for our battering train, every part of our force was ready to act many days before it did, & the last that joined were the Germans from Rugen, who could not on many accounts be brought away before. Since the troops have landed our operations have not gone on so rapidly as people in general expected. But it must be recollected that Copenhagen is a fortified town, & therefore if it did not yield to the first panic & surrender on the summons, there are but two ways in which it can be taken, by storm, or by siege. Lord Cathcart thought that he could take it by the former, but wisely, I think, preferred the latter. But though as certain it is of course slower. The process of a siege is to carry certain ditches & banks up to positions near the walls of the town & then to erect batteries which are to destroy the works & dismount the enemies' guns. This must necessarily be a work of some days when the place is extensive; on the 26th great progress had been made, with very little interruption on the part of the enemy, & I have no conception that when our works are finished & our batteries begin their fire, the town will hold out a day. Their garrison consists of but 4,000 regulars, while our besieging force by land amounts to 26 or 28,000 men. Our last accounts did not give us any precise guess as to when the attack would be made, but one should imagine it was not deferred longer than the first or second of this month at the furthest.

But apropos of disgraceful failures what think you of Genl White-lock's exploit.[1] It is a most lamentable business both as it deprives us of the footing we had gained in South America & as it lowers our military reputation. Till we hear what Whitelock has to *say* for himself it would be unfair to pronounce any but a suspended opinion, for in his dispatch he seems so well satisfied with his prowess & to have so little foreseen that any fault could be found with his proceedings that he has left us pretty much to our own conjectures. But by his own statement he appears to have been guilty of most inconceivable folly in every part of his arrangements. It surely could not be necessary in the first place to make his troops beat all the snipe bogs in the country for two days before they got to the town & by that means not only fag themselves when they were wanted to be fresh but lose all their provisions & great part of their ammunition. In the next place his previous knowledge that the inhabitants meant to fire from the tops of the houses, seems a curious reason for his ordering his men to scour the streets with empty muskets. Nor do the *two corporals* with hammers & mallets who were to walk *at the head* of each division to break open the doors as they went along, appear very likely to have long continued their morning's walk without being shot, or if they had, were they capable of committing much burglary with any effect. But then to crown the whole, after he had succeeded in a great part of his plan & had got possession of some of these great squares & flat roofs which it was the whole object of his arrangement to seize, he finds out what he might without being a conjuror, have previously discovered that the people of the town & country are very ill disposed towards us, & therefore he concludes we would derive no advantage from the possession of the country; now if this fact was so convincing he might as well have come to the same conclusion before the action; for it received no such additional proof by the mere circumstance of the inhabitants of the town liking the fun of popping off his men with-out any danger, as to make the whole difference between conquest & evacuation and if we are never to conquer any place unless the people are *civil* to us, I fear our victories will not be very numerous. The danger in which our prisoners were, might be very distressing, but he should have reminded Liniers that we had Spaniards in our power upon whom we could retaliate, and after all, however shocking to his feelings it might be to think he was at all contributing to their death, he ought to have had other considerations of public duty to

---

[1] Gen. Whitelock had made a humiliating withdrawal from the campaign in the River Plate during the summer.

his country that should have outweighed his private sensibility.[2] War is not child's play, & if he signed the capitulation for no better reasons than the displeasure of the mob, & the threat of putting to death our prisoners, I think he has much to answer for. I am tempted however to suspect that he was in no very pleasant situation himself. All this I beg you would take as my *private* opinion. I do not as yet know what govt think of the matter though I fancy they do not much approve of Whitelock's conduct.

I am glad to hear you are going to Walcot, as I think it not impossible you may be persuaded to take Broadlands in your way home! Pray think of it; it is very little out of your way & I need not say how glad we shall all be to see your party. I am rejoiced you are all now fairly at open war. I can tell you Ly M. is outrageous. She would have foresworn you but for the pleasure of abusing you. You must recant politically & sentimentally before you can shew yourself safely at Park Place. I have been down at Broadlands for ten days, I shot 4 days & killed 16 brace of partridges. At Clive's you will commit absolute murder. This being a very fine year for birds, I dare say he has a great number. I shall remain here till Ward[3] comes to town which is a time representable by *x* for I am wholly ignorant when he will be here but fancy it will be towards the conclusion of this month.

[*PS.*] I will enclose you a letter received from Matthew Stewart.

48. *Broadlands. 20 Nov. 1807.*

Pray believe that my not having sooner obeyed your order proceeded from no other cause than a proper degree of obstinacy which ran rusty at so peremptory an injunction & not at all from any diurnal delay of a diurnal intention of writing. You seem to have made a very pleasant tour particularly the latter part of it & knowing the perpetual series of amusements which must have occupied you while at Powys Castle I really wondered that you found time to write to me during your stay there. I am very sorry to hear that poor Clive has been so ill since you left him. He is now almost well, but I understand his illness is attributed intirely to the fatigue which your riots produced to him, & a long course of quiet is prescribed as a remedy. The lady you point out to me as a *fortune*, I have known for many years & we

---

[2] The Spanish commander had offered to release his British prisoners if Whitelock agreed to withdraw British forces altogether from the River Plate, at the same time indicating that he might otherwise not be able to protect them from the anger of the inhabitants of Buenos Aires.

[3] Robert Plumer Ward was one of Palmerston's colleagues at the Admiralty. Three commissioners always had to be on hand to sign the Board's orders.

have long been sworn friends. But your hint is somewhat like the Irishman's maxim that the best way of winning a rich widow was to court her during her husband's lifetime.[1] You wish you say for some explanation of our noble conduct (as you call it) to Louis 18 & our *concessions* to America. I really am not aware what there is relative to the King of France or America that particularly requires explanation. With regard to the former, he came over here without giving any previous intimation of his intended visit, & till his arrival in Yarmouth Roads government knew nothing more than what the newspapers told them. He came as Ct De Lisle, & therefore could not be received as King of France. But Mr Bagot was sent down to meet him, as soon as his arrival was known, & Holyrood House was ordered to be prepared for his reception. But it appears he does not mean to stay, & professes not to be come in search of a refuge, but merely upon some scheme of his own. If it is any plan connected with his re-establishment in France, one cannot help regretting that a man in his situation should be so deficient in judgment as to conceive the present moment the most proper for entertaining schemes of that nature. If he is running away from Buonaparte it is odd that he should have left his wife & family behind him. As to the person sent down to meet him I suppose it was right that it should be some official person, & as the King came in his private capacity, it could not be any of the Principal Secretaries of State. With respect to the other topic I can *guess* what you mean by *concessions* to America, but cannot agree in the propriety of the term. *Concessions* we have made none, but ministers have not suffered themselves to be led by the ignorance or intemperance of an officer into the assertion of claims which could be supported upon no grounds either of practice or of right.[2] The right of searching the *men of war* of friendly states for deserters, we never have claimed or avowedly exercised except in cases in which (as happened with the Dutch States) the privilege was secured to us by treaty. So that in disavowing any such pretension with regard to America while we maintain that of searching merchant men, we are placing our cause upon its proper & real basis. In fact if you will but consider the question one instant, you must see that we cannot insist upon any right of that nature being granted us by an independent power unless we consent to a perfect reciprocity on our part. Independant nations must in such matters be treated upon the footing of equality; & whatever such hotheaded fellows as Cobbet may say no system of public law

---

[1] Sulivan had reported a visit to a Mrs Wheler where Mrs Bromley (the wife of Palmerston's housemaster at Harrow, perhaps) had talked so glowingly of Palmerston that Sulivan banteringly suggested that if unfortunately widowed she would accept his friend's proposal (4 Nov., S.P.).

[2] The reference is to Vice-Adm. Sir George Berkeley, whose order had led directly to the *Chesapeake* affair.

can be permanent that is not founded upon the principles of reciprocal justice. We may indeed have the power *at present* to enforce an obedience to our existing maritime dominion, but if we are wise & wish it to be lasting we shall not attempt to establish it by tyranny and oppression. Now as to allowing the Americans to search our men of war, there is not an officer in the navy that would hear of it with patience. The obvious inconveniences are so many, that it would be useless to enumerate them; you would have a little Yankee privateer running up into your Brest fleet & ordering all hands on deck on board Ld Gardner's ship to search for two deserters. In fact there can be no reason why you should interchange with America a right, which no other nation on the earth grants, or receives from you. Thus you see we have not made (nor are we likely I think to make) any concession. We have taken our stand upon our real & necessary claims & if the Americans should be so absurd as to go to war with us upon these grounds, I think every sensible person here & there will admit that we have not thought it beneath our dignity to be just, but have reserved our firmness for a proper object. But apropos of concessions how fortunate it is that the Americans were so absurd as to reject the very ample ones which were made to their commerce in the treaty of the two noble lords. You see that by it the neutral carrying trade between the enemies' colonies & the mother country was positively sanctioned. They will find thus when the last Order of Council reaches them that there are golden opportunities which if missed do not again offer themselves. I hope this order will satisfy you that the system now acted upon is one of energy & vigour, & that ministers do not mean to sit down with their hands before them under the idea that the one effort at Copenhagen is sufficient for the glory of a whole administration. But I must say you are a little unfair upon this point. I remember that when I was finding fault with the Talents last spring for having done nothing during the whole of their reign you defended them upon the ground tht they had not had time, or opportunity, or something or other (I thought *sense*), to do much; and yet this advocate for inactivity in [*the*] spring, becomes so energetic a politician in the autumn, that, even before the Danish prizes are all arrived in port, he begins (like the children) crying out for *more*; & lashes at the ministry for thinking, as he is pleased to suppose, that they have done enough & that they may now go to sleep. Undoubtedly according to Lord Howick's disposition of time, there has been exertion enough during the last three months to intitle government to a nap of half a century if they were not disturbed in their slumbers by apparitions of six months' transports, & contractors demanding payment for stores & copper bottoms. By the bye though, I quite forgot all this time that I was writing about an expedition, which though well planned & conceived, had been so *diabolically mismanaged* in the execution, & had failed completely from the army not [*having*] been provided with a *battering train!!* But however as this shame and disgrace must lie upon Lds Cathcart & Gambier, it is lucky they have been put into the House of Peers, where you may have an opportunity of making your legal debut at their impeachment.

I certainly do not mean to run mute always in the St Stephen's covers, but I admire your style of exhortation, first recommending me to open, & then shutting my potatoe trap immediately by a gentle hint of what a loss of character the Fusty may sustain by its being opened. You have not studied Cicero *de cohortatione.*

We have had the Harris family here in succession. Ly Malmy seems a little less incensed against you than she was. Her violent and ungovernable rage seems to have subsided into *calm & settled aversion*, so that you need have no *personal* apprehensions in case you visit Park Place, but must only prepare yourself for a cool & ungracious reception. She indeed dropped some hints while here about Jacobins, suspicious persons, Secretaries for the Home Department, Bow Street Officers, & Cold Bath Fields; but as she only muttered to herself in broken sentences I could not collect whether she alluded to any particular persons, or only referred to general measures of precaution. I shall not be long at Park Place this Christmas but probably shall spend a day or two there in my way to town. I shall wish to remain here as long as my official duties will permit. I have a good deal of country business on my hands. There has been some necessary change in the departments of administration of the farm & garden, & not having been here much for some years past, I find things a good deal out of order.

I have had no sport in the bagging way having indeed scarcely taken out my gun since I have been down. I have however had several wet jackets in company with the hounds, but our weather has been so unfavourable that we have done very little with them.

I had a letter not long ago from Fiott[3] & Bruce dated Helsingborg. They had both been for some time at Head Quarters in Zealand & had consequently seen a good deal of what was going on there. They must probably both be returned before now. I am glad to find that our losses in the late violent gales have been so small. The *Neptunus* is the only ship of war we lost. She went aground in the Baltic & was burnt by us after her men & stores had been taken out & Barrow wrote me word some days ago that there were only 17 transports unaccounted for then, & most of them have I believe come in since.

You have probably heard of Mrs Cranston's death.[4] Her age &

---

[3] John Fiott (afterwards Lee: 1783–1866) had been a pensioner at St John's.
[4] Mrs Cranstoun, the widowed mother of Mrs Dugald Stewart, had died on 27 Oct.

state of health rendered it a desirable event both for herself & her friends. I was glad to find that the young Ly Ashburton was with Mrs Stewart during Mrs Cranston's illness & was of course very kindly received. I cannot for Stewart's sake wish that he should be upon a footing of very intimate intercourse with Ashburton but it is much more comfortable that at least the niece should be reconciled with them. We shall possibly meet at Park Place, but if not I presume I am sure of finding you when I come to town. I suppose Shee's nuptials are soon approaching. I should like to see him in the character of a *bridegroom.*[5]

49. *Broadlands. 8 Dec. 1807.*

There is no resisting your *gentle solicitations* to write, so as a determined snow makes it *extremely convenient* to do so, I proceed to answer your last letter. To premise then, I must confess that I cannot unravel the meaning of your *premise*, really if you *plead* in such unintelligible sentences you must not address a *popular* Jury. I have no doubt that when explained it will be perfectly perspicuous, but at present it is to me a riddle. The sentence in question is as follows. 'I must *premise* that you are not yet a thoroughly accomplished *partizan*, for altho' I believe you are tolerably staunch, yet, by some degree of unfairness when on opposite sides and by reviving the recollection of this when on the same side, you will not gain your number of converts or keep them if gained.' This really sounds like the figure of a country dance, there is such a changing of sides, but I must beg you to lead me down the middle, & tell me who these *sides* refer to. The general meaning however seems to be that I have not set about *bringing you over* with sufficient dexterity. To this charge I can only reply that if I had entertained any hopes of inspiring you with a suitable portion of party

---

[5] Shee had written to Palmerston as long ago as 30 Aug. 1806 (B.P., G.C./SH no. 77) that he could not carry out his plan to marry because his father would not give him a big enough allowance. But he persisted in his hopes. In some undated letters written about this time (Shee Papers) his father 'again' complained about his inflated projects and pretensions. In one letter he spoke of an epistle Shee had sent his mother, 'the style of some parts of which appears to me to be self sufficient & presumptuous & the sentiments to have been picked up from the novels of a circulating library'. In another he made what must have been a reference to Palmerston: 'I thought you of a different turn of mind or I should never have made the melancholy mistake I did in placing you in a situation to contract intimacies with young men of great fortune & high pretensions.' Shee, on the contrary, had no chance of his father's finding him an office and no prospect of a fortune. The largest allowance he could expect was £300 a year, and at his father's death £1,000 Irish per annum. Nor were there any better prospects from the family of his intended bride. For Jane Young was the eldest of ten children and her father, William Young of Hexton House in Hertfordshire, merely a former Puisne Judge in India. But the elder Shee evidently miscalculated his son's future prospects from the marriage (see no. 168).

spirit a little *wheedling* might have been attempted, but as I fear you
are incorrigibly tinctured with some oldfashioned antiquated notions
of independance & some ideas about public men & measures which
are now quite exploded, I despair of making anything of you as a
partizan, & look upon you as a sort of *no man's land* which may be
attacked & badgered at pleasure, since although nothing is to be
gained by it there is also nothing to be lost. But I am sorry to find
that you were not convinced by my explanation of our motives for
disavowing the right of searching men of war. You assert it to be a
pretension that has before existed, has been enforced & never formally
abandoned. To this I can only in reply assure you that you are mistaken as to the point of fact. Holland was the only nation against
which as far as I am aware we ever had such a pretension, & that
was founded upon particular treaties & not upon general principles.
In the time of Charles the Second this right was enforced by the
captain of a man of war in the *Downes* (not in a *Dutch port*) who
took some deserters out of the Dutch admiral. A remonstrance was
made by the ambassador of the States, which was referred to the
Judge Advocate, & it was determined after much discussion that no
reparation could be made, because each party was bound by treaty to
give up deserters to the other. But we never asserted such a right with
regard to any other state, and in this case it was evidently *mutual*.
That such seizures may have been made at times I do not deny,
though I do not know that they have, & I am certain that if they had
been made the subject of a remonstrance to the court, they would
have been disavowed as unauthorized acts of violence. So far then
from this right never having been formally *abandoned* it never has been
formally *asserted*, and therefore in the present case the question was
not whether we should give up a right we previously possessed, but
whether we should establish a new one—and here with all due
deference to your Cobbettian maxim that *might* makes *right*, I still
must maintain that we could require of the Americans no more than
we were prepared to concede to them in return. All your arguments
drawn from the present state of Europe & our new system of vigour
adapted to it, are wholly irrelevant to the point. You seem to have
intirely overlooked the wide difference between establishing a general
principle & doing a particular act. The expedition to Copenhagen &
other measures of the same nature we allow to be contrary to the
usual law of nations but urge that they are rendered necessary by the
present state of the continent, but does not this very defence imply
that they are to be considered as special exceptions to our general
rules of conduct, which are necessarily suspended by the aggressions
of France, and not as establishing a principle by which our subsequent
relations with neutrals are to be guided. So far indeed they do so, that

if ever the conduct of a third power, a belligerent, shall destroy the free agency of the neutral we may be obliged in self defence to have recourse to similar measures, but no man will infer that from what has been done we wish to establish the maxim, that in any future war we may, *apropos de bottes*, sail into the harbour of a neutral & bring out his fleet. But in the question with America the case was widely different. We were not to decide upon an individual act, but upon a general *principle* by which our future acts were to be guided, and in that decision, I repeat, we were bound to abide by the maxims of *reciprocal justice*. It may be necessary sometimes to act contrary to law, but it never can be so to enact an unjust one. How any set of ministers could have ventured to defend to the Parliament & the Country such a conduct as you seem to wish the present to have adopted I know not, but I should have thought it a very bad symptom of the state of the public mind had it met with their approbation. Possibly the Americans might have been intimidated into concession, probably had they gone to war we might have beat them into acquiesence but would that have compensated to us for the injury which the public principle & political integrity of the nation would have sustained. Depend upon it that in a free government like this which as it were subsists by its credit & its conscious probity, every thing that tends to debase the national character strikes a deadly blow at the sources of its power & existence. I am convinced therefore that ministers have been correct in their *calculations*, and that a right which could not be reconciled with justice was not *worth* enforcing.

You object to my expressions about Berkeley; I accompanied them, if I remember, with a caveat, that as his conduct would probably be inquired into, I would not be understood decidedly to condemn it, but I own that to me he does appear not to have acted correctly. His fault, or perhaps one should term it *mistake*, seems to have been the conceiving that he was authorized to take the men by force, & accordingly in his order he lays down the law of nations with as much confidence as Puffendorf or Grotius; granting that he was right in his principles, he acted upon it with as much circumspection & modera-tion as the case would admit, but he was wrong in the outset. Instead of taking such vigorous redress it would perhaps have been more prudent, though I admit less like a British sailor, to have remon-strated through the Minister to the government of the States, and left the question to be decided by the two governments instead of cutting the knot himself. But it certainly is a case that must rest upon its own grounds & considering the provocation he met with, his conduct is not to be wondered at or much disapproved. But what I said referred more to what ministers were to do in consequence, than to the merits of the thing itself. Very possibly you may be right in the inference you draw from the conduct of Russia that we were wise in letting her fight our battle by herself, although it seems to me rather an odd conclusion that because she was beat when left to sustain alone the whole pressure of the war, she would have been so equally if we had allowed our merchants to lend her money to clothe, arm & provision her army, & had sent 40 or 50 thousand men to join the Swedish troops & cause a diversion in the rear of the French army. No one certainly ever denied that had the expedition to Constantinople succeeded it would have been attended with very important results, but the wisdom of the planners does not seem much proved by sending a force incompetent from its numbers & nature to accomplish the object for which it was destined. You ask whether Whitelocke was sent out by the present government. I cannot conceive how such a report could have obtained. He certainly was not, nor was it I believe possible in point of time that he could. He was Windham's own choice. The Duke of York it is said wished Sr A. Wellesley to go. I am glad however that towards the conclusion of your letter you mollify a little towards the present set. I do not care what *ites* you consider them provided you will but like them. The affairs of Ireland will I fancy occupy a good deal of attention next session & doubtless have not been neglected during the recess.

So you have finally determined upon the law in earnest; you certainly are right. The *premier pas*, must to be sure be disagreable, but I cannot think that with your abilities success is at all doubtful— and the prize is great.

My motions are not quite settled as they must depend in a degree upon how my colleagues feel about my absence. I shall however pass a few days at Park Place, in my way to town, & that will probably be about the first week in January but I fear not later. I find from Ly Malmy that Shee's marriage is at length announced.[1] What I referred to about you was an account I heard of some person having dined at Mr Wheeler's, & having said that he met there a bride & bride-groom. The latter was yourself, but whether the former was Miss Wheeler or Mlle Mertellari it remains for you to tell us.[2]

I had a letter of three sheets of paper chuck full from Ashburton not long ago. He asked about you the same question which you ask about him, whether I had heard from you lately. His political speculations are slightly curious & whimsical; we will compare *folios* (not *notes*) when we meet.

Winter seems setting in in good earnest. I do hate snow most cordially, and I fear we are likely to have a good deal of it. How squashy you must be in London. Have you heard anything of Clive

---

[1] Shee married Jane Young on 4 Jan. 1808.
[2] The references are obscure, but see no. 48.

lately. I mean to give his memory a jog soon; he is without doubt a much worse correspondent than I am, which is very satisfactory to my feelings; one likes to be better than *some*thing or *some*body.

50. *Broadlands. 24 Dec. 1807.*

With the punctuality that belongs to a man of business I lose not a moment in answering the question contained in your letter of yesterday, and begin by informing you that it is our intention to be at Park Place on the fifth or sixth of next month. I shall remain there a few days, and then proceed to resume my functions at the Board. I hope this will suit you as I have laid my account with meeting you at P. Place.

I am sorry my simily did not please you but must contend that it was much more genteel as well as appropriate than your metaphor about *grubbing* & *pounding*.

The emigration of the Braganzas is really a very singular & important event and cannot fail to produce very beneficial results to our commerce. Query? will the Cambridge Duchess be seized with a sympathetic wish to remove to a milder region. I think I shall publish a certain essay that appeared on this subject in the Fusty, & contest with Burke the palm of political prophecy. How do you like the declaration against Russia?[1] I think it is inferior to none of Canning's former state papers, & that is saying everything. Would not Shee call it *refined sarcasm*? It calls Alexander, though in gentlemanlike circumlocutions, a fool, a liar & a coward. If he reads it, & has any sense of shame left, it must make his cheeks tingle, but he appears too far sunk even to feel his degradation. I wish we could make him change places with the King of Sweden; by the bye is it not curious that the only two sovereigns who besides ours have shown any spirit & energy in these times should have been the King of Sweden & the Prince of Portugal who have been constantly represented by the opposition the one as a madman & the other an idiot. The affairs of Spain seem incomprehensible, but the enigma will most likely be solved by the sudden disappearance of the Prince of Asturias. Buonaparte *sometimes* can act upon the maxim *qu'il faut reculer pour mieux sauter*, & when he does take his leap into Spain it will be a highflyer.

I am sorry to hear that you have been attacked by your old winter companion, but considering the weather we have had it is not very wonderful. It is lucky however that he waited till you were disengaged from business & I hope he will have the good manners to quit you

---

[1] Of 18 Dec., replying to Russia's breaking off of relations.

before you resume your occupations. William comes to us tomorrow morning or this evening if he can. He threatens utter extermination to all the snipes in the neighbourhood. Countess Woronzow's marriage has given great pleasure to all her friends.[2] Ld Pembroke is certainly a good deal older than she is, but her habits are more formed than those of most young women of her age, and he bears his years lightly, and as they have been intimate from her childhood the objection is not strong. The Count of course is delighted. It always was his wish that his daughter might be fixed in England, and Ld Pembroke was the man to whom of all others he was most desirous of being indebted for such an arrangement.

I cannot but approve of your matrimonial designs upon *La belle jardinière*, but if you are not quick in your operations I think the Count will anticipate you. He *must* marry her in self defence, she cannot any longer live with him upon any other footing & what is to become of him if left entirely by himself after being so long used to female society of so agreeable a kind? For to do Wiskerandos justice she *can* be very pleasant & entertaining when she chuses, & to him of course her inclinations are usually favourable. I declare I think it would be a very *pretty* match.[3]

[*PS.*] I am just going down to Romsey to superintend the distribution of rewards & Prizes to the young ladies of Fanny's & Lilly's school. I can assure you there are some cards equal to any of your *sketches*.

51. *To Elizabeth Temple. Admiralty. 4 Feb. 1808.*

Cf. *Bulwer & Ashley, i. 80–1.*

Palmerston reports his maiden speech in the Commons. The manuscript continues: William was persuaded to stay for the debate & sets out by the mail this evening. He saw Phipps yesterday who gave a very good report of his eye which he said was quite well & refused to accept the fee.

We have no news to day but the loss of the *Leda* frigate in Milford Haven; all the crew saved. It appears to have been owing to the imprudence of the pilot in entering the harbour when it was pitch dark by which means he cd not see the headlands.

---

[2] Count Woronzow's only daughter, Catherine, became the second wife of the 11th Earl of Pembroke on 25 Jan. 1808. Their only son was Sidney Herbert.
[3] It is not known to what these remarks refer.

52. *To Elizabeth Temple. Admiralty. 6 Feb. 1808.*

B.P.W.; cf. Bulwer & Ashley, i. 81–3.

Palmerston reports the substance of his speech in the Commons and his lack of success in the search for a suitable house to rent in London. The sentence omitted by Bulwer reads: The forwardness & preparation of their fleet & stores gave additional proofs of their hostile intentions, & their silence when Portugal communicated to us the demands by Buonaparte of her fleet.

53. *Albany.*[1] *23 Mar. 1808.*

I am *free to confess* that I am open to censure for not having sooner performed the promise I made of writing to you, but your letter could not have come at a moment better calculated to obtain immediate acknowledgement. I have since Sunday been confined with an agreeable mixture of a bilious headache and a *rash*; which as they require to be treated in exactly opposite manners, have timed their visit most disagreeably for me; however I have nearly got rid of both & hope in the course of tomorrow to be released from imprisonment. I am particularly glad that you have been so well pleased with your tour, & are likely to derive some useful information from it as well as pleasant acquaintances.[2] I expect to see you return with a blooming countenance that will put to shame all of us cockneys—I was going to say to the *blush*; but that is the only thing Londoners are not capable of doing.

I have not a great deal to tell you in the way of news of a private nature & all the public of course reaches such learned persons as yourself. Shee I have not seen this age, indeed we have of late been so uncommonly occupied in the House with long debates, and my mornings have been so well filled with attendance at the Admty & the West India Committee that I have scarcely seen a soul except in the way of business. The last time I saw him we took a long Sunday walk & he seemed to mean to leave London early in the spring on account of the health of his *cara sposa*. I am very glad Clive is allowed a little longer holydays, as he stood much in need of them & the work we have had in the House during the last fortnight would have quite knocked

---

[1] His own house in Hanover Square had been let as it was expensive to run and larger than his family needed. When he was on his own in London Palmerston lived in hotels, the Albany or the Admiralty. But something more suitable had to be found when the rest of the family came up for the season. In 1811 he finally settled on Stanhope St (now Stanhope Gate), taking a lease first of no. 12 and two years later of no. 9.

[2] Sulivan had been on circuit.

him up. Percy contrary to your predictions has been voting with us *occasionally* but has certainly not been very regular in his attendance, however quite enough so, to shew his general disposition. Ld Welles-ley's business you see is not allowed to sleep at rest even after the very decisive vote on Folkestone's motion.[3] The history of Ld Archibald's intended motion is this. The opposition meant to adjourn the debate on Folkestone's motion a second time & have *three nights* of it, and accordingly at about one o'clock Ld Archibald beginning to be a little drowzy marched out with his speech & his papers, & told a friend at the door, he should not speak *that night* but reserve himself for the next Friday, the day to which it was intended to adjourn; at this time no proposition of adjournment had been hinted at, but at about 2, William Smith, I believe, moved the adjournment, a division took place on it, and afterwards the House agreed to resume the discussion which was continued till 7 in the morning. But my Lord Archibald, who does not like to be choused out of his speech, has given this notice in order to have an opportunity of making it. I should not imagine however it would lead to much more discussion as the subject seemed pretty well exhausted in the last debate.

We have not heard yet of the Toulon & Rochefort squadrons, but we had yesterday intelligence from Sr Sidney at Gibr dated Feby 29 that the Carthagena squadron of 6 had made an unsuccessful effort to join the Toulon & had put back to a port in Majorca on the 25 of that month. There is therefore a possibility that Strachan might hear of them and *draw* them in his way to the *great earth*. There can be no apprehensions for Sicily; the Rochefort consists of 6 of ye line & the Toulon of 5 & Collingwood has 10 or 11 at Palermo & Syracuse.

I am happy to say I *have* got a house & have let my own in Hanr Sqr to Ld Cawdor who takes it on. The house I have got is Ld Wm Beauclerk's in Lower Brook Str. which was occupied by Lord Lake. It is very roomy though the furniture is not very new & clean, the situation is very good for the *young ladies* but not as near the House as I could have *wished* though much more so than I was afraid of being forced to go. On the whole I am very well pleased, & so I believe are they to get a house *any where*. They come to town the end of this week or beginning of next according as the house is ready for them. The Malmesburys and Harrises are well, but Fitzharris has the ophthalmia. It is but a slight attack fortunately although very unpleasant to the sufferer even in its mitigated degree. Orator Milnes is going to be

---

[3] The debate on Lord Folkestone's condemnation of the Marquess Wellesley's policy towards Oude had several times been adjourned, for the last time on 10 Mar. at the suggestion of William Smith. The debate resumed on 15 Mar., when another attempt at adjournment and the resolutions attacking Wellesley were heavily defeated. Lord Archibald Hamilton attempted to reopen the debate on 31 Mar. (1 *Hansard*, x. 1042, 1146–8 and 1290–3.)

married but I forget to whom, & Petty was to be turned off today or tomorrow.[4] He has been the most cool lover I ever heard of; his fair one has been ill in the country but he has preferred badgering his Majesty's ministers to the detriment of his own health as well as theirs, to the gentler and more amiable office of soothing the sufferings of his charmer. I have read *Marmion* and do not like it so well as the *Lay*. Nobody does. It is good, the story more interesting, but it does not contain any of those very brilliant passages that arrested one's attention in the other poem. Adieu My dear Sulivan. I shall always be glad to profit by your impiety whenever it occurs though sorry for the circumstance.[5]

54. *Cambridge. Monday [4 July 1808].*

The ball being tonight I suppose you will hardly think it worth while to come down as everybody will be gone by Wednesday. I am going on pretty prosperously in the new M.A.s.[1] Petty is not down & I am told by Clarke that Cauldwell[2] says he has expressed his determination never to stand again. Ld John Townshend however is here as his deputy.[3] Euston is here & Gibbs was yesterday but was obliged to return last night. I shall be in town on Wednesday evening.[4]

55. *Admiralty. 17 Aug. 1808.*

For once your intentions of keeping me in the basket have failed, as I have heard of your notable exploit in chousing poor Primrose of his only brief, & I wonder your conscience did not smite you for taking the *bread out of a poor fellow's* mouth, & depriving him of the means of earning his *wittels*.

As you do not chuse to communicate to me anything relative to your shop it would be serving you right if I were to be equally costive about mine. In fact however I have nothing in the way of news to tell you

---

[4] Robert Pemberton Milnes was married on 22 Aug. 1808 and became the father of the 1st Baron Houghton. Lord Henry Petty was married on 30 Mar. 1808.

[5] Sulivan's last letter had been written on a Sunday.

[1] Palmerston was still nursing his Cambridge interest for the next election.

[2] Probably George Caldwell, a fellow of Jesus.

[3] Lord John Townshend (1757–1833) was the first Marquess Townshend's younger son and a former member for the University. The nest year, however, Palmerston found Petty at the Commencement Ball (Palmerston to Malmesbury, 6 July 1809, Malmesbury Papers).

[4] In fact he did not arrive in London until the Thursday, having slept en route at Ware. The next day he reported to his sister: 'Our ball was pretty good. The display of female beauty was certainly not great; but there were many *masters of arts*. We had a gay but very cold gala on Tuesday evening at Dr Clarke's. The house being very small, the majority of the company was sent into the gardens where there was dancing, fireworks & supper. . . . I dined with a party of my committee afterwards.' (B.P.W.)

more than you see in the paper. Spanish affairs have gone on as well as could have been wished, & as I always expected; this victory of Castanos must I think be decisive of the war in the Peninsula & cannot fail to influence materially the operations of any contest Buonaparte may engage in with Austria. It is not easy to foresee exactly what he will do. He has lost since the beginning of May near seventy thousand men in Spain & Portugal (including Junot's army which I look upon as certain of being taken) and in order to carry on the contest with any prospect of success he must send in at least a hundred thousand more. Even with that force the event would probably be favourable to the Spaniards, whose forces trained & encouraged by three months' services & successes, would with the assistance of about 50,000 British who will soon be in Spain be able to bid defiance to any army the French could possibly collect. But if Buonaparte makes war with Austria, he must give up Spain as he cannot find men for both & it seems very probable that such is his present intention. He finds the Spaniards too tough for him while Austria is able to menace his frontier, & hopes perhaps by crushing her, to divert the attention of the French from his recent disasters, & then to be able to turn his whole force to the reduction of the Peninsula. The Spaniards at present invincible while defending their own territories, are too little organized to be very formidable to him as an invading army and he doubtless hopes to be able to break the bundle stick by stick. The Austrians however are in a better state of defence than they have been since the beginning of the revolutionary war. Their army amounts to near 200,000 effective men besides their militia & levy *en masse*, which together amount to 200,000 more; the Arch Duke Charles since the peace of Presburgh has been working heartily & cordially with the Government & has succeeded in placing the army upon an excellent footing, & in any future war their operations will not be marred by those unfortunate dissentions to which the Arch Duke's opposition was perpetually giving rise. Besides the events in Spain must produce a wonderful moral effect upon both parties, & the popular spirit which has so effectually displayed itself in that country will most likely extend itself to Hungary & Bohemia. Russia too may be considered as a probable ally of Austria in the event of a war with France. The French have latterly been detaining Russian merchant men in the Mediterranian & I have some shrewd suspicions that there have been some conciliatory communications between our Court & that of Petersburgh. These two circumstances however are *strictly between ourselves*. If the Russians & Swedes should unite to support Austria, the skeleton of Prussia would afford all the *negative* co-operation in her power & much may be hoped to result from such a general confederacy.

Buonaparte would be obliged to have recourse to another antici-
pated conscription for ye year 18*10* & when the knowledge of what
has happened in Spain spreads itself through France, such a measure
could not be carried into effect without causing very serious dis-
turbances. In such an event 50,000 English floating about in the
Mediterranian would be a most formidable force, & might be landed
as occasion might offer either in France or Italy so as to produce a
powerful diversion in favour of the Austrians. We have not yet heard
of Wellesley's operations but there can be no doubt of his success.
Junot's force has been variously estimated from ten to seventeen
thousand, but Cotton's last accounts state it at under eleven. Wellesley
joined by Spencer will land 15,000 & will in a few days after be
reinforced by 5,000 more under Anstruther. These 20,000 English
assisted by ten or twelve thousand effective Portugeze must be sufficient to reduce Junot, but should he hold out ten days Burrard's
division of 10,000 men will arrive at the Tagus to make sure of it.
I trust the Spaniards will be able to intercept Joseph's army in its
retreat to France, but at any rate they will harrass his rear, and considerably diminish his force before he reaches the Pyrenees. His army
is calculated at between thirty & forty thousand including a reinforce-
ment which he brought with him, & Bessières' division which retreated from Asturia. The great want of the Spanish army in the
north has been of cavalry, of which if they had had two thousand
Cuesta would have given a better account of Bessières' army than he
did. The gratitude expressed by the whole of Spain to England for
the ready & disinterested assistance afforded them is not to be
described. The Junta of Oviedo have begged the King to accept 2,000
sheep with a proper proportion of rams as a token of their gratitude
& regard, & we have sent out orders to some transports to bring them
home. One of our officers who landed at Gihon some time ago was
received with every possible attention and one of the handsomest
women of the place provided for his entertainment. I am afraid
government have not been quite as attentive to the *comforts* of the
Spanish Deputies here.

I have been at Park Place for a few days as I do not mean to pass
there in my way to Ireland. They were all in high health & had
recovered from their royal visit. William comes to town on Monday
next & on the Wednesday we set out for Ireland. I expect to be absent
from hence about five weeks which will enable me to do all I want
there & take a few days' shooting on my return.[1] Should you pass by
Broadlands in your way home you will of course not forget us.

---

[1] From Frances Temple's diary (B.P.W.) it would seem that Palmerston and William
Temple left London on 25 Aug. and arrived back at Broadlands on 4 Oct.

56. *To Elizabeth Temple. Florence Court. 12 Sept. 1808.*

Cf. *Airlie, i, 33–9, and Bulwer & Ashley, i, 85–8.*[1]

Palmerston reports upon his first visit to Ireland. Among those he has visited are the first Earl of Enniskillen, from whose seat he writes, Enniskillen's son-in-law Owen Wynne (ob. *1841*), *who lived near Palmerston's estates in Sligo, Charles O'Hara of Annaghmore* (*1746–1822*), *M.P. for Co. Sligo, and the first Viscount Lorton, whose four younger brothers had all been at Harrow, two of them in Palmerston's time.*[2]

Palmerston's main purpose, however, was to inspect his property in Dublin and Co. Sligo. Dublin, he had already reported to Frances Temple,[3] *he thought 'in point of publick buildings one of the handsomest' towns he had ever seen. In general, too, he sensed a 'spirit of improvement'. 'Instead of seeing the grass grow in the streets as was prophesied by the anti-unionists one cannot turn a corner without seeing some new work carrying on.' He admitted, however, that there was 'a military look throughout that brings to one's recollection what things have happened, & proves that the argument most relied upon to secure the tranquillity of the people is the point of the bayonet. The people in fact are at all times ready for a rising.' He spent much less time than he had expected in Dublin and a mere couple of days inspecting his property there. 'It is an extensive but not a profitable possession', he reported, 'the greatest & best part of it being let upon leases renewable forever. As an instance I am nominally the owner of 8 acres of ground in the center of this town, covered with some of the best houses in it. For this I receive the annual rent of £49. 10s. 0d. whilst the actual value of the ground is not far short of 15,000 pr. annum. These leases were all made between the years 1710 & 1720 by Sir John Temple, to whom the property was granted by Charles 2nd. The intention probably was to encourage English settlers, but the effect has been to diminish in a wonderful degree the value of the property. There is hardly any prospect of improvement in any part of this property for many years & none immediately.'*

He had also been led, he reported to his elder sister, to believe that for some time to come it would not be possible to make any improvements on his Sligo estate beyond, perhaps, the encouragement of linen manufacture. But after the sub-agent in Sligo[4] *had taken him round, he made plans for the extensive*

---

[1] Lady Airlie's version, though slightly inaccurate, is more complete and more reliable than Bulwer's. Lady Airlie's p. 34, line 25 should read 'assist' not 'adjust', p. 35, line 26 'Here', not 'When', p. 35, line 28 'us', not 'me', and p. 36, line 1 'intermission', not 'interruption'. Coching was Palmerston's butler in London until about 1823. Thomas Hold had been butler or valet to the 2nd Viscount and his sister Anne was housekeeper for the 3rd at Broadlands. Anne Hold wrote on 24 July 1818, her seventy-ninth birthday, to say she thought it time she retired; but she stayed on until Oct. 1824 and died on 26 Mar. 1835. (B.P.W.)

[2] Lorton's elder brother had succeeded as 3rd Earl of Kingston in 1799, though Palmerston persists in calling him by his former courtesy title of Viscount Kingsborough.

[3] 31 Aug., B.P.W.

[4] The sub-agent, Chambers, who was also an Anglican minister, died in Dec. 1810

improvements he now outlines to Elizabeth—three schools for the tenants'
children, roads for bringing sand from the sea-shore to mix with the bog, the
construction of a pier and harbour at Mullaghmore and the gradual elimination
of 'the middle-men or petty landlords'—on all of which he laid out large sums
in subsequent years. His letter ends with a postscript not printed by Airlie:
William thinks it unnecessary to send a duplicate of this by the same
post tho' he is in Ireland.

57. *Wednesday, Nov. 1808.*

Many thanks for your kindness in attending so early to my request
about providing William with a pleader.[1] I should feel very great
satisfaction indeed if Dampier would be prevailed upon to take him,
& I think I could venture to answer for his attending to the business
of the office. I have had an answer about the chambers the lowest
price of which furniture included is 1,500£ & I think there can be no
doubt about the expediency of taking them. William seems to see the
propriety of commencing his studies early, & I shall give Lane[2] my
answer tomorrow.

Will you dine with me on Friday to meet Goulburn at ½ past five.
We mean to go to the Haymarket afterwards.

[*PS.*] Ld Malmy wants to know whether you *ever* mean to go to P.
Place. If you dont you will be put on a footing with *Garrow*.[3]

58. *Broadlands. 15 Dec. 1808.*

As I have known such things happen as young *gentlemen* changing
their minds, I take the chance of such an event having possibly happened with you, and beg to restate all the pretty things I said when
last I saw you of the pleasure etc. it would give us to see you here. In
short William tells me he means to come down to us the beginning

---

and was replaced by James Walker. His superior in Dublin was Henry Stewart, the
son of the man the 2nd Viscount had appointed as his agent in 1788. In 1805 Stewart
had taken an Irish barrister, Graves Swan, as his partner, but when Swan died in
1829 he formed a new partnership with an employee, Joseph Kincaid. The firm of
Stewart & Kincaid continued to act for Palmerston for the rest of his life. (Connell,
pp. 356–7, and B.P.W.)

[1] Sulivan had studied under Henry Dampier.

[2] Thomas Lane was Steward of Lincoln's Inn.

[3] Probably Joseph Garrow (1789–1857), a Johnian but an illegitimate child of the
secretary to the C.-in-C. in Madras by a native woman.

of next week, & why could you not accompany him? Should you be afraid of making too long a stay, I can offer you the happiness of my agreeable society to town on the ensuing *Sunday* (I know you are fond of appropriating that day to prophane purposes) as I am summoned to mount guard for a few days on the Monday. I mean after I am released from the Board which I hope to be in a very few days to run down for a day to Cambridge previous to returning here & I shall then get another fortnight's hunting before the meeting of Parlt. What a *good* man Perceval is to put it off to the 19th that members may not be induced to travel on a Sunday. I send you back L[*ane*]'s letter. I think the French bulletins give us much less unfavourable accounts of Spanish affairs than our own officers send us; it appears that instead of being dispersed & annihilated, Castanos was only forced to retreat about 20 miles with the loss of 3,000 prisoners & 4,000 killed, (French reckoning too). I thought it would turn out to be less disastrous than Baird represented it. He is a terrible croaker, and hasty in giving credit to reports, but he should be admonished to be more cautious in future in dispersing a whole army without its consent. Buonaparte has a fair chance of being beat still if the Spaniards are what we take them for & they have hitherto shewn themselves to be. The Malmesburys etc. are here & remain till Monday sennight & I believe your only chance of retaining any footing in Ly M.s good graces is by coming down with William, as I have now a good opportunity of retailing all your treachery, & *cramming* her as much about you, as you are in the habit of doing about me. So look to yourself, I give you fair warning.

59. *Broadlands. 27 Dec. 1808.*

I am really very much obliged to you for the very kind manner in which you have stated the change in your intentions about staying with Dampier, & should certainly have thought it rather inconsistent with the sort of intimacy which has subsisted between us, if the certain scruples which you mention had prevented you from frankly mentioning the circumstance.[1] Of course it is unnecessary for me to say that William cannot & must not in any way interfere with your arrangements, & I am sure that after all the kindness which both he & I have experienced from you, it would be utterly impossible for either of us to harbour a wish of that nature. Indeed I am not sure whether upon

[1] Sulivan had been admitted to the bar in July and had evidently indicated earlier that he intended leaving Dampier's chambers. But he wrote again on 23 Dec. to say that he would probably stay after all and that there would then be no room for William Temple (S.P.).

the whole he would not derive as much advantage from attending the Courts for the first year and reading by himself as from dashing at once into the business of a pleader's office, but upon that point we can decide before he returns to town. My chief reason for wishing William to go to a pleader's office as soon as he could was the idea that by being under the eye of such a person he would have got more into habits of regular attendance, than if left to his own energies in attending the courts; but I am not sure that there is much weight in it, & Dampier's opinion as to the expediency of a previous attendance in the courts is certainly a strong argument in favour of that plan. I am inclined to think too that Dampier is worth waiting for, as William has the time to spare & can employ the intermediate interval to advantage. I shall be in town for a few days in the course of next week and we can then talk the matter over more fully; but in the mean time, I certainly think that William should not give up his *turn* upon Dampier's list if the latter will allow him to retain it.

60. *Admiralty. 9 Feb. 1809.*

I mentioned to Rose two days ago what you wished.[1] He said that the subject was under the consideration of Govt & had been for some time; that it was certainly their wish to afford every possible encouragement to the trade of our N. American colonies, but that with regard to the *mode* of so doing there was considerable difficulty & delicacy in deciding. It is obvious that in the present state of our relations with the United States, it would be improper to hazard any additional duties upon their importations, but in point of fact their embargo acts as the most effectual encouragement to our colonies, since although it is worth while for the Americans to break the embargo with articles of small bulk in proportion to their value, it would not answer to run the risk with bulky cargoes in articles such as alone are exported from our N.A. colonies. Should your friend however have any particular questions to ask or any information to communicate upon this subject, Rose promised to answer the one as well as he could, & would be much obliged for the other, & in this case I would give to Rose any written statement which you might transmit to me.

[1] George Rose (1744–1818), Vice-President of the Board of Trade and Treasurer of the Navy from 1807–12, was a Hampshire landowner and closely acquainted with Palmerston through Malmesbury.

61. *Admiralty. 13 April 1809.*

I certainly was much edified by the exemplary discretion of your last letter in which without hazarding any questions of a political nature you very prudently confine your inquiries to the proceedings in the gay world. I was not however at the time I received your letter in a situation to answer this requisition; having got down to Broadlands for a few days, which were spent much to my satisfaction in the rural amusements of hunting, farming & looking over & marking timber. My excursion increased my physical knowledge as I discovered that a north east wind is most decidedly a different thing in the country from what it is in town & I mistook it at first for a southwester. The *gay world* has not of late been remarkably gay & I rather fancy you will be in time to christen your new pumps at the first ball of any note that will be given this season, for as yet I have heard of nothing of the kind. You will have read in last night's *Gazette* an abundance of good news, which will be followed up today by the details of the capture of Cayenne. Our loss in these affairs has been wonderfully small compared with the advantages obtained. The capture of Martinique is highly important with a view to warlike operations, as it was the only naval station the French had in the West Indies where line of battle ships could lie protected from attack: & Cayenne was an endless source of privateers which annoyed our trade excessively. The surrender of the French at Vigo is also very encouraging, as far as it shows that the Spaniards are plucking up courage again and are determined to persevere in harrassing the French wherever they can muster numbers sufficient to cope with them. Romagna was advancing to Astorga with a very considerable force and as the French had nearly evacuated all Gallicia it was hoped he might perhaps retake Ferroll or at least establish himself in its neighbourhood. Wellesley I am sorry to say has not yet sailed and this S.W. wind will I fear prevent him. I wish he was in the Tagus, as the French were supposed to be advancing in considerable numbers against Lisbon; but I think if he can get there in time he will make a very good fight against them. We have no accounts from Austria, but it is hardly possible to imagine that France will suffer her to remain quiet & it is to be feared that in the event of a rupture between them Russia will scarcely remain neuter. She is however at a good distance and if she can do no more to hurt Austria than experience has proved her able to accomplish in her defence Turkey may find pretty full employment for her army. I suppose you have been busily employed with your brother barristers in sowing wide the *seeds of sedition, & preparing* the Country for Parliamentary Reform. All the outcry and meetings we have had are certainly unpleasant but I cannot say I am one of those who apprehend any serious or alarming consequences. It is an ebullition of the popular feeling which has been strongly excited; but it seems to be referable to a particular cause which it will probably not long survive. A great deal has been & will be said & done that is detestably mischievous in its tendency & intention; but one should rather have thought less favourably of the state of the Country had the questions which have of late been agitated produced less sensation in the publick mind. The subject *ought* to have been strongly felt; and as it was one in which misrepresentation had so fair a field to act in, it was impossible but that if the mass of the people were as alive as they should be to publick events, many should not be very *properly wrong & factious*. But I trust the tide will soon slacken & that all the puffing & blowing of Cobbett & his gang of revolutionists will be unable to prevent the waves from subsiding. Wellesley's appointment to Portugal creates a vacancy which I am told is to be filled up by Robert Dundas from the Board of Controul but as this arrangement is not yet announced & may possibly not take place, pray do not repeat it. Cholmeley is almost gone mad with joy at what Cobbett calls the *heart cheering* scenes in the Common Hall & ye Hackney meeting.[1] He says a set of *genuine whigs* are gone down to different parts to bring up petitions for Parliamentary Reform; & I believe he already imagines himself member of the *Conservative Senate*. He says the city meeting was evidently composed of free & independant people because they so strictly refused to hear more than one side of the question. The Powys's are come to town, Ly P. looking remarkably well, & the *young ladies* also in high feather. Clive has not yet made his appearance.

62. *Brocket Hall.*[1] *15 Sept. 1809.*

I really feel very considerable compunction when I bring to mind how long it is since I wrote to you, or rather I believe I should speak more correctly if I were to say, since I heard from you. I find from Shee whom I saw in town a little while ago that you were to be at Scarborough to which place I direct, taking it for granted that if you have left it you have had the sagacity to leave your direction with

[1] *Cobbett's Political Register*, xv. 516–24, reported a meeting of the aldermen and liverymen of the City of London on 1 April supporting Wardle's attack on the Duke of York, and pp. 564–6 a similar meeting of the Middlesex freeholders in Hackney on 11 April.

[1] Palmerston had known the Lambs since childhood. But quite when he made an adult friendship, apparently first with William Lamb and then with his sister Lady Cowper, is uncertain. It was certainly before this stay at Brocket or the visit he made at the same time with a party of Lambs and Cowpers to the latter's newly rebuilt house at Panshanger.

the postmaster. I hope that this northern excursion will not so far alter your previous plans, as to prevent you from making good your promise of a visit to Broadlands; I shall be there about the latter end of next week, & from that time to the meeting of Parliament with the exception of about three weeks in the beginning of November I shall be there, & most happy to see you. William, Fanny & Elizabeth have been down there since the beginning of this month. The former has been doing considerable execution among the partridges, and though our breed has been tolerably abundant, yet unless you come soon I cannot promise that you will find many to have escaped from the united volleys of his gun and mine. My aunt, Culverden, & Emma are still at the Lavender, but will join us towards the latter end of this month. My aunt is wonderfully recovered, but did not find herself quite equal to the journey when my sisters removed, & thought that it would be better for her to remain a little longer quiet at home. I thought Shee was looking remarkably well when I saw him in town. He came up for one day from Tunbridge Wells where he had left Mrs Shee. She has again miscarried & I fear seems to have acquired a confirmed habit of that kind of failure. Cholmeley is spending his honeymoon in a small cottage on *Putney Common* by way of being very rural. I suppose the great advantage of the situation must be the near neighbourhood of Sir Harry & his *fair* damsel.[2] I have been half tempted to go down & beat up his quarters but thought it fair to allow him to enjoy his matrimonial retirement undisturbed a little longer. I think however it will be practicable to attack him before I leave London entirely.

As to politics one is really quite sick of them. It is quite wretched to think that such an expedition as that to the Scheldt should have had such a termination. What will be the result time alone can shew. Some partial change of administration appears probable at present, & whether the failure will lead to a total change after Parliament has taken the thing in hand it is not easy to foresee. The Opposition are certainly strong in the Commons, & they never can have a better point to attack us upon. Much remains to be explained as to the history of this misadventure & upon the imperfect data which one at present possesses it is unfair to form a decided opinion, but it is difficult not to think that had Lord Chatham possessed the energy even of a child he must have succeeded. There certainly were no troops of any consequence collected at Antwerp when our army landed in Bevelandt, & one does not understand why during the siege of Flushing that part of our army which was in the former place were not pushed

[2] Francis Cholmeley had been married on 22 Aug. His maternal uncle, Sir Henry Charles Englefield (1754–1822), was a notable antiquary and a close friend of Palmerston's parents.

over to the attack of Lillo which if taken would have protected our flotilla in its advance up the Scheldt & have enabled both services to cooperate in the reduction of Antwerp. However all this reasoning depends upon an accurate knowledge of dates & distances which can only be obtained by a court martial & of which the public *must* be ignorant.

I think the only point upon which we are vulnerable is the appointment of our staff, Ld Chatham, Coote, & Grosvenor, who certainly are none of them fit for the situation in which they were placed; the object of the expedition certainly was practicable, its importance if accomplished no one can deny, & if it was to be done at all the force we sent out was as to its numbers, composition & appointments (I mean equipment, not officers) fully competent to the undertaking. It was a considerable time delayed by contrary winds & other circumstances before it sailed, but still so little could that have marred the end, that the enemy certainly were ignorant of its destination till it arrived off Walcheren, conceiving it destined for the north of Germany, & in one of their reports they say that we changed our point of attack in consequence of the armistice. If then the failure arose from delay it must have been delay after the landing & the question is whether that was unavoidably occasioned by the weather or by Lord Chatham's indolence; I believe the latter. The attack then I conceive must be for having sent out a man whom his employers must or ought to have known incapable of the service; & this it will be difficult to parry; the only thing to be said, is, that though known to be habitually indolent he certainly is a man of a very strong understanding, and of unimpeachable honour, & that therefore it might naturally have been expected that a sense of the importance & responsibility of the situation in which he was placed would have roused him to exertion, & stimulated him for a time to break through his natural habits. And the more active & energetic those persons were who had to decide upon his appointment, the more difficult would it be for them to conceive the insurmountable force which his habits of indolence had acquired. It is also said, & perhaps with some truth that it would have been impossible considering the number of troops we now have on foreign service to have found officers of sufficient standing for so large a force as was sent out, unless you took your commander in chief high up upon the list. Had Hope for instance been appointed Ld Huntley & Paget, and Ld Rosslyn could not have served, being all senior to him, and deficient as our list of generals is it would have been a great loss to have cut out such good officers. Then taking a man of Ld Chatham's standing the choice was nearly reduced to a question between him & Ld Moira, & certainly whatever one might think now that one has been tried, one should not *a priori* have hesitated an instant in preferring Ld Chatham.

They say Castlereagh is to troop; I think it is rather hard upon him. No one complains that there was any deficiency in his department as to the equipment of the army, & though as War Secretary it may be supposed to have the recommendation or suggestion of a commander in chief, I should conceive that the whole Cabinet or at least the majority must have acquiesced & thereby rendered themselves to the full as responsible. However if a victim is to be sacrificed to appease the fury of the many headed monster, I know no one whose loss would perhaps be less felt than poor Cas[*tlereagh*], since whatever his talents for business may be, & I confess I rather think highly of them, he is dreadfully unpopular & is somewhat of a millstone about the necks of his friends. The old Duke[3] they say is also to retire but I know nothing as certain or authentic, & if he does so it can only be from finding his infirmities increase, but at present he is in a very good state of health. Ld Wellington seems to have made good his retreat in a very able manner, but nothing can now be expected from his exertions. The termination of the war in Austria, & the inconceivable apathy & folly of the Spaniards have extinguished every hope in that quarter. It really is not to be borne that while we are straining every nerve to supply them with money & means to raise armies of their own, & shedding our best blood in their defence, in the center of their kingdom they should literally starve our troops although their own were provided with provisions of every sort in abundance. The Spanish spirit & enthusiasm seems to have been a mere *pet en air*, it made a great noise at first, but broke immediately & has left very unpleasant consequences behind it. It is singular that they should scarcely have found one man of any ability among them, & not one capable of commanding an army, I do not except even Palafox for I much doubt whether he would have made much of a figure out of the walls of Sarragossa. We shall now soon be again in a state of siege but I think the battle of Talavera has pretty well relieved us from any fears about invasion if any still remained. Adieu my dear Sulivan.

I find I have advanced so near the limits of my privilege that if I do not conclude I shall make you *pay* dearly for my loquacity.

[*PS.*] By the bye, pray consider my speculations etc. in the political part of this letter as *strictly confidential*; as Shee would say. I came here yesterday for a day or two & shall return to town Sunday or Monday.

[3] The Duke of Portland resigned shortly before his death in Oct.

63. *Brocket. 17 Sept. 1809.*

In case a long letter which I directed to you at Scarborough two days ago should not be punctually forwarded, I write two lines merely to say that I shall be at Broadlands on Monday or Tuesday next, and shall be most happy to see you there as soon as you can come & for as long as you will stay.

64. *Admiralty. 28 Oct. 1809.*

I entered yesterday upon the functions of my new office, & have only delayed writing to you in order that I might be able better to ascertain the point with regard to the private secretaryship, and as the thing concerns us both equally I think the best way will be for me to state exactly what I have collected upon the subject.[1] It appears then that in point of practice the priv. sec. has usually been taken from the office, since Sir G. Younge, who took Mr Merry, now one of the principal people in the office, but who came in at first as his priv. sec. Granville Leveson followed the custom, & took Sr J. Pulteney's, instead of the person who had been with him in Russia in a similar situation.[2] He of course advised me to do the same. Mr Moore,[3] Deputy Sec. at War, is certainly of that opinion & the

[1] It was not finally settled that Palmerston should be Secretary at War until 26 Oct. His predecessor Lord Granville Leveson Gower (afterwards 1st Earl Granville) introduced him to the office the same day and Palmerston entered on his duties the following morning (Granville to Palmerston, 26 Oct., B.P./GMC no. 15). But he spoke to Sulivan about becoming his private secretary as early as 24 Oct. and Sulivan had replied the following day that it would be *'peculiarly* agreeable to me at all accounts' (B.P./GMC no. 16).

[2] William Merry (*c.* 1762–1855) had entered government service in 1778 and become private secretary to Sir George Yonge in 1782. He had stayed on in the War Office, becoming Chief Examiner of Accounts in 1801. (Merry to Pulteney, Nov. 1808, enclosure no. 10A in W.O. to Treasury, 28 July 1809, P.R.O., W.O. 4/429.) He was Palmerston's Deputy Secretary from Dec. 1809 until his retirement in 1826. His second son, also named William, became a War Office clerk in 1810 and was Palmerston's last private secretary in the office. The junior clerk who acted as private secretary to Sir James Murray-Pulteney and Leveson Gower was Robert Wilkinson.

[3] Francis Moore (*ob.* 1854), who was Sir John Moore's youngest brother, decided to retire in December, after only a few weeks under Palmerston. Politics may have had something to do with it, but his family was reputedly rich (J. Greig, ed., *The Farington Diary*, 1922–5, v. 201). He retired on a pension of £1,800 per annum, £800 of which was in respect of previous service as a Foreign Office clerk. Ten years later he voluntarily gave up the £800, saying that he did not need so much in Italy where he lived. The fact was widely advertised by the Government in the hope of encouraging others. In 1843 Moore wrote to complain about income tax being deducted. He was admitted to have a good case; but it proved impossible to waive the deduction and special arrangements had to be made to repay the tax to him regularly. (W.O. to Moore, 28 Sept. 1829, and to Treasury, 7 Oct. 1831, P.R.O., W.O. 4/724; P.R.O., W.O. 43/525.)

reasons he assigns for it are the convenience to the Sec. at War of having somebody close at hand to whom he can refer upon points that may arise, involving matters of precedent, or official routine & detail, & upon which probably a great portion of the private correspondence of the Sec. at War would turn; and the advantage to the priv. sec., who it appears has the arranging of the different applications for pensions upon the compassionate fund list, to have a previous knowledge of the usages of the service. Merry who is next to Moore in the office did not see the same objection to a new person coming in, but said at the same time, that the business of the office was much changed & enlarged since his time, as instead of about 30 clerks which there were then, the establishment now amounts to above 100; but all agree that I have a perfect right to name whomsoever I please & that nobody in the office can have a pretence to complain at another being put into the situation. The practice therefore can only be binding on me so far as it suits my convenience to follow it. Now it certainly appears that at first there might be some little inconvenience arising from the Priv. Sec. not being conversant with the business of the office, but it seems to me that this detail & routine & precedent cannot be the *grand arcanum of nature* & must be [*?apt*] to be learnt in some period, & by some means, or other; & even if the clerks etc. should not like the idea of a new person coming in, yet when they found he was on a footing of intimacy with the Sec. at War, they would soon understand that it was their interest *to be civil*. Now Moore's opinion which certainly was very decided, although intitled to weight from his long experience in the office, must yet be taken with the allowance arising from one's knowledge of the force of habit upon geniuses of that sort—a man gets a sort of set of official ideas & whatever is new is to him *therefore* objectionable & difficult. As to the compassionate fund list as that is made up only once a year it might easily be managed. And with regard to the other point of convenience, viewing it merely & intirely as it regards myself, I should willingly submit to any slight inconvenience of that sort at first for the pleasure & advantage of having you there afterwards. I cannot conceive that the inconvenience can be very great, as it cannot make much difference whether these references are made to Moore or to my priv. secy. At all events the inconvenience would be temporary & the advantage permanent. I do not imagine that the business would be very entertaining but on the other hand I should not think it would be very laborious at least to a person like to you in the habits of application. What strikes me upon the whole as perhaps the best arrangement, is that you should come and at least *try* it. If upon experiment you find it the sort of thing you like, nothing would gratify me more than your remaining. If on the whole you thought it not worth your while, your giving it up at any time would create no embarrassment to me as I should always find plenty of persons in the office ready to take it and probably at this particular season you might give the thing a sufficient trial without at all interfering with any other pursuits should you not ultimately like it. I find I was wrong in the salary which is £300 not 430 as I believe I stated.[4]

I almost fear upon reading this letter over that I may appear as wishing to dissuade you from coming, which I can assure you was not my intention. I thought it but right & fair by you to state exactly what I had learnt upon the subject, but the bias of my mind is that the best plan would be for you to give it the trial I propose.

65. *Admiralty. 30 Oct. 1809.*

I have settled every thing in the most satisfactory manner with Moore etc. Wilkinson has behaved very well. He said that he felt he had no claim whatever to be continued, but that he would most willingly remain to *act* as long as I wished, and that when you came, he would with the greatest pleasure do anything he could to shew you the best mode of getting into the business of the office. If therefore it should be at all more convenient to you to remain another day at Ponsborn Thursday will do just as well as Wednesday for the commencement of your official labours.

66. *War Office. 17 Nov. [?1809].*[1]

I am sorry to hear that your face is playing you one of its old tricks, but the only inconvenience sustained by it will be felt by yourself in the quantum of pain you have to suffer.

I am fearful I cannot postpone Bayley[2] from tomorrow as I wish to gain all the information I can from him previous to meeting Perceval on Monday to discuss the new arrangements, but I shall probably have occasion for the said Mr Bayley's services on more days than one so that you will still have an opportunity of hearing him narrate again.

---

[4] The usual emolument was £300, but it was supposed to be reduced to £100 if the private secretary was also a salaried clerk. Sometimes, however, the Minister had authorised the payment of both emoluments in full.

[1] The year is uncertain, though the watermark of the letter is 1808. The 'new arrangements' mentioned in the text most probably concerned the review of the clerical establishment that had been left uncompleted by Palmerston's immediate predecessors.

[2] Richard Baily was a clerk in the Accounts Department of the War Office.

67. *War Office. Monday [?Dec. 1809].*[1]

I inclose my opera ticket to be returned on my return. I shall not be here till Thursday morning; I have been attending a conclave of the most heterogeneous composition, consisting of an Archbishop, a Bishop, a Chancellor of the Exchequer, a Commander in Chief, a Quarter Master General and a Secy at War. The Archbishop played his part to admiration, expressed the reluctance with which he undertook the onus imposed upon him, but he yielded to Perceval's intreaties from his regard for the public good, although he did not view it as any accession of *patronage* or *power*. It appears that the holding of any other preferment will be a bar to the continuance of a Garrison Chaplain, & that all Chaplains will be liable to be called upon to go on service though of course where there are great bodies of troops generally stationed that call will be less probable than elsewhere.

68. *Broadlands. 10 Dec. 1809.*

I shall not return to town till Tuesday evening as I find there is nothing in the office which particularly presses & it will be very convenient for me to remain here another day. I wish therefore you would send me my letters by Monday's post. I ordered the messenger to send them as usual to my house in the red box, & enclose you the key of it in case he should have shut it before you come down to the office. I have been particularly lucky in my weather, yesterday was very fine, and I had a most glorious run. Pitch behaved incomparably as he always does and it was generally agreed that the hounds had not had a better run this season. I dine today at the Sloanes. Mrs Stephen is at Paultons quite subdued & upon her good behaviour.[1] Tomorrow I hunt at Paultons.

[*PS.*] Were you or William the person taken up in the pit on Friday with a lawyer's wig for making a row?

---

[1] The system of appointing chaplains and the determination of their duties were both overhauled in Dec. 1809.

[1] The Sloanes were neighbours of Palmerston's in Hampshire. Hans Sloane (1739–1827) had been one of his father's closest friends. He had inherited Paulton's from a cousin and later changed his name to Sloane Stanley. His younger son Stephen, who had married as early as Nov. 1800, was still a struggling undergraduate at Trinity when Palmerston went up to Cambridge. He finally graduated in 1805, but died in 1812. His elder brother William (1781–1860) had married the youngest daughter of the Earl of Carlisle in 1806.

69. *Broadlands. 27 April 1810.*

We do not return till Sunday, as I find so much to do in the *rural economicks*. I inclose a very fat letter from Shee, which I think would gain the prize, if Freeling[1] was to have an annual show like Ld Somerville. Who Wm Anderson is I know not but perhaps you may be able to find out. I suppose Mrs Stewart's letter might be consigned to that endless Mr Meheux[2] who would probably take good care of it. I shall thank you to tell the messenger to send me the *Chronicle* tomorrow as usual & he may get a *Courier* to add to it.

70. *Park Place. 5 Aug. 1810.*

The Cattery[1] goes on very well, but I begin already to feel a disposition to purr & mew, & an amazing inclination to go a rat catching. This will however wear off again probably before the next session of Parliament as an aversion so decided to that species of animal might be inconvenient in St Stephen's. The rain has been incessant yesterday & today though I got down on Friday without one drop. I shall probably return Tuesday.

71. *Park Place. 23 Aug. 1810.*

Add. MSS.

I beg you will desire William to pay into the hands of my agent the sum of 2s. 6d., being the amount of a bet I won yesterday by arriving here in full time. The Duke did not come till near ten o'clock as he came from Windsor.[1] He has talked most incessantly ever since. We are however particularly fortunate in our weather, as we are enabled to take him out & there one can bear a loud talker better than in a close room. My box is not arrived, did you forget to send it or has it miscarried. If the former you need not send it, as I shall return Saturday and it would therefore be no use to me. Pray inquire & let me know by return of post whether the appointment of Mr Creswell Detacht Paymaster at the Opthalmia Depot was not made out & signed by me some time ago, & whether it is known if he has begun to act or the Committee of Paymasters still remains.

---

[1] Francis Freeling (1764–1836) was secretary to the G.P.O.
[2] Not identified.
[1] Palmerston's term for Lady Malmesbury and her two, as yet unmarried, daughters.
[1] According to the *Courier* of 23 Aug., the Duke of York had been at Windsor on the 22nd for the Duke of Clarence's birthday celebrations.

[*PS.*] I suppose Merry is come back as brown as a moorfowl & with hands unpolluted by blood.

Will you also ascertain from Torrens whether the Col. Wyndham who has been taken prisoner in Portugal is son to the member for Wiltshire.[2]

72. *Park Place. 28 Sept. 1810.*

Lady Malmesbury informed you yesterday of the melancholy result of our journey.[1] I confess that from the first account I but too much feared that there were scarcely any hopes to be entertained but I did not expect so rapid a termination. However all is for the best, and though the suddenness of the event deprived us of the consolation of seeing her again, yet as it shortened her sufferings we must derive comfort from that consideration, & the knowledge that even to the last moment there was no perceptible expression of pain. My sisters, Culverden & Emma are as well as could possibly be expected & Culverden indeed has shewn more firmness & fortitude than I could have hoped from him. William arrived today. It is now very late & I have not time to write more, but you shall hear from me soon again. I shall of course not be able to come to town so soon as I intended.

73. *Park Place. 1 Oct. 1810.*

All here continue as well as could be expected, & indeed although the event was at the moment it happened unexpected, yet all who had witnessed & watched the general decline of health which had been taking place for some time past must have contemplated it as a thing but too much to be apprehended, upon any recurrence of former attacks. We shall remain here probably till the latter end of this week, & then I fancy William & my sisters will return to Broadlands with Culverden & Emma, & I proceed to London. Will you be so good as to put in extenso the memoranda on the corners of the inclosed.

74. *Park Place. 3 Oct. 1810.*

This place is at length sold. Mr Morse has been here two days in the greatest possible agitation of mind urged to buy by his wife,

[2] Henry Torrens was Military Secretary at the Horse Guards. Henry Penruddocke Wyndham (1736–1819) was member for Wiltshire; his second son, Thomas Norton Wyndham (1774–1839), had been taken prisoner in July (H. A. Wyndham, *A Family History 1688–1837*, 1950, p. 288).

[1] Mrs Culverden had died on 26 Sept.

reminded of economy by his father, & having neither taste, opinion nor judgment of his own. Alarmed by the fall of stocks, frightened out of the wits he has not by Ld Malmy & Webb he seemed hardly to know whether he stood on his head or his heels. The day he came he seemed resolved to purchase, last night he formally declared off, & said he could not or would not. This morning again he sent at 7 o'clock to Webb's room to say he had passed a very restless night & must see him before he went. He was again closetted with him & Ld Malmy for three or four hours, & went off at 2 to Reading having agreed to agree when he arrived there. The articles were to be drawn up there & sent here tonight or tomorrow morning. The only thing in which all who have seen him concur is his excessive folly, & he himself confirms this opinion having told Ld Malmy that his whole property did not exceed 100 thousand pounds, out of which he is about to expend 70 thousand in a place.[1]

My sisters return to Broadlands on Saturday with Culverden & Emma & William, & I shall come on to town.

75. *To Elizabeth Temple. Privy Gardens.*[1] *29 Jan. 1811.*

You will see by the papers that we did extremely well in the House of Lords last night & had a larger majority than was expected. We had reckoned upon 9, & had 15, upon the peerage restriction question. Ashburton spoke but unfortunately I did not hear him. I am afraid he did not acquit himself particularly well; Lygon told me he did not shew one ray of talent or genius, but that I can hardly believe; he says he did not speak one sixth part of what he had intended & he is to send me his speech to read. The Regent will probably be installed in the course of next week,—& from the improvement in the King's health it begins to be very doubtful whether any change will be made.

I have not yet found a house & indeed it is uncommonly difficult at present, but I have a good many agents employed & hope before long to be able to do so. In the mean time I can assure you I am very comfortably lodged here. I have the library to myself & have my own writing table, some of my books & all my boxes, so that I suffer as little inconvenience as possible & as to dinners one is always able to dine with a pleasant party at the Alfred if one has no other engagement. As to Kinnaird he certainly has acted oddly but it is hardly fair to abuse him as much as you young ladies have been

[1] Morse, whoever he was, seems to have changed his mind again, for Park Place was not sold until 1816. Webb was Malmesbury's agent.

[1] Palmerston had leased Lord Kinnaird's house in Lower Grosvenor St in Dec. 1809 and when suddenly he had to leave it in Jan. 1811 he took refuge with Mrs Robinson in Privy Gardens in Whitehall until he could find the house he wanted in Stanhope St.

doing. It was evidently my business to have come to a clear understanding with him before the end of the year by means of our agents,
& he could not know that I had no other house. Our conversation
took place in September, & though he then volunteered to tell me I
might have the house another year there was time enough for him to
alter his mind, & if he really wanted to return to his own house I
do not well see upon what pretence I could keep him out of it. He
might certainly have given me a little earlier notice of his intentions,
but that after all is the only thing I have any right to complain of. My
books, furniture is safely deposited at Skidds & my pictures at
Tathams so that I am ready to establish myself [*rest lacking*].

76. *Sun Inn* [*Cambridge*]. *24 Mar. 1811.*

We are going on very well here, 309 promises this morning besides
20 probable Johnians.[1] Pray send a bottle of Eau d'Husson to Mr
Blackman, Symmonds Inn Coffee House & Dr Weston, Amen Corner
& desire them to take half a bottle at night.[2] This seriously. We have
had several votes in the course of the day. I think it might be a good
thing to send immediately a paragraph to the *Courier* to say, 'we
understand that the greatest exertions are making by Mr Smith &
Ld P. and the contest is expected to be a very hard one. It is probable
that the successful candidate will carry it by only a very few votes.'
Or something to this effect, as they have been spreading about the
idea that I am secure & have canvassed votes on that ground saying
that I do not want them & they may oblige a friend without hurting
me. I think however I shall carry it without doubt.[3] Very few people
are arrived as yet. The Duke of Rutland has been here today & stays
till tomorrow evening.[4] Burghersh is come.[5]

[*PS.*] They are drawing up some paragraph here which will probably
be nonsense; but I cannot very civilly tell them so, you had better

[1] The death of the Duke of Grafton on 14 Mar. and the translation of Lord Euston
to the upper House had brought on a by-election in Cambridge. Petty had also been
translated to the Lords as Marquess of Lansdowne. So Palmerston's opponent in a
straight fight was John Henry Smyth (1780–1822) of Heath Hall, York, a Browne
medallist from Trinity and a nephew of Euston's.

[2] John Blackman was a graduate from Queens'. Dr Samuel Ryde Weston (1747–
1821), a Johnian and a Canon of St Paul's, was at first inclined to support
Palmerston but was persuaded by Hardwicke not to do so (Weston to Hardwicke,
21 and 23 Mar., Hardwicke Papers, Add. MS. 35658).

[3] Palmerston defeated Smyth by 451 votes to 345, but Smyth secured the other seat
on Gibbs's appointment to the Bench in 1812 and held it until his death.

[4] Rutland was a candidate for the Chancellorship, now also vacant by Grafton's
death.

[5] Burghersh was also a Cambridge graduate.

therefore send to Street of the *Courier* immediately to take care that he does not insert any thing but what you send; all are very zealous & active here.[6] I inclose two letters for Mr R. Cockburn[7] to press him to come. They should be sent by express if there is no means of letting him have it early tomorrow morning.

77. *Broadlands. 14 April 1811.*

We reached Bath on Friday morning & found everything going on better than I had expected.[1] Fanny & I left it yesterday afternoon & came hither. Emma, William & Elizabeth follow today. I left Ld Malmesbury there drinking the waters & in great health & spirits; he always enjoys the convenience and independance of Bath, & Ld & Ly Pembroke being there gives him agreeable society. I have received a letter from Stratton[2] about some article the produce of his estate which he does not name, but which he conceives might be usefully manufactured if some small duty were laid upon the importation of the same commodity from N. America. I suppose he means hemp or flax. He wished me to mention the thing to Perceval but *no one else.* He comes to town tomorrow & wished to see Perceval Tuesday or Wednesday. I do not know where he lives in town; therefore I wish you would try to find out & write him a line from me to tell him *merely* that I have sent his letter by today's post to Perceval & that if he calls in Downing Street I have no doubt that Perceval will see him *if he can* & that I am sorry my absence from London has prevented me from seeing him. On second thoughts I enclose a note which perhaps you will convey to him. The country is looking beautiful & the weather is delightful. What glorious news all this is from Portugal. It really is altogether taking all its bearings & consequences, the greatest national military advantage achieved in any period of our history.

78. *Broadlands. 16 April 1811.*

I conjectured that Gordon wanted his information with some such view as you have stated, & I think you can need no better proof than the mode in which he has set about his object to be satisfied how

---

[6] T. G. Street was editor and joint proprietor of the *Courier.* An appropriate comment appeared in the *Courier* the following day.

[7] The Rev. Richard Cockburn was a former fellow of St John's.

[1] Culverden had died on 7 April.

[2] Probably John Stratton (*ob.* 1819), a former fellow-commoner of St John's.

little qualified he is to give Bankes any useful assistance: what man who knew *anything* about regimental accounts would think the disallowances on *one pay list* sufficient data for a general scheme of audit. Depend upon it the less you tell him & the fewer things you put into his hands the better. He knows very little of the matter, has I daresay very decided opinions on the subject, which nothing that you can say on them will at all alter, & will notwithstanding tell all the world that *he* has new modelled the War Office. He is a devilish clever active fellow, but inordinately vain, & self-opinionated.[1]

I can assure you I feel as strongly as you can do the necessity of making some arrangement for the accounts, current & arrear; but I am quite sensible that no good can be done unless the thing is taken up in good earnest & my days consist but of 24 hours, & my head is of a limited capacity & cannot apply to very many things at once; & for some time past the addition of Estimates, militia bill, election, canal bills, thankings, etc., to the ordinary business of attendance of office & the House has rendered it ridiculous to think of doing anything effectual with the office accounts & if you think otherwise all I can say is, you are as unreasonable as Lady Malmesbury herself.

I trust the account of Ney's surrender may prove true, but not if it is to be compensated by Ld Wellington's death, which would not be made amends for by the capture of Massena & all his ragamuffins. I return on Thursday as I originally intended, William will I believe stay on some days longer.

[*PS.*] I shall wait for the post on Thursday so if there is any great news pray send it.

---

[1] Col. (later Gen. Sir) James Willoughby Gordon (1773–1851) was Commissary-in-Chief and involved about this time in a dispute with the War Office over the possible transfer of some accounts to his department. Henry Bankes (W. J. Bankes's father) was chairman of the Committee on Public Expenditure, whose tenth report he laid before the Commons on 24 June. The Committee took evidence from Gordon and reported, among other things, that the accounts in question 'should be transferred forthwith'. At the same time Bankes drew the attention of the House more especially to 'the tardy examination of military and regimental accounts'. (*Parliamentary Papers*, 1810–11, iii. 1001–54; 1 *Hansard*, xx. 758.) But Palmerston may also have been aware that Gordon was a candidate for his own position in the event that the Whigs displaced the Government during the Regency crisis of 1810–11. Gordon had the impression that the Prince looked to him not only to make the War Office more efficient but also to make the Secretary 'submit to the controul of a Commander-in-Chief'. Certainly Gordon was consulted by the Prince about the growing quarrel between Palmerston and Sir David Dundas, the Commander-in-Chief during the Duke of York's brief disgrace. (*P.O.W.*, vii. 47 and 186–8; see also in the Grey Papers, Gordon to Grey, 5 Mar. 1810, enclosing a 'Confidential Memorandum upon the Military offices' in which he advocated the consolidation of the various departments into a 'Board of War'.)

79. *War Office. 27 July 1811.*

Elizabeth has shewn me your note, & commissioned me to convey to you her answer; her feelings on the subject are such as I could have wished, & you deserve.[1] If you can step over here we will talk more fully about it, but in the mean time you will believe that the existence of these feelings on the part of two persons so dear to me & so well worthy of each other is the source of the greatest pleasure & satisfaction to me.

80. *Broadlands. 6 Sept. 1811.*

I send you for observation amendment etc. a draught of an answer to Foveaux & Stewart's letter.[1]

I wish you could come down here to see how *bad* our sport is this year. There are scarcely a dozen coveys on the whole manor, but the weather is very fine & it is very pleasant walking across the fields. The Campbells[2] are here but he has not yet ventured out with his gun. He is a hero at walking. We took him upon a moderate calculation 18 miles yesterday, in the morning, & walked him for an hour & a half after dinner, & made him say he *liked it*. The *ladies* are all very well & Mrs C. has a *curled flaxen wig* that is quite delightful; I long to borrow it for *Coachie*.[3]

81. *Broadlands. 13 Sept. 1811.*

I have despatched your note & will send you the answer when I receive it, I hope the parties to be blown up are *plushites*.[1] Your large unconscionable parcel for Ireland is also franked—I am truly sorry for what you tell me of Goulburn & the more so, as the thing having occurred after a period of relaxation is not to be attributed to over official exertion. As to Stuart [*Stewart*], I should think indeed he would soon cease to be a *rear* Superintendant, as that part of his person must be pretty well wasted by this time. I hope however that he will soon set you free to come down here. Our weather had been really

---

[1] Sulivan had proposed to Elizabeth Temple, possibly not for the first time.

[1] Michael Foveaux and John Stewart were two of the three Superintendents of Military Accounts Palmerston had appointed in Dec. 1809 in order to catch up on the vast arrears of business. The third had retired in Jan. 1811 and Palmerston had appointed Sulivan in his place. Encouraged by his friend, Palmerston had begun during the summer to reorganise their work. The enclosure is lacking.

[2] The Rev. Henry Campbell and his wife.

[3] Perhaps a nickname for Coaching.

[1] Word unknown.

delicious, & not at all too hot even for shooting although perhaps so deliquescent a person as yourself might have complained of it. Our sport has improved & we have found & killed more birds, but Shee has lost the knack, & finds his gun as crooked as Bob Clive's.[2] We have had a great misfortune in the family. Nibbs[3] gave me a fine lively turtle with divers directions to the cook how to keep it; he even brought it bodkin in his chaise between himself & Mrs Nibbs. The turtle came in perfect health & not materially affected by having sat looking at Mrs Nibbs all the way; it was to be kept in water with the chill taken off, but my cook thinking that poor turtle could not have too much warmth literally I believe *slow boiled* the poor animal to death. It expired last Monday & I have to make its funeral apologies to a numerous party who will assemble here today at six of the clock for the purpose of eating the same.

82. *War Office. 18 Oct. 1811.*

Many thanks for your communication of Ld Malmy's letters which I will send back to you as soon as I go home.[1] I will immediately forward to Forster the paraphrase & commentary on the memorandum of Ld Malmy, & I think that even if the Devil himself were to ink his fingers & put on a black coat he could not now pretend to mid-understand the matter. I cannot however help adding in closing this business that I do very sincerely trust that there has not at any time existed in your mind the least idea that there was *on my part* any doubt of the propriety of the arrangement contained in Ld M.'s mem. or any wish to make the least alteration in it, as I can with truth assure you that was not the case.

I will write today to FitzHarris to communicate the thing to him & ask him to be trustee; indeed I know no great reason why it should be any longer a mystery, particularly as Ld Malmy tells me that Emma has inadvertently let the cat out in Essex, & it will be difficult to confine her to one county when once she is loose. Will you dine with me tomorrow & I will try to get Peel. He is the only one of the sub cabinet[2] I believe in town. By the bye I fancy Croker is come back, I will try him.

[2] Lord Clive's younger brother, Robert (1789–1854).
[3] James Nibbs was a Hampshire acquaintance.
[1] There had been a misunderstanding or difference of opinion about Elizabeth Temple's marriage settlement as drawn up by Palmerston's solicitor, Forster (Malmesbury to Palmerston, 14 Oct., B.P., G.C./MA no. 162).
[2] Probably a reference to the junior ministers among the Alfred set.

83. *To Elizabeth Temple. War Office. 25 [?23] Oct. 1811.*

I believe I told you there was some doubt whether I could be your trustee, & I found upon consulting with Forster that I could not properly be so as your fortune consists in part in a mortgage on my property. FitzHarris was suggested by Ld Malmesbury & I thought I might venture to write to him without further consultation with you as Sulivan seemed to think he was a very good person for the *difficult office*. I enclose a very kind note which I have received in reply.

London is uncommonly gay, so I go every night to the play, I belong to a private box which gives me the run of Convent Garden & the Lyceum all week about which is very pleasant.

I sold my two horses very well, Harlequin who was likely to be blind & lame for 100 guineas, & Firefly who was not quite sound for 87. This was a good riddance of bad rubbish. Pitch is in high feather but not quite in such high kick as when he was less worked. I was extremely sorry to hear of the death of poor Sir Nathaniel. What was the cause of it? He was looking so well when he was at Broadlands.[1]

I believe *really* that the comet is the cause of our fine weather, for really we have had scarce any other since the appearance of this *awfully splendid stranger.*[2]

There is no news stirring in Portugal. The army is in cantonment & not likely to move till November. They have been *miserable* sick, but they are getting a little better.

[*PS.*] Did Ly Malm. borrow Philip 2d & 3d Quartos from the book room. She has sent them to me back but I did not know she had them.

84. *Broadlands. 27 Sept. 1812.*

I shall be in town tomorrow night as I find the diss[*olutio*]n is on Tuesday. I take it the only thing to be done will be to go down to Cambridge immediately and canvass the gyps & porters who probably are at present the chief occupiers of the colleges; but however I trust we shall not have much trouble this time as I do not anticipate a contest.[1] I send you a letter I recd yesterday from Ld Liverpool. I write to Wood today.

---

[1] Sir Nathaniel Dance Holland, the painter, had died on 15 Oct. 1811. He lived at Cranbury House, near Winchester, and was evidently known socially to Palmerston. He had also painted his uncle, Benjamin Mee.
[2] First observed at Viviers by Flaugergues on 25 Mar.
[1] Palmerston was returned unopposed.

85. *Broadlands. 23 Feb. 1814.*

I send you the return up to the latest period. The numbers you see are a good deal increased in the course of today.[1] I kept the men till after their dinner & dismissed them at ½ past one by which time I thought the volunteering was quite over. I made an example of the sergeant and 3 corporals who would not volunteer. I took off the sergeant's sash & sword belt in the middle of the market place and invested with them a deserving corporal of the same company. The three corporals I degraded to the ranks and took three men to succeed them out of the company which had turned out most volunteers. The sergeant offered afterwards to volunteer if restored but I refused to accept him on any terms. The corporals solicited & obtained leave to volunteer as privates.

I have desired Holmes[2] to write today to all the subdivision clerks who have still to send men to request they will endeavour to enrol them at once for extended service, and draw upon Holmes for the five shillings if they succeed; I shall attend the enrolment at Romsey on Saturday & send Needham[3] over to that at Winchester, and I think we may very likely get 40 or 50 men more which will make three tolerable companies.

The South East are said not to have turned out nearly so many as we have.

I have no time to add more as it is late, the return having only just been made out.

[1] Soon after becoming Lord Lieutenant of Hampshire in Aug. 1807 Malmesbury had Palmerston made one of his deputies. In that capacity Palmerston was given the command of a new regiment of local militia in Jan. 1809 and gazetted its paid Lieutenant Colonel commanding the following Mar. On 16 Jan. Malmesbury wrote to his sister, Mrs Robinson: 'I have been delivered of my local militia—*twins*—your old friend Waller nurses one & Palmerston the other. They are fine children but not at their full growth. I have given Palmerston a dry Scotch nurse to assist him.' (Malmesbury Papers, Merton College, Oxford, Box F33b.) Palmerston commanded the South West Hampshire Regiment; Lt Col. John Abel Waller the South East. Palmerston's 'dry Scotch nurse' was Lt Col. E. P. Buckley. Among the other officers to be found at one time or another in the South West Regiment were William Temple, George Rich and two of his brothers, Shee and Sulivan. The regiment had been assembled for volunteering on 21 Feb. 1814. It never assembled again, being reduced in April 1816. (Col. Lloyd-Verney, *Records of the Infantry Militia Battalions of the County of Southampton from A.D. 1757 to 1894*, 1894, pp. 291–6.)

[2] Henry Holmes was a Hampshire lawyer as well as lieutenant quartermaster in Palmerston's regiment. He was also Palmerston's agent in Romsey from 1823 until 1842 when he was discovered to have been using his client's money as his own and at no profit to either of them.

[3] James Needham was Captain and Adjutant from 1813.

86. *Broadlands. 25 Feb. 1814.*

I sent my return yesterday a little augmented since the one I sent you. Three or four have dropped in since from newly enrolled men & I think we shall make three good companies which I wish as we have already too many for two.

I do not like the accounts from the allies. If you look at the map you will see that they intended to play off the same trick which succeeded so well before the battle of Leipzig & turn both Buonaparte's flanks at once; but he would not let them give him scholar's mate twice running and first drove both Blucher & then Swarzenburgh. Completely foiled in this project they seem now to have altered their plan and are concentrating their whole force at Troyes to make a joint attack which I trust will be more successful but they had got within forty miles of Paris and have been driven at least that distance back away from it. I should like to see Robinson.[1] He will be devoured by questioners.

87. *To Mrs Sulivan. Le Havre. Wednesday night [30 Aug. 1815].*[1]

Cf. *Airlie, i. 95–7.*

Palmerston reports his crossing from Southampton to France. He was accompanied by two servants from Stanhope St, Joseph and Brooks, and among his fellow-passengers were William Alexander Madocks (1774–1828), who was Mrs Blackburn's uncle, and Robert Heathcote (ob. 1823), the younger son of Sir Gilbert Heathcote, third Bart, and a popular drinking companion, who in April 1817 had married the 'Columbine' of Drury Lane Theatre, Elizabeth Searle.[2] In Le Havre Palmerston has been joined by Gally Knight who is to travel with him to Paris. The manuscript continues: Brooks was a proof that people do not *die* of sea sickness but I should think he could have [*rest lacking*]

88. *To Mrs Sulivan. Hotel de Londres, Place Vendome [Paris. 3 Sept. 1815].*

Gally Knight & I arrived here last night at about eight o'clock after a very pleasant though not very rapid journey. We did not get away from Havre on Thursday till the middle of the day near eleven o'clock,

---

[1] Frederick Robinson was in Europe with Castlereagh in 1813–14.
[1] Airlie gives the date as 'September 1821', but Guedalla, p. 468, gives it correctly. This was Palmerston's first visit to the mainland of Europe since 1794. The account given in the published version of *Palmerston's Journals*, pp. 7–37, is very full, but some entries have been been wrongly dated or run together by the editor.
[2] *Glenbervie Diaries*, ii. 134–5.

& did not proceed further than Rouen; on Friday morning we walked all over Rouen and started at two, & slept at Vernon which we reached just by dusk and yesterday we left Vernon at eight. As we stopped every where to see every thing that appeared worth looking at our progress was slow & our delays were increased by getting into conversation with every body we found who seemed likely to be willing to talk to us. We just looked into Malmaison as we drove by but had not time to see it to our satisfaction as it was growing dark. I have been this morning to a review of about 20,000 Prussians in the Champ de Mars; they are very fine looking troops all newly dressed & very neat & soldierlike in their appearance. There were 9,000 of the Guards. I am going now to the Gallery, having disposed of divers considerable packets which I found waiting here. The people all abuse the Prussians, but in Normandy at least we could only learn two or three instances of personal injury done to the inhabitants & then it seemed to have arisen from disputes, but they rob upon a grand scale. Several people however said 'Qu'ils fussent ce qu'ils veulent; ils ne pourront jamais nous rendre ce que nous leur avons pris'. A dirty fellow this morning was saying to his comrade after the review, 'Eh bien nous avons vus la même chose dans leur ville, il n'y a pas d'affront'.

The state of debasement of the nation as far as we have seen it is complete. Every vestige of independent spirit seems destroyed; in Normandy the people all believe that our troops are come to take permanent possession of the country, and they all tried to persuade us that they wished it extremely. The old beadle who shews the cathedral at Rouen assured us that 'deux tiers de la ville le souhaiteroit beaucoup'; a fellow at Bolbec asked us whether we meant to establish ourselves meaning Gally Knight & myself in that place, half joke & half serious. Nobody will talk decidedly on politics but all seem afraid of committing themselves by giving an opinion, 'eh! qu'est ce ca nous fait que nous gouverne pourvu qu'en nous laisse gagner la vie, tout ce que nous desirons c'est la tranquillité'. We asked a bourgeois at Vernon if it was the Emperor who had planned the canal. He said yes. He did a great deal in the way of public works did he not? 'Monsieur il a fait apporter ces pierres ici', was the reply; 'eh bien donc', we said, you are probably not sorry on the whole that he is gone. 'Messieurs c'est par là qu'en va au pont', was his answer. If Louis can only get rid of the army & substitute for it one attached to himself he need fear nothing, but without bayonets no man can govern France.

The place I am told is full of English & Ly Castlereagh's midnight suppers are going on very prosperously. The heat is extreme and as my present room is immediately over a stable & dunghill the air is not very balsamic, I move tomorrow however into a better. Brooks is come in safely but wonders at the stupidity of the people for not understanding him when he tells them to rub down a horse, & is astonished at not having found one hostler who had such a thing as a curry comb or a bit of spunge to wash the horse's eyes with. I am now however in England for Ld Hawke's coachman who is rubbing down a horse under my window is conversing with it in the native & emphatic dialect of a London stableman. The Place de Louis 15 & all this part of the town is certainly magnificent but I console myself by reflecting that little of it is due to Buonaparte.

89. *To Mrs Sulivan. Paris. Wednesday, 6 Sept. [1815].*

I take advantage of an offer of Maddocks to take a letter as he leaves Paris this morning. Gally Knight & myself arrived here on Saturday after a pleasant journey by Rouen & Vernon. I have now got some very comfortable rooms in the Hotel de Londres which is an excellent situation, being near everything one wishes to see. I have been to a review every morning but have not made much progress through the Louvre. It is really a most appalling sight from the number of pictures. Very few have been removed as yet & those are of no particular merit. Clancarty has however been through the Gallery on behalf of the King of the Netherlands and has marked a considerable cargo for removal. Cannova is come to claim the property of the Pope both canvas & stone, so that altogether there is I trust a fair chance of a little dispersion.

Ney is going to be tried at last, Jourdan is to be President of the court martial.

90. *To Mrs Sulivan. Paris. 14 Sept. 1815.*

It is needless to say how much grieved one feels at the most melancholy intelligence from Heron Court[1] for which however the previous accounts had in a great measure prepared one. I am glad to hear however that Lord Malmesbury's health has not suffered materially.

I succeeded in getting to the review[2] with Sir Chas Greville, Brooke's brother. We were disappointed by a man who had engaged to supply us with horses on the road & made a desperate trial for post horses which everybody said were quite out of the question. However by having set out a few hours earlier than the shoal of

[1] Lady Fitzharris had died on 4 Sept.
[2] The review of the Russian Army at Vertus not Vestres as in *Palmerston's Journals*, pp. 20–1.

sovereigns etc., we got on without any difficulty. It was really a most magnificent sight; 160,000 men including 25,000 infantry on an immense plain in the middle of which rises a hill like Arthur's Seat on the top of which is a flat where we all stood. The army were first drawn up in three great lines; they then formed a hollow square, round which we rode; we then reascended the hill; they broke into lines again & fired. The whole lasted about four or five hours. The troops were beautifully equipped all spick & span new at the expence of the French, and every regiment was as good as the rest—there seemed to be no difference. I saw Michel[3] looking very well. Adieu, one has no time to write except to sign one's name to D— War Office papers. Clive is very well & Castlereagh recovering from his kick.[4]

91. *To Mrs Sulivan. Paris. 25 Sept. 1815.*

  B.P.W.; cf. Ashley, i. 81–2.

I am delighted to hear that you have at length done the sensible thing & settled yourself at Broadlands. It is quite the fashion now a days to take up one's quarters in people's houses, but I hope you will behave well & not carry off any of the pictures or marbles; as to the books I have no hopes for them, as they pack so easily. *Palmerston then gives an account of the Allies' recovery of the pictures seized by the French. The manuscript continues:* All the [*rest lacking*]

92. *Heron Court. 24 Dec. 1815.*

I am sure it cannot be necessary for me to say how much I sympathize with your feelings upon the melancholy event which your note which reached me yesterday evening announced, & which has been rendered more distressing by the sudden & unexpected manner of its occurrence.[1] For Mr Sulivan too I am much grieved, the shock must have been a severe one to him, as the loss is indeed great, but I trust & hope that he bears it as well as under the circumstances can be expected. To yourself I will not attempt to point out those subjects of consolation, if one may so call them, which your own good sense and strength of mind must of themselves have suggested, but although the immediate attack has been sudden you must I am sure in common with others who have had opportunities of witnessing her state of

---

[3] Probably Michael Woronzow, the Russian commander and brother of the former Russian ambassador in England, rather than Michael Bruce, though Palmerston also encountered Bruce in Paris.

[4] See *Palmerston's Journals*, pp. 25–6.

[1] Sulivan's mother had just died.

health for some considerable time past, have felt that there was much occasional suffering from ailment and much reason to look upon the event which has happened as one which in the course of events might not be very far distant.

Fanny will accompany me to town on Tuesday & will remain with Elizabeth during my absence at Cambridge. I am glad to hear so favourable a report of Eliz. and hope to find her considerably better upon our arrival in London. We found FitzHarris as well as one could expect and though his feelings are sometimes with difficulty controuled yet he fights up against them with a firmness & resolution which one cannot but admire though from the strength of his mind one was prepared to expect it.

93. *War Office. 2 Feb. 1816.*

Ld Sidmouth has no objection to turn the Loc. Mil. Quartermaster to the right about & I I [*sic*] [*am*] much inclined to think one might safely do so, and make the adjutant take charge of the accounts so as to get some work out of him for his eight shillings a day; but I wish to know what you think of this before anything is decided. Of course none of the regts will be called out this year, but it might happen that in the event of a corps being suddenly assembled for the suppression of riots the adjutant would have more to do with a raw undisciplined set of men & an inexperienced set of officers than would allow him the time necessary for the payment of the corps. This ought to be weighed & considered.

I hope you mean to stay till the end of the next week.[1] This frost I believe agrees both with you & Elizabeth, & however fine it may be in the country it is so dark & foggy here that I could scarcely see to shave this morning, though you know I seldom rise *before* the sun & almost poked my nose through the window to obtain all possible light.

Ld Buckinghamshire is scarcely expected to live, his strength is failing him rapidly & his physicians are not decided as to his disorder though the symptoms look like water in the chest. He is come to London.[2]

[*PS.*] Mat says the Nepaulese say we are the oddest people in the world for when we go to war with our neighbours whether we lick them or they lick us we always end by taking half their country from them.[3] He says they fought with the most extraordinary bravery,

---

[1] The Sulivans were at Broadlands.
[2] The 4th Earl of Buckinghamshire died on 4 Feb.
[3] Dugald Stewart's son, Matthew Stewart, had gone to India in 1807 as aide de camp to Lord Minto and had pursued his military career there subsequently.

and as one instance a fellow came dancing up with a silver standard which he planted in the ground *a foot* from the mouth of one of our field pieces; he was knocked down by one of the men with the long ram rod of the gun & bayonetted under it.

Let me hear from you about Qtr Mrs if you can by Sunday's post.

Clive is in town looking tolerably well but a little thin. I do not know whether it is from a tender passion for Ly Emma Edgecumbe.[4]

Brougham M.P. for *Winchelsea* had the impudence yesterday in his speech to talk of 'our constituents *if any of us have any* constituents'.

Mr Thomas of Irish Ordnance will wait upon you & Emma with his portmanteau of deeds for your signature.[5]

94. *To Mrs Sulivan. Tours. 1 Sept. 1816.*

I am just arrived here at 11 this morning after a very prosperous journey by sea & by land & as I am going forward I have not time to write you a very long letter.[1] I embarked at Southampton on Tuesday 27 and reached Havre by half past four the next day; on Thursday 29 I crossed the ferry to Honfleur and slept at Caen, a pretty country but infamous road. On Friday 30 I got to Alencon, through a pretty country rich & well wooded & inclosed; passing through Falaise a remarkably picturesque town, with the ruins of a very fine old castle, and a beautiful round tower 200 feet high in almost perfect preservation though built by William the Conqueror whose birth place this was. They still shew you an old shabby house in the market place in which he is said to have been born. From Alencon I came on yesterday through Le Mans to Chateau du Loir, from whence I proceeded this morning to this place. The roads have in general been very bad & deep & not accidentally but systematically so. This line is however reckoned a road de traverse and therefore it is thought fair to neglect it. Thursday & Friday were very fine but yesterday & today have proved rainy again & I begin to fear that the sun will not favour the rest of my tour. The harvest has however been as they

[4] Lord Mount Edgecumbe's elder daughter did not marry until 1828; Clive married Lady Lucy Graham in 1818.

[5] Palmerston was selling some land in Dublin to the Board of Ordnance and was having checked the mortgages he had given for loans received from his brother and sisters in order to ensure that they did not concern the land in question (Palmerston to Board of Ordnance, copy, 11 Jan., B.P.W.).

[1] Palmerston had intended to meet Lady Malmesbury, who was in Paris with her daughter and Palmerston's sister Frances, but was delayed in starting off from England by a fierce debate in Parliament. Since he was anxious to catch up with Lady Cowper, who had gone off to Switzerland in pursuit of her errant sister-in-law, Mrs George Lamb, he had decided to cut Paris and to push on to Geneva. (Lady Malmesbury to Anna Maria, Lady Minto, 31 Aug., Minto Papers; see also Palmerston's 'Journal of Tour in France, Italy & Swizzerland in 1816', B.P.W.)

say *superbe* in spite of the season and the grapes are the only produce which has failed. The apples are abundant & they must drink sour cyder instead of generous wine. I hear of many English being at Caen, Le Mans & this place but have not fallen in with any nor been able to learn any names; except an old school fellow of mine by name dirty Hinxman whom I met at Caen near which he has taken a chateau & whom I had not seen before since he used to whine lamentations through his nose at Harrow for being licked because he was fat & slovenly. You must or may remember his speaking, the next boy to me.[2] I mean to get to Lyons on the 5th and to Geneva on the 7th unless I am detained a little longer by bad roads which may make me a day later. I will write to you again either from the one or the other. They ask one perpetually for one's passport & last night I was very minutely examined upon my motions by a gens d'arme who came to the inn & took down every particular not omitting the exact hour of my arrival & intended departure. The maid of the inn however observed to him that he had not put down my name. 'Bah!', replied he, '*qu'est ce que cela signifie.* J'ai bien tout le reste'—so that his information was 'Seigneur Anglais arrivant du Mans allant à Tours'.

95. *To Mrs Sulivan. Lyons. 7 Sept. 1816.*

   B.P.W.

   I arrived here last night after a successful but slowish progress from Tours. I passed through Limoges & Clermont, the road is good as far as the former but thence to the latter abominably rough & excessively hilly & even mountainous, the horses wretched & the inns miserable. The country however is interesting & picturesque, which indeed its very inequality accompanied as that is with an abundance of trees is sufficient to produce. The Spanish chesnut is the predominant tree & grows to a considerable size. The people of Auvergne indeed are very Spanish, their patois is more Spanish than French. 'Jo sabe muy bien', 'Chi ti comandè de far ceci, nous montarem et puis descenderem', have lost much of the French character & idiom. The people are short & swarthy, with black hair & coal heaver hats. But one cannot help as one passes through the country blessing the memory of King William, if as Ashburton records, he saved us from popery, slavery & *wooden shoes*, for it is wretched to see a whole people tied to the ground by their sabots, any exertion such as running or even walking fast is impossible in those unyielding coverings &

   [2] Henry Hinxman (*ob.* 1854) had entered Harrow the same year as Palmerston, in 1795, and first performed in the speeches there in 1800. He was Head of the School in 1802.

the fellows stump about in them apparently as helpless as a cat in walnuts on the ice. Tours is a fine town & in a rich valley but Touraine is much overrated as far as a traveller is concerned; the soil is doubtless rich but it lies flat & undistinguished by any prominent features. Berry is beautiful & the Limousin & Auvergne wild but less pretty, something like the lowlands of Scotland. Clermont is beautiful; a magnificently rich plain surrounded by an amphitheatre of hills of the most varied & picturesque outline necessarily makes an interesting spot & it really may be called the garden of France. The town itself is poor, & indeed anybody who has seen the auld toon of Edinburgh has seen all that can be seen in the way of towns in France, and I do not know that his other senses would inform him of much difference. I leave this tomorrow for Chambery, shall cross Mt Cenis to Turin thence to Milan over Simplon to Chamouny & Montanvert, & Geneva, then take ten or twelve days through Swizzerland to Basle where I expect to be by the 30th and from thence six days will carry me to Calais & you know how far that is from London. I have of course heard nothing of the motions of Fanny & Ly Malmy & shall not till I reach Geneva where I shall be the 17 or 18 at latest. I found George Cornewall[1] here, he set off today for Geneva & I gave him a line for Fanny in case they are still in that neighbourhood. 'Oh monsieur', said the innkeeper at Pont au Mur between Limoges & Clermont, 'dans cet endroit on est beaucoup plus du côté du roi que de celui de l'empereur.' 'Are you,' said I, 'but I think then you would have done well to have given some proofs of it.' 'Ah mon dieu nous l'avons bien montré; donc, eh nous avons beaucoup plus fêté le retour du roi que celui de l'autre.' I thought this intrinsically French.

96. *To Mrs Sulivan. Milan. 15 Sept. 1816.*

I write two lines to say that I am just setting off from hence for Como, Lugano & Lago Maggiore in my way over the Simplon to Geneva; I arrived here on the 12 at night & have staid two days. I got to Turin in three days from Lyons, staid one day at Turin, and came in one from thence here.[1] The best road I have yet met with was from Chamberry to Turin, as to Mount Cenis it exists no more but really

---

[1] George Cornewall, afterwards 3rd Bart (1774–1835), was the nephew of Lady Malmesbury and the Dowager Lady Minto.

[1] Palmerston had probably changed his plan about going direct from Lyons to Geneva because he expected Lady Cowper to have left Switzerland by this time. But she had waited in Geneva, possibly because of alarming tales of robbers in the Italian passes. By the time Palmerston reached Geneva, Lady Malmesbury and Frances Temple, having missed him all along, had given up and returned to Paris.

& seriously if that single hill could be lifted out of the way you might travel two good days' journey from Chamberry to Turin without a single hill to stop your horses from a trot; the whole line of road from Chamberry has been new laid & incomparably well done all by Piementese engineers, & between Lyons, or rather Port Beauvoisin & Chamberry the great pass of Les Echelles de Savoie is already extinguished by a perforation through the heart of a solid mountain. The road is not yet made but the tunnel is completed, & is 900 feet long & 24 high & wide, and all blasted by gunpowder, the rock being too hard to cut. Buonaparte was certainly was [sic] a capital maker or rather employed capital makers of roads & bridges; to be sure it was an object of primary importance to him to establish an easy communication between Italy & France. There is much worth seeing here & one could have spent a week or ten days with pleasure in going through the different collections of pictures, churches, etc., but I have seen all the principal objects; & bought two pictures which I am now expecting every minute to be brought to me rolled up, a Titian & a Paulo Veronese, quite masterpieces *of course*. I hope they will turn out better than the Seville speculation. I met young Cornewall the Bishop's son last night at the opera, he came from Genoa & is going to Florence.[2] La Scala is a magnificent house, and if well lighted would really beat our Opera; I need not say how much it must excel anything at Paris. Buonaparte built or rather made the Milanese build a regular amphitheatre where he gave 40,000 spectators the exhibition of Roman games, races of men on foot, of chariots, and afterwards filling the place with water boat fights & races; however I will venture to say the latter could not equal our display on the Serpentine. I met three Cantabs here whom Suln will know, Hailstone Professr—Gosli, now Carrigan & a third.[3] Ld Lansdowne & Brougham are here. I expect to be at Geneva the 20, stay there a day, see Swizzerland in 10 days, and hold good my time as to the remainder. Adieu, my love to Stephen.

[*PS.*] Cornewall says the Genoese were much struck & delighted with our victory at Algiers. Well they may.

Our weather is fine. I call it hot—the Italians *freschetto*.

He also tried to avoid the Dowager Lady Minto who lived nearby in retirement; but she ran into him in Geneva, arm in arm with Lady Cowper. (Lady Malmesbury to Lady Frances Cole, 12 Oct., Lowry Cole Papers, P.R.O. 30/43.)

[2] Folliott Herbert Walker Cornewall (1754–1831), a relative of Clive's, was Bishop of Worcester.

[3] John Hailstone (1759–1847) was the Woodwardian Professor of Geology at Cambridge; Arthur Judd Gosli, afterwards Carrigan (*ob.* 1845), was a fellow of St John's.

People know much of our politics here, the man of whom I bought my pictures & who has a magnificent Albano, said he was sure that when the Princess of Wales came back which is soon expected she will buy it as a present for the Regent but he begged me not to mention this as he meant it in strict confidence.

97. *To Mrs Sulivan. War Office. 14 Oct. 1816.*

Many thanks for your letter which I received this morning. I arrived last night at ten o'clock after a very prosperous journey. From Geneva which I left on the 25 ult. I went by Lausanne, Fribourg, Berne & Thun to Lauterbrunne, a celebrated valley, from thence by Grindelwald & over the pass of the Scheidek to Meyringen, thence over the Brunig to Luzern, down the lake to Weggis up Mount Righi, & by Arth, to Zug and Zurich, thence to Schaffhausen to see the fall of the Rhine, and on to Basle which I got to (or at least to Rheinfeld the next stage to it), on Saturday 5th. I breakfasted at Basle on the 6th and got to Cambray by Nancy, Verdun & Mezieres on Friday last about one o'clock. I found Fanny Cole & her young lady in great health.[1] Sir Lowry was out and I did not see him, for as Fanny told me there was to be a review of all the cavalry of the army on Saturday morning at 11 o'clock near St Omer I pushed on immediately & by travelling all night arrived in time for the shew. I got on to Calais that evening and sailed at two o'clock yesterday morning, landed at Dover at ten and after some little delay in getting my carriage to rights set off at one and found myself in Stanhope Street by ten o'clock in the evening.

I mean to publish a map of my tour to rival Sir John Sinclair's. He I believe visited most of the capitals of Europe in six months. I have made a complete tour of France, Swizzerland & the northern part of Italy in less than seven weeks; it will be that time tomorrow since I embarked at Havre. I send you by Sulivan my last letters from Fanny & William. Adieu I have not time to add more.

98. *Broadlands. 17 Dec. 1817.*

   Add. MSS.

I was sorry I could not answer your letter yesterday but I was out early with the hounds. I really do not know what to advise but I think the best way is to treat the matter with contempt.[1]

[1] Frances Harris had married Lt Gen. Sir Galbraith Lowry Cole in June 1815, three days before Waterloo.

[1] The *Morning Chronicle* of 27 Nov. had commented adversely on Sulivan's promotion over the heads of his seniors in the War Office and suggested it was due to his connection by marriage with Palmerston rather than to his talents.

Your proposed letter to Perry[2] would be a very good one upon one supposition namely that it was addressed to a man of gentlemanlike feeling, but I doubt its making any effect upon such a fellow as Perry; however the only harm it could do would be enabling him to shew it to the blackguard in the office whoever he may be from whom the attack originates & perhaps gratifying him by making him think that his purpose of annoyance has been answered. Upon the letter itself I would just make one remark, might not Perry say that though he cannot *in honour* (for no doubt he affects such a quality) give up the name of his informant, yet that he *has* stated what that person conceives to be a just cause of complaint, namely the appointment of a person to a high situation in the office who had not risen to it through the gradation of inferior appointments. The true answer is that it was an appointment which the Secy at War for the time being had a full right to make and that the result has most completely proved its expediency, and a comparison of the state of the accounts for the six years from 1811 to 1816 both inclusive with that of the accounts of the six years preceding 1810, in Decr 1816, would speak for itself, but I am inclined to think that as yet the attack does not deserve the honour of a reply, unless it were to call upon the attackers to shew that the business has not been better conducted since your appointment than before.

The weather has been tolerably good since the frost but a little too strong for much sport. We had however a pretty run yesterday.

We go on Tuesday to Heron Court & I shall come from thence to town on Friday, and if Mr Sulivan will be prepared, I mean to start for Cambridge on Sunday, and remain there till the Friday morning following.[3]

[*PS.*] Since writing this I have sketched out a paragraph for the *Courier* which might perhaps check the *Chronicle*'s informer. If sent with a note & my comp[*limen*]ts to Street he would insert it immediately. Put 'Private' on the note & my name at the bottom of the cover.

[*Enclosure referred to in the postscript:*]

We are often amused by the garrulous indiscretion of the

---

[2] Sulivan had sent Palmerston a draft retort to the editor of the *Chronicle*. However nothing further seems to have been printed on the matter in either the *Chronicle* or the *Courier*.

[3] Palmerston had written to William Temple on 5 Dec.: 'I am at length free from Estimates & go down to Broadlands on Monday & shall remain there until Parliament meets, with the episode of my usual excursion to Cambridge at Christmas, which is more than ever necessary this year, as the dissolution cannot be far off ... Old Sulivan means to go down to Cambridge with me & looks forward with great delight to the whist, the punch and the turkey pie of the Combination Room.' (B.P., G.C./TE no. 151.) Parliament was dissolved in June 1818 and Palmerston was again returned unopposed.

Chronicle, & it is diverting to see how it has *let the cat out of the bag* in the late renewal of its attack upon the War Office; its information it seems '*is not solely derived from the dry Army List*' (Lucky *Chronicle* not to have applied this epithet to the *Navy* list!) The plain English of which is that it comes from some discontented Clerk in the Office, whose merits have not been rewarded according to *his own* estimation of his deserts. We thank the *Chronicle* for this hint, and as it has such good sources of intelligence, we intreat it to favour us with some information as to the progress which has been made in the examination & settlement of the accounts of the Army since the end of 1810, the period from which it appears by returns presented to Parliament Mr Sulivan's responsibility commences. We shrewdly suspect that such an enquiry would shew that as usual the *Chronicle* is most fretful & splenetic when the public business is best conducted and that while the accounts of former years are greatly in arrear, those which have been placed under Mr Sulivan's superintendence have been promptly and regularly settled. If this *should happen* to be the state of the case, whatever may be the disappointment of the *Chronicle* and its official informer we think the public will not regret the appointment.

99. *Stanhope St. [8 April 1818].*

Immediate
A thousand thanks for your affectionate kindness. Astley Cooper has put a *wet handkerchief* to my back which is all that the nature of the case requires & I am quite well.[1]

100. *Stanhope St. Wednesday evening [8 April 1818].*

Pray beg the gentlemen in your department to accept my best thanks & acknowledgements for the letter which they have transmitted to me through you.

101. *Stanhope St. 10 April 1818.*

I am sorry to hear that you have caught *cold* by being so *warm* in my service, but I hope that it will not confine you for any time. Merry

---

[1] Palmerston had been shot at by a deranged ex-officer as he arrived at the War Office about 1 p.m. He was badly bruised, though not wounded, and a subordinate had sent for Cooper who lived nearby.

saw Markland[1] to day & I desired him to say that I should be ready
to attend at the office any day after tomorrow & that Markland had
better settle the time with Astley Cooper whose hours are less at his
command than mine. I am much better today; they have taken
off the cold application & put on a plaister, and the soreness about
the part wounded has much diminished, so that I hope to be quite
free from inconvenience in a few days.

102. *Broadlands. 3 Sept. 1818.*
   Add. MSS.

The Duke of York has been proposing to Liverpool among other
sources of retrenchment to abolish the office of Regimental Paymaster
as useless and unnecessarily expensive alledging that any subaltern of
the regiment acting under the agent could as formerly carry on the
finance & keep the accounts.[1] Liverpool does not seem at all impressed
with the force of the Duke's reasoning, but as this is a sort of declaration
of war I think it a fair opportunity to recommend to the Treasury
what would I really believe be perfectly equitable, a reduction in the
rate of agency. I had got the accompanying papers some time ago
with a view to think of such a question, but they contain but little
information as to the grounds upon which such a measure could either
be recommended or resisted. I wish you would just give me any thing
that occurs to you upon the subject; but do not let any one know
anything of the matter as I do not wish it to be supposed at present
that I entertain such an intention, and do not mention to any one
the Duke's proposal which as yet is only privately made to Liverpool.

103. *Broadlands. 3 Sept. 1818.*

I have I believe no other papers of yours than these; & I have to
apologize to your leather breeches for having so long detained one of
their back strings from its proper vocation.
   I really think that chestnut horse may by a little quiet practice &
some low feeding be brought to carry Elizabeth, but one shall be better
able to judge when I have had him a little longer, but he seems so

---

[1] Possibly James Heywood Markland (1788–1864), a London solicitor.
[1] It had been decided in 1798 that regimental paymasters should not be serving
officers. In this way the influence over them of their regimental colonels was deliberately diminished and, consequently, the role of the Secretary at War in matters
of pay enhanced at the expense of the Horse Guards. Inevitably, therefore, it became
an issue in the grand dispute between the Minister and the C.-in-C. The Duke, however, was unsuccessful.

very gentle and docile & to have so tender a mouth that I think with you, the only doubt is as to the rider.

At length it rains but in the most genteel manner, soft & mizzling & wafted by a warm southerly breeze. We already begin to look greener. We have a good breed of partridges but very little cover for them; but I am well off for dogs, and have now by the addition of Ld Stawell's deputation of Mitchelmarsh a very extensive range of manor.[1]

104. *Broadlands. 9 Sept. 1818.*

I have bought a poney which is *intended* for Fanny but which will I think while she makes up her mind about it carry Elizabeth perfectly. It is quite gentle and quiet & has just as good & as safe action as the chestnut horse; it belonged to the Stockbridge waggoner, & I met it the other day going merrily along the road with a man of 16 stone on its back so that although it is small there can be no doubt of its being strong enough to carry Elizabeth.

[*PS.*] Stephen's poney will be most welcome in the park.

105. *War Office. 10 Oct. 1818.*

I have received your papers about agency which when complete will afford useful information towards coming to a decision on the point, and I shall now postpone making any proposal to Liverpool till I come back from Cambray by which time he will probably be in town.[1] So I will leave the papers directed to you. I mean to set out on Monday evng or Tuesday morning: I cannot quite ascertain when & where the Reviews[2] are to be, some say the English one is to be at Cambray on the 16th, some that the Austrian will be the first & will at at Sedan on the 17th; by getting off as I propose I should be in time for either. I shall leave directions with Brooks to hand over the chestnut horse to you, on your arrival in London. I have written to Shee & hope he will be in town tomorrow.

[*PS.*] The time of my return will of course be uncertain as it must depend on the time of the Reviews but probably the 23 or 24 of the month will bring me back to London.

---

[1] Lord Stawell had inherited Michelmersh, near Romsey, from his grandfather.

[1] The rate of commission to be deducted by regimental agents involved another perennial dispute between Secretary at War and C.-in-C. The War Office, with economy in mind, sought to reduce it; the Horse Guards with the interest of the colonels in mind, to keep it at its existing level.

[2] By the allied armies of occupation prior to their evacuation of France in Nov.

106. *Calais. Tuesday evening, 13 Oct. 1818.*

So far we have safely proceeded though not expeditiously upon our journey; we reached Dover this morning at a little before 8, & embarked at ½ past 9. The wind was southerly and the sea very rough with a heavy swell and we were all of us very sick, even I who seldom suffer on such occasions was laid upon my back. Our passage was long & we did not get on shore till seven o'clock this evening. But having recruited our strength & spirits with a good dinner and a sufficient quantity of claret we are preparing ourselves for a good night's rest & mean to be off early tomorrow morning. This is not the land for quick travellers; customs houses, passports & fortified places check one at every turn, but if we can get off in tolerable time tomorrow we shall do well enough. We had a large ship's company amounting to forty; among the rest a gentlemanlike man of the name of Frazer who has been employed at Macao, and knows young Davis very well; he is a Dorsetshire man & has a brother in the 7 Hussars, & like us is bound to see the Review—a great number of people seem to have gone upon the same errand.[1] I write to you as you are I understand in London & you will forward this report to Fanny. Darkness & seasickness have hitherto prevented Shee from expressing any great wonder at the change of scene.[2]

107. *Cambray. 15 Oct. 1818.*

We arrived here this morning at eight o'clock, having pushed on without stopping from Calais which we left at about eleven yesterday morning: we were delayed longer than we expected by all the different ceremonies of custom house, hiring a carriage etc., but we got a very good open barouche with a head apron & a box for the servants which being rather narrow and somewhat rough kept them nice & warm all night especially Joseph to whom Fitzclarence[1] was as good as a second box coat. The country between Calais & this you know and it is needless to say that it did not gain in picturesque effect by being seen for the second time. We found the Coles & Catherine[2] very well and a good breakfast soon ready for us. The Review has

[1] Sir William Fraser of Ledeclune (1787–1827) had a younger brother who had been on the staff at Waterloo and succeeded him as 3rd Bart. John Francis Davis (1795–1890) had been a writer in the factory at Canton since 1813.
[2] Shee accompanied Palmerston on this journey to France.
[1] Not identified.
[2] Lowry Cole commanded a division of the British Army of Occupation. Lady Catherine Harris, the Malmesburys' elder daughter, married Gen. Sir John Bell in June 1821.

been postponed till Wednesday the 21st and is to be between Bouchain & Valenciennes. The Prussians & Austrians are to be reviewed afterwards near Sedan. We mean to employ the interval by going tomorrow to Compiegne which we shall see on Saturday and shall return here on Sunday; on Monday we shall go to Valenciennes, on Tuesday there is a preparatory Review of the Russians, on Wednesday the grand review, on Thursday we shall go to Charleroi & so by Waterloo to Brussells & from thence by Ghent along the coast to Calais. This will take us a few days longer than we intended, but being here it is as well to see whatever is in our way.

[*PS.*] Our weather is beautiful. Send this on to Fanny.

108. *To Mrs Sulivan. Cambray. 20 Oct. 1818.*

We returned to this place yesterday morning after a very agreeable excursion. We left this on Friday morning & reached Compiegne that night. The country pretty uniformly ugly & uninteresting. On Saturday morning we saw the palace & garden at Compiegne which I believe you know & which therefore I shall not describe. We were much pleased with the palace which is I think the best palace I ever saw. Some of the rooms are very handsomely furnished but at the same time there was no look of private comfort or the appearance of such furniture as one should require if one occupied a room—a remarkable scarcity of tables for instance. In the Duke of Berry's great drawing room 50 feet long there was only one little circular marble table with an elevated ridge round the rim, & about 3 feet diameter upon a high pedestal; & there was no such thing as a book stand in any room but the library. That indeed is a remarkably comfortable room & fit for any *gentleman*, which is saying more than calling it fit for a prince. The great gallery or ball room is nearly finished & will be a most magnificent apartment. Cannova's two groups of Cupid & Psyche, the one a duplicate of that which was at Malmaison, the other, with Cupid's wings extended, are alone worth going the whole distance from here to Compiegne to see.

After having seen the palace we looked at a review of a regiment of hussars of the *Garde*, which was inspected in a field close by, & in spite of all national prejudice I must confess they are a very fine body of men remarkably well equipped & looking very like soldiers. They were however but indifferent horsemen, rode with immensely long stirrups & reins, & seemed to have but little command of their steeds. One officer in particular having checked his horse rather unexpectedly in a canter was thrown up about a yard from his saddle and was within an ace of being off. He seemed much annoyed at our having observed it, & rode past us several times afterwards making his horse prance & curvet *gently*, as if to shew that he really could ride in spite of his mishap. Having finished our inspections at Compiegne we left it about the middle of the day & reached Soissons at night. On Sunday morning we walked about Soissons, saw the cathedral which is a fine building though not so handsome in point of style as the church at Compiegne, both being Gothic; we then pushed on to Laon the scene of action between Blucher & Woronzow & the French, and one of the most remarkably picturesque situations I ever saw. It is a very high ridge like a hog's back rising by itself out of a great plain. The summit is covered by a very old & irregular town the outline of which is broke by windmills, towers, churches etc. As a military position it must be impregnable to any force that could be brought against it & to make it stronger there are abundance of fine springs on the hill itself. There is an old tower in the town at the door of which a well dressed Frenchman informed us Charles the 5th lost *120,000* men 'et ce ruisseau que vous voyez là Monsieur couloit de sang tout comme s'il y avait eu un ouragan'. A Frenchman *can* not tell a word of truth about anything in which his personal or national vanity is concerned, & there are few subjects that have not some connection with his feelings in one of those relations.

We left Laon about seven on Sunday evening & travelling on through a very cold night reached this by eight o'clock yesterday morning; our journey was lengthened 4 posts by the necessity of going round by Marles & Cerisy to avoid La Fere the commandant of which is a most inexorably sound sleeper & will not hear anybody who knocks at the town gates after eight o'clock in the evening. Upon our arrival here we found that we need not have hurried, as the sovereigns have found more to do at Aix la Chappelle than they expected & have put off the Review till Friday next & the previous inspection of the Russian army to the day before (Thursday). We found the Coles therefore still here & took a ride with them to see an old ruined chateau called Esnes about 7 miles off. Today we are going to ride to Vaucelles about a similar distance. Tomorrow we go to Valenciennes early in order to look about us & see the town. Thursday we see the Russian inspection, Friday the Grand Review & a great ball afterwards. Saturday we shall go to Brussells, Sunday see Waterloo, Monday probably leave Brussells & get to Ghent, Wednesday will probably bring us to Calais & then our return to town must depend upon winds & waves. We have been highly delighted with our tours hitherto & though we quarrel all day like cat & dog yet as we left our duelling pistols at home no fatal consequences have yet ensued, & as to hours, it is difficult to say which is the earliest or the most punctual to appointed times. The weather continues beautiful though rather *freschetto*, and the Review will doubtless go off admirably well.

[*PS.*] Send this on to Fanny. We have given up all idea of the Sedan Review as it appears that Alexander goes straight to Paris on Saturday to *dine* with Louis, & then returns to Sedan, so that that affair will be too late for me.

109. *To Mrs Sulivan. Valenciennes. 24 Oct. 1818.*

I have only just time to say I received yesterday your letter of the 20th for which I thank you. Our review yesterday was magnificent and most gratifying to honest English pride. The whole army were admirable but as Alexander said to Cole '*votre* (that is *notre*) armée a un charme'. We are just going to commit ourselves to two Russian artillery drivers & horses who look as if they would eat us before they reach Maubeuge where Woronzow has commissioned them to take us to be present at a ball tonight. Tomorrow we shall go on to Sedan for the Prussian review on Monday; not for the sake of that sight but because it is just possible that William[1] may upon the receipt of my letter have gone there.

110. *To Mrs Sulivan. Brussels. 29 Oct. 1818.*
     B.P.W.; cf. Ashley, i. 85–6.

We left Cambray on Wedy 21st as I believe I told you, reached Valenciennes & saw the grand review on Friday 23rd & the inspection of the Russians on Thursday 22nd. It is needless to say that both but especially the grand review were magnificent sights & that we were gratified beyond measure. Fred Ponsonby lent us two troop horses, which carried us remarkably well. On Saturday we went on to Maubeuge, a dirty filthy hole fit only for a Russian army but I wonder that Woronzow should not have managed better for himself. We were put into an unoccupied & unfurnished building out of which a Russian major had been turned to make room for us, and every civility was offered us by two servants who spoke no language but their mother tongue & wanted only to be tatooed & covered with a mat to pass for South Sea savages. Woronzow gave us a very good ball in the evening at which the Emperor & the K[*ing*] of Prussia & D. of Wellington were present.

On Sunday we started soon after daybreak & got on to Sedan by
_____
[1] William Temple was Secretary of Legation in Frankfurt.

3 o'clock the following morning. We travelled very slow for the Russian artillery drivers had such an invincible affinity for ditches into one of which we actually descended and just stopped upon the brink of several that we soon discarded them & took to the French post, but the horses were always either tired or engaged & we worked our way slowly on by means of cart-horses & ploughboys. At Sedan we found a comfortable quarter in the Duke's house, and on Monday went to see the Prussian review on the plain of Donchery about three or four miles to the westward of the town. At ½ past 2 we dined with the King & went to a ball in the theatre. The dinner was in a riding-house, very neatly fitted up with the Russia duck prepared for the soldiers' trowzers & the scarlet cloth of which their facings are made, and the ball-room was ornamented with the same materials, none of which were cut so as to be less useful afterwards. I could hear no tidings of William, who probably did not get my letter in time to make his arrangements for coming & very probably was absent from Frankfurt when it arrived there. The Prussian troops amounted to about 25,000 and made a very pretty review. They are in most respects of dress & discipline an imitation of the Russians, but with a great deal of their steadiness they combine much of our quickness & activity & seem a more manageable army.

We did not leave Sedan till near ten o'clock on Tuesday 27th, and got on very slowly as there were swarms of Grand Dukes & Generals, etc. travelling the same road who greatly interfered with our motions. However, we reached Dinant to breakfast yesterday morning the 28th & pushed on to Namur where we arrived about 4 in the afternoon, time enough to walk around & up the new fortifications they are making. The drive from Givet to Namur is almost all pretty but the latter half of the road from Givet to Dinant & the whole way from Dinant to Namur is beautiful. The road winds along the valley of the Meuse, & to eyes which had ever since landing at Calais seen nothing but open flat country without one single feature of any sort or kind, fit only for war & corn, the sight of rocks & wood & a winding river was a prodigious treat & we were all admiration. The fortress now making at Namur is on top of a hill 400 feet from the level of the river, a steep ascent. It will be strong, but I did not like to hear the engineer who superintended the works expatiate so much as he did upon the advantage of some works 'pour *encourager* la garnison' and the aptitude of others to 'faire *peur* à l'ennemi.' I am afraid our allies the Belgians want much of that 'spirit never to submit or yield' which is necessary to enable them successfully to defend their territory. We slept at Namur & came on to this place today, seeing Quatre Bras & Waterloo in our way. By the assistance of a good plan & description & some peasants we met on the ground we satisfied ourselves completely about Waterloo, walked over the position of our army, picked some bullets out of the orchards of La Haie Sainte & Hougomont, cut a bundle of sticks at the latter enough to beat clothes with during the rest of our lives, bought a French sword which probably never saw the battle, & came here by ½ past eight this evening. Tomorrow we see this town, the next day go to Antwerp, & shall probably be at Calais on Wednesday evening. We go by Ghent & Tournay. We are in the Hotel D'Angleterre where we have been rejoiced to find a clean well furnished room with a carpet & mahogany table, articles of luxury which we had not met with since Kelliacks.[1]

111. *To Mrs Sulivan. Brussels. 3 Nov. 1818.*

We have been detained here by one of my bilious headaches brought on by being overheated in travelling & perhaps by partaking too copiously of the good things given us by our royal entertainers. There is a very good English physician here a Dr Doratt whom I have feed for telling me what I knew before, & for giving me some calomel which I should have taken without his advice. I am better to day, and if I am able to do without another charge of calomel we shall probably set out the day after tomorrow; if another is required it may detain us a day or two longer. At all events I must now give up Antwerp and shall return to Calais by the direct road.[1] Our weather continues fine & warm, the thermometer standing at 60 in the open air.

[*PS.*] Send this on to Fanny.

112. *Stanhope St. 15 Nov. 1818.*

You are in my debt just *nil*; if the animal turns out to be just as well suited to the purpose as I think he is, I shall find my account well balanced by having contributed to Elizabeth's health & amusement.[1]

---

[1] Not identified.
[1] He reached Calais on 9 Nov. and Dover at 3 p.m. the following day.
[1] The chestnut intended for Elizabeth had cost Palmerston £115. 10s. 0d.; the pony intended for Fanny just ten guineas.

113. *To Mrs Sulivan. Stanhope St. 18 [or possibly 12] Nov. 1818.*

I can assure you that if the chesnut answers our expectations it will give me infinitely more pleasure to see you upon him than it would to have ridden him myself and therefore you see I have been consulting my own gratification in giving it to you. I was much pleased yesterday by hearing a high character of him from Fozard[1] whom I met in the Park & I hope he will continue to deserve it.

114. *Stanhope St. 21 Oct. 1819.*

I do not see that there can be any reason whatever for you to hurry your return to London and I am sure that you had better take your *quantum suff* of country air.

Pong is wellcome to remain as long as he pleases.[1] I cannot understand how people can submit to such degradation as the Whig aristocracy had to undergo at York.[2]

[*PS.*] What a change of weather. This day week our thermometer at B[*roadlan*]ds was I think bordering upon 70, and at this moment it is actually *snowing*.

115. *War Office. 22 Oct. 1819.*

I suppose some of you have the *Courier* but in case you should not I send you a copy that you may see how well our List looks in uprights. I also furnished Street with the paragraph of comment.[1] Government decided yesterday morning to have a call of outpensioners to raise 10,000 men to be formed into Veteran Battalions. The call is to take place as soon as it is possible to carry it into effect. The men can hardly be got together in less than a month as the proclamation is not to go out till tomorrow week to give the officers

---

[1] So the name appears to be. But the only person of such a name traced in the London directories of the period is a Joseph Fozard of 140 Edgware Rd, a dealer in spruce and ginger beer.

[1] Possibly a horse belonging to one of the Sulivans, who had recently been staying at Broadlands.

[2] The assembly in York, which had met on 14 Oct. to demand an inquiry into the 'Peterloo Massacre', had been called and conducted by members of the local aristocracy. Earl Fitzwilliam was dismissed from his Lord Lieutenancy of the West Riding for his part in the affair.

[1] The *Courier* on 22 Oct. published a list of the signatories of a counterpetition against the holding of a public meeting in Hampshire to protest against the 'Peterloo Massacre'. The list was headed by Malmesbury and Wellington and included Palmerston. There were also several paragraphs of approving editorial comment.

who are selected for the regts which are to be formed time to get down to the places of assembly before the men come in. I do not see that this measure need make any difference in your arrangements. Everything in which your department is concerned is a matter of routine & there is a precedent in 1815 which with slight alterations will serve as a complete guide.

[*PS.*] The snow was two inches deep this morning & everything as white as Spitzbergen.

116. *Broadlands. 13 Feb. 1820.*

I wish you joy of Elizabeth's safe confinement. She seems to have managed her arrangements remarkably well, and I am glad that she has equalized the sexes in your family.[1]

We have had some very good runs with the hounds, & I think I shall be tempted to play truant till the end of this week as there can be nothing on Thursday & Friday except effusions of loyalty, my concurrence in which will I trust be taken for granted. Heathcote's resignation surprised all who did not know that he has for 3 years intended to slip his neck out of the collar at the first opportunity. I had not heard of his meditated retreat till a few days ago. Fleming will I fancy come in unopposed.[2] The honor of representing a county is one which I think one rather covets for one's friend than for oneself & I do not wonder at Heathcote's handing the feather out of his own cap after having worn it long enough for glory.

117. *Broadlands. 16 Feb. 1820.*

   Add. MSS.

Many thanks for your intelligence; I am glad to hear that ministers have been so stout, as I am perfectly sure that to agitate the question of divorce without evidence absolutely indisputable, would be the most unfortunate measure that could be undertaken. If the opposition agree to come in upon the basis of supporting a proceeding which this administration have refused to countenance because they thought

---

[1] Mrs Sulivan's second daughter, Mary Catherine Henriette, was born 8 Feb. 1820.
[2] The sitting M.P.s for Hampshire, Chute and Sir Thomas Freeman-Heathcote, 4th Bart, both declined to stand at the 1820 General Election. Palmerston approached Sir John Pollen, 2nd Bart (1784–1863), and Henry Combe Compton (1789–1866), but John Willis Fleming (*ob.* 1844) and George Purefoy Jervoise (1770–1847) were returned unopposed. (Palmerston to Pollen, 19 Feb., and to Compton, 22 Feb. 1820, B.P.W.)

the evidence insufficient, well and good, we shall not envy them their triumph and they need not be proud of their victory. But I shall not believe that matters will take this turn, till it is announced as a fact. I will stake my existence that the King will give in, and that like an angry woman when he finds that neither tears nor scolding neither threats nor entreaties neither promises nor upbraidings will carry his point, he will dry up his tears and eat up his words & very quietly sit down to bear his disappointment & pocket the affront.

I know that there is no occasion whatever for me to be in town before Monday, because the Estimates are not ready to be presented on Friday & that is the first thing to be done by me, and nothing can take place in the House tomorrow or Friday that can involve a division. But however I shall come up tomorrow so as to be in the House on Friday.

118. *St John's. 6 Mar. 1820.*

Many thanks for your note which is not a bit more minute than I wished it to be, for nothing is more unsatisfactory than a general report of a person's health which means nothing unless it is as explan-tory as yours is.[1]

I shall be anxious to get tomorrow's account as I do not at all like this one.

All is quiet here and instead of a contest we have only one candidate for Smyth is not well enough to come down in person. The election is on Wednesday, & I shall therefore not be in town till Thursday.[2]

[*PS.*] Wood has just obtained from Sidmouth a new statute for the college throwing open all the county fellowships.[3] This has caused great rejoicing in the college and is a very important benefit to the body.

[1] This probably refers to the recurrent illnesses of Stephen Henry Sulivan.
[2] Palmerston and Smyth were re-elected unopposed at the General Election following the death of George III.
[3] James Wood was Master of St John's from 1815 to 1839. Palmerston had written to his brother on 19 June 1818:

> Wood of St John's has not been very well of late; he is an instance of the vanity of human wishes for I really believe he has not been so comfortable since he has been Master as he was before; at least since the first novelty of the promotion has passed away. He lives of course a great deal more by himself & misses the daily society of the Hall dinner & wine party afterwards which came unsought and had a tendency to keep up his spirits, & as Master he misses the occupation he had before & he has not provided himself 'in a wife that controversy which lasts for life'. (B.P., G.C./TE no. 159.)

119. *Broadlands. 10 June 1821.*

The severing of the earliest and closest ties is always one of the most painful events in the life of man; but perhaps if there are any circumstances which can mitigate the acuteness of the feeling they are those under which the loss has fallen upon you; when on the one hand those who have sustained the deprivation have been for some time prepared in the ordinary course of nature to expect it, and when those whom we lament have not in their latter moments suffered more than is unavoidably connected with the termination of existence, and have had the happiness during the last years of their life not only to be free from the painful diseases which so often afflict the evening of life, but have closed their days with a *cloudless sunset* cheered to the very last by all the comforts which domestic affection can impart.[1]

120. *To Mrs Sulivan. Ferrybridge.*[1] *5 Nov. 1821.*

I have made a very pleasant progress hitherto having spent agreeably two days at Newmarket & three at Apethorpe, & having seen on my way the Cambridgeshire Fens, Ely Cathedral, & the Bedford Level, and the plate & cutlery manufactures at Sheffield. From the latter I send you a small pair of scissors; I would have sent you the knife with 1818 blades & instruments, but that I feared it would be too heavy for a frank. I am going on after I have done what I want here, to Leeds Manchester & Liverpool & shall take Nottingham in my way back & shall be in town probably by tomorrow week.[2] The Sheffield people are almost all at work and their trade is thriving— but the wages being considerably lower than they were a few years ago the prices of their goods have proportionately fallen.

In the principal parish of the town they paid in 1819 poor rates at the amount of from 5 to 600£ a week & now in the same parish they pay only about 100£; but the rough workman who used to have 3s. a day now has little more than 1s.

We had a perfect tornado of wind & rain on Sunday & I expect

[1] Stephen Sulivan, Laurence's father, had died on 9 June.

[1] Palmerston was paying a rare visit to the only estate he had in England outside Hampshire, at Fairburn in Yorkshire. He was making considerable improvements and investments there about this time, especially in a lime works. But when he ran into financial difficulties a few years later Fairburn was the property he was most inclined to sell.

[2] His plans were changed when he received a sudden invitation, at the instance of Lady Gertrude Sloane Stanley, to her father's place at Castle Howard. 'He was very agreeable & pleasant', reported Lady Georgiana Morpeth to her brother (17 Nov., Chatsworth Papers, 6th Duke/561).

to find the valley of the Air tomorrow morning under water. I spent
this morning in seeing Sheffield & arrived here this evening.

121. *War Office. 12 Aug. 1822.*

  Cf. *Airlie, i. 99–100.*

Palmerston reports Londonderry's suicide at Cray.

122. *Stanhope St. 19 Aug. 1822.*

I am glad to hear that your tour has answered so well. As to rain
at the Lakes you might as well expect to have no smoke at Wolver-
hampton & if you can ever see the sun at either you should rejoice &
be thankful. It now appears that my first idea about the nature of
poor Ld L.'s disorder was erroneous, it was not a bodily and accidental
inflammation settling upon and affecting the brain, but a gradual
& regular mental disorder which had been coming on for some time
& which perhaps would have been incurable even if he had lived. His
family are subject to it. The late Ld Hertford was quite out of his
mind for above a year before he died. The present Ld Drogheda has
long been confined, Ld Wm Seymour is next to deranged, & Ld
Henry odd. Many little circumstances disregarded at the time but
now remembered by those who have been in daily habits of intercourse with Ld L. prove that for the last two months his mind has
been affected. The lowness & depression was ascribed to fatigue but
it now is proved to have been the beginning of the disorder. His
notion was as he himself said more than once that his mind was
extinct, that Parliament was too much for him, that he was worn &
broken down by it, that he never could go through another session.
He fancied that people shunned and avoided him, that there was some
dark intrigue & secret conspiracy carrying on against him among his
own friends. He is reported to have said to Lieven six weeks ago that
a plot was formed against him & that he suspected Wellington to be
at the bottom of it but that he would take him home in his carriage
& probe his soul to the bottom, that some days afterwards feeling
that he had exposed himself he tried to laugh it off. On the Friday
he was quite insane. After he had gone through his business with the
King in his usual masterly manner he began about himself, said he
was an outcast of society, that everyone shunned & avoided him, that
plots were formed against him, that he hoped it was not yet too late
to fly the Country, that his horses were there waiting at the door of
Carlton House, that he had not ordered them, that his servants must

have sent them, & that this proved that even they thought he ought to fly the Country. The King spoke to Wellington about it & sent for Liverpool & Bankhead was immediately sent to Ld L. but on the Saturday with the sort of acuteness that is peculiar to that state of mind Ld L. wrote to the King to thank him for his attention to his health, to say that he had been cupped, was much relieved & quite composed & by Bankhead's permission was going down to Cray with Ly L. to keep himself quite quiet for a few days. How Bankhead could have allowed him to be alone for five seconds without a man, or how he could have permitted Ly L. to pass the night in the room with him I cannot conceive. He had expressed a great desire to have his pistols, & to shave *himself,* which he seldom did, & in consequence his pistols & razors were removed & locked up, but when precautions to such an extent are thought necessary I cannot understand by what infatuation the utmost precaution should have been omitted. He should have been watched like a person insane & there was no longer any question about feelings & delicacy, when so much more important considerations were at stake. By the peculiar mode in which he ended his existence he must have previously contemplated the act & have studied the subject with that view; it was scarcely possible that it could have been the hit of the moment.

No one could be a greater loss to his friends for a tender more generous or noble mind never existed and by the public his loss will be long & severely felt. I quite agree with you that there are many difficulties & objections to be overcome if Canning should be appointed. The King hates him, the Cabinet distrusts him, the Hs. [*of*] Cns do not respect him & the Public have little confidence in him. In the other side of the account are his *preeminent* talents as an orator which in a constitution that is carried on by speaking in one room, the Hs. [*of*] Cns, form a most important consideration.

The difficulty is not to decide whether he or Peel would best lead the House because fresh as Peel is to the task no man who has seen him do his work can doubt that in discretion, in personal following, in high mindedness he is superior to Canning & though not so eloquent an orator yet speaks quite up to the situation of Leader, but the point is whether the Government having lost Londonderry would stand as they could wish in the Commons without the accession of Canning, & if he joins them what should be his situation on the Treasy Bench. I do not see that it would be impossible for Canning to come in as Secy of State yielding the nominal lead to Peel. You may say it would not be a proud eminence considering the past, but yet also considering the past it is not impossible. Liverpool who is the person most interested on personal grounds in not placing the Govt in the Hs. of Cns so much in the hands of Canning as his being Leader would imply, is perhaps from private regard the most likely to urge his claims. On the other hand he certainly wishes well to & thinks highly of Peel.

Canning Leader of the Commons wd be to Liverpool a difft person from Londonderry. The latter was all good faith & honour & disinterestedness; he never was playing a personal & counter game, never tried to make to himself any party separate from Liverpool's, & the latter might always be sure that whatever Londonderry reported to him was dictated by the clearest discernment and the most scrupulous good faith; this might not always be the case with Canning. In short it is a fair & even bet either way & if you like to put a sovereign upon it you shall chuse your own side.

The King seems to have been well received at Edinburgh & to have been rewarded by the success of his voyage for that provident prudence which made him refuse to set out on Friday, it being an *unlucky* day. But do not mention *this*.

[*PS.*] How snug Liverpool has kept his intended marriage.

123. *Stanhope St. 31 Aug. 1822.*

You are right in your conjecture that you would not find me in town on Monday; I am going down to Bds tomorrow with Wilmot[1] to shoot Monday & Tuesday & come back on Wed. to see & hear what is going on. I shd think that a very few days or hours will settle the main question whether Canning comes in or not, and I would lay a wager that he does & that Peel will lead the Commons. I suspect that Canning has written to Peel to intimate that he should not object to such an arrang[emen]t but of this pray say nothing.

I flatter myself you will kill more at Bds than you have done on the the moors though you may not have such beautiful & extensive prospects.

[*PS.*] Pray thank Ld Normanton for this answer to my inquiry.[2]

124. *Ryde. 30 Nov. 1822.*

I confess I was rather surprized by the result of the Cambridge election, I thought Ld Hervey wd have come in.[1] This certainly shews

---

[1] Probably Robert John Wilmot, afterwards 3rd Bart (1784–1841), the undersecretary at the Colonial Office. He assumed the surname of Horton in 1823.
[2] The 2nd Earl of Normanton was Pembroke's son-in-law.
[1] Smyth had died in Oct. and there was a fierce contest in the by-election that

that Protestantism is very rife at Cambridge, but still I do not fear a general election; at least I do not see with what face people who have year after year promised me support knowing my sentiments on the Catholic question can all of a sudden turn round & leave me because a Protestant enters the field agst me; but however one must take one's chance and let things come as they will. The diminution of Protestant feeling which I had observed was among the residents but as 900 people voted the residents of course formed but a small part of the pollers, and the non-resident clergy are all of them Protestants.

I certainly took a very effectual mode of making my journey a secret by giving *Merry* my direction. I did not succeed however in taking the pier by surprize as they had completed its defences before my arrival though in other respects the defences of the place are in a favourable state for an attack as Buckingham's cannon are dismounted.

If you will *not* send my warrants in my own pet bag, it is your fault & not mine that they go astray.

125. *Lulworth.*[1] *21 Dec.* [*1822*].

Just look at these papers & let me know if any thing occurs to you upon them. We have had very good sport here & have seen an immense quantity of game of all sorts & kinds; our party consists of Ld Melville, Robinson, Huskisson, Daly & Henry Baring.[2] I have killed from 12 to 16 head every day, having shot ill the first day. I go to Bds tomorrow, to London on Monday & to Cambridge on Tuesday, to be ready to start fair with the Combination Room festivities on Christmas Day.

I congratulate you on this hard frost which will I hope do you good as well as give you pleasure.

This is a fine wild place. The house is just like Inverary only rather smaller & without a center tower. The grounds are extensive & pretty in a wild style. You may judge of the quantity of game

---

followed. Three candidates eventually appeared, William John Bankes, the Trinity student who had once spied on a meeting of the Fusty, Lord Hervey, who was the Earl of Bristol's son and Liverpool's nephew, and James Scarlett, afterwards 1st Baron Abinger. Bankes won by a wide margin as a 'Protestant' Tory, and the consequent opinion was that the other, 'Catholic', member for Cambridge would not last much longer: 'The common talk of London since the election is that Lord P. must look out for some other seat in one of the two Houses of Parliament at the period of the next general election.' (Lord Colchester to Charles Yorke, 30 Nov., Hardwicke Papers, Add. MS. 45037.)

[1] Peel was the tenant of Lulworth Castle in Dorset.

[2] James Daly (1782–1847) was M.P. for Co. Galway and afterwards Baron Dunsandle; Henry Baring (1777–1848) was a younger brother of Alexander Baring, afterwards Baron Ashburton.

when I tell you that the first morning upon putting my head out of window I counted upwards of a hundred cock pheasants feeding on the lawn before the house.

[*PS.*] Cracking a Bottle. The Irish say they threw the bottle at their Ld Lieut. as they had no other chance of cracking one with him.[3]

126. *St John's. 26 Dec. 1822.*

Protestantism is abroad certainly, but I am under no apprehensions as to its results. Bankes is here still, feasting with his constituents— my friends however remain apparently unchanged. The Cambridge paper of last week announces that Grant means to stand at the next opportunity.[1] Most of his votes went to Bankes, & I suppose he thinks he should succeed to Scarlet's interest. I shall remain here till Monday evng, then go to town for a day, & perhaps go for a few days to Middleton[2] in my way to Bds.

127. *Broadlands. 5 Jan. 1822 [1823].*

Nicholl[1] meets tomorrow at Ashley not far from Fritham, on Wednesday probably somewhere near the kennell but no place is mentioned; Thursday at Bistern, and Saturday at Norley inclosure about two miles due east of Lymington.

I arrived here at five this morning after a long & tedious journey, the road from Hertford Bridge to Winchester being excessively bad & full of holes from the effect of the frost on the chalk substratum.

I dine to day at the Flemings.[2] Malmesbury[3] & Merry come to see me on Wednesday to shoot. They say in London that the appointment of Ld F. Canningham by Mr Canning was a capital hit;[4] congratulate Robinson *privately* on succeeding Van but do not

---

[3] On 14 Dec. there had been a demonstration at the visit of Lord Wellesley to the theatre in Dublin and a number of missiles were thrown in his direction (*Annual Register*, 1822, Chronicle, p. 231).
[1] Robert Grant had canvassed support in the recent by-election, but withdrew shortly before the poll.
[2] Lady Jersey's place near Bicester.
[1] A local M.F.H.
[2] John Fleming's place was Stoneham Park, near Southampton.
[3] The 2nd Earl; Palmerston's old guardian had died in 1820.
[4] Lord Francis Conyngham had been appointed Canning's undersecretary at the Foreign Office. The appointment served to conciliate the King, but not everyone approved.

blow him up. I hope it is to be so; it is reported.[5] I take [*it*] you will come here soon.

128. *War Office. 10 Feb. 1823.*

I have heard nothing yet from Liverpool but the Duke sent me yesterday copy of a long rigmarole etc. which he wrote on Saty to Liverpool in reply to mine to Ld L. sending the copies, and in which he repeats his complaint of my encroachments, complains that I have misconstrued his arguments & drawn incorrect conclusions from them but repeats that his act was produced by the encroachments which provoked it.[1] I have sent a reply to Liverpool pointing out that my statement of the D.'s principle is borne out by his own act and Taylor's letters,[2] restating that I have never contended because it was unnecess[*ar*]y that the act was not *produced* by my encroachments, but that my argument is that it cannot be *justified* by any previous encroachment; that I wholly deny the alledged encroachment but cannot now enter into that question; my objections to the D.'s act being equally applicable whether encroachment is proved or disproved. I suppose I shall hear something from Liverpool tomorrow.

I was sorry not to see you before you left town because I was anxious to hear the result of your medical consultation, pray let me know. We shall have no Hs. [*of*] Cns business this week of any importance.

129. *House of Commons. 12 Feb. [1823].*

Long[1] spoke to me yesterday in ye Hs. upon the subject. He said Liverpool was in a fever & in despair, not knowing what to do, bored with the length of the papers, disliking contact with ye D[*uke*] & in short labouring under the *Weaks*. L. had begged Long to try to make matters up & to talk to me about the difficulty of dealing with Princes

---

[5] Fred Robinson succeeded Vansittart as Chancellor of the Exchequer on 31 Jan.

[1] A new round of conflict between C.-in-C. and Secretary at War had opened in Jan. when Palmerston issued a direct order to commanders on foreign stations to dispense with a number of superfluous clerks although by a compromise agreement of 1812 he was supposed to clear such orders first with the Horse Guards. The Duke of York immediately retaliated by ordering all commanders to ignore any communications from the Secretary that were not sent through the Horse Guards. Palmerston complained to the Prime Minister on 6 Feb., the Duke countered with his 'long rigmarole' on 8 Feb. and Palmerston wrote again on 10 Feb. (Liverpool Papers, Add. MSS. 38194 and 38292.)

[2] Herbert Taylor was Military Secretary at the Horse Guards.

[1] Charles Long, afterwards Baron Farnborough, was Paymaster-General. See his memo., 12 Feb., Liverpool Papers, Add. MS. 38370.

of the Blood, that though right I perhaps pushed my rightness to extremes, & that it was more than could be expected of D. to degrade himself by cancelling an order known to his clerks etc. I replied by such answers as of course will occur to you, & told Long that L. must make what he can of the matter, that I felt every respect for Princes of the Blood but could not admit they have a right to give an affront any more than any other peer of the realm. I shall I think propose to L. in order to save D. from having formally & of his own accord to cancel order that L. should write to him to say that he thinks it improper, & if L. agrees to that it will satisfy me as well.[2] The proposition I should submit to L. is that no servant of Crown is competent to order disobedience to the order of another who conveys avowedly the King's commands, unless the King's pleasure is specifically taken to that effect, that such a signification of the King's pleasure is tantamount to dismissing the offr in question, and that it is the head of the Govt & not the C. in C. who should take King's pleasure as to dismissing Secy at Wr—and that head of Govt would not act justly if he were to do so without previous communication with Secy at Wr to give him opportunity to explain & defend himself.

Adieu in gt hurry

130. *House of Commons. 14 Feb. 1823.*

Liverpool has sent a mem.[1] to C. in C. & to me of which the following is the pith. After expressions of regret & stating that he must treat the matter as a dispute of two depart[*ment*]s without ref. to station of parties or high rank of the illustrious person who is one he says:—

I certainly am of opinion that in any dispute between two departments of Gov. on the subject of their respective authority or jurisdiction, it cannot be adviseable that one of them shd give orders, to authorities which must be considered as in some degree subordinate to both, *not to comply with the instructions of the other.* Such an order could in my opinion only be justified as a matter of *dernier ressort* after explanation had been demanded & refused, & even in such case, I should think it by no means the proper mode of bringing the existing difference to an issue.

I must however now observe that the order referred to by the Secy at Wr had not been *actually issued*, & the *issue of it* being suspended I cannot conceive that the Secy at War is warranted in declining to discuss the merits of the original question until the offensive order was removed from the records of the Commr in C.'s office.

[2] Palmerston to Liverpool, 12 Feb., P.R.O., W.O. 18/10.
[1] *Cf.* Liverpool's draft 'opinion', 13 Feb., Liverpool Papers, Add. MS. 38370.

Upon the subject of the order which has given rise to the discussion I have referred to the King's warrant signed by H.R.H. [*the*] P.R. on 29 May 1812.

It certainly appears to me that by this warrant the Secy at Wr ought not to have issued ye orders in question to ye offrs on for[*eig*]n stations without *previously communicating them* to C. in C. & in event of C. in C. making any objection to such order a ref. shd have been made to one of the offrs of state designated in ye warrant in order that H. Majesty's pleasure might be taken on propriety of carrying it into execution.

I am further of opinion that if H.M. shd be pleased to approve of such order or if C. in C. had not originally objected to it as it regarded matter of finance and account it was within the province of the Secy at Wr to issue the order to the stations abroad.

He ends by saying he leaves the cases of Ross & Ford to be settled between us unless we require him to go into them.[2]

The first part of this is nearly satisfactory to me & is tantamount to the cancelling of the letter because *of course* C. in C. could not issue the l[*ette*]r after such an opinion nor again have recourse to the same proceeding, but I shall state to Ld L. that my principle goes a little further than his position because I hold that one officer can not use his delegated authority to command disobedience to the delegated authority of another without a special command of King to that effect, that such a command wd be tantamount to the dismissal of the officer, and that the head of the Govt is the person who ought to take the King's pleasure upon dismissal of a member of the Govt.

I wrote immediately to Ld L. to observe that he had decided that my letter was at variance with the warrant of 1812 without having heard a syllable from me on that point & he has replied that he gave his opinion as he had formed it but that he was quite ready to receive any further explanations, but deprecated the continuance of the discussion etc.[3] Adieu I must finish, it is 6 o'clock.

131. *War Office. 15 Feb. 1823.*

I send you the inclosed which you will like to see.[1] Return them

[2] In two coincidental disputes, the C.-in-C. had reprimanded a regimental commander for submitting a claim for travelling expenses direct to the War Office and clashed with the Secretary at War over the appointment of a regimental paymaster.
[3] Palmerston to Liverpool, 13 Feb., P.R.O., W.O. 18/14, and Liverpool to Palmerston, 14 Feb., P.R.O., W.O. 18/15.
[1] Probably copies of the letters he had exchanged with Liverpool on 13 and 14

to me when you have done with them. Upon thinking over Liverpool's minute I do not mean to urge the question of the forbidding order any further. Liverpool decides that it would not be proper to issue it under any circumstances, & there is no use in arguing with him that I think it improper upon different grounds from those on which he has so declared it; and he has put his opinion in general terms as between two departments, so that it cuts both ways & does not give to C. in C. any supposed power to issue such an order as a *dernier ressort* against Secy at War, which it does not equally give to Secy at Wr against C. in C.

I shall state to him why my circular does not appear to me to be at variance with the warrant of 1812. Merry says that Long tells him that the Duke is very angry with Liverpool's minute. I have not seen Long since nor have I been able to catch Taylor today the D. being still at York House & not coming to the H[or]s[e] Gds.

[*PS.*] Liverpool's minute decides in my favor the point which was the real question with the Duke, namely whether I am the proper offr to communicate on such points with Genl Offrs abroad.

132. *Stanhope St. 24 Feb.* [*1823*].

    Add. MSS.

C. in C. & Secy at Wr are going on smoothly. Civil letters have passed on both sides,[1] & the Duke has of his own accord cancelled the objectionable circular, & has offered to recall his letter to Col. Ross. I have thanked him but with regard to the last have preferred letting the matter rest till he & I come to a clear understanding as to the point at issue. I will send you the papers in a day or two as you will like to see the whole correspondence.

Robinson did *most admirably.*[2] There were not two opinions in the House on that point; the Opposition were all captivated.

[*PS.*] Were you not sorry for poor Ashburton.[3]

Feb. Palmerston half took the Prime Minister's hint not to pursue the matter, merely leaving his case on record in a further memo. of 17 Feb. (Liverpool Papers, Add. MS. 38370.)

[1] Taylor to Palmerston, 20 Feb., and Palmerston to Taylor, 21 Feb., copies in Liverpool Papers, Add. MS. 38292.

[2] The new Chancellor had presented his first budget on 21 Feb.

[3] Ashburton had died on 15 Feb.

133. *25 Mar. 1823.*

  Add. MSS.

I have mentioned to Wilmot Blackburn's name & have told him that if there would be time to communicate with legal authorities I have no doubt that satisfactory testimonies of legal competency can be obtained, & have stated my own opinion of personal character, and my knowledge of the interest which Clive takes in B.'s welfare.[1]

Wilmot says that nothing shall be done for ten days that shall preclude B.'s claim from receiving a fair consideration.

He does not think it at all probable that the salary could under any revision be brought below 3000£.

[*PS.*] I shall sound the Attorney General to see whether a direct reference to him without previous communication with Park would be expedient.[2]

134. *Broadlands. 6 April [1823].*

I send you the inclosed. Return me Wilmot's letter which is private.[1]

Shee doubts whether Blackburn's prospects at home are not good enough to be preferred to the colonial situation & he is rather against taking it. I advised him to write to you about it.

135. *Stanhope St. 15 Aug. 1823.*

Read this project with attention, and consider whether there is any reason why you & Elizabeth & I should not carry it into practical execution;[1] I am not at present aware of any and as the harvest will be late this year there will be no good partridge shooting till the second week in September. I should propose taking no carriage but trusting to the vehicles of the country and carrying as small a retinue as might be consistent with absolute comfort. I think I have allowed full time for everything & that we should be more likely to be a day less than a day more.

[1] Blackburn's Cambridge friends were inquiring on his behalf about the Chief Justiceship in Mauritius.

[2] The Attorney-General was Sir Robert Gifford (afterwards Baron Gifford); James Parke (afterwards Baron Wensleydale) was an old Cambridge acquaintance.

[1] The enclosures were Colonial Office responses about the expenses of the passage and of living in Mauritius.

[1] Unusually, there is no surviving journal of the trip Palmerston made to the Netherlands and Belgium. The Sulivans did not accompany him.

I find from Canning that William cannot come away till he is relieved by his successor & therefore he would not be here till after our return.[2]

[*Enclosure in Palmerston's hand:*]

			Leagues	Miles
Monday	25 Aug.	By sea to Rotterdam		
Tuesday	26	See Rotterdam & to Hague	5	15
Wednesday	27	See The Hague		
Thursday	28	Leyden & to Haarlem	12	36
Friday	29	To Amsterdam & see it	$3\frac{1}{2}$	10
Saturday	30	To Utrecht & see it	$14\frac{1}{2}$	44
Sunday	31	To Breda	16	48
Monday	1 Septr	To Antwerp	12	36
Tuesday	2	See it		
Wednesday	3	To Bergenopzoom	14	42
Thursday	4	To Antwerp	14	42
Friday	5	To Ghent & see it	13	39
Saturday	6	To Bruges & see it	11	33
Sunday	7	To Ostend & embark	$7\frac{1}{2}$	22
Monday	8	To London by steam		

136. *To Mrs Sulivan. Rotterdam. 28 Aug. 1823.*

B.P.W.

I embarked at the Tower yesterday at ten o'clock & after a very prosperous steaming arrived here at two o'clock this afternoon; our vessel the *Rapid* was a very good & roomy one, 460 tons according to sailing admeasurement & very spacious though not extremely clean. We had not many people on board but the few we had were some of them agreeable and the rest exhibited specimens of various kinds of the human race; among the agreeables were Sir Edward & Lady Hamilton of the navy, with a boy & girl, the latter a little Welsh girl of 8 or 10 uncommonly sharp & clever [&] a man from Durham whose name I know not but who was tolerably well informed though his chief authorities for his anecdotes were the newspapers. He had a doughy companion who added not much to our society. There were besides a German Jewish priest with a long robe, a small black gaberdine on his head, a flowing hair & long beard & a most picturesque countenance; a West Indian planter born at Manheim who

[2] William Temple had accepted the Secretaryship of Legation in Berlin, but as Fred Lamb, his chief in Frankfurt, was on leave he could not take it up until the autumn.

was going home to his Country after 30 years abroad. His father having specially enjoined him never to return home as long as there was a war in Europe, he probably left the W. Indies without having heard of the entrance of the French into Spain. He had been taken prisoner by the English in his youth, was sent into the West Indies, became a negro driver & then at last a planter. We had also a Scotch youth from Peterhead, besides an old clothes man, the companion of the Jewish priest and several mates to fill up the *dramatis personae*. To amuse us in the night we ran foul of a fishing smack; one should have thought the North Sea wide enough for two vessels. No very material harm however was done to the fisherman & none whatsoever to us. The wind was smack in our teeth, & the tide against us so that we had the fullest opportunity of enjoying by experience all the advantages of the steam engine. Ly Hamilton reminded me that she had seen me years ago at Sécheron when I came to play with her brothers; was she sister to John & Arthur Marthamartha?[1] She is too well-informed & ladylike to seem to be the sister of Macnamara who is a bad raff.

I lost no time after landing in providing myself with a guide & setting off to walk round the town & up the steeple. This is emphatic- ally a Dutch town, and one of the completest specimens of the real froggery. It is not unpleasing from the mixture of trees & houses, but as for the inhabitants, I can conceive nothing more gloomy than having a row of high elms within ten feet of the front of one's house completely obstructing every ray of the son [*sic*], and collecting all the damp which the canals & climate can afford. There is not much to see here except the general appearance of the town. There are some few private collections of pictures of which I saw one belonging to a Baron Lockhurst, among which is the Temptation of St Anthony by Teniers, and a good picture by John Steen. There is a statue of Erasmus on one of the canals & two or three good monuments in the Great Church.

I shall start tomorrow morning betimes for the Hague—and dare say I shall be able to make my tour good in the fortnight. I have become master of a Dutch dictionary, grammar & book of dialogues & flatter myself that before I return I shall be in a fit state to hold high converse in Low Dutch with Fagel[2] or Lilliput himself. The weather here has not been much better than ours but the apricots here *are* ripe & I have seen none in that state in England. When I hope to be an adept in Dutch my expectations are founded upon my

---

[1] Adm. Sir Edward Hamilton (1772–1851) had married in 1804 Frances, daughter of John Macnamara of Llangoed Castle, Co. Brecon. Palmerston had stayed at Sécheron, on the northern outskirts of Geneva, with his parents in 1792 (Connell, p. 267).
[2] See no. 225.

intended locomotion for if one remained here one could have no inducement as every body one meets speaks English and in the bookseller's shop I went to nothing was to be seen but English books, Walter Scott, Byron, English Poets, Travels, Philosophy, etc., and it was only here & there that a solitary foreign book ventured to shew (not its face but) its back. Really the Dutch Language is *too* ridiculous to an English ear, & it is hardly possible to hear some of their serious names of things & places without an affronting laugh.

[*PS.*] I inquired if there was a play tonight; they said not & that they have not a play *every night*. How often have you then; oh Sir at least once a fortnight in the gay season of the year, & the players come from the Hague on purpose. I am writing in the nicest smoking room that ever was seen, a little square building projecting into a canal at the end of a small garden, with windows all round, the outside of which (as they never open them) were nicely covered with spiders' webs. I am afraid I have disturbed some of these industrious tenants. The only windows however that are not beautifully clean are those over the canal, for all the others are cleaned daily with a small water engine. As I have now been in Holland at least ten hours I ought to send you a full account political & statistical of the Country, with general remarks on the character, manners & habits of the people, but as you may read it all in a little book which I have bought I shall spare you the manuscript accounts and I am afraid if I keep my letter open much longer it will go laden with some overpowering fumes of tobacco which have this instant invaded my peaceful retreat and make me almost fancy myself a slug on a gooseberry back attacked by an industrious gardener.

137. *To Mrs Sulivan. Amsterdam. 2 Sept. 1823.*

So far I have made a prosperous & very amusing journey. I left Rotterdam the morning after I arrived there, that is to say on Friday the 29th and seeing Delft in my way got to the Hague by eleven o'clock, so as to have time that day to see everything at the Hague including Schevening & the house in the wood.[1] The collection of Flemish & Dutch pictures in the Royal Gallery is beautiful, the Italian are bad; but the Paul Potters, the Metzus, the Mieris's are first rate, and I was excessively delighted with them. The King is not at the Hague but comes there in October, so that I had nothing to interrupt me in seeing the place. I left the Hague early on Saturday

---

[1] Scheveningen, two miles north-west of The Hague. The House in the Wood (Huis ten Bosch) is a royal residence between The Hague and Scheveningen.

30th and seeing Leyden in my way got to Haarlem at night. Leyden is not a very interesting town though there are several things one is taken to see. Sunday being a bad seeing day I was obliged to halt at Haarlem, but made my time out by hearing a long Dutch sermon, listening for an hour afterwards to the magnificent organ in the great church & by taking a drive to a place about 9 miles off called Velsen where there is a country seat of an Amsterdam merchant by name Gull. The Dutch Protestant service is like the Scotch, it consists of a psalm sung lustily by the whole congregation to whose credit at Haarlem I must say that they nearly drowned the organ, a long *soi-disant* extempore prayer by the clergyman, another short psalm and then an immensely long sermon. After the service I & three other Englishmen (one by the bye a constituent, a Cornish clergyman; I always meet constituents when I travel) hired the organist to play to us & really the powers of that organ exceed anything I ever heard. The man played us a thunderstorm not omitting the heavy rain with which it is accompanied, & really the thing was so naturally done that one began to regret that one had not brought one's umbrella & galoshes to walk home with. The trumpet & *vox humana* stop are admirable, & the latter really is what the name denotes & not merely *vox Hollandeia*. The drive to Velsen is very pretty & I had the advantage of seeing a modern Dutch garden which is as different from one of the days of William 3d as the dress & appearance of Admiral Schimmelpenninch of the Royal *Nederlandische* service from the warlike habiliments of De Ruyter or Van Tromp. The straight alleys, clipped hedges, leaden cupids and sputtering dolphins are all banished, and their serpentine and curvilinear walks have reached the *ne plus ultra* of labyrinthic involution. The effect however is very pretty & the garden in question is like one of the prettiest possible English flower gardens; but as you cannot expel nature & can only improve her, the slow and turbid stream that used to stagnate in the straight canal now creeps silently but not very offensively through the meanderings of a picturesque piece of water, sometimes narrowed to the span of a Chinese bridge, sometimes swelling out to the majestic dignity of a mimic ferry.

On Monday morning, that is yesterday, I saw a collection of good pictures at Haarlem belonging to a Madlle Hoffman, and then came on to this place; today I went in the morning to the little village of Broek[2] in North Holland which is like a thing in a top shop from the extreme neatness & tidyness of all the houses. It is built round a little bay, the streets are narrow & paved with bricks & are merely alleys not being meant for carriages or horses. All the houses are as smart as yellow & green & other coloured paint can make them and extra-

[2] Broek in Waterland, a few miles north-east of Amsterdam.

ordinary to say there are two which aspire to all the pride and
splendour of Grecian architecture, columns, pilasters, friezes, & pedi-
ments, & which evidently belong to persons of some property & must
have cost a good deal of money. It is difficult to conceive how any
body who had money enough to build such houses should place them
in a spot from which they could throw a biscuit on one side into the
muddy branch of the Zuyder Zee on which they stand and on the
other across a narrow ditch into a great meadow like Hern Mead[3]
which stretches as far as the eye can reach uninterrupted even by a
single willow for the space of several miles. I also saw today the royal
collection of pictures here which contains some magnificent Vander-
veldes & Rembrandts besides a great many other very excellent
pictures. Tomorrow I shall see some private collections & the next day
I leave this rich & populous, and industrious, pile-supported and
stinking city. There is not one house out of the 25,000, of which
Amsterdam consists that is not built upon piles. About half the streets
have canals running through them & not one out of the many
thousand boats that are constantly moving through those canals,
traverses ten yards without stirring up from the bottom a mud of such
irresistible power that any but a nose bred & born in the town takes
immediate refuge in the productions of Cambray or India. I must
say however that this is the only town in which I have been informed
by any other sense than sight that such things as canals existed. I find
I get on so quick & this country is so small that I cannot well spin
out the time till Thursday the 12th, the day on which I meant to
embark at Ostend on my return to London, & so as I have more time
than I know what to do with I shall take a week longer—a good Irish
resolve you will say, but this additional week will just enable me to
see the Rhine and pay William a visit at Frankfort, which visit I hope
he will speedily return me at Bds. I shall run from hence to Cologne
which is only 150 miles, from thence by Coblentz to Frankfort is only
110 more; I shall stay one or perhaps two days at Frankfort; if William
is not ready to come back with me I shall return again down the
Rhine to Cologne, strike across by Brussels to Antwerp & there fall
again into my original route & get to Ostend on the evening of Wedy
17th so as to embark on Thursday morning per steam for London.
This will be a very considerable addition to the amusement & interest
of my tour & is well worth the additional week which it will occupy.
If any letters have come to me from William you may open them &
read them as they can contain no secrets and may give you intelligence
of him. I have made considerable progress in Dutch in spite of the
people who will all talk English to me, but the provoking thing is
that though I never can remember a word of German when I want

[3] Hurn Mead, near Christchurch, Hampshire.

to talk it, it is always coming to my tongue's end when I try to speak Dutch, but by walking about with a little dictionary always in one's hand one manages to get on capitally; the language too is not very difficult to an Englishman, one has only to speak broad or broken English, 'Wat is Dat' is good Dutch, & '*Ik dank ur*' perfectly classical.

[*PS.*] I went to a Dutch play last night & am going again tonight. It is rather amusing but the house emptier than anything I ever saw.
I shall expect you at Broadlands on Saturday the 20th. Mind that.

138. *To Mrs Sulivan. Frankfort. 9 Sept. 1823.*

I have made good my expedition to this place where I arrived yesterday morning at 5 o'clock; I found William perfectly well & not surprized to see me as he had got my letter telling him I was going upon a tour & he thought it not impossible I might stretch on here. I have been much pleased with the Rhine though I cannot say that it has quite equalled my expectations but that was my fault for expecting so much & not its defect in not performing more than nature enabled it to do. We drove over to day to Hamberg & saw there the old Queen of Wurtemberg (Ye Pss Royal), the Princess Augusta & the Dss of Cambridge.[1] We dined there at ½ past one & returned here & have been to a German play, a conjuror's & a tea party. We are now going to bed to be up at five tomorrow (*my regular hour*) to set off for Heidlebergh, from thence we shall go to Baden, and thence back to Mayence where William will leave me, he returning here & I going back to Antwerp; this will not take me above 3 or 4 days more than I intended & I think I shall be at Ostend on the morning of Saturday the 19th to come over by the steam-boat on that day. Tell Sulivan that I shall be in town therefore unless some unexpected sand or bad drivers should befall me in time to sign the warrants before the 24 of the month.

William has not yet heard when he is likely to get his leave.

Adieu my dear Elizabeth. I have not time to write more & am not quite sure that you will get this much before I myself arrive.

[*PS.*] My motions are as far as I can judge—

Wedy 10   Heidelbergh
Thursday 11   Baden

---

[1] Charlotte, the widow of Frederick I of Würtemberg, and her unmarried sister Augusta Sophia, were children of George III; the Duchess of Cambridge was their sister-in-law.

Frid. 12	back to Carlsruhe
Saty 13	Mayence
Sundy 14	Andernach
Mondy 15	to Liege
Tuesdy 16	Antwerp
Wedy 17	see it
Thursdy 18	Ghent
Fridy 19	Ostend

Weather has been beautiful. Who should turn up here but Henry Elliot.[2]

139. *Broadlands. 5 Oct. 1823.*

By some stupid mistake of Hold & Harrison[1] a bag which I had directed to Merry this day week just before I set out for Lulworth & in which I had put a mem[*oran*]d[*um*] explaining my motions, was allowed to slumber on my table & I found it here yesterday on my return. You must have thought me the most careless or mysterious of mortals. I meant to have returned on Thursday but the shooting was good, the party agreeable & Malmy asked to meet me so I staid till yesterday. I killed about 50 brace in the week which considering the wildness of the weather & the occasional crookedness of my powder proves the quantity of birds. Indeed they swarm. We had the landlord Mr Weld there, who came to expel the dry rot from his Catholic chapel, easier than from his flock perhaps. He is a quiet, harmless man, & to hear him talk you would not think him such a fool as he must be to leave such a place with 16,000 acres round it to go and say mass in a chapel in Sloane Street.[2]

The Shees came yesterday. I grow less of a Tory every time I see Shee whose head makes me wish for the *Wigs*, though unlike Burke I should appeal from the old to the new Wigs. The Flemings & Ly

[2] Henry Elliot (1789–1848) was the grandson of Samuel Glasse (1735–1812), a chaplain to the Dukes of Cumberland and Cambridge and friend and collaborator of Palmerston's maternal relatives, Robert Raikes and William Man Godschall. His father, the Rev. George Henry Glasse, was a scholar but a spendthrift. George Glasse's name was mentioned in the Mrs Clarke–Duke of York affair in 1809 and, though he was said to be innocent, he hanged himself shortly afterwards. Henry Glasse subsequently assumed the name of a family benefactor and succeeded Sulivan as Palmerston's private secretary at the War Office.

[1] Harrison was housekeeper or butler in Stanhope St in 1823–4.

[2] Thomas Weld (1773–1837), Peel's landlord at Lulworth Castle and the son of the founder of Stonyhurst, had taken holy orders in 1821 after the death of his first wife. He became a Roman Catholic bishop in 1826 and a cardinal in 1830. According to the *D.N.B.* he had already transferred Lulworth to his younger brother Joseph.

Gertrude [*Sloane Stanley*] come to day for a day & I presume Fanny & Bowles will be here tomorrow.[3]

[*PS.*] I wish you would at your leisure give this to your *architect*: the commission it contains will not materially interfere with your works.[4]

140. *Broadlands. 15 Oct. 1823.*

> *From typescript; MS. not found.*

Brown complained that Codd's room is a constant drain on the arrear, from the illness & absence of clerks in Codd's room. I hold that Codd's business must be kept up because in one sense it is current business, and therefore that any wants of hands in it must be made up from the arrear. Brown proposes to have it put under [? *his*] section & that any failure of hands in it should be made up from Lukin's branch & I am disposed to think this not an inexpedient arrangement as I believe that Lukin's people have comparatively less to do than yours or Brown's though it is difficult to get Merry to own this or to remedy it. What is your objection to the transfer? The other mode of remedying the evil would be to transfer a clerk from Lukin to Brown; Brown certainly has a large number & it is chiefly from a wish to reduce Lukin's number or give them more to do that I thought of adopting the proposal.[1]

141. *Broadlands. 19 Oct. 1823.*

I send you some game for your own private eating, & I also send you a basket with 3 brace of pheasants which I wish you would by means of Doyle have forwarded to Langley Heyland Esq. Consul at Ostend with my compliments—it will go by the steam boat & Doyle should pay the carriage & let me know what it comes to.[1]

Will you also send this letter to the Foreign Office.

[3] Frances Temple had married Capt. (afterwards Adm. of the Fleet Sir) William Bowles on 9 Aug. 1820.

[4] It is not known to what this refers.

[1] This letter seems to be referring to Philip Codd, who had been a Senior Clerk in the Correspondence Department, rather than to Harrison G. Codd, a Junior Clerk. Philip Codd had been compulsorily retired after twenty-eight years' service early in 1822 as part of Palmerston's economies. If the letter is correctly dated, therefore, it would seem to be referring to the internal redistribution of work following his retirement. Richard Brown was the Principal Clerk, that is the no. three in the office, and according to Foveaux, had been pensioned off at the same time as Codd, a particular favourite of Palmerston's. Brown took general charge of the arrears of accounts and succeeded Sulivan as Chief Examiner in 1826. Robert Lukin, the First Clerk, or no. two in the Correspondence Department, was one of several close relatives William Windham had placed in the office; another relative, James W. Lukin, had married a daughter of Merry's.

[1] George Doyle was the head messenger at the War Office.

142. *Catton.*[1] *23 Nov. 1823.*

We have had two very fair days' shooting though yesterday was by no means a fair day. Our party consists of the Granvilles, Littletons & Hay, Ld Melville's Secy.[2] Wilmot, Littleton & myself are going on tonight to Chatsworth to shoot tomorrow & Tuesday & I think I shall return to Hatfield on Wednesday. Ld Granville was taken the day before yesterday with an attack of gout which has completely tied him by the leg.

This place has some capability but requires a good deal of improvement. The house is a large square mass of the reddest brick placed on a flat near one branch of the sluggish Trent & at the extremity of what might with very little trouble be made a handsome park. The ground rises at a little distance from the house & the upper ground is clothed with plantations of various ages which will soon form into good woods. The shooting establishment is in its infancy but for a first season we have had a very tolerable sport & though pheasants are not numerous hares & rabbits abound.

The Duke of York is expected tomorrow at Ld Anglesea's at Beau Desert in this neighbourhood. I must be back in town on Friday morning because I am subpoenaed to a trial of Murray the late Life Guard Colonel against Genl Arabin & it comes on Saturday & I must have a talk with Merry on the subject before I can be prepared to go into court. I hope you are going on better [*?than*] in Hill Street.[3]

143. *Chatsworth. 25 Nov. 1823.*

I am very sorry to hear of poor Mr Pondret's[1] death because besides my regret for the loss of an apparently very deserving person I know

---

[1] Catton Hall was Wilmot Horton's place near Burton-on-Trent.

[2] *Cf.* Lady Granville to Devonshire, 24–25 Nov., F. Leveson Gower, ed., *Letters of Harriet Countess Granville 1810–1845*, 1894, i. 232–5. Edward John Littleton (afterwards Baron Hatherton) was apparently already a friend of Palmerston's. Robert William Hay (1786–1851) was Melville's private secretary at the Admiralty, 1812–25, and undersecretary at the Colonial Office, 1825–35.

[3] According to Palmerston to William Temple, 29 Oct. 1823 (B.P., G.C./TE no. 170), the Sulivans had already moved out of Hill St on account of the constant illness among them. When his father had threatened to sell Ponsborne House in 1809, Sulivan had told Palmerston that he did not care since it had been in the family only sixty or seventy years and in any case he could not 'endure the country' (28 July 1809, B.P., G.C./SU no. 17). Ponsborne was not sold until 1818. In the summer of 1823 Sulivan bought Broom House in Fulham, no doubt as a compromise between the unhealthiness of the West End and the boredom of the country. Palmerston reported that same year to his brother that the move 'had not served', but he subsequently reported differently (Bulwer & Ashley, i. 158), and Broom House remained the Sulivans' home.

[1] Not identified.

that it will have distressed you & Elizabeth. I am equally concerned to hear that Stephen's attacks grow more serious in their character & symptoms because whatever the cause of the disorder may be those effects are unpleasant & their increased severity proves that the cause be it what it may has not hitherto been successfully treated. I hope to hear better accounts but I own your note of yesterday makes me uneasy.

We came on here on Sunday night; our party consists of Wm Ponsonby, Wortley & Ly Caroline, Miss Stewart, Littleton, Sr Joseph Copley, Wilmot & myself.[2] Ld Granville was so lame with the gout that he & Ly Granville remained at Catton. The shooting is so good here that I shall stay tomorrow & next day & I shall set off after shooting on Thursday & get to town on Friday afternoon. Yesterday I killed with my own gun 51 head, today our sport was not quite so good & I killed only 18 head. The alterations & additions which the Duke is making here are upon a most magnificent scale & when completed seven years hence will make the house one of the best & most splendid in the kingdom, but at a cost of about 100,000.

144. *War Office. 14 Feb. 1824.*

If I mistake not you seemed to think that you could not well spare this man, but let me know if I am right in so supposing.

I have not yet given final instructions about the new List but I am satisfied that the Ex[amine]r was a higher offr than First Clerk as to nature of duties & degree of personal responsibility & that latterly at least he stood first in the List though in earlier periods the First Clerk stood the first.[1]

I hope your colds are better and that you find Stephen on the whole making progress in recovery. We are at slack water in the House but next week we shall begin to do some business, & my Estimates come on next Friday. I have been out twice with the King's hounds yesterday & yesterday week:—capital runs both days;

---

[2] William Ponsonby was probably the friend who later became 1st Baron de Mauley. James Archibald Stuart-Wortley-Mackenzie, afterwards 1st Baron Wharncliffe, was married to a daughter of Earl Erne. Sir Joseph Copley (1769–1839), 3rd Bart, later became father-in-law to the 3rd Earl Grey. Miss Stewart was Granville's natural daughter by Lady Bessborough; in 1824 she married George Godolphin Osborne, afterwards 8th Duke of Leeds. There was also a George Stewart who acted as private secretary to his father.

[1] With the appointment of the three Superintendents of Military Accounts in 1809, the office of Chief Examiner had become superfluous and on the retirement of George Collings in 1817 it had been left unfilled. But Palmerston subsequently decided to meet the demands of economy by eliminating the offices of Superintendent instead. In 1824 the last of the Superintendents was eliminated by reviving the office of Chief Examiner and giving it to Sulivan.

yesterday from Longford near Colnbrook to Watford in Herts, 15 miles from point to point—Thomas[*?'s*] horse performing beautifully, & (*tell Shee*) much improved by a snaffle.

The Duke of Wellington's acct of the quarrel between Rice & O'Grady is that the latter told the former that Ld Limerick was an honest man, for he is quite sure that that is the only assertion with respect to Limerick that any man of honour could retract.[2]

145. *Stanhope St. 26 Feb. 1824.*

From typescript; MS. not found.

Did I give you the sheet return of the arrear accounts; if I did will you send it to me.

[*PS.*] Estimates went off like smoke from a steam engine or Shee from Weymouth.

146. *Monday evening [?29 Mar. 1824].*[1]

I saw Seguier, he thinks the Netchers to be by the best master of that name & thinks them worth 25 or 30 £ each; the picture of Sir William Temple without a number Christie had discovered; Seguier thinks it an original Sir Peter Lely and worth probably about 50 £. My directions to him are to bid for any of the lots 2, 3, 10, 12, 13, 14, 15, that go cheap: they have no great value as works of art, but I should like to have them; as to the pictures he is to buy lot 25 (two copies) if it goes cheap, lot 29 if it does not go for more than about 25 £, it is evidently a relation & perhaps I could find out who. Lots 42, 43, 45, 53, if they go for little; lots 65, 66, 67 if they do not go extravagantly dear, & he is to bid for the unnumbered Sir William as far as about 50 £. If lot 29 goes dear, he is to skip 42, 43, 45 & 53, & reserve his fire for 65.[2]

[*PS.*] I will dine with you tomorrow if you dine at home.

[2] Thomas Spring Rice (afterwards 1st Baron Monteagle) was married to a daughter of the 1st Earl of Limerick. A Mr Waller O'Grady had apparently insulted Lord Limerick and a duel with Spring Rice was supposed to follow. But the intervention of the police gave time for an accommodation to be made (*The Times*, 14 Feb.).
[1] The MS. is endorsed Mar. 1824; the sale to which it refers was to take place on 30 Mar.
[2] The sale was of a major part of the classical marbles and family pictures collected at Moor Park, in Farnham, Surrey, by Sir William Temple (1628–99). John Seguier was a notable London expert. In B.P.W. there are a copy of Christie's catalogue and a fuller list obtained some time earlier from the owner, Mr Kenrick Bacon, whose

147. *Broadlands. 20 April 1824.*

I am very glad to hear so good an account of Elizabeth, but extremely sorry to have so bad a one of Stephen. It is very distressing that he should fall ill again just as he was beginning to recover his health & strength, & it is the more annoying as the disorder with which he is threatened is one generally of long continuance. I shall be anxious for further accounts.

148. *Hatfield. 7 Jan. 1825.*

Give me back this card when you have looked it over.[1] I think it is no bad report of progress & proves that Brown has been at work.

I shall be in town tomorrow & shall go down on Sunday morning. The D. of Wellington & Ld Melville cannot come, but I hope that Peel & Huskisson & Esterhazy will. Have you a mind to run down with me I could take you on Sunday & what is more could lodge you at Bds without the assistance of the White Horse.[2]

You were much regretted at Cambridge. We had some very pleasant parties, & I found things looking very prosperous. The Speaker will probably not stand; his friends there have taken amiss his summer excursion to the continent with Mrs Purvis; which certainly was an ill-advised measure for so big a wig.[3]

---

ancestor, Nicholas Bacon, had married a grandaughter of Sir William. Palmerston's accompanying notes and correspondence show that he got most of what he wanted either at the sale or subsequently, together with some portraits not included in the sale direct from Mr Bacon, for a total expenditure, according to his separate accounts, of £278. 15s. 0d. These included: from the sale, the Lely of Sir William for £21, a child by Netscher for £10. 10s. 0d. (Lot 29) and two further Netschers, one of which was another portrait of Sir William, for £81. 18s. 0d. (Lot 65); and direct from Mr Bacon, further portraits by Lely, Dahl and Cornelius Jansen of Sir William's parents and brother, who were direct ancestors of Palmerston's.

[1] Presumably a statement of the progress made in winding up the last remnants of arrears in the War Office accounts.

[2] In Romsey.

[3] Charles Manners-Sutton (1780–1845), Speaker of the House of Commons, 1817–35, and afterwards 1st Viscount Canterbury, had contemplated contesting the other university seat in Nov. 1822. As a 'Protestant' Tory and a Trinity man, as the son of the Archbishop of Canterbury and cousin of the Duke of Rutland, he had considerable advantages. But he squandered them by running off with Mrs Purves, the notorious sister of the notorious Lady Blessington. Manners-Sutton was a widower; but Mr Purves did not die until 1827. The delinquents were married the following year.

149. *Stanhope St. 8 Jan. 1825.*

I am sorry you cannot come but if you & Eliz. should either or both of you find yourselves able to come I have room for either or both. Eliz. might like to take out the last of William.[1]

I send you the enclosed to read because I am sure this picture of rural felicity enjoyed by your friend Halliday[2] must gratify & amuse you.

150. *Stanhope St. 8 Aug. 1825.*

The call is for 10£ a share & I therefore return you this draught.[1]

If sailing is your occupation you will not be baulked by want of that primum mobile wind. I hope the blowing you will have will do you both good & that you will prolong your stay till you are turned out of doors.[2] You see I did them pretty handsomely at Salisbury, having won five out of the eight races that were run there, & have got a cup that exactly matches the Southampton one.[3]

151. *Tuesday evening, 23 Aug. [1825].*

I arrived here[1] this evening & shall embark tomorrow morning at six per steam for Dublin. All the sailing packets by the bye are given up, and as if to add insult to injury the only two vessels of that sort which remained were at last turned into *colliers* to supply the steamers with fuel. The road through Wales when completed will really be worthy of that great continental *highwayman* Buonaparte. But it is not quite completed & the bridge over the Menai will not be passable till this time next year; the two abutments are nearly finished and the chains are bedded into the rock at each end. I went over to see Blenheim from Middleton. The house is getting into bad repair & there are a plentiful scarcity of servants in it, but the Duke is enlarging his flower garden & has 30 men constantly employed in his garden;

---

[1] According to the *Courier* of 17 Jan. there was a large party at Broadlands, including on 15 Jan. the Duke of York, Peel and Huskisson as well as William Temple and the Bowleses. Shortly afterwards several of them, including Palmerston, were at a similar shooting party at Stratfield Saye (*Arbuthnot Journal*, i. 371).

[2] Sir Andrew Halliday (1789–1839) was a physician with military connections.

[1] Sulivan evidently joined Palmerston in his unfortunate Stock Market speculations of 1825. The call was for a second instalment on their shares in the Cornwall and Devon Mining Co. (Palmerston to William Temple, 5 Aug., Bulwer & Ashley, i. 157).

[2] The Sulivans were at the Flemings' near Southampton (*ibid.*, i. 158).

[3] See Palmerston to William Temple, 8 Aug., *ibid.*, i. 159–60.

[1] Probably Holyhead.

but his plants were advertised for sale under an execution a little while ago so that plant as he may he is not quite sure of reposing under the shade of his own fig tree.

[*PS.*] Will you send this packet of books to Stanhope Street. There is no use in lugging *Red Gauntlet* about when he is done. I cannot say that he entertained me as much as the rest of his predecessors have done.

152. *Sligo. 2 Sept. 1825.*

I send you two packets which I wish you would take care of for me till I return to town; they contain my Welsh Iron shares which I had left with the secretary before I went away, to have inserted in them the receipts for the last instalment, & which have been sent to me here by mistake, and so much iron is too heavy an article to be dragged about all the country.[1]

153. *Cliffony.[1] 12 Sept. 1825.*

I am still here & shall continue here another day or two. I then return to Sligo for a couple of days & thence back to Dublin, my further motions are unsettled. I have here Nimmo the engineer, an Aberdeen man, a keen, shrewd, ingenious Scotchman, accused by the practical antitheorists of our side, of the crime of being too speculative, anglice of thinking & inventing, and suspected by the Whigs of holding heretical doctrines upon certain points in Political Economy. I have however found him hitherto a very ingenious & useful counsellor and I trust that he & I, as the organ blower said, will succeed in making very considerable improvements both in the value of my property and in the condition of my tenantry; of course, the full execution of our plans must be the work of some time but I am convinced that no good is to be done in the way of such improvements without striking off at first a large outline, which you may fill up afterwards as means & time will allow.

I have upon this part of my estate about 1500 Irish or nearly 2000 English acres of unprofitable bog, and I think we see our way, through a vista of a certain length to be true, to the conversion of the whole of it into land as good as any I have. My harbour goes

---

[1] The Welsh Iron and Coal Co. was another speculative investment of Palmerston and Sulivan.

[1] The principal village on Palmerston's Sligo estates.

on well though slowly, but the natural position is a security against failure & insures its success.[2]

I began this letter a few days ago at Cliffony from whence I returned yesterday having made a voyage in my way to Ennismurray, an island on the coast which belongs to me. I go tomorrow to Cooper's the c[ount]y member[3] & on to Dublin on Monday. I shall probably be at Powys Castle for a day on Friday & mean then to stretch across to Ferrybridge for a day & thence come down to Bds.

Your very discreet & mysterious inuendo letter about slate does not much surprise me. I suppose you had a quarrel between Barret & Wilks: the latter I am sure is a bit of a rogue if nature writes a legible hand, at the same time he is a clever fellow & as long as his interest goes hand in hand with ours will probably do well by us. I shall not fail to look at the works in my way.[4]

154. *Broadlands. 24 Oct. 1825.*

I have written a letter to Raper which will settle the matter I trust, highly complimentary to him, but pointing out what nonsense his objections are; if two detachments of the same corps are brought together the senior officer must take the command; and the Foreign Branch has long ago & much for its advantage been declared an integral part of the office.[1]

[2] Palmerston had made at least two visits to Ireland since 1808, in 1813 and 1824, and though little is known about them he evidently on each occasion set some improvements in train on his estates, including the construction of a pier and harbour at Mullaghmore. On his 1824 visit he seems to have engaged Alexander Nimmo (1783–1832) to survey his uncultivated bog lands. Nimmo recommended that Palmerston build a short line of railway from Mullaghmore to the peat bogs in order to carry sand to the bogs and peat for export from the harbour. But though he favoured it at first, Palmerston seems in the end to have preferred to go on building and improving roads. He built houses, inns and schools, brought hundreds of acres of bog under cultivation and tried to encourage the local fishing and manufacturing industries. He spent very large sums of money but the work seemed endless. Mullaghmore harbour in particular defied all of Palmerston's expenditure and optimism and all the efforts of Nimmo and his successor, Robert Stevenson.

[3] Edward Synge Cooper of Markree Castle was M.P. for Sligo until his death in 1830.

[4] Samuel Barrett Moulton Barrett was M.P. for Richmond and chairman of the Welsh Slate Co. John Wilks (*ob.* 1846), another M.P., was solicitor for the Welsh Slate Co., the Welsh Iron and Coal Co, and the Cornwall and Devon Mining Co. Palmerston was a major shareholder and a director of all three. His doubts about Wilks's honesty were all too well founded. The Slate Co.'s quarries were at Tan y Bwlch, near Portmadoc.

[1] Charles Chamier Raper was the clerk in charge of the arrears of foreign soldiers formerly in British service. As the work on the British arrears had been going so well a number of clerks had been transferred to accelerate the work on the foreign arrears. Shortly afterwards the whole of Richard Brown's section was transferred. Raper evidently felt it all reflected in some way on his competence and resented in particular Brown's taking over as the more senior in rank. There is a copy

155. *Stanhope St. 20 Nov. 1825.*

I am going down to Brighton for a couple of days. Send my letters there till you hear from me again, direct to the Post Office.

156. *Stanhope St. 2 Dec. 1825.*

B.P., G.C./SU no. 30; cf. Bulwer & Ashley, i. 164.

Although the General Election is not due until the following summer, Palmerston has just heard that two other candidates have already opened a canvass in Cambridge and consequently he writes to Sulivan asking his opinion, particularly in reference to the Catholic question, of the enclosed election circular, now in the S.P.:

Stanhope St. Dec. 1825.

An active canvass for the representation of the University of Cambridge in the next Parliament having already been commenced I hope it will not be thought premature in me, if I thus early solicit a renewal of that confidence with which I have so long been honoured.

In performing those duties in Parliament which the choice of the University devolved upon me, it has been my earnest endeavour faithfully to guard the interests of my constituents, and steadily and honestly to pursue upon all occasions that course, which appeared to me best calculated to promote the welfare of the Empire, and to maintain and strengthen our Constitution in Church and State.

I trust that I am not too sanguine when I indulge a hope that I may again enjoy the distinguished honour of representing the University in Parliament, and I beg most earnestly to solicit the favour of your vote and interest.

I have the Honour to be

Sir,

Your very obedient

Humble servant

157. *Cambridge. 4 Dec. 1825.*

B.P., G.C./SU no. 31; cf. Bulwer & Ashley, i. 184–6.

Palmerston reports the progress of his canvass in St John's and Trinity, where, despite all the other candidates—Bankes, John Singleton Copley (the Attorney-General and afterwards Baron Lyndhurst) and Henry Goulburn (the

---

of Palmerston's 'complimentary' letter of 20 Oct. to Raper in the Palmerston Papers, Add. MS. 48420.

Irish Secretary)—being Trinity men, he believes he has the support of the majority of its members. The manuscript continues with a postscript:

I had a long note today from Trench which must have been written three days ago, & dated from Radnor about his cursed quay![1] I wonder what people are made of.

158. *St John's. 9 Dec. 1825.*

I am going on extremely well & as far as the residents are concerned shall have a large majority, and at all events they are on the spot, and one vote here is worth two promises elsewhere.[1] I shall finish tomorrow morning & return to town I think tomorrow evening. My strength lies in St John's, Trinity, Christ's; Peterhouse, Emmanuel & Clare are mostly against me & in the other colleges I stand well.

The Attorney General makes way & Bankes loses ground very fast.

159. *Stanhope St. 31 Dec. 1824 [1825].*

We are doing well at Cambridge, & have a very active committee. With few exceptions all those whose support is worth having are with me. But the clergymen are terribly Protestant. The Whigs are cordial, & there is this in my favor that Hervey & Scarlett together, being both Catholics polled more than Bankes by a good many. If the election is later than the Commencement the inceptors of this year will come into play & I shall be strong among them; the Catholic Question has always been carried in the Union, the enlarged Fusty. Your speculations about Liverpool are too refined. He simply will not stir or do *anything*, so at least I infer from having heard nothing from Lushington.[1] I wrote to the Chancellor as a bit of fun the letter of which I inclose a copy & send you his answer which is just what I

[1] Palmerston's 'Analysis of Expenditure from 1818 downwards' (B.P.W.) shows that he contributed £50 towards the provision of technical drawings for Col. Trench's Thames Embankment scheme.

[1] But he wrote to George Canning on 22 Dec.: 'I have met with the greatest success among the resident members at Cambridge and among the London voters, but the number of these bears so small a proportion to the 1,600 who have their names on the boards that it is impossible for me not to feel much uneasiness as to the possible result of the contest, until I have been able to ascertain the sentiments of the out-voters. A great majority of the non-residents are country clergymen and it remains to be seen to what extent the anti-Catholic feeling can be excited among them.' (George Canning Papers, Leeds Public Library.)

[1] Stephen Rumbold Lushington (1776–1868) was Joint Secretary of the Treasury, 1824–7.

expected & an amusing specimen of his hypocritical humbug; as to his retirement he will be as long making up his mind to resign as to give judgements & will be surprised by the agonies of death in the agonies of doubt.[2]

I returned last night & go back on Monday or Tuesday. I have about 210 promises & can reckon near 20 other votes as certain though not actually promised but 500 will be little enough to insure success & we have a long way yet to go.

[*PS.*] I am inclined to suspect that my friend the D. of York was the prime instigator of the Atty Genl, & if this is so it accounts in some

[2] Having become only too well aware that several members of the Government were very far from giving him their support in Cambridge, Palmerston had written some rather pointed letters to those he most distrusted. The first he seems to have picked upon was the Chancellor, perhaps because Eldon was not only a notorious anti-Catholic but also a close relation of Bankes by marriage. Palmerston's 'bit of fun' went in part: 'Your first wishes must of course be for my colleague Bankes; but I trust that I am not mistaken in hoping that your Oxford predisposition towards sitting members and your official feeling towards a member of the Government who has so long been in possession of his seat, may give me upon this occasion the second place in your good wishes.' Eldon's 'hypocritical humbug' of a reply, undated and delayed by gout, began 'The report was so current that we were to have you in the House of Lords that your letter rather surprised me', and after having pleaded the conflicting claims of the candidates upon him and the lack of any influence at Cambridge, admitted to a 'natural wish' for Bankes's success while disclaiming any 'actual active influence'. 'I think I must be passive', Eldon concluded; 'I am not aware that I would do you any good, be assured I have no inclination to do anything adverse.' (Palmerston to Eldon, 26 Dec. 1825, and Eldon to Palmerston, n.d., B.P., G.C./EL no. 1.)

Palmerston must have sent a similarly ingenuous inquiry in the direction of another anti-Catholic, the Colonial Secretary, Lord Bathurst. For Bathurst wrote on 10 Jan. 1826 that while he felt the University owed it to Palmerston's long service to return him, his own 'little interest' must go to Goulburn with whom he had had a long official connection in the Colonial Office (B.P.W.). For some reason this response rather than Eldon's seems to have annoyed Palmerston who sent a very sharp reply on 12 Jan. (H.M.C., *Report on the Manuscripts of Earl Bathurst*, 1923, p. 598). But he sent both his colleagues' letters with a long complaint to Liverpool on 20 Jan. (Palmerston took great pains with this letter. There are a much amended draft and a fair copy, both dated 19 Jan., in B.P.W. The copy has been printed in A. Aspinall and E. A. Smith, eds., *English Historical Documents 1783–1832*, 1959, xi. 105–8. But the letter sent, now in the Perkins Library, Duke University, is dated 20 Jan.)

To Palmerston's complaint that at the very least the Government's neutrality on the Catholic question was being breached, the Prime Minister replied on 23 Jan. that though himself a 'Protestant' he had in 1822 personally supported a 'Catholic' relation (Hervey) against a more distant anti-Catholic one (Bankes) and that in the present case, as both Bankes and Goulburn were relatives—very distant ones in fact—the most the sitting members could expect was 'an explicit declaration that I was of opinion that they ought not to be disturbed & that I should take no active part in soliciting votes for anyone'. Moreover, he went on, 'the elections for the University have always been considered as standing on distinct grounds from any other elections. They are contests for personal distinction ... [*and*] it is not unnatural that the Universities should feel a particular interest in the Roman Catholic Question ... I admit that there is a great difference between electing a member for the first time & declining to reelect him:— but for this you must blame the principle upon which the University of Cambridge think proper to act, which I have always considered as rendering a seat for that University one of the least desirable seats in the Kingdom.' (B.P.W.)

degree for Liverpool's shabbiness though it only makes his conduct the more shabby.[3]

160. *Stanhope St. 8 Jan. 1826.*

I only returned at an early hour this morning—I am going on well but very *piano*. I have got about 300 actual promises and perhaps 30 more expectations which may be reckoned almost as good as promises —but the general complexion of affairs is good. The Popery panic is dying away within the University. The Atty Genl is the strongest in the aggregate, having had some day this last week 340 promises. Bankes I understand is not making way; his numbers I cannot learn, but the general impression at Cambridge is that he has got nearly as much strength as he ever will. Of Goulburn I do not hear much; his numbers were about 150 some days ago. Among the residents I am first, attorney next & I conjecture Bankes & Goulburn nearly equal. I should *think* that I am equal to Bankes in the aggregate, but I have as I said no accurate information as to his numbers. The Johnians are zealous & active, & the few resident *Dissenters* are beginning to *conform*. The Trinity men are doing well, & the Whigs are helping me but from this time foward each vote must be picked up singly; & the majority if I get one, built up vote by vote. Cludde is for; Mortimer against. The two Clives & Swainson with me, but Wm Clive adverse. I will be with you at a little before seven today.[1]

161. *Stanhope St. 15 Jan. 1826.*

I can easily defer sending my notes till after I return from you this evening, but I confess I do not see the force of your objection; I am perfectly convinced that without a committee I am defeated and that nothing but the cordial & active assistance of the Whigs can effectually aid me even by means of a committee. My desire to

[3] The Duke of York was taking a very active part against Palmerston and for Copley. Palmerston knew that the other Joint Secretary of the Treasury, J. C. Herries, had got the Foreign Office to frank some of Copley's canvassing letters. What he probably did not know was that it was also Herries who had prompted the Duke. (Canning to Palmerston, 21 Dec., B.P., G.C./CA no. 79; Peel to Goulburn, 24 Nov., Peel Papers, Add. MS. 40331.)

[1] Both Shee and Sulivan, as well as Palmerston, had put pressure on Fitzherbert and, probably, Cludde. These two old 'Protestant' Johnians compromised by supporting Palmerston and the anti-Catholic Bankes. (Palmerston to Fitzherbert, 21 Dec., Cludde to Fitzherbert, 27 Dec. 1825, Shee to Fitzherbert, 3 Jan., and Sulivan to Fitzherbert, 7 June 1826, Fitzherbert Papers.) Hans Sanders Mortimer (*ob.* 1846) was a former fellow-commoner at St John's. Christopher Swainson (1775–1854) was the Clives' former family tutor. William Clive (1795–1883) was a cousin of Palmerston's friend.

succeed is I confess increased by the wish to frustrate an underhand Protestant cabal and on this occasion those who support me are my friends be they Whig or Tory; and if you want people to help you, you do not go the best way to work by shewing that you receive their aid distrustfully or reluctantly.

[*PS.*] There is inconvenience no doubt in being driven to the Opposition for support, but I see no distinction worth drawing between courting them personally & by letter, and having them as members of my committee.[1]

162. *Broadlands.*[1] *29 Jan. 1826.*

Add. MSS.

I send you a list of additional promises received by me, & also Henslow's Cambridge report.[2] I have now got down 458 in my book, and about 180 more names of probables & possibles which I have sent to Henslow to correct.

I am on the whole rather sorry that you wrote to Dean as it has produced the inclosed letter from Copley which it is difficult to answer, without either going into a useless altercation with him, or appearing to shrink from expressing to him opinions which I have strongly expressed to others. I have however sent him an answer of which I inclose a copy in which I think I have steered clear of both, but I have not found it easy to please myself. There could be no possible use in entering *now* with him into a statement of grievance; and yet to express general satisfaction at his explanation which explains & denies nothing would be impossible.[3]

[1] Sulivan, as usual, managed Palmerston's committee in London, with William Bowles acting for him when he was obliged to go to Cambridge. In London they also had the assistance of Henry Elliot and Michael Bruce. (Mrs Sulivan to William Temple, 16 June 1826, B.P.W.) Possibly it was Bruce to whom Sulivan objected; more probably it was the Whigs in Cambridge. In Cambridge Wood probably still assisted Palmerston, but he was growing lukewarm on account of the Catholic question and the most active organiser would seem, from Palmerston's accounts and expenses, to have been the Bursar of St John's, Charles Blick. Palmerston was also in active communication with such notable Cambridge Whigs as Professors William Whewell and J. S. Henslow. It is not clear, however, if there was a joint committee. But some of the Cambridge Whigs, too, found their new alliance rather strange (Professor Sedgwick to W. Ainger, 29 Dec. 1825, *Sedgwick*, i. 268).
[1] 'Where', Palmerston explained to Copley on 29 Jan., 'I have taken refuge for a few days from the labours of canvassing.' (B.P.W.)
[2] Lacking.
[3] Copley had written to say that, having heard from a supporter canvassed for Palmerston by a Mr Dean that Sulivan had suggested the Attorney-General had come forward against Palmerston, he wished to remind Palmerston that in 1822 he had intended to contest the seat subsequently gained by Bankes, that it was therefore Bankes he was now opposing, and that he had 'not in the slightest degree interfered

I wish you would send the inclosed to John Thoroton I do not know his address—it is to thank him.[4] We had an excellent day's sport yesterday & shall do well I hope tomorrow.

163. *Stanhope St. 20 April 1826.*

I am sorry to hear that Elizabeth has knocked herself up but I hope that a little care & quiet will set her right again, especially as I trust that from the precautions you have taken about Harry his attack will be more mild than Stephen's & will not cause you so much anxiety.

I am going to the Iron meeting & will let you know the result.[1]

164. *Sun Inn [Cambridge]. Monday [12 June 1826].*
    Add. MSS.

I arrived here by ½ past 7 this morning, & have been on foot a good part of the day; I found all the other three [*candidates*] here but few voters arrived, though a great many have been coming in during the course of the day. Bankes has been writing some violent letter to Goulburn which he is now shewing about & in which he again urged the comparison of strength for the retirement of the weakest; but which proposition Goulburn of course rejected.[1] A great deal of angry feeling has been created between the Goulburnites & Bankites which is so far in our favor, and it also will prove favourable to Goulburn; some of Copley's second votes who meant to go for Bankes say he has behaved so ill that they will vote for Goulburn. There is in short a general feeling in the University that Bankes's behaviour to Goulburn has been ungentlemanlike & unfair. We have got some few additional votes & not many additional defaulters. Some very distant men have arrived, Sir John Douglas of Spring Park, & Halton from the north[2] & they left behind them a batch of votes waiting for horses. Henslow has written to you, & sent you a list of additional declarations. Our travelling arrangements work out very well & we have stuck up in

---

with the interests or expressed an opinion or a wish in favour of either of the other candidates'. (B.P.W.) Palmerston had therefore sent the reply whose essence is quoted by T. Martin, *A Life of Lord Lyndhurst*, 1884, p. 207, n. 1.
    [4] John Thoroton was a former pensioner of Trinity and a connection of Rutland's.
    [1] The Welsh Iron and Coal Co. had also run into trouble.
    [1] See *Sedgwick*, i. 276–7.
    [2] This seems to identify the John James Douglas in *Alumni Cantab.* as Sir James Scott-Douglas, 3rd Bart of Springwood Park, Roxburghshire (1792–1836). Immanuel Halton was a clergyman from Derbyshire.

the old committee room a board with the rates to be paid for horses, places, etc.[3] Bankes has been bringing his people up & evidently means to make a push tomorrow. Goulburn is not quite so strong in men up. We shall keep pretty near them. I am writing in the committee room with a dozen people talking to me and the post is just going out but I have nothing particular to say; I think we shall do well. Bankes looks very downcast & I am sure we shall beat him.

[*PS.*] We have been negotiating about exchanges with Copley & Goulburn but not with Bankes.

165. *Sun Inn* [*Cambridge*]. *10* [*p.m.*] *Tuesday* [*13 June 1826*].[1]
Add. MSS.

The poll is just closed for tonight

Copley — — —	319
Pal. — — —	239
Bank. — — —	222
Goulb. — — —	203

We have kept back our votes as much as possible. Bankes & Goulburn have pressed on theirs as much as they could. Copley has let his alone. I think he will decidedly lead & I am equally convinced in my own mind that we shall beat Bankes. I judge more from the defeated faces of Bankes & his friends than anything else. Paynter & Brand pro-

---

[3] The correspondence relating to the 1806 and 1807 elections (see nos. 23, 39, 41) shows that Teignmouth, i. 303, is wrong in saying that Bankes had in 1822 'introduced the payment of voters' travelling expenses'. Probably Bankes, who was rich, had refused to agree to the sort of limitation arranged between the committees in 1807. The account given in *Sedgwick*, i. 277–8, therefore seems more likely, that while the candidates had for some years past paid the expenses of non-resident voters, Bankes had spent 'a vast sum' in 1822 and, inevitably, caused all the candidates to be swindled. Since matters threatened to be even worse in 1826, an attempt was made to get the committees to compromise, but Bankes refused even to discuss it. Palmerston's 'Analysis of Expenditure from 1818 downwards' (B.P.W.) shows his expenditure as follows:

	£	s.	d.
Coleman, committee room	111.	8.	11.
Wiltshire, messenger	24.	4.	4.
Hire of stage coaches	131.	0.	6.
Monk, Waltham Cross horses	63.	7.	6.
Price, Ware	68.	5.	0.
Crawley, Buntingford	59.	12.	6.
Pitt, Royston	83.	13.	6.
Clough, chaise	1.	4.	0.
Blick, Cambridge expenses	181.	1.	8.
King, lithographing letters	28.	18.	4.
Total	752.	16.	3.

[1] The first of what were intended to be three days of polling.

posed the bribery oath which has been taken by every voter all day. The greatest indignation has been felt at this by all & at last when dinner had rouzed minds to more than morning calmness it broke out & we had a scene in the Senate House which ended in a tumultuous debate round the Vice Chancellor's table which Price of Downing at length mounted, the Vice Chancellor having retired. The proposers then gave up their oath & the polling continued the last hour without it.[2]

166. *Stanhope St. 15 Aug.* [*1826*].
    Add. MSS.

I suppose Fisher has told you that he has succeeded in getting Wilks to assign over to us all his interest in the Mines for 200£. This is a grand stroke for though I never feared any serious or ultimate danger from Wilks yet it is a great relief to have extinguished him intirely.[1]

167. *Dublin. 23 Sept. 1826.*

I arrived here at 4 today after a good journey & fair passage, rather rollypoly & some of the party suffering, though I escaped. I go on to Shee's tomorrow, shall stay with him Monday & probably Tuesday & go on to Sligo on Wednesday. Go on directing to Dublin till you hear to the contrary from me. Menai Bridge looked grand in the dark, & must be magnificent by day light.

---

[2] According to *Sedgwick*, i. 278, since Bankes had refused to discuss payment of voters' expenses, Henslow and the Master of Corpus Christi, John Lamb, had drawn up a 'recommendation' against it and this was signed by 102 members of the Senate, seven heads of colleges and ten professors including Sedgwick himself. Evidently encouraged by this, two other members of the Senate insisted that the bribery oath should be administered to each elector as he came to the Vice-Chancellor's table. These two were evidently former students of Trinity, John Brand and, probably, Thomas Paynter, a barrister and an expert on election practices. Samuel Grove Price (1793–1839) was afterwards M.P. for Sandwich. At Bankes's insistence the poll was kept open for a further day, but the result, on 16 June, was: Copley, 772; Palmerston, 631; Bankes, 508; Goulburn, 437.

[1] Lord William Powlett (afterwards 3rd Duke of Cleveland), whose family owned the land the Cornwall and Devon Co. had been formed to exploit and who was himself a shareholder and director in that company, wrote to Brougham on 2 Feb. 1827 (Brougham Papers) that J. H. Fisher (of Fisher and Rhodes of Davies St), who was Palmerston's 'private solicitor', had taken over as company solicitor when it was found that Wilks had been 'acting improperly'.

168. *Dunmore.*[1] *25 Sept. 1826.*

Upon this note the application may be considered as withdrawn & the papers may be put away with a mem. to that effect.

I arrived here late last night & found Shee & his lady prospering, the place a regular *Irish* place, & of course therefore wholly deficient in those circumstances of neatness, finish & comfort to which Englishmen are accustomed, & in fact it consists of a house & no place at all; but the house (for an *Irish* one again) is not a bad one, as it contains two very good rooms on the ground floor each of them nearly as big as the whole of Mudeford Hall; and the place will be, when it is made not ugly, & indeed may, when certain plantations which are now only in contemplation shall have grown to a good size, be rather pretty. The estate however is a very good one, contains 10 or 11,000 English acres, & Shee seems managing it very sensibly & judiciously & with great success; it has given him an object of interesting occupation, health & comfort and I do not know when I have seen him look so well & so happy. He is doing a great deal of good to his tenants while he is very materially increasing his own income; and the annual visits which he will certainly make to this place will be of great advantage both to him & to the neighbourhood. She (with one e) is much more rational than I have ever seen her before & greatly improved in health; I say nothing about looks. Fat John is the admiration of the country and they all long to visit the land which can produce such thriving bipeds. I go on to Sligo on Wednesday.

169. *Cliffony. 2 [possibly 1] Oct. 1826.*

Is this Catherine Boileau's husband?[1] I have been tolerably lucky in weather since I have been here & have been greatly pleased with

---

[1] Dunmore was the Shees' family place in Co. Galway. Probably it was entailed and came directly to Shee upon his father's death in Dec. 1825. But the English property, including Lockleys, a place near Welwyn that his father had bought in 1814, had passed to his mother. Shee endeavoured to persuade the Dowager Lady Shee that his father would have altered his will had he lived a little longer and that she had discretion in any case to pass Lockleys to him. But upon her death in 1838 it passed to his sister and her husband, Robert Dering. Mudeford Hall was a place near Christchurch, Hampshire, that Shee had rented in 1813, in order to get his wife away from her parents, he said. When his father objected on the ground of expense, he was told Mudeford would cost only 160 guineas a year; what Shee neglected to say, according to Palmerston, was that his father-in-law was paying for it. Evidently the elder Shee had misunderstood his daughter-in-law's prospects and, though she may have been one of ten children, they were all girls it would seem and she the eldest of them. (George Shee to Sir George Shee, 25 and 26 Jan. 1813, and George Shee to his mother, 13 Dec. 1825, Shee Papers; Palmerston to William Temple, 5 Aug. 1817, B.P., G.C./TE no. 141.)

[1] The 1st Earl of Minto's youngest daughter had married on 14 Nov. 1825 John Peter Boileau, afterwards 1st Bart.

the progress of my various improvements since I was here last year. My harbour is getting on well & I have about 40 acres which were wet bog last year at this time & which now are growing turnips, potatoes & rape. The people too are beginning to understand how to labour & that is the first step in civilization.

You seem by your account to have attained a very high state in that condition but why do you not send from Brown or Lukin.

170. *Cliffony. 6 Oct. 1826.*

If you think the inclosed memorandum will do, give it out forthwith for the satisfaction of Brown, & return me a copy of it with Merry's draught & memorandum. I shall stay another day here & then return to Sligo. I have been very prosperous here till the evening when returning across the sands of Mullaghmore late in the dusk & the wind blowing strong off shore my poor hat grew frisky, quitted my crown & went off at such a pace that it got out of sight before I could catch it; this where a hat cannot be had within twelve miles is a bore.

171. *Sligo. 15 Oct. 1826.*

You were quite right about the militia clothing; I had settled with Peel that the unserviceable part should be given to the relief committees instead of being returned to store. I have finished all my business here & am going tomorrow to Ld Belmore's near Enniskillen & from thence round by Londonderry, the Giants' Causeway & Belfast to Dublin. I have never seen the North of Ireland & have long wished to do so. This will probably take me a week; so go on directing to Dublin till you hear from me to the contrary.

There is a good deal of animosity & ferment all over the country arising out of the elections & that detestable Catholic Question. I wonder whether the Govt & Parliament will ever find out that so long as a people think only of quarrelling & fighting between themselves they cannot advance in industry & prosperity, & that internal concord is necessary for national wealth as well as foreign peace.

172. *Londonderry. 20 Oct. 1826.*

I shall probably leave Dublin on *Friday next*, & therefore do not send any more letters to me at Dublin after you receive this letter but keep them till you hear from me again; as I cannot at present exactly arrange where I can be hit on given days.

I left Sligo on Monday & went to Ld Belmore's place called Castle Coole near Enniskillen, a very magnificent palace built by his father upon a plan by old Wyatt who never was at the place, and faced with stone brought from the Isle of Portland. I staid there Tuesday & Wednesday; & yesterday came along the northern bank of Loch Ern to Ballyshannon & thence to Donegal, & today by Stranerland & Strabane to this place; my motions not very rapid, as I had to take the same horses the whole way from Enniskillen to Strabane, a distance of 68 Irish miles or nearly 90 English; at every place where I had intended to change I was promised horses the next morning if I would remain the night, but at Donegal where I did sleep that promise was not made good. The weather has been for some time, indeed for the last fortnight, cold & rainy, with now & then a fine day, but that is a pretty fair account of Irish weather at all times. I go on to Coleraine tomorrow, shall from thence visit the Causeway & so go by Belfast to Dublin.

[*PS.*] By some mistake of Strachan's[1] I have found no letters here & have received none since those which reached Sligo last Sunday; I suppose I shall find them at Coleraine.

173. *Dublin. 27 Oct. 1826.*

I arrived here yesterday afternoon, having been rather longer than I had expected in going round the North of Ireland; I wished to see the country & therefore did not travel after dark. I was much pleased with the coast from the Giants' Causeway to Belfast; parts of it on the shores of Antrim are very fine & bold. I had a beautiful day for the Causeway & was able to navigate along the coast for some distance; I mean to leave this the day after tomorrow and shall be at Broadlands probably on Tuesday, & shall stay there a few days before I return to town. Send my letters thither as soon as you receive this.

174. *Monday.*[1]

I would not for the world expose Mrs Jacket to such a soaking as she would probably get on horseback today, so whether your visit be to Παν with an *a* or with an *e* I should recommend the carriage.

[1] M. Strachan was a messenger at the War Office.
[1] Both the date and the substance of the letter are obscure. 'Old Pan' was a name Palmerston sometimes applied to his old Harrow housemaster, Dr Thomas Bromley

175. *19 April 1827.*

I am to be Chanr of Exqr but to avoid tumbling into Goulburn's contest have preferred remaining as I am till the end of the Session, as there was no middle term; but am immediately to be in the Cabinet.[1] I had rather my intended official removal were not known for the present & until matters settle themselves at Cambridge so do not mention it, though probably others will.[2] Canning says he has told Tindal that he must not stand against me, though he may of course against anybody else, & that he has persuaded Ld Bristol to keep back Ld Jermyn, which however was hardly necessary for the Cantabs would have sent him back quicker than he went.[3] I send you two letters from Cambridge on the state of affairs there. I am quite sure that I have judged right in letting Goulburn's contest take precedence of my reelection.

I am off for Bds today but shall probably be back the middle of the week.

[*PS.*] The Home Office is not filled yet. I believe the Speaker & Ld Farnborough have both declined it; I only hope Bexley will not be put there. I suspect that Leech will go Chancellor to Ireland & Plunkett be Master of the Rolls here, but this is only guess.

(1749–1827). Possibly Sulivan had written about a journey he was to make, but leaving Palmerston uncertain whether he meant to 'Pan' or to 'Penn'.

[1] On 14 April Canning had promised Palmerston either the Exchequer or the Home Office. The other seat in Cambridge was made vacant by Copley's translation to the Lords as Lord Lyndhurst and Lord Chancellor. Palmerston left two, rather different, accounts of his arrangement with Canning, that in his 'Autobiographical Sketch' (Bulwer & Ashley, i. 374–5), and another in the form of a memo. on the back of the summons from Canning of 14 April (printed, with minor inaccuracies, in Lorne, pp. 40–3, from B.P., G.C./CA no. 80). In the first Palmerston relates how, after 'a great dinner ... at the Foreign Office just before the recess', Canning urged him to take the Exchequer immediately but Croker 'artfully suggested' the postponement. Croker may have made the suggestion, though it hardly seems fair to call it 'artful'. Palmerston presumably really meant to say *after* the recess, since Parliament had risen for Easter on 12 April and the dinner followed on the 18th. The second, but probably earlier written, account stresses the convenience of the whole arrangement to Palmerston himself and makes no mention of Croker. Nor does a letter Palmerston wrote to William Temple, also on 19 April (Bulwer & Ashley, i. 188).

[2] They did. See, for example, A. Aspinall, ed., *The Diary of Henry Hobhouse*, 1947, p. 129.

[3] Goulburn retired the day before the poll and Bankes was again beaten, this time by the Solicitor General, Sir Nicholas Tindal. Immediately afterwards Bankes and Lord Jermyn (the Lord Hervey of 1822) both announced that they intended to try again at the earliest opportunity. (*Sedgwick*, i. 279; Henry Gunning to Palmerston, 23 May, B.P.W.) But since Canning afterwards withdrew his offer of a new office for Palmerston, he did not have to seek re-election until the next dissolution.

176. *Wednesday [? April 1827].*[1]

Add. MSS.

The removal of officers from the half pay was a matter on which the D. of York & Torrens were frequently squabbling & encroaching, and I have a vague recollection of some case just before the Duke's death in which I declined to carry into effect the King's pleasure as to striking an officer off the half pay communicated to me by the C. in C. I think it was a medical officer in Scotland who declined serving. The C. in C. has not *the means* of effecting his own purpose on the subject; the half pay list is made out by the Secy at War, and submitted by him with a warrant to the King, and the only way, in which practically a man can be struck off the half pay, is either his being omitted from the new list so sent to the King, & afterwards sent to the Paymr Genl; or else, the Secy at War taking the King's pleasure & communicating it to Paymr Genl, for striking a man's name out of a standing establishment of ½ pay on which it has previously been put by King's warrant at the advice of Secy at War.

Half pay is a pecuniary allowance, and can therefore be taken away only by the financial authority of the Secy at War; it is not a matter of discipline; the genl rule is that offrs on full pay are subject to martial law and to the Commr in Chief, officers on half pay not subject to martial law, & under the Secy at War. At the same time as the loss or retention of half pay, involve also the loss or retention of rank in the army, the C. in C. seems to be to a certain degree entitled to a concurrent voice in the matter where it is a question of discretion, not provided for by existing regulations; and in such cases the Secy at War would communicate before-hand to the C. in C. his intention to submit to the King the removal of an officer if C. in C. should concur in opinion with him, but certainly if Secy at War had a decided opinion, he might do it even if C. in C. differed. I think that the rule to which I brought Torrens & the Duke at last was that when C. in C. thought an offr ought to be removed from half pay, he should communicate that opinion to the Secy at War, & request him to take the necessary steps for doing so, but that the C. in C. should not himself take the King's pleasure upon it, in order not to expose the C. in C's King to the chance of having his orders counter ordered or neglected by the Secy at Wr's King.

Still I believe that the Duke to keep up his own notions used to

[1] The subject of this letter was so persistent a problem that the letter is difficult to date. It is possible that it concerned some question that Sulivan had put even after Palmerston had resigned from the War Office. But from a letter Wellington addressed to Palmerston on 30 April 1827 (S.P.) it seems very likely that Palmerston's letter was written earlier that same month. Wellington's letter concerned the conviction of a half pay officer as a felon and his sentence to transportation.

take the King's pleasure sometimes to remove a man *from the Army*,
after I had done the same to *strike him off the half pay*. When the officer
is high in rank & has a brevet commission, besides that by which he
draws half pay, the C. in C. seems more necessarily a concurrent
party. I am pretty sure that the question came to issue in the last
two years of the Duke's life, in the case of some medical officer on
half pay who declined to serve when called upon by McGregor,[2] that
the Duke signified the King's pleasure to strike him off, & that I nevertheless took time to consider, & did not strike him off, & that I either
got the C. in C.'s letter withdrawn or else answered it assigning reasons
why he had acted irregularly. I am convinced that the books of the
office will shew something conclusive on the question.

[*PS.*] Look to see what was done in Sir R. Wilson's case. But then
he was a Genl Offr receiving unattached pay which is held to be in
the nature of full pay.

I apprehend that the Paymsr Genl having a warrant under the sign
manual for placing A.B. on the half pay, could not legally strike A.B.
off the half pay upon any other authority but a sign manual, taken
by the same adviser who submitted to the King the warrant and as
the C. in C. never communicates the King's pleasure to the Paymsr
Genl he has not the means of striking a man off the half pay.

177. *Memorandum. 11 June 1827.*

   Add. MSS.

When the specific appointment of Commander in Chief is vacant
the Secretary at War by the antient constitution of his office becomes
the responsible adviser of the King for the Government of the Army,
& without any first commission or appointment is virtually Commander in Chief though not bearing that appellation but retaining
his appellation of Secretary at War; and he is the officer who then
advises the King to order the sentence of the court martial to be
carried into execution, or to mitigate capital punishment to transportation as referred to in Sectn 9 of Mutiny Act. The Secry at War
therefore seems now to be the officer of the Crown intended by the
words 'Commander in Chief' used in the Mutiny Act inasmuch as
he is the responsible adviser of the Crown for the command of the
Army.[1]

[2] Sir James McGrigor, Director-General of the Army Medical Department.
[1] As Secretary at War Palmerston became acting C.-in-C. between the death of the
Duke of York and Wellington's appointment in Jan. 1827, and again from Wellington's
resignation on 5 May until his reappointment on 27 Aug. 1827.

178. *To Mrs Sulivan. London. 7 Aug. 1827.*

The bulletin of 8 this morning states the danger to be more urgent than last night. I consider this as announcing a speedy termination.[1] What a loss! not merely to parties but to nations, not to his friends only but to mankind. It was

> The fiery soul which working out its way,
> Fretted the unequal body to decay
> And o'er informed the tenement of clay.[2]

What the result will be it is difficult to say. I will let you know what I may hear but nothing probably will be thought of till next week at the soonest.

179. *War Office. 9 Aug. 1827.*

Yesterday Lansdowne went down to the King to announce Canning's death, it being his duty as Home Secy to do so. The King said he was perfectly right to do so, but told him that he had sent for Goderich & Bourne; & stated to him the nature of the communication he meant to make to them. Lansdowne on his return met Goderich on his road, got into his carriage & stated to him what had passed between him & the King. Goderich did not know till then that Bourne had been sent for & Bourne did not know that Goderich was sent for till he reached Windsor.

The King stated to Goderich that he wished to continue the Government with as little change as possible and to place him at the head of it, and that he wished Bourne to lead the Government in the House of Commons.[1] He entered into no details stating that as charges of intrigue had been thrown out against various persons when the last arrangements were made he was determined in order to prevent this on the present occasion to put in writing his communication to the Cabinet & should send it this day. Goderich stated that as the King meant to make a written statement he would of course excuse him if he made no answer whatever to the intimation with which he had honoured him; Bourne however expressed his disinclination to

---

[1] Canning died shortly before 4 a.m. the following day.
[2] *Cf.* Dryden, *Absalom and Achitophel,* i, lines 156–8.
[1] Bourne was to be Chancellor of the Exchequer, according to Goderich (*Ripon,* ii. 331). In any case, despite what Palmerston relates in his 'Autobiographical Sketch', Goderich had clearly not 'immediately requested' Palmerston to be his Chancellor (Bulwer & Ashley, i. 377). There are many other inaccuracies in Palmerston's account, which is strongly refuted by *Herries,* i. 154 and 193, n. 7.

undertake the task which the King wished to impose upon him. Both returned last night.

Today the Cabinet met at one & Goderich stated to them what I have related & read the written communication which he had received this morning from the King.[2] This paper states the King desires not to dissolve his Government; that he wishes to conduct his administration upon the same principles upon which he has acted during his regency & from thence to the present time; that when he formed his last or present Govt, whichever it may be called, he explained to Canning that he did not wish to have an exclusively Tory Govt because that wd deprive him of the services of many members of the present Govt, but that he had an understanding with Canning on several points; that he & Canning agreed that the destructive measure of Parliamentary Reform was to be resisted; that on the Catholic Question while on the one hand he did not expect Canning to abjure his own deliberate & deeply rooted opinions so on the other hand there was an understanding with Canning that the King's conscientious sentiments on this subject and his *unalterable determination* agst the question were to be respected, & that if ever Canning shd be forced to bring this question on as a Government measure the Govt should be considered as from that moment dissolved; that if the Cabinet are willing to go on upon these principles he proposes to place Goderich at the head & wishes to know our intentions as soon as they can conveniently be given.

He has also sent to Lyndhurst to go to Windsor tomorrow but without stating for what purpose.[3] We are to meet tonight at ½ past nine for the purpose of obtaining from the King an explanation of his passage about the Catholic Question which as worded may seem to imply something different from the real fact, and to mean that Canning had engaged never to propose the question in the Cabinet, whereas he distinctly reserved to himself & every other member of the Cabinet the full right of proposing it whenever he chose, the King of course being at liberty *then* to deal with his Cabinet so advising him, as he might think fit.

Ld Harrowby retires having long meant to do so on acct of health. All this of course is in strictest confidence, as to every body but Elizabeth; to all else say only what the *Courier* may announce.

[2] The King's Memorandum, 8 Aug., *George IV*, iii. 275–6.

[3] Evidently to receive a paper, for transmission to Goderich, outlining the King's views about the new Government. It included the suggestion that Herries should have the Exchequer since the King understood Bourne was unwilling to take it and the hope that Bourne would therefore remain at the Home Office. (*Ripon*, ii. 331–2; the King to Goderich, 10 Aug., *George IV*, iii. 279–80.)

180. *War Office. 7 o'clock, 10 Aug.* [*1827*].

We met last night at ½ past 9 and prepared an answer to the King's letter, in which we stated our understanding of the footing on which Canning's Govt stood with respect to the Catholic Question submitting that as our interpretation of his letter. This was sent early this morning and at half past five this afternoon we received an answer stating that he is anxious to retain his present Govt and accepts their explanation in the sense in which they give it adding however that the Govt are in possession of his sentiments on the Catholic Question, & asking what seems strange to have a copy of his former letter as he had kept none.[1] All this is well. Goderich is now charged with the formation of the Govt and a few days will probably decide the arrangts.[2]

181. *London. 13 Aug. 1827.*

Nothing new today but the D. of Portland succeeds Ld Harrowby as President of Council & Goderich is gone to Windsor.

182. *Stanhope St. 14 Aug. 1827.*

      B.P., G.C./SU no. 32; cf. Bulwer & Ashley, i. 194–6.

Palmerston agrees that Huskisson is the best fitted for the lead in the House of Commons, a position Palmerston himself would particularly dislike as it would place him 'in a perpetual state of canvass'. He also insists that Lord Holland 'must in some way or other' be in the Cabinet.[1]

183. *15 Aug. 1827.*

      B.P., G.C./SU no. 33; cf. Bulwer & Ashley, i. 196–7.

Palmerston announces that Goderich had written to the King the previous day that, as Herries had refused the Exchequer, Palmerston must have it.[1]

---

[1] Goderich to the King, 9 Aug., and the King to Goderich, 10 Aug., *George IV*, iii. 276–8.

[2] Lyndhurst had apparently communicated the King's suggestion to the Cabinet at the meeting of the previous night (*Herries*, i. 154). Bourne did not write to the King to refuse the Exchequer until 11 Aug. (*George IV*, iii. 282–3).

[1] Yet the King had already made unmistakably clear to Goderich that he would not have Holland in the Cabinet (*Ripon*, ii. 332).

[1] Goderich's letter to the King is, however, dated 15 Aug. (*George IV*, iii. 286; see also *Ripon*, ii. 332, and *Herries*, i. 156–7).

184. *Stanhope St. 16 Aug. 1827.*

My precautionary injunction of silence to you was not vain. Goderich tells me to day that the King insists upon seeing & talking to Herries before he finally determines not to take the Exchequer so that the matter is still uncertain, but will probably be settled by tomorrow.[1]

The funeral was fully attended and the streets lined with people. Tomorrow there is a Council at Windsor.[2]

185. *Stanhope St. 18 Aug. 1827.*

I could not write to you yesterday as we did not get away from Windsor till six o'clock & of course I was not in town till after post time. The Council was held to prorogue Parliament & to declare the D. of Portland President in the room of Ld Harrowby. We all met at the Castle at two and the King arrived half an hour afterwards and the business of the Council did not occupy more than the last ten minutes of our stay—all the intermediate time was taken up in audiences or rather discussions, & the end of the affair was that Herries did *not* receive the Seals of the Exchequer as all the papers this morning say he did, and that the arrangement of this *weighty* matter is postponed till Huskisson's return which will soon take place.[1] The state of the matter is that the King has set his heart upon having Herries; on the other hand Herries does not wish to take the office, Goderich does not wish him to have it because he would rather have me there, and the Whigs are outrageous at the idea of it, because they consider his selection for that office, and the refusal to admit Ld Holland into the Cabinet as indications of political sentiments wholly incompatible with those views & intentions upon the faith of which they originally joined the Govt & have since agreed to continue with it. In the course of yesterday the King saw Goderich several times, Herries more than once, Bourne & Lansdowne. The Whigs

---

[1] 'Lord Palmerston made no difficulties' (*Ripon*, ii. 333).

[2] Canning's funeral procession moved off from the old Foreign Office about 1 p.m. on 16 Aug. This letter therefore seems (like *Ripon*, ii. 333) to confirm the version in Palmerston's 'Autobiographical Sketch' (Bulwer & Ashley, i. 377), that Goderich spoke to him as they were assembling beforehand. The dating of the Council on 12 rather than 17 Aug. is clearly a slip.

[1] This and the following letter confirm that while there were two Council meetings, on 17 and 21 Aug., the crucial decision to wait for Huskisson's return from France was taken at the first. In attributing it to the second, A. Aspinall, 'The Coalition Ministries of 1827. Part II. The Goderich Ministry', *English Historical Review*, xlii, 1927, p. 539, has misinterpreted a reference in Planta's report to Huskisson about 'a second interview' between Goderich and the King.

namely Lansdowne, Carlisle,[2] Tierney looked black as thunder, Goderich uncommonly annoyed, & poor Herries like a victim about to be cast into a den of lions ready to devour him.

Well, you will say, what is the key to all this, for more there must be in it than at first meets the eye. Why this is the clue—Knighton considers Herries as his creature, and fancies that if he could get him into the Exchequer a hundred questions connected with the Privy Purse, the crown revenue and royal expenditure which are constantly arising, would be determined in conformity with Knighton's wishes & probably interests. He it is who proposed Herries to the King & who urges him to insist upon having him, the King no doubt sharing in Knighton's feeling of the convenience that would arise from placing in the situation of controuler a person who should owe his political existence to those whom it would be his duty to controul. In all these calculations I firmly believe they would be mistaken. Herries is an honourable fellow, and would do his duty under any circumstances in which he might be placed. But this is the very reason which makes him so little anxious to be placed in a position that might become so embarrassing to him & where he would be liable to be urged on one side by solicitations & appeals very difficult to be resisted, and on the other to be bound by public duty and a parliamentary responsibility, open, immediate and inevitable. He knows too the strong dislike with which many of his intended colleagues look to his accession to their body, and then his health is really such as to require temporary relaxation rather than a recommencement of labour.

Goderich I conclude is aware of the source from whence the urgency comes but I shall give him a hint if he is not. The Whigs are quite upon a wrong scent, and ascribe to political feeling that with which it has next to nothing to do; at the same time they would to a certain degree be right even if they knew the real motive which points the choice, because the effect of the appointment upon the public mind & the impression it would create would be the same whatever the secret cause of it may be. I suspect that this may have had some share in Canning's decision, that is to say that the strong representations made to him of the expediency of his continuing to hold the office (which however I think were perfectly just) might have sprung from the same views which suggest the appointment of Herries. For while Canning was First Lord, Leader in the Commons, chief of the Government, effectively though not ostensibly Foreign Secy, it is obvious that Herries was substantially though not nominally Chancellor of the Exchequer.[3]

[2] Carlisle's undated 'Notes of Interview with the King. George IV's Formation of Ministry' have survived among the C.H.P., but are filed out of place in series 2/154.
[3] This letter confirms the further strictures on Palmerston's 'Autobiographical Sketch'

Nothing can be more kind & handsome than Goderich has been to me upon this matter, and all he has said & done would convince *my friends* of that which no result could lead *me* to doubt, namely that I was quite right in avoiding to put myself in his way or to seek any communication with him from the first moment that he was sent for by the King—and when you say you are sorry to see that I am not in his confidence so much as some of his newer friends, this is the reason, namely, that I studiously avoided going near him till he sent for me, that he might not think I wanted to embarrass him by putting forward any personal objects of my own—directly or indirectly. After all Herries would really be an excellent man for the office. His knowledge of all the details of the subject would render him most valuable to Goderich; he has been at the work in some shape or other since Perceval first came into office, now twenty years ago. He is a very intelligent, clearheaded man, and I believe a man of strict integrity and of honourable feeling. He has not at present perhaps the scope of mind which belongs to a Cabinet situation, but a man's views expand very rapidly with his position, if he has the natural talent to form them, and though I fear that the Catholic Question is not the only subject on which he agrees with the illiberals, and that though he may not go quite so far as Tierney says Westmoreland did & declare himself an enemy to every measure founded upon the principles of liberty & humanity, yet *at present* his opinions all lie in that direction. Still he would soon imbibe the sentiments of those he would act with.

If I hear any thing more today I will send you another note.

[*PS.*] Of course I need not imitate Ld Wellesley & put '*Secret*' upon this letter, though there is so much better reason to do so than there is for such an inscription upon a letter to Lansdowne inclosing a report from a police officer of the row at Tipperary & the depositions of a dozen soldiers taken before a Bench of Justices. But this is strictly confidential to you & Elizabeth.

186. *War Office. 21 Aug. 1827.*

The King saw Goderich, the Chancellor & Ld Carlisle to day before the Council & expressed to them a fixed determination to have Herries, though the matter as a final arrangement is still to stand over

in *Herries*, i. 162, n. 5. It also suggests that he is right to be sceptical (i. 197) about the private interview Palmerson recalled having had that day with the King. Probably Palmerston was confusing this visit to Windsor with the similar occurrences of 4 Sept. (see no. 192).

till Huskisson's return if that is soon to be looked for, which will be known in a few days. It remains to be seen therefore whether the King or the Whigs will give way. I think the former will not & the latter will be very foolish if they do not. To break up the Govt about a man would be unwise & would place them in a position in which they could assign no intelligible public ground for their secession; and as it must be presumed they came in on public grounds & public principles it strikes me that they would do themselves little credit by going out upon a personal question. They may think Herries an enemy: perhaps he *has* been, but it does not follow that he *will* be. He has not been sufficiently marked & prominent to have committed himself publicly to any particular line of conduct at variance with the views of the Govt, & though he differs with the majority of the Cabinet on the Catholic Question, that is not a reason which can be assigned by the Whigs for quitting the Govt. I confess I think it would be very unfortunate if this were to be the result for there can be nothing less desirable than to have the Govt thrown back again into the hands of the prejudiced old Tories from whom it has been as it were by a miracle rescued. If they were to come in they would soon overpower Goderich & the few that agreed with him & place them in a very unpleasant situation; we should have over again all the inconveniences of a divided Cabinet squabbling over every measure of public policy foreign & domestic and even if the liberals were not intirely thwarted they would constantly be driven to compromize their real views, & forego their own objects to prevent a disruption of the Govt. The D. of Wellington of course would in such a case come in; how could he go on with Huskisson? How could he co-operate with Goderich? Which is to give up his opinion? The Duke who as to foreign affairs is an apostolical & holy alliance politician, or those who are embarked in measures founded upon intirely opposite principles. There is a fate about the Whigs & therefore I expect them in trying circumstances to do the foolish thing. But if they have common sense they will swallow Herries, Knighton & all & trust to parliamentary controul to get the Govt out of any difficulties arising from Herries's connection with Knighton, and to time & the preponderance of liberal views in the Cabinet to neutralize any Tory propensities which he may have.

The Duke will probably be gazetted on Friday. Taylor goes immediately & FitzRoy Somerset will come in at once with the Duke.[1]

---

[1] Wellington returned to the Horse Guards on Monday, 27 Aug., with Fitzroy Somerset as his Military Secretary. Sir Herbert Taylor had been conducting affairs at the Horse Guards as a special Deputy Secretary of the War Office while Palmerston was acting C.-in-C. Palmerston wrote to Wellington on 25 Aug.: 'I have swept your table up clear to the day, and I trust you will find that ... I have done no mischief.' (B.P./WO no. 56.)

187. *War Office. 24 Aug. 1827.*

The Duke will be gazetted tonight of which I shall be right glad upon every possible account. It is a great advantage to have him at the head of the army & I shall not be sorry to be relieved from a very troublesome addition to my own proper business.

Huskisson got to Paris on the 20th, & will be here next week. I think somehow or other that matters will be arranged.

I took an opportunity yesterday of stating my thoughts on the subject to Lansdowne saying that I felt I was taking a liberty I had no right to, but there could be no harm in stating to him how the matter struck a person not in a party sense concerned in it as he was, & though he stated forcible objections to the whole arrangt which the King wants to effect, as indications of a general system of detailed interference in matters which constitutionally should be left to his responsible ministers, & also the peculiar objections which he & his friends have to Herries individually yet still I think that unless the evil star of the Whigs still predominates they will not sacrifice great public objects for a personal question. Herries's connections with Roschildt etc. may be objectionable, his political opinions may all be wrong & his views narrow & illiberal but he is only one among 14, & the deuce is in it, if he governs us instead of our governing him; & as to the way in which the King has done this I took the liberty of telling Ld L. that those who determined not to continue in office when their King took steps of this sort which they think & justly at variance with the proper & constitutional course of proceeding must make up their minds not to be ministers during the reign of George the 4th. But that the only way is to get rid of these little matters as well as one can for the sake of greater objects with respect to which the King does *not* thwart his Govt.

[*PS.*] I think either Huskisson will say he must be Exchequer to lead the House, or Bourne the King's first choice may be persuaded to devote himself for a Session in order to save the Govt.

188. *Stanhope St. 27 Aug. 1827.*

Huskisson is not yet come but will probably be here tomorrow or next day. All parties seem now likely to fall into the arrangement which would make him Chancellor of the Exchequer.[1] I take it that

---

[1] Evidently, then, the idea was canvassed before Lansdowne wrote to Huskisson on the evening of 28 Aug. (*Goderich*, p. 164). Perhaps Palmerston had suggested it to Lansdowne at their meeting on 23 Aug. The Duke of Devonshire also mentioned it in a letter to Lady Granville of 21–24 Aug. (Chatsworth Papers).

the King would do anything short of breaking up the Govt to get Herries into that office & the Whigs would go exactly the same length to keep him out of it. Brougham whose price is still unpaid, writes to intreat them not to stickle about individuals & protests that he is ready to serve *even under Planta* if it be agreeable to the King. The King has certainly no wish to go back to the Tories whom he still has in dudgeon. He resents the D. of Wellington's hardness as he calls it, and there was some angry explanation between him & Peel when the latter went out which the King has not yet forgiven—besides he hates being troubled & he knows that a change in such a direction would bring a great deal of trouble upon him. He looks to Huskisson's return with all the anxiety with which an imprudent skaiter on the Serpentine who has made a flourish too much & finds the ice breaking under him casts about for the agent of the Humane Society. Whether if Huskisson goes to the Exchequer the King will insist upon Herries having the Colonies remains to be seen. He certainly dislikes me & would be glad to get rid of me *any*how as the Irish say. He said to Mad. Lieven the other day, 'Connaissez vous Palmerston', & then went on, 'il y a quelque chose en lui qui me déplait, il a toujours l'air si fière [*sic*]'. She ought to have said, 'il est fière [*sic*] Sire d'être votre sujet'. I shall bow next time several degrees nearer to a right angle. But if this is his view of requisites for his service I wonder he has not cast some ray of favour upon Sir Alexander Grant in all the recent changes.[2] However I am determined to take no *hints* & to understand nothing short of a positive intimation that my room would be more agreeable than my company—a seat in the Cabinet may enable a man to do some good now & then, and as to the rest it moveth one rather to smile than to be angered.

Winter seems over today & summer is returning though the wind is still north.

189. *Stanhope St. 28 Aug. 1827.*

I send you a proposed addition to the clothing warrant as prepared by Marshall[1] & amended by me. Look it over & see if you can improve it.

If I hear any news before the post goes out I will send it you. I cannot resist also sending you a letter I had from Brougham this morning which would make even a condemned culprit laugh. It is in reply to a few lines I wrote to him on this subject the other day in a note which had reference to another matter. It is amusing to trace all the

---

[2] Sir Alexander Cray Grant, 8th Bart, was chairman of committees.
[1] Edward Marshall was one of the senior clerks in the War Office.

different calculations of personal advantage & convenience, and all the individual views which run through his note; it is quite a picture of the man, so pray return it to me. However there is much truth in some of the reasons which he gives for the policy of not urging extreme principles of etiquette on the present occasion & I have no doubt that his letters to his friends will have done good.[2]

190. *War Office. 29 Aug. 1827.*

Huskisson arrived yesterday & is gone down today to the King, so that tonight or tomorrow we shall know what is to become of us. He is prepared I believe to be Chanr of Excr if that would save the Govt though he would himself chuse the Colonies, but if he agrees to take the former will the King give up Herries? Probably yes, & if so all will be well. But Taylor who came back today from Windsor says the King spoke to him in a very determined manner on the subject. I think that even if Herries is forced in the Whigs will remain, for each man appears willing to digest it though each says that all the rest will not. I suspect Ld Carlisle is the stiffest; Tierney affects to be so but will any man living believe that he would willingly go out if he had a decent pretence for staying in? Macdonald, Abercromby, & Maurice FitzGerald are all for remaining.[1] The fact is that though the appointment is very objectionable they will not have any broad & adequate public reason to give for their secession; should they go out, [*it*] remains to be seen what will happen.

[*PS.*] Send this on to Fanny.

Bourne says that if the fate of the Govt depends on his taking the Exchqr, the Govt must prepare for dissolution, for that on no consideration will he do any such thing.[2] Huskisson is better but not by

---

[2] Brougham had written of the King's determination to have Herries on 26 Aug. (B.P., G.C./BR no. 64) that 'to be sure, everything that *we can* possibly & without loss of character & publick confidence submit to, must positively be swallowed'. So far as the rumours about Herries and the Rothschilds were concerned, he also suggested that the question be put directly to Herries: 'Have you on your honour ever in your life, since being in a place of trust, directly or indirectly, benefited by stock in any manner of way?' He then went on to commiserate with Palmerston, saying that since it was always necessary to take more from Kings than from others it was necessary 'to bridle your temper & calm your sense of private honour in such emergencies. For my part I look to your power a year hence as incalculably greater for every good purpose.'

[1] Sir James Macdonald, James Abercromby and Maurice FitzGerald were all junior members of the Government.

[2] Huskisson, who was unwilling to take the Exchequer, had raised the possibility of falling back again on Bourne as a temporary expedient.

any means fully re-established, & of course much affected by the loss of Canning, & harrassed by the present state of things.

191. *War Office. 1 Sept. [1827].*

I have only time to say that matters are not yet settled. Lansdowne went to Windsor today & was to go on to Bowood but wd write to Goderich from Windsor to report the result. It came to this at last that Bourne would not & therefore the King insists upon Herries.[1] But the Whigs are softened & matters have been so explained to them that unless there is any expression dropped by either L. or the King in their conversation today which blows up a flame I think the Whigs will acquiesce.

Yrs in haste

192. *Broadlands. 4 Sept. 1827.*

I arrived here last night having taken Windsor in my way to attend a Council which was held to swear in Huskisson & Charles Grant & to give the seals to Herries. The King was enchanted at having got out of his difficulty so well & has been persuaded that *he* was able to prevail upon Lansdowne to remain after everybody else had failed. He was perfectly determined not to go back to the seceders of April even if the Whigs had left us & would have set Goderich to work to make up the best government he could without either Whigs or Tories. He said he should follow the example of his father when left by Pitt & if none of his present ministers would serve him he would go into the streets for a government & would be sure to find one (he did not add but probably meant) as good as Ld Sidmouth's. He sent for me into him to say divers very civil things about the handsome manner in which he thought I had behaved about the Exchequer in not pressing my claim etc. etc., all of which was I knew an echo of what Goderich had told him & suggested to him to tell me. I of course was overpowered with a sense of His Majesty's condescending kindness, & only anxious to do anything in my power to be useful to His Majesty & his Govt, & perfectly conscious how much more fit a Chancellor he had got & so we parted *very* great friends.

I expect a party over from Cowes to day for a week. I shall be in town again for a day or two on the 9th or 10th.

[1] Bourne had been persuaded after all to accept the Exchequer on 30 Aug.; then Herries took umbrage and refused an alternative office. By the time Herries had been placated, Bourne had again, and finally, changed his mind. Palmerston wrote to Bourne that evening pleading with him to take the Exchequer in order to save *Canning's* Government (B.P./GMC no. 17).

I return you the inclosed as I do not like now to be meddling with Commr in Chief's business. Your friend will not suffer by the delay, for though he talks of not losing a moment in getting an unattached Company as if it could be got ready made like a boat cloak. I can tell you that the facilities of getting such a step have ceased with the sale of half pay, & all that can now be done is to put a man's name down on a long list where he will find himself waiting in excellent company.

193. *To Mrs Sulivan. Ryde. 21 Sept. 1827.*

I have turned yatcher for a few days & have done what I always wanted to do & had never yet accomplished, circumnavigated that large island from which I now write. We set sail yesterday in the *Thérèse*, Ld Chesterfield's, at one from Cowes, and by nine in the evening had returned there after encountering all the perils of the Needles & Bembridge Ledge; making a most prosperous & very agreeable voyage. It is quite comical to see the mania. We boarded this morning the *Scorpion* [*belonging to*] Mr Greville who was just returned from Dieppe to which he had been for the purpose of seeing the town, but no sooner did he enter the harbour than the Duchesse de Berrie & all the population entered his yatch & he was kept bowing & receiving upwards of 500 people the best part of two days & never could set foot on shore, & at last came away in despair—leaving the French charmed with everything on board & especially at finding ices there, which they seemed to fancy he had brought with him on purpose for them, instead of recognizing the handicraft of their well known confectioner. His yatch is of 110 tons, carries 2 six pounders, 2 four pounders & 2 three pounders, & his cabin is decorated with ten rifles & ten pistols, and his deck bordered with an appropriate number of cannon balls neatly disposed. The club have about 140 vessels & 1200 men. They are quite a naval power & beat hollow *Pappenheim* & *Hilburghshausen* that made such a figure in the war. The experimental squadron are still here but are at St Helens waiting till the equinoctial gales begin, & when their ships come into port for refuge they will it is supposed take to the sea.

I like Ld Chesterfield very much; he improves greatly upon acquaintance. He is natural & unaffected with all the feelings & notions of a grand seigneur, not much read, as might be supposed from his having had nobody to look after him; but with a good deal of quickness & intelligence. I think he will be something more than a dandy bye & bye.

I went to see Nash's castle; what a beautiful thing it is, & what a delightful winter garden he has. I never saw such a variety of choice plants so well disposed & producing so much effect.

I have had very good shooting at Bds & have quantities of birds. The Flemings were with me for a few days, & have given up their French tour which indeed I believe neither of them very much wished for.

194. *To Mrs Sulivan. Dublin. 23 Oct. 1827.*

I arrived here yesterday (Monday) at 4 o'clock having had a good journey & voyage though the latter a little rolly poly, but of the usual duration namely from 8 in the morning to about 3 in the afternoon. I am off tomorrow morning quite early for Sligo, where I shall be early on the following morning, and shall probably be back again here by the 5th or 6th of November. To be sure they have shortened the time of communication by letter between this & London; you may write to Dublin from London, on Saturday night & have your answer on Wednesday morning. Dublin is as much deserted as London. Ld Wellesley is living 15 miles off. Lamb is today with him, Sir G. Murray inspecting his districts & all the nobility & gentry minding their country affairs. The only people I have seen are George Rich & Hercules Pakenham both looking prosperously, but the former un- luckily going to add another to an unprovided family[1]—Pakenham is helping Longford to attend upon Ly Longford who is occupied in the same way as Ly Rich. Everything in this Island is quiet, & the violence of party is venting itself in bible discussions instead of political outrage.

195. *Cliffony. 3 Nov. 1827.*

I am truly grieved to hear the sad account of poor Ld Pembroke's death which though an event that one has long considered not im- probable his improvement latterly had made one cease to entertain any immediate fears of. It will *indeed* be a loss to Ly Pembroke and all his family; I hope however that he has been able to make such ar- rangements as will render her independent in all ways of Ld Herbert.[1]

I shall leave this on Monday and on Wednesday leave Sligo for Dublin, which I shall reach on Thursday morning—on Friday I shall

---

[1] George Rich was Chamberlain of the Vice-Regal Court in Ireland. Palmerston had provided for his younger brother, William Osborne Rich, by making him a clerk in the War Office. Sir Hercules Pakenham was Longford's younger brother.

[1] The 11th Earl of Pembroke had died on 26 Oct. His heir, Lord Herbert, who was Lady Pembroke's step-son, had given a good deal of trouble on account of his clandes- tine marriage with the Princess Buttera.

embark & make the best of my way to London. I find everything going on well here, and my improvements though somewhat more expensive than I had reckoned yet satisfactory and nearly brought to an end. I am at present engaged in a battle royal with Priest & Bishop about my school but I think that by a little bullying & swaggering & two or three very oppressive acts towards my tenants I shall bring these holy personages to some reasonable terms.[2] I had the pleasure of fining the priest 6£ 10s. yesterday, having compelled one of my tenants to pay up his arrears of rent amounting to that sum, in consequence of some uncivil & contumacious demeanor of his wife with reference to the school, & I am sure by the manner in which the man paid the money, without any complaint or grumbling & rather with a cheerful countenance that it was given him by the priest. That is exactly what I should have wished, & the rap has been handed to the right knuckles.

[*PS.*] I have been pursuing a rigorous system of sea bathing before

---

[2] Palmerston had required in his schools that 'those scholars who have learnt to read should by the daily perusal of a part of the Testament acquire that moral instruction which that volume is so well calculated to convey'. But this had led to unexpected trouble with the Catholic schoolmaster who, when told by Palmerston that he must obey orders or go, had decided he could not resist his priest (McHugh). This had left the schoolmaster's Protestant colleague, Miss Plunket, alone and frightened among an overwhelming majority of Catholic children. Consequently, while he looked for a new master, Palmerston made a formal agreement with the Roman Catholic Bishop of Elphin. Written in his own hand, it reads:

Lord Palmerton will select for the boys school at Cliffony a Catholic schoolmaster. Miss Plunket who was appointed last year to the girls school, will continue to have charge of it, under the following regulations, which are to apply both to the boys school and to the girls school:—
No books of any kind shall be introduced into, or used in the school, until one copy of such book shall have been signed in the inner cover as approved by Ld Palmerston & Ld P. engages not to approve or sign any book without previously submitting it for the inspection of Dr Burke or Mr McKue [*sic*], & he also engages not to introduce any book to which they shall have any objection upon religious grounds.
A stated time shall be set apart in one day in each week, during which the Roman Catholic children of each sex shall be instructed in the Catechism of their Church as published by Dr Butler.
No attempts shall be made directly or indirectly to influence the religious opinions & feelings of the children either Catholic or Protestant with the view of changing their religion, and Ld Palmerston will immediately take such steps as the occasion may require if any such attempts shall be made & reported to him.

P.   6 Novr 1827

[*It continues, in another hand:*]
Convinced of the fair and liberal views of the Rt Honble Viscount Palmerston, I feel pleasure in acceding to his wishes, and arrangement as set forth in this sheet, in his Lordship's hand-writing.

Patrick Burke *R C*
6th Novr 1827   Bishop of Elphin
(B.P.W.)

breakfast though I can tell you that to dress & undress in a November morning on the bare rocks of Mullaghmore is by no means a warm occupation.

196. *War Office. 18 Dec. [1827].*

I have departed from the ever to be observed maxim of doing to others as one would be done by—but the enclosed note from Lady Pembroke seemed to be so pressing that I thought you would excuse me for complying with her request. I accordingly desired Mr Stewart[1] to look & see if he could find me a large letter answering her description and he brought me that of which I inclose the cover, and as it *palpably* contained a sealed letter within, I ventured to open it, and sent the enclosure to Ly Pembroke to whom it was addressed.

There is nothing more known to day as to ministerial changes, but Goderich is returned to town.[2]

197. *War Office. ½ past 6, Wednesday [19 Dec. 1827].*

All is right again; Harrowby declined & Goderich remains, & the proposition as to Holland & Wellesley is for the moment postponed; the only thing we must labour to do, is to make it well understood by the public that the idea of Goderich's retirement arose intirely out of private & personal considerations and that there has been no difference of opinion whatever upon public measures either between the members of the Cabinet, or between the Cabinet & the King.[1]

Yrs affly & in haste

198. *Stanhope St. 31 Dec. [1827].*

I was in a great hurry just now being rather late for my Don.[1] I am off to Cambridge & shall return on Wedy after the post comes

[1] R. Hardinge Stewart was Sulivan's private secretary at the War Office.

[2] Goderich had written to the King on 11 Dec. saying that he would have to resign if both Wellesley and Holland were not admitted to the Government. The King had chosen to treat this as a definite offer of resignation and had asked Harrowby to be Prime Minister. Meanwhile, Goderich retreated to the country. Palmerston, like most of the Cabinet, was kept in ignorance of all this for about ten days. Apparently he gave Huskisson the impression that he was hurt by this lack of confidence. (Goderich to Palmerston, 17 Dec., B.P., G.C./GO no. 20.)

[1] Palmerston had hardly written this than Huskisson and Herries plunged the Government into a new and fatal crisis. This time Palmerston was let into the secret much earlier because Huskisson had been at Broadlands for Christmas.

[1] Dom Miguel arrived in London on 30 Dec. Bulwer & Ashley omitted (i. 210) from a letter to William Temple a comment Palmerston made about Miguel at this time. 'He will do very well in Portugal.' (B.P., G.C./TE no. 193 of 8 Jan. 1828.)

in, so you may send my letters thither tomorrow, but Wednesday's letters to Stanhope Street.

199. *Stanhope St. 3 June 1828.*

I send you in this box all the War Office papers which I have got to act upon; I will look over my Estimate papers & send down by the messenger tomorrow those which will be useful to Hardinge, distinguishing those of which I should like myself to retain copies.

Huskisson's explanation was I think remarkably well received by the House last night, & seemed to satisfy his hearers that he had no choice but to receive his dismissal.

200. *Stanhope St. 4 June 1828.*

I send you in this box all the Estimate papers I have which can be of any use to Hardinge; those which I have marked with X in pencil I would like to have back again *before the day* the Estimates come on.

I enclose a nominal return of gentlemen in Parliament who may be supposed as agreeing pretty much in opinion & likely to find themselves voting the same way. I think the list is respectable both in its number & composition.

[*Enclosure:*] List of the ejected liberals as mustered in Hs. of Commons on 3rd June 1828.[1]

Huskisson	A. Ellis—Honble
Palmerston	John Wortley
Lamb	Denison
Grant	Wm Lascelles
Sturges Bourne	Loch—(Ld Stafford's)
Wilmot Horton	Acland
Frankland Lewis	Robt Grant
F. L. Gower	Ld Spencer Chichester
Sandon	J. Fitzgerald (M.P. for Seaford)

[1] *Cf.* the list from Palmerston's Journal (Bulwer & Ashley, i. 278) and A. Aspinall, 'The Canningite Party', *Transactions of the Royal Historical Society*, 4th Ser., xvii, 1934, pp. 224–6. There is a third list of Palmerston's in a letter to William Temple of 8 June (B.P., G.C./TE no. 200). In all these Palmerston makes the apparent error of 'Lord Spencer Chichester' for Arthur Chichester; that of 'John Worsley' for John Wortley in the Journal is an error of transcription by Bulwer. Similarly the qualification 'Pub.' against some of the names in Bulwer's list is an error for 'Prob.'. The list in Palmerston's letter to his brother differs from that to Sulivan in that it does not include Robert Grant and does not qualify Lennard as a 'probable'. In addition it includes Carlisle, Harrowby and Wharncliffe among the Lords, and Morpeth and Normanby among the 'well-disposed' in the Commons.

Stratford Canning	Liddell—probable
Jermyn	Lennard—do
Littleton	Spencer Perceval—do
Warrender	G. Bentinck—do

House of Lords

Dudley	Morley
Goderich	Haddington
Seaford	Granville
Howard de Walden	Stafford
Bristol	Gower

201. *Stanhope St. 10 June 1828.*

I send you the proceedings of the Finance Committee but pray do not forget to send them back to me as I do not wish to lose them.

I am glad Beresford's letters have at last been noticed in Parliament but something ought to be said about them in the Lords; the Duke saw them & the answers to them as they went on, & yet was instructing Lamb in a different sense; this is rather going near the wind.[1] Ld Salisbury's speech last night is looked upon as a sort of demi official intimation of a readiness to *parley* at least, on the Catholic Question.[2] The Duke must be sick of that question when he finds it such an obstacle to forming any government that can be creditable to its chief. The various refusals he has met with must make him wish the Catholics emancipated or damned.

202. *Stanhope St. 19 June 1828.*

Thank you for sending me the inclosed; I have sent my 10 gs. I had quite forgot the birds.[1]

I can assure you I miss very much our daily talk, which I have so often found as *useful* as it was agreeable.

So we have now got very much the Govt I foretold to Tierney last year—a Tory dish with a garnish of Liberal Catholics; Calcraft & Vesey [*Fitzgerald*], I always saw were destined to join; but Francis

---

[1] Fred Lamb had complained that Lord Beresford's Portuguese correspondence had conveyed notions of the Government's policy which were at odds with that he was attempting to convey as British Minister in Lisbon. Wellington wrote on 18 June asking Beresford to be more cautious (*W.N.D.*, iv. 491–2). Reference was also made to this matter in the Commons on 9 June and Beresford replied in the Lords on 12 June (2 *Hansard*, xix, 1203 and 1315–17).

[2] See *ibid.*, xix, 1161–2.

[1] In Palmerston's 'Analysis of Expenditure from 1818 downwards' (B.P.W.) there is an entry of 1828 for ten guineas for 'Cambridge Collection of Birds'.

Gower surprizes me; if he had gone out on impulse, he might have repented on reflection, but having maturely deliberated on his retirement, it does seem strange that he should in 10 days return, without any new event except an unmeaning speech in the Hs. of Lds leaving the Cath. Question very much as it was before. He must clearly be a very undecided youth although a clever one. When I remember that a few weeks ago when the Duke told the Cabinet that the repeal of the Sacramental Test must be resisted as a Govt question, and some of us said that the only ground on which we *could* resist it would be that it was the lesser question, & that the greater one of the Catholics ought to be settled first, when I remember I say that upon this being stated, he put it to our serious & earnest consideration whether such a course of argument would not tend to unite the Dissenters & Catholics to make a common cause & thus to create great embarrassment; & stated *that* to be an evil by all means to be avoided, & when I know the strong feeling of the King & of all those hidden personages who are working upon the Duke without his owning it to himself, I confess *I* cannot *yet* bring myself to believe that he has any serious intention whatever, to take himself a single step in the question; particularly as his doing so would probably break up his Government by driving out Peel & Bathurst & Goulburn. Time will shew; but I think he has only meant to palaver the Catholics, & not being quite as skilful in maneuvring words as men, has said a *little* more than he meant.

[*PS.*] The sending of Ld Heytesbury I find does not proceed from any change of feeling here, but from Metternich having as I always thought he would changed sides & gone round to the Russians & determined to send an Austrian ambassador to the head quarters. Do not mention this.[2]

203. *Stanhope St. 13 July [1828].*

Many thanks for your kind note about Brockenhurst, but she was a gift & not a loan, and even if she had been the latter she would long e'er this have been liable 'to be sold to pay for her keep'. I have no use for her myself as I am over horsed like most other people, & I know no friend who wants one. Yes by the bye I remember I do know one, and a man very likely to buy it & that is Dudley who commissioned me some time ago to get him a Forest pony which

[2] Lady Cowper wrote to her brother Fred Lamb on 14 June that this was 'a thing that he [Wellington] was quite furious in the Cabinet with Ld P. for proposing a month ago—as it was a thing that he *never* would consent to'. (Panshanger Papers, County Record Office, Hertford.)

I have hitherto been unable to do, and I advise you therefore to write a note to Dudley telling him that I bought this pony some time ago for Stephen from a man in the Forest between Lyndhurst & Lymington, that he is a genuine Forester & that Stephen no longer wanting it he Dudley may see & try it & buy it if it suits him. It is very like a favourite pony mare which he bought some years ago from Edward Montagu who brought her from Naples & I should not be surprized if Dudley bought her.

204. *Stanhope St. 26 July 1828.*
    Add. MSS.

My chief reason for not attending the Chelsea Boards more frequently than I used to do, was that the business generally transacted there was of the most unimportant & uninteresting kind, consisting of a great variety of little domestic details about contracts for coals & beer & soap, etc., but transacted with great pomp & gravity in all the detailed ceremonial of the Privy Council; the result of attendance usually was to lose a whole day in doing nothing, and as there is always a Board ready made by the local authorities & the Paymsr General who is necessarily a member of the Board, I seldom threw a day away in going there unless I was told that there was anything to be done that was of real importance, & on those occasions I have frequently been present. During the last year that I was in office the duties of the Cabinet being added to those of the War Office made me less disposed to give unnecessary attendance at Chelsea. But I never felt any difficulty as to attending the Chelsea Board in consequence of any idea that the Secy at War was a controuling authority over them; in fact he has long ceased to be so, by Windham's arrangement; and they have duties imposed upon them by their present patent, for the performance of which they are themselves responsible. Merry always clung to the old arrangement & used to contend for the controuling authority of the Secy at War, but I do not think he was borne out, by the instructions under which the commissioners are constituted & the acts which give them power.

205. *Stanhope St. 3 Aug. 1828.*
    Add. MSS.

As to Dr Renny,[1] I remember that I felt that his case was one which might be argued either way, but on the whole I satisfied myself that

---

[1] Dr George Renny was McGrigor's counterpart in Ireland, Director-General of Hospitals and Chief of the Army Medical Department.

the decision I had at first given was right, & I stated at some length
on one of the papers the reasons upon which that opinion was founded,
& perhaps I had better refer you to that mem. written when the matter
was fresh in my mind, than trust to my recollection of it now. I should
say however generally speaking, that the thing to be proved is, *not*
that the *increase* of *salary* (for it is neither more nor less than that)
should be *withheld* from Renny, but that there is any good reason for
granting it to him. When the currency of Ireland was raised to the
standard of England one unavoidable consequence of that measure
was an increase of pay to the army in Ireland. The pay of the soldier
is fixed by a regulation, upon the faith of which he inlists, at a certain
nominal daily rate, and upon the change of currency one of two things
became inevitable, either that this nominal rate should in Ireland be
reduced, or that the real pay of the soldier in Ireland should be increased by his receiving the same nominal pay in a more valuable
currency; the last alternative was considered for various reasons the
one which it was necessary to adopt. The same reasons however were
not thought applicable either to the salary of civil officers or even
to military allowances of a local nature, & not fixed by general regulations extending every where, or at least both to England & Ireland,
& these salaries & allowances were translated into the new denomination with a due regard to their original import & value. Now Renny's
appointment is either civil or military. I think it is one of the *civil
departments of the army*, & that his salary whether reckoned by a daily
rate or by an annual sum is perfectly & correctly speaking the salary
of an official situation, & not the pay of a *soldier* (including in that
general term an officer). I consider McGregor's salary to be of the
same nature, & the *official* salary of Torrens & Gordon to be something
of the same kind, though in their case there is this difference that their
duties extend wherever the army extends & might be exercised from
any given center as well as from London, whereas the duties of Renny
& McGregor are not borne upon the military part of the Army Estimates, they are not included in the staff vote but are voted in the
public departments, and I should say that Renny's situation is quite of
a civil nature or rather of an official nature though connected with
the superintendence of the army; & saying this I am aware that he
does occasionally give medical advice to officers & soldiers. But even
supposing his appointment to be considered as a military one, it is
purely a *local* appointment; he is not like an Inspector of Hospitals
who may be stationed in Ireland, a member of a class in the army,
accidentally stationed in Ireland but liable to be removed any where
else and holding a commission which forms a link in the great chain
of the army, & to which the *general* regulations attach a specific rate
of pay. Renny is on the contrary an insulated & local officer, he is

a tumour which might be cut out without affecting the organization of the body & not a member naturally belonging to the system; his duties are intirely confined to Ireland, & if he was removed from Ireland his military existence would I apprehend to a great degree cease, or at least his military *functions* such as they now are, *must* cease. If you move a Depy Adjutant or Quarter Mr Genl from Ireland to England or any other station, he may be Depy Adjt or Qtr Mr Genl still, but if you moved Renny from Ireland you would extinguish him; he is Director Genl of Hospitals *in Ireland,* and *no where else.*

If then it should be thought (upon which point however others may differ from me) that Renny has not under the arrangements connected with the change of currency, a *right* to British currency the only question is whether there is any reason for giving him in that way an increase of salary; & whatever may be his merits it did not seem to me that there was any good reason for so doing. His office is one which ought to have been abolished, as there is no earthly reason why the Medical Board in London should superintend & controul the medical service at the Antipodes and yet have no cognizance of it next door in Ireland. The only ground upon which the appointment was agreed to be retained so long as Renny should hold it, was that he was a very meritorious individual, a great favourite, & very deservedly I believe, of Goulburn's, & that he performed duties & rendered services to the Irish Government quite unconnected with the ordinary details of the army, for which it was very convenient to pay him by keeping up his appointment. But the very temporary nature of the existence of his office seems to make it necessary to have so much the stronger reasons for increasing its salary. This is all that occurs to me at present—except that it may be well to consider whether there are any other amphibious appointments which might found claims upon the precedent of Renny if his pay was increased in this way.

206. *Stanhope St. 3 Aug. 1828.*

Thank you for remembering my request about 'Piccolissimo' for so your pony should be called; I will let you know in a day or two whether I shall take advantage of your offer. As to Brockenhurst I gave 20 gs for her in Octr 1824 she being then I think 3 yrs old; she must now be seven, therefore, and all the better for the work she has had. I should say that she is honestly worth 30 gs at the present moment to any body who wants such an animal. I was asked that price, or I believe even more, last spring for a *three year old* pony in the Forest, that Vivian mentioned to me as likely to suit Dudley, but the account which Turner gave me of it did not induce me to mention it to Dudley. I should not advise you however to refuse pounds or even to break off for 25 gs.

207. *Stanhope St. Friday [4 Aug. 1828].*

Prince & Princess Lieven to whom I have shewn your pony are delighted with him and will take him at 12 gs, the price I told them you had put upon it.

Let me know whether I shall send the saddle & bridle back to you; or if you do not want those appendages, supposing them not to be big enough for any larger animal let me know what I am to add to the price of the pony on account of them.

208. *Stanhope St. 11 Aug. 1828.*

Read over this letter from Shee & let me send him your reflections thereupon together with mine.[1]

The fact is, that I doubt much whether the contingency to which his statement refers will ever happen, that is a fresh election for Galway before the Catholic Question is settled. There is a very strong opinion prevalent that the Government mean to settle this question before next Session, & from some words which fell incautiously from Fitzgerald yesterday at a dinner where I met him I am *positively certain* that a communication is to be opened with the Pope with a view to make some arrangement on this subject. In this state of things the Government cannot be so foolish as to risk a second affront in Galway, when by keeping back Daly's peerage a few months they might probably avoid it. However Shee must decide as if nothing of this kind were to happen & determine what he would do upon the offer thrown out to him. There is much to be said both ways. In some respects it would be objectionable to be brought in as the protégé & creature

[1] With the aid of his inheritance from his father and of Palmerston's friendship and support, Shee had been thinking of a parliamentary seat for a year or two. In Mar. 1828 he had turned down an opportunity of government support at Ennis, under the mistaken impression that he could not have continued as Sheriff of Galway—a position he had accepted only the previous month. He had therefore resumed his search in April, telling Palmerston that he would be willing to pay some £1,200 or £1,500. Palmerston's resignation did not deter him. When the prospect loomed up of a vacant seat in Galway, by the elevation of James Daly to the peerage, Shee, though professing to be 'a staunch Protestant and a King's Man', accepted the support of the Catholic Association and pledged himself to oppose the Wellington Government. With the example of the Clare election before them, however, the Government decided another vacancy had better be avoided in Galway. Daly's patent had already been signed by the Lord Lieutenant; but he had to wait till 1845 to receive the peerage. (Shee to Palmerston, 28 Mar., 13 April and 7 Aug. 1828, B.P., G.C./SH nos. 93, 94 and 95; Sulivan to Palmerston, 26 Aug., B.P., G.C./SU no. 18; Peel to Wellington, 26 Aug., and Wellington to Peel, 27 Aug., *W.N.D.*, iv. 670 and 673.)

of the Association. On the other hand if there is a distinct understanding with them that their support is accepted upon the clear condition that no pledge is to be given upon any subject but the Catholic question, and the only engagement is to forward that Question by all proper means & to oppose any & every government that will not take up that question as a government to settle it, *I* should not object myself to give such a pledge; for I have pretty well made up my own mind henceforward to make the Catholic question a *sine qua non* to my return to office.

As to being brought in by the Catholic rent, I do not share in Shee's objection. The law which forbad the collection of that rent has expired, & the collection is therefore no longer *illegal* and I do not think it, in its nature improper; on the contrary my own opinion is that the Catholic Association are good patriots, & that all their *measures* (I say nothing of their *speeches*) have been adapted to the attainment of a most legitimate object, with much temper & great judgement. This language would not be commended in St John's Combination Room, but I am inclined to think it will be the verdict of future History.

I have got pony's price to give you & will hand it over to you when we meet.

209. *Stanhope St. 12 Aug. 1828.*

I send you the 12 gs for the pony; as the saddle & bridle fit pony & young Lieven I have left them there as a present to Master George,[1] & you must allow me to fit out Squire Harry with a new saddle & bridle for the quadruped whatever it may be that he will mount.

210. *Stanhope St. 14 Aug. 1828.*

I am glad to find we take so much the same view of Shee's affair; I shall send him your note.[1]

I will dine with you tomorrow instead of today.

I have discovered that the Govt certainly mean to settle the Catholic Question & to negotiate with the Pope for a concordat.

Reports are rife of differences between the Duke & Peel; I should rather say *disputes* for *differences* have existed between them in opinions, ever since January.

I do not see why Peel should go out on the Cath. Question if it is settled by those who like him have always opposed it, though he

[1] Princess Lieven's fourth son.
[1] B.P., G.C./SU no. 18 of 26 Aug.

might not have been able to stay in with Canning under similar circumstances.

I am glad to see that the Greek slaves are in a fair way to be rescued;[2] I have taken some pains on this subject, & had a long talk with Polignac on it, two days after the Prorogation. His Govt were then for buying them back. I reminded him of the way we had *bought* back the slaves at Algiers & suggested that Ibrahim & his army should be made answerable for the release of these slaves in Egypt. The French seem now to be going the right way to work. I also got Lieven to take an interest in the matter. As to our own Government, when the account of these outrages came to us in March last Bathurst treated the matter as a good joke, Aberdeen as the exercise of a just right, & Ellenborough as a laudable action. We certainly are going rapidly downwards in the public estimation of Europe, & shall continue to do so, as long as we have the leaden weight of Tory narrowmindedness hanging about our necks.

I have heard & from pretty good authority that the Duke begins to find that it is not quite so pleasant a thing as he thought it, in the long run, to do everything himself; & that the subserviency of his colleagues does not quite compensate for the helplessness which arises from that want of energy & information by which alone that subserviency & absence of individual opinion can be created; & that he greatly misses the assistance of Huskisson & it is generally thought that before Parliament meets some changes must take place. The Duke brings little to his extensive duties but narrow prejudices & an obstinate will to act upon them, but that forms a slender capital upon which to govern a nation and keep her up to her station among the improving nations of civilized Europe.

France is taking a great start & putting us into the shade.

211. *To Mrs Sulivan. Stapleton.*[1] *17 Sept. 1828.*

I arrived here on Sunday night after a journey long & tiresome for want of horses at the latter stages. I found a house full of people & a very gay assemblage at Doncaster. The great race, the St Leger, was won yesterday by Petre's horse the Colonel easily; the winnings in money are however not great as most people had what is called 'hedged', that is had betted both ways so as to bring their possible loss & gain within narrow compass. Ly Petre is in extasy, at her success, & pray tell Harry that she & the Miss Petres talk of nothing but

[2] See Bulwer & Ashley, i. 290–5.
[1] The place, outside Doncaster, of the Hon. Robert Edward Petre, a younger son of the 9th Baron Petre.

the race & him. Ly Petre's first observation to me was how much little Harry would be delighted when he heard of her victory, & she means to send him a list, & an ivory knife with the race engraved upon it; instead of bringing him up to the Law or any other profession I think you should bring him up to marry Lady Petre. This house is excellent & capacious as you may fancy when we sit down every day 28 or 30 inmates to dinner. To be sure two of the last arrivals live at the bailiff's. Tonight there is a grand ball & I believe another tomorrow. Friday & Saturday I shall give to Fairburn; next week I shall go to the York Music Festival. I shall like to hear an oratorio in the Minster; it will be a fine thing. After that I may probably go for a day or two to Castle Howard, & possibly to Newby;[2] Ireland will do any time in October.

Camden's appointment is obviously *provisional*, he brings neither strength in Parliament nor wisdom in Council.[3] Offers of office have been made to Sir Jas Graham & to Poulett Thompson & refused. This shows that the Govt feel their weakness in the Hs. of Cns. In fact they could hardly scramble through a stormy Session, & if the Cath. Question is not settled a stormy Session they will have; if on the other hand that settlement is proposed it will break up the Govt, for I hear there has been a correspondence between Oxford & Peel in which Peel tells his constituents that he never will remain member of a government which intends to carry that question. Here then the Duke is in a cleft stick. Without the question he will be hard driven if not beat; with it he *must* take people with whom he *cannot* have his own way in other things. It is quite curious to see how very little he is known & understood as a statesman; people all ascribe to him the enlarged views & opinions which he *ought* to have, & nobody is aware to how great a degree he has them *not*. Time & events however must either give him what he wants, or betray to the public what he wants, to be a real statesman. Petre tells me that the Pope is very willing to agree to any reasonable arrangement about the Catholics, but then Petre knows only & speaks only as to the English Catholics; the Irish treat for themselves & in fact will probably end by making themselves independent of the Pope, to the great scandal of the faithful in all parts of the Catholic world.

212. *Stapleton. 20 Sept. 1828.*

I send you some letters inclosed in the cover from Cole which you sent me the other day, & which I wish you would forward. I also

---

[2] Grantham's place near Ripon.
[3] There was a rumour that Camden was to succeed Ellenborough as Privy Seal.

send a letter which I have received from William & which I wish you would send on to Fanny.

Pray when next you write tell me some news. We hear much of Cabinet quarrels, journies to Windsor to lay statements of differences before the King etc. etc. and Ly Georgiana Ellis writes to Ly Caroline Lascelles that the other day at Geneva she met a King's Messenger searching for Huskisson who was somewhere in Swizzerland. What does this mean? Is it an invitation to him to join the Govt or is it a commission to go on to Rome & negotiate with the Pope for a concordat. I conclude the former, but the latter is not impossible. Melville's return to the Admty proves the destitution of the Govt as they would not have compelled him against his will to go there if they could have got any respectable person to go, & Camden's appointment if it takes place to the Privy Seal is evidently *provisional*. The truth is there never was so insulated and *individual* a government, or rather it is a dual administration consisting of Peel on one hand & the Duke & his staff & hangers on on the other; it is cut off from all communion with public men and will not long rest upon the support of public opinion. Sir James Graham of Netherby & Poulett Thompson of Dover have both refused office; the offering it to them proves that the Govt feel themselves in need of assistance. It seems quite clear that many months cannot pass away without some very material changes & indeed I suspect that we shall very soon hear something thereupon. This communication with Huskisson must be about something important. The Duke's friends gave out that they were sure of him whenever he was wanted & that he would come in by himself. I am pretty confident however they will find themselves deceived.

I have had a very pleasant week—good racing, agreeable society & fine weather. Today I am going on to Worksop to the Surreys,[1] on Wednesday to York for the Music Meeting, on Saturday to Castle Howard, for a day or two, then to Chatsworth for a few days & after that I shall proceed to my further destination in Ireland. My direction will always be known in Stanhope Street.

Ly Petre is very tender about little Harry. I hope he will write her an equally affectionate answer to her note.

213. *Worksop. 24 Sept. 1828.*

Thank Elizabeth for her letter which I received this morning. I go on to York tomorrow & to Castle Howard on Saturday.

[1] The 12th Duke of Norfolk's eldest son was married to the Marquess of Stafford's elder daughter.

[*PS.*] This place is fine & magnificent but dull; our party consists of the Stanleys,[1] Surreys, Ld G. Bentinck & a Miss Howard, niece of the D. of Norfolk.

214. *To Mrs Sulivan. Castle Howard. 27 Sept. 1828.*

I arrived here yesterday after the York Festival which was really quite worth going a considerable distance to see. The oratorio in the Minster in the morning was the finest *coup d'œil* & *coup d'oreille* that can be conceived. There were on Thursday 4900 people besides 600 performers, & yet so well was everything aranged that they all melted away & vanished in ten minutes after the thing was over. The expence was 14,000£ and the receipts about 17,000. This meeting was not so full as the last at which there were upwards of 6000 people, & money taken to the amount of 21,000£. We had a concert on Thursday & a fancy ball on Friday, the latter half a masquerade, many people coming in fancy characters as well as dresses. There were two thousand four hundred people at the ball; a *select* party, but wonderfully well behaved considering their numbers; they were all contained in two rooms which you may conceive must be tolerably large to do; one was built a few years ago for 6000£ out of the surplus produce of the balls. The three most striking sights in their respective ways I ever remember to have seen are this Festival, the Coronation & the Russian Review of 160,000 men at Vertus.[1] I met quantities of people I knew; first of all Cambridge men by shoals, but those one meets everywhere. The first man I fell in with in the Minster was Cholmeley with white wand & red ribband officiating as steward, amateur connoisseur & admirateur. Strickland I dined with on Thursday;[2] Vernons are to be found by the dozen at York; Fitzwilliams & Harewoods of course abound. There were not however many strangers, the assemblage being almost intirely Yorkshire people. I was two days at Worksop with the Sloane Stanleys & Surreys. I stay here tomorrow & Tuesday, go on Wednesday morning to Cholmeley who is only a few miles off, & on Thursday to Chatsworth where I shall stay a few days & thence go on to Ireland.

We are told here that Westmoreland is to be Privy Seal; if that is [*so*], it will clearly indicate the renewed ascendancy of pig tails & simplify matters extremely; it will be a clear proof that the Catholic question is not to be carried this next year. Nothing more has been heard of the messenger sent or supposed to be sent to Huskisson, but

---

[1] William Sloane Stanley and Lady Gertrude.
[1] See no. 90.
[2] Cholmeley's sister was married to Jarrard Edward Strickland (1784–1844).

Huskisson was expected at Venice & had not arrived. This may either
be that he had changed his plans or that he was going home in consequence of the messenger's dispatches. I should advise him if he were
to consult me absolutely to refuse to join any government that would
not settle the Catholic question. The state of Ireland is becoming daily
more alarming, and matters cannot remain as they are much longer;
if the question is not settled there will inevitably be an explosion &
blood shed, & I for one should be sorry to put myself in a way to
be responsible for the measures of severity which will be required to
preserve the peace of the Country when so much easier methods would
produce the effect in a more satisfactory manner.

[*PS.*] If you write next week direct to Chatsworth, Bakewell.

215. *Castle Howard. 29 Sept. 1828.*
   Add. MSS.

I do not know where Ly Malmy is & I fear Miss Cozens would be
overweight if I was to frank her. I do not wonder at troops being
sent to Ireland. The Govt must chuse between the pen & the sword
between a bill of conciliation & martial law; & I envy not those who
may make themselves responsible for the latter branch of the alternative.

216. *Sligo. 17 Oct. 1828.*
   Add. MSS. and, for the second sheet, S.P.

The woman who gave me these papers says she has received only
two payments, one of 1£. 8s. 0d., & the other of 3£. 10s. 7d., & that
she knows nothing of the other two sums stated to have been paid
to her order; perhaps you would oblige me by letting one of your
people ascertain the facts of the case & send me an explanatory
memorandum. I conjecture that the other sums were paid to some
agent who has failed & pocketed the money.

We are all as quiet here as Orange & Brunswick Clubs will let us
be, but it is quite impossible I should hope, that Parliament can determine that it is fitting to go on permanently governing a Country as
we now do this, by sword & bayonet; at least if this is the right way,
we have all been in a great mistake about the British Constitution.

There will however be no serious disturbance at present, the Catholic leaders are keeping the King's Peace for the King's Government.

But their legions are living on hope, and as soon as that food fails them they will begin to be clamorous.

It is difficult to make out what the Duke intends, but I rather think he has no settled intention, but means to meet Parliament with things as they are & see what comes out of the next debate on the question, & then side with the strongest party. I have pretty good reason to believe that the Catholics would be very tractable about arrangements if they saw any real intention to relieve them, but while [*second sheet*] there is no appearance of this of course they vapour & talk big.

The crops here have been rather deficient & prices of grain are unusually high. Potatoes however are plentiful. I find my affairs going on well & satisfactorily as far as I can hitherto collect, but I have only been here a day. I am just setting off for Cliffony. I saw Ld Anglesey & Ld F. Gower while in Dublin, the former tolerably well in health at the moment but he has been suffering much from his complaint & will I fear continue to do so, as the moistness of the climate is said to be unfavourable to his disorder. Ld F. appeared well pleased with his duties & relaxes his coldness & reserve as much as the most vigorous efforts to conquer nature can enable him to do. I do not know where Ly Malmy is so I send you the inclosed for her.

[*PS.*] If you want any clerks here you may find a cheap one in Paris; I cut this out of a French paper[1]—what would Hume give for such a document for a debate on Estimates.

217. *Cliffony. 26 Oct. 1828.*

Thank you for enabling me to correct what was a palpable mistake in the joint recollection of Wm Merry & myself; I am glad that my successor's courtesy has discovered his [*Merry's*] extreme utility which certainly formed no part of my memorandum or recollection.

I am still here & shall remain a few days longer. I find the place & the people improving very much and all the elements of civilization which I have brought together are beginning to operate. I had as Molière says to begin at the beginning, as we had neither inn, market, chapel or school, all of which are now in a sort of way established, besides some good roads made unlike *all* the other roads in Ireland at the expense of the proprietor through whose estate they run. My harbour is I may say finished and will answer perfectly;[1] it already is thronged with fishing boats, and I have people wanting a corn store

---

[1] Lacking.

[1] His confidence, however, proved unfounded; the harbour continued throughout his life to require major repairs and improvements.

there, in order to export grain from thence, & I have no doubt but that in a couple of years there will be a smartish trade of that sort carried on there. We had also this last summer a great outcry for lodging houses there from gentlemen who wanted to perform their annual ablutions in the sea in this neighbourhood and I expect that Mullaghmore will not only be the Liverpool but also the Brighton of the neighbouring counties. My schools are prospering & I am hand & glove with my Priest & Bishop. Our weather has been beautiful, warm & dry & I have had no occasion this year for my waterproofs.

I had some interesting conversation with Ld Anglesey as I passed through Dublin. He seems to be doing very sensibly & is satisfying the Catholics & the impartial (no there are none such in Ireland) I will rather say the Liberal Protestants. The Orangemen of course are furious against him. George Villiers[2] who passed by here two days ago on a tour, said he was at Clancarty's & asked whether a picture of Lord Strafford was an original. 'Yes', said Clancarty, 'it is, & I wish to god we had a good & accurate copy now in the Castle at Dublin.' In short the Orangemen breathe nothing but blood & slaughter. However the Govt will be able for the present to keep them quiet & the Association will do the same by the Catholics, till the next Session, & then we shall see what will happen. For it is idle to speculate upon matters upon which one has no materials to judge by. I am told that Anglesey & F. Gower do not quite harmonize. The former wants to act without check or controul, & the latter considers himself as more immediately in the confidence of the Duke. Ld A. seems I think to feel that he is not on a confidential footing with the Government, & the Govt I am told rather think that Ld A. separates himself too much from them in his acts & language. This is only between ourselves.

I believe the Catholics would be very tractable as to arrangements if there was any serious intention to make any with them.

[*PS.*] You may judge what a spirit of improvement has sprung up here when I tell you that a working mason offered to build a two storied, slated house at Mullaghmore at his own expence, if I would only find the timber, wood-work & glass for him, pay him for his own labour & let him take the stones, lime & slates from my quarry; & upon those conditions he further offered to live in the house when built (provided a suitable garden was added to it) rent free for as many years as I might require. Who will say there is no enterprise in Ireland.

---

[2] George Villiers, afterwards 4th Earl of Clarendon, had been sent, as Commissioner of Customs, to arrange the amalgamation of the English and Irish Boards of Excise.

218. *Cliffony. 27 Oct. 1828.*

Add. MSS.

I have received your note of the 23d about the mode of proceeding on resolutions.

This is one of the many anomalies in the practice of the two offices, upon matters in which the gradual internal usage of the one has departed from the principles which ought to guide both, & till at last that departure has been tacitly acquiesced in by the other. I rather think the actual practise as to augmentations & reductions has been that C. in C. has not only taken the King's pleasure by a written memorandum submitted, but that he has also communicated that pleasure to Secy at Wr; that the Secy at Wr has not actually himself taken the King's pleasure again, but has communicated the King's Orders to the Army, as if he had so taken it—acting upon no other grounds than the communication received from C. in C. The true principle on this matter I take to be, that C. in C. is the responsible military adviser of the Crown as to the government & discipline of the army, whatever that army may consist of (by government I mean the administration of the existing law martial but not the alteration or creation of that law, which matters rest with Secy at Wr who prepares the code called Articles of War). But though C. in C. governs the army that *is*, he being a purely military officer cannot properly advise the King as to what shall be the amount of his army, that being a matter involving constitutional political & financial considerations; upon this subject the King's civil council, that is his Privy Council, that is his Cabinet, are the proper advisers, & though every augmentation or reduction of a regt may not be a matter requiring such vindices, yet their concurrence & sanction must be assured. The Secy at War then is the civil officer whose departmental duty it is on behalf of the Cabinet to execute the details of augmentations & reductions, & he is the officer who *ought* to take the King's pleasure on such measures & communicate that pleasure to the C. in C. and to the army; of course it being understood that the Cabinet would not come to any such decision without having taken previously the C. in C. into their counsel & either obtained his concurrence, or taken upon themselves the responsibility of acting against his advice.

This is what I think would be the true & proper course, but it is nearly the reverse of the existing practice, but as the difference involves speculative objections rather than practical inconvenience I never thought it worth while to stir up from the muddy bottom of the official pool a new subject of litigation in addition to the many others which arose of their own accord. It might have seemed offensive to the C. in C. & certainly would have been so considered by either of the Dukes I had to do with, to have proposed the change & to have prescribed to them what should be their communications with the King, so long as they did not *act* upon those communications in a manner to contravene the proper principles of office. The King's pleasure taken by C. in C. for reduction can be of no avail until it is re-taken or adopted by the Secy at War. This the C. in C. has never disputed, & consequently the substantial principle has been preserved though the practical course has in point of form been defective. I am glad to hear the question is arising as I conclude we are going to have a reduction of army, and this implies a settlement of the Catholic Question, without which I should doubt our having too many troops. I to be sure should have diminished some of our foreign garrisons if I had continued acting as C. in C., at least if the Colonial Secry had agreed to do so. Murray is a sensible man & he perhaps may be wise enough to see the absurdity of keeping up so many men in some of our islands, where they have nothing to do but to get sick.

I have just been told that I am to be invited today to attend a dinner of Liberals & Catholics at Sligo on Thursday but I shall excuse myself; a man who has been in the Cabinet & means to be there again, has no business to go chattering at tavern dinners if he can possibly help it, especially in such ticklish times & on such ticklish subjects as would be brought into discussion, so I shall thank my friends & express my high sense of the honor they intend me but plead off, [*?without*] telling them my real reason.

I shall probably return to Dublin on Saturday & embark for England a few days afterwards.

[*PS.*] I wonder when the widows & soldiers' wives will find out that I am no longer Secy at Wr.

219. *Stanhope St. 17 Nov. 1828.*

I send you the materials which I once prepared with a view to reconstruct the Mutiny Act. The ink amendments are Wm Harrison's,[1] the pencil ones mine. I gave up the intention for several reasons. However clumsy some of the old drawing, I thought William Harrison's verbiage would be no improvement, & yet could not easily be set aside; and even if I had taken my friend Becket's[2] pen instead, I should not have gained much. To have announced a general remodelling of the Act would have drawn upon me at once the discussion of various questions connected with it, upon which the Duke of

---

[1] Law Clerk in the War Office.
[2] Sir John Beckett, 2nd Bart (1775–1847), was Judge Advocate General.

York & Co., on the one hand, & I on the other, never could have agreed; & upon most of which I knew I should have no help from Beckett, but the contrary. These questions were all kept in abeyance as long as the Act was passed annually *in a hurry*, and I could say, there was no time to consider important changes. The same consideration applied to the House of Commons, in which the want of time, and the absence of any material changes from the Bill of the preceding year, parried many an intended discussion. There is something too of respect attaching to the idea of its being King William's Bill, though there is little enough of the original remaining; but the antique phraseology of some of the clauses, though somewhat unlike Harrison's legislation, is perhaps as good as more modern expressions would be.

Instead therefore of remodelling the whole, I kept from time to time mending its details, & though it is still susceptible of improvement it is much better than I found it. You will recollect how difficult we always found it to get the C. in C. for the time being to agree to anything, when I remind you that even the *Duke of Wellington* objected to my proposal of substituting in the first section of the first Article of War the punishment of '*confinement*' for the now obsolete punishment of 'being laid in irons for 12 hours' which that article denounces as the penalty of irreverent behaviour at Church, but which I apprehend has not for very many years been inflicted.[3]

220. *Stanhope St. 20 Nov. 1828.*

I mean to be at Broadlands from about the 5th of Decr till Christmas. Do try & contrive to get down to me during that period. I am not sure about January, as it is possible I may run over to Paris in that month.

221. *Stanhope St. 7 Jan. 1829.*
          Add. MSS.
     I shall be much obliged to you if you will frank on to

                    J. Kincaid Esq.,
                    Leinster Street,
                    Dublin

two or three deeds which will be sent under cover to you for that purpose.

---

[3] Wellington had not produced any serious objection, 'save that it would appear to be made in deference to the marked sentiment of the times'. Beckett had conceded that

I would, if I was you, be rather cautious in what terms or at least in whose presence, I expressed myself about the Duke of Wellington just at present; walls & ministers have long ears & he might take offence at any very strong expressions from a person in office; at all events it might create some awkwardness between you & Hardinge.

222. *To Mrs Sulivan. Hotel du Rhin, Place Vendome [Paris]. 12 Jan. 1829.*

I left London on Wednesday evening & arrived here on Saturday morning between five & six. I had a pretty good passage to Boulogne, for which the wind was fair, and as the weather was too cold to stop to sleep anywhere, or to hope to find any place in a French inn as warm as one's post chaise, I travelled on till I reached this. The frost is sharp & the streets covered with ice, which the French call *verglas*, but for which we, thanks I suppose to our warmer & more genial climate, have no word. I am dating by anticipation as to residence, as I do not get to the Rhine till this evening; being now in a bad *entresol* in the Hotel de Bath, the only place I could find on my arrival; where, there being a gaping void under every door big enough to let a kitten through I sit writing by the fire in my travelling cap & cloak & by this means do tolerably well. All day yesterday & Saturday I was going my rounds & paying visits. I find a great number of people I know & they have all been very kind & civil, & what with original acquaintances & persons to whom I have letters, I shall get through my three weeks very agreeably. I found Mad. Flahaut whom I know very well, having pleasant parties; she took me on Saturday to the Opera & Mad. Girardin's & last night she had a party at home. Today I dine with Pozzo di Borgo, & tomorrow with Mad. de Bourke.[1] Of English there were at Mad. Flahaut's, Burdett & his daughters, Sligo, the Leitrims, the Albemarles, the Berrys (at least Agnes), Ly Charlotte Lindsay; of Portugueze, the Villa Flors, Barboza (Pedro's minister) & divers others; of French the Neuvilles, Girardins & several others of those who ought to be known.

I saw Mad. de Rully[2] yesterday who begged to be remembered to you. La Ferronays the Minister for Foreign Affairs has recently had a paralytic seizure, the result of a long course of previous bad health. If he gets well enough to be moved, he is to go to Nice. No

the old phrase gave ammunition to the 'anti-punishment gang', but wanted to preserve it as an alternative against the day when flogging might have to be abolished. They therefore compromised on the substitution of 'corporal punishment'. (Beckett to Palmerston, 19 Mar., and Wellington to Palmerston, 20 Mar. 1827, B.P., G.C./BE no. 572 and WE no. 33.)

[1] The widow of Count Edmond Bourke, formerly Danish minister in Madrid, London and Paris.

[2] See C. Nicoullaud, ed., *Memoirs of the Comtesse de Boigne (1781–1814)*, 1907, p. 303.

successor is appointed nor is it yet determined who is to hold his office *ad interim*; there is a struggle between the ultras & liberals about this. Hyde de Neuville who is *now* liberal, though at one time violent ultra wants to have Chateaubriand; Martignac who though liberal leans to the court party, wanted Pasquier; but the Baron Agier a leader of about 40 independents went to him to say that if Pasquier was appointed, he & his squadron should oppose. So the matter rests for the present.

The people here are generally Russian and anti-Turkish, but their real wishes or feelings are directed towards certain territories between their present frontier & the Rhine, now held by the Netherlands; & all parties would support any minister who would regain them these. If as is at present probable the war in Turkey goes on into a second campaign there is no saying what chances may turn up, to set matters stirring in Europe, and to give them an opportunity of making an attempt.

Paris does not look much to advantage in its snowy veil, but there seems to have been a good deal of new building since I was here last though nothing compared with the additions to London in the interval. As far as one could judge of the appearance of the country as I drove along, though the hours of daylight are short and one's glasses in a frost are not very transparent, I thought there was visibly a great improvement perceptible; many new houses built & building in the towns, & in a more comfortable style, & the inns are wonderfully improved. What strikes one most on the Continent is the general prodigality of space and the size of their farmyards etc., & they remind one of the observation of a Fen farmer who was met by a Trinity College fellow at the Panorama of Waterloo, & who in reply to a remark that it was a most interesting sight, said, 'yes it is indeed Sir', and, pointing to Hougomont & La Haie Sainte, added, 'what capital out buildings they have in them countries'.

There is great expectation here of some counter movement at Lisbon, & doubts were entertained there of Miguel's existence as nobody had actually seen him, but *one* captain of Royal Volunteers; at all events it was suspected that if alive, he was gone mad.

Ld Stewart does not seem to have succeeded here much on his second arrival.[3] When he went people thought it was for good, & everybody began to talk & canvass freely the innumerable anecdotes which had accumulated during his long residence. Now that he comes back again those who have thus committed themselves to each other about him, of course feel shy of courting a man of whom they have openly & unreservedly expressed very disparaging opinions. He has

[3] Lord Stuart de Rothesay was Ambassador in Paris, 1814, 1815–24 and 1828–31. Lord Granville was his predecessor in 1824–8 as well as his successor in 1831.

done too, several shabby things, especially about some furniture &
pictures of Ld Granville's which he refused to buy, & when compelled
to do so by Aberdeen sold by auction, hiring inferior articles in their
stead. It is said that just at that time the King was very ill & he specu-
lated upon a new reign & a new ambassador. He gave a ball the other
night, and asked Da Ponte, Miguel's unacknowledged minister, &
left out Barboza, the minister of Pedro, though he had invited Mad.
Loulé, & had asked her which of the two she visited & she had told
him Barboza & then he & Ly Elizabeth went to their rooms & left
the Loulés waiting for their carriage in the hall till two in the morning.
These things are *gaucheries*. But he has turned all the attachés out of
the apartments they had with the Granvilles & given two of them
only, bare walls of rooms over the porter's lodge leaving them to furnish & even paper them. The Duchesse de Berri gives a ball tomorrow
at which there are to be quadrilles of nothing but ladies, & she has
her ladies to drill six hours a day till they are ready to drop.

223. *13 Jan. 1829.*

    Bulwer & Ashley, i. 325; MS. not found.

    Palmerston reports further on his stay in Paris.

224. *Hotel du Rhin, Place Vendome. 19 Jan.* [*1829*].

    Add. MSS.

We are still dark & frosty, though not quite so cold as we have
been, but January is certainly not the month I should advise any
friend to chuse to see Paris to advantage.

Nothing was settled yesterday about the Govt here; but Polignac
has been sent for & is expected to arrive today; not as Minister of
Foreign affairs, but to be talked to and consulted & probably to have
the place offered him. The King is very fond of him & wishes to have
him; the liberals & even moderate ultras fear his high Tory & Jesuitic
propensities, & great efforts were made with the King all yesterday
to dissuade him from such a choice.

Whatever happens however the best informed seem to think that
this Govt cannot stand & that it must be succeeded by one more intirely liberal consisting probably of Chateaubriand, Casimir Perrier,
Royer Collard, the D. of Broglie who married Albertine Stael, Sebastiani, & others of that sort. People in general distrust Chateaubriand
as a mountebank without discretion or judgement & even those of
his party laugh at Mackintosh's comparison of him with Canning in

the *Keepsake*.[1] The *tendency* of a more liberal government would be less friendly to England. There are many motives which point to war; a strong desire to regain the country on the north east between France & the Rhine; a great hankering after Savoy & Piedmont & the Milanese; a wonderful itching for promotion in the army, who all declare that three years more of peace will superannuate every rank & put them hors de combat as a military nation. On the other hand though their finances are good & flourishing still they could not make *war* without a loan, & that would derange their affairs considerably, and unless the war was popular with all parties, the Chambers would not vote the supplies. Pozzo on the part of Russia is holding out to the French every kind of promise to induce them to side with Russia in the event of a scuffle in Europe next spring. But Prussia though generally speaking the follower of Russia would little like to see France advancing to the Rhine, & would require very large bribes in the shape of Austrian dismemberment to induce her to be consenting to such arrangements. Belgium I fear would be a very willing prey to France & Italy would rise with gladness to hail any Power that would offer emancipation from the stupid tyranny of Metternich. In the mean time this country is making the most rapid intellectual improvement, sound & rational notions of government & of national interest are finding their way through all ranks, and as old Soult said, with whom I had a very long & entertaining conversation yesterday, men of *his* day are a wonderful improvement on the old regime, but the young men of the present day beat them as much as they did their predecessors; and enlightened views are if possible more prevalent in the young men of the Faubourg St Germain (that is the quarter where the old Tory nobility chiefly reside) than among other classes of society. The fine ladies complain that they have lost all their influence in public affairs—when politics were settled in drawing rooms & cabinets, they could do what they liked, but now that ministers must answer to Chambers & explain their reasons & conduct to the satisfaction of Deputies, the case is wholly altered & ladies become only the ornament of society. The habits of the members of Parliament during a session are these—at two the Houses meet, at six they all go to dinner, & no human eloquence nor any national interest could keep a man to listen beyond that critical hour. During the Hundred Days when Buonaparte had fled from Waterloo & the allies were sweeping upon Paris, when the deepest interests of France & of individuals were at stake, at six o'clock the electrified assembly used to rise, & assure the orator who wanted to detain them, that they did not undervalue the importance of the subject, nor the force of his reason-

[1] See 'Sketch of a Fragment of the History of the Nineteenth Century by J. M.', *The Keepsake for MDCCCXXIX*, pp. 242–3.

ing, but it was six o'clock & dinner was already on the table at their home & go therefore they must, compelled by *ineluctabile Fatum*. People generally admit the absurdity of not admitting Deputies under 40, & talk of bringing the age down to 30. In the mean time the young men form a spouting club called the *Parlotte* where they do what the law does not allow them to do in the Chambers, discuss & vote upon all the transactions of the day.[2] At eight o'clock all the Deputies go away from their homes to certain reunions or meetings at the houses of leading members, where till ten or eleven, they rediscuss the debate of the day or anticipate that of the morrow & settle what course they shall pursue. There are four or five of these party meetings, made up according to the various shades of political opinion. Every thing here is more or less military, & so are their party divisions; they have center, and right & left & center right & center left & extreme right, & extreme left. The President too instead of taking the chair preceded by a chaplain & prayers like our Speaker, marches up to his seat with a military band at ordinary time.

So Ireland has been offered to the D. of Northumberland; I shall be curious to learn his decision. In ordinary times & common circumstances he might do well, but if he is wise he will decline it now. He would take it under great disadvantages. However my guess is that he will accept. I would rather have seen Verulam there, & because I think he is more a man of the world than the D. of N. The Duke has one of the most inconvenient weaknesses for a Ld Lieut.—a great proning to toadies; & the Irish are such capital toadies that he will have a flight of such vermin settle upon him at once; and in the shape of men whom with his political bias he will not distrust, but will naturally look to as his supporters & advisers. At all events this appointment is a new crisis in the opinion & politics of our General in Chief; for last year he was resolved to send a *moderate Catholic*, in the event of Ld Anglesey retiring, and the D. of Northd at best is only a moderate *anti*-Catholic.[3]

This system of government *will* not & *can* not do; & on this *rock* the Duke's vessel will split. I was talking the evening before last with the D. of Orleans on these matters & he said what is quite true that

[2] Palmerston himself was elected a member the following year (Airlie, i. 167).

[3] Palmerston perhaps still nursed his Cambridge grudge against Northumberland, but his poor opinion of Northumberland personally and of the appointment, which the Duke accepted, was widely shared. In society Northumberland was still probably what he had appeared to be in 1810—'a chattering, good-humoured civil young man' (Mrs Warrenne Blake, *An Irish Beauty of the Regency Compiled from 'Mes Souvenirs',— the Unpublished Journals of the Hon. Mrs Calvert 1789–1822*, 1911, p. 163). But in 1829 opinions as wide apart politically as Charles Greville's and Lady Holland's condemned him as a nonentity. Greville said he was 'an absolute nullity, a bore beyond all bores'; Lady Holland that he was 'a poor creature, vain, ostentatious & null'. (*Greville Memoirs*, i. 312; the Earl of Ilchester, ed., *Elizabeth, Lady Holland to her Son 1821–1845*, 1946, p. 94.)

the foundation of the King's obstinate resistance to the question is a
confused & jumbled idea that his title to the throne rests solely upon
the principle of entire Catholic exclusion; & that if once Catholics
were deemed eligible to anything, they ought to be so equally to the
throne, & he ought to make his bow to the King of Sardinia & would
become virtually an usurper.

What trash this is, & yet how likely to catch the magical & un-
methodized mind of a royal person.

225. *To Mrs Sulivan. Hotel du Rhin, Place Vendome. 19 Jan. 1829.*

The weather continues excessively cold & disagreeable, & not one
ray of sunshine have I seen since I came to Paris; the sky has been
invariably a fine iron grey. I have however been well enough amused,
have found many old acquaintances & have made several new ones—
among the former Fanny Jarratt now Mrs Fitzwilliam who is settled
here for life, turned French woman bringing up her girls to speak
French through their little *nez retroussés* like natives, & meaning to
marry them here. She inquired very kindly after you all & her old
flame William. The Greffier Fagel is here & his brother is better.[1]
I went to Court yesterday & here it is an operation, as you go first to
the King, then to the Dauphin, then to the Duaphine & then to the
Dss of Berry. The King is wonderfully stout & well for his age, &
several years younger than our King in constitution.

The Dss of Berry received us in the apartment of ye D. de Bourdeaux
from the furniture of which it seems they mean to make him a great
captain. The walls are hung with pictures of battles, there are suits of
child's armour stuck up like those in the Tower, & under the side
board is an army of little soldiers half a foot high whom his Royal
Highness knocks over like nine pins.

Nothing was settled last night about the successor to La Ferronays,
but the idea was that Polignac would be appointed & the Duc de
Fitzjames be sent to London to succeed him. This would be a very
bad arrangement. Polignac is high Tory & Jesuit, & probably an
entire change of Govt would be the consequence whenever the
Chambers meet. Hyde de Neuville will most likely retire if Polignac
comes in. I saw Soult & his pictures—they are very beautiful, & he an
ugly ruffian—but tolerably civil as a showman, especially under the
idea that one should puff the pictures to the Govt & help him to sell

---

[1] Baron Henry Fagel (1765–1838), who had been appointed Secretary of the States
General in 1787, continued to be known by that title though he was Netherlands
ambassador in London 1813–24, in order to distinguish him from his brothers and
especially from Baron Robert Fagel (1771–1856), who was Minister in Paris 1814–54.

them which *now* he would be glad to do. As to sights I have been to none. The weather is too cold & comfortless to see anything, & the ground where it had not been beaten & trodden & covered with lime & rubbish, so slippery with ice that there is no walking or standing on it. I very nearly knocked my brains out by tumbling with my head within an inch of one of their granite posts on the Place of Louis 15. I went last night to wait on the D. & Dss of Orleans; they were very civil, asked me a great deal about Broadlands etc. He is probably the richest subject in Europe, & has an income of about 300,000£ a year, of which they say he annually lays bye two thirds to provide for his nine children & yet lives like a little sovereign—as well he may upon 100,000£ a year in France. This country is certainly making great progress in civilization & improvement & if they only keep the peace for twenty or thirty years longer will be a very flourishing kingdom. It is curious however to see a state of society so much resembling in many things what England was 100 years ago; their great festoons of cloth *hung out* of their upper windows to denote that they sell that article; the huge stockings & gigantic hats & gloves that cover the walls of the houses, to indicate dealers in those commodities; their primitive vehicles that rumble along the streets like caravans at fairs only filled with human beings instead of wild beasts; the above ground sewers, & the private dung-hills at every door like those in an Irish village; their immense fire-places & drawing room gales that oblige everybody to entrench themselves behind screens as our grandmothers used to do—all these things are more or less uncivilized, but still they are improving. *I* do not add to the catalogue a *six* o'clock dinner though that certainly is a Gothic practise.

I shall stay here till Saturday the 31st & shall probably be in town on the 2nd of Feby.

[*PS.*] Send this on to Fanny & one shot will hit both. Mad. de Rully desires her best regards.

226. [*Paris*]. *Friday, 23 Jan.* [*1829*].

I send you a letter I have just recd from William; we are not quite as cold as he has been but my thermometer outside my window is now at ½ past 3 standing at 12° of Fahrenheit or 20° below freezing.

I believe Mortemart will succeed La Ferronays, or else Rayneval will.

[*PS.*] I leave this tomorrow week.[1]

[1] He reached Stanhope St at 5 a.m. on Tuesday, 3 Feb. (B.P./D no. 5). Hobhouse crossed from Calais with him the day before (*Broughton*, iii. 300).

227. *Stanhope St. 10 Feb. 1829.*

I certainly consider myself as *landed* at Cambridge by this division of the Govt, & therefore care but little whether this petition is carried or not.[1] I think however that as it will probably be supported by all my Johnian friends it would not be taken as a particular compliment to them if you were to make your first appearance at Cambridge after a long absence, among a small squad of Londoners come down to defeat them; as far as *I* am concerned therefore I should rather wish you to plead inevitable official engagements which at so short a notice cannot be arranged so as to admit of your leaving town.

228. *Stanhope St. 13 Mar. 1829.*

Many thanks for your copies of the Mutiny Bill; you have done it very well and judging from the trouble it took one merely to hunt out the places of the clauses in the old and new bill, the arrangement must have been a work of no small labour.

229. *Broadlands. 24 Sept. 1829.*

The Aberdeens are not in the least Evangelical; what Abercorn & Ld Claude may be I know not, as I am not acquainted with them.

The tutor I mentioned to you is a Mr Anderson and is not the man with whom Abercorn has been; a friend of mine had a son at Anderson's and in about a year's time the lad took the most extraordinary Methodistical twist. Anderson himself is highly Evangelical & there is a little knot of Methodists at Brighton who seize & fasten upon any young men they can get hold of; the Elliots of Trinity College, friends of Calthorpe, are the chiefs of the click. Goulburn & Buxton are all more or less in the same line, and I would advise you to make some further inquiries about the man in question before you do anything further about him.[1]

[1] Thomas Flower Ellis, a barrister and former fellow of Trinity College, had written that day to warn Sulivan that an attempt was to be made at Cambridge the following day to carry an anti-Catholic petition (S.P.).

[1] Henry Venn Elliott (1792–1865) and Edward Bishop Elliott (1793–1875) were both Trinity men, members of the Clapham Sect and evangelicals. Henry was first chaplain of St Mary's, the chapel his father had built in Brighton. In Brighton, until 1832, he also took in pupils, among them the 2nd Marquess of Abercorn and his brother Lord Claud Hamilton, and the sons of Thomas Fowell Buxton, Lord Aberdeen and Henry Goulburn. (Josiah Bateson, *The Life of the Rev. Venn Elliott*, 3rd ed., 1872, pp. 98–9.) The Rev. Robert Anderson (*ob.* 1843) was perpetual curate of Trinity Chapel, Brighton; George Peacock (1791–1850) was then tutor at Trinity; and the 3rd Baron Calthorpe was both Harrovian and Johnian.

I forget his name, but he belongs to Trinity College and is a clever man; probably Peacock or Ellis may know something more about him, & the ways of his house. But those people are so artful and indefatigable and work upon the imagination and vanity and love of distinction of a young man with the most astonishing dexterity. The lad I allude to was intended for the army and all of a sudden wrote word to say that he was determined to go into the church; of course he was taken away, & was soon cured, but it shews how they try to unsettle minds & interfere with people's arrangements. Do not mention the circumstance pray, because it was told me in confidence with a view to some inquiry.

[*PS.*] I think Gordon & Muffling seem to have humbugged Diebitch, who they say is not a very sharp fellow though a good officer.[2]

230. *Ryde.*[1] *27 Sept. 1829.*

I return you the inclosed which does not belong to me, but as I know not my correspondent I cannot, as I usually do on these occasions send the packet back to him referring him to the *Annual Register* for May 1828.

I shall start in a day or two upon my peregrinations making some visits in my way to Ireland, to Baring, Littleton, Ld Anson & probably Lord Anglesea.

So it seems certain that Gordon & Guilleminot have bamboozled Diebitch and stopped him on pretence of insurrections at Constantinople. If I had been him I would have said that was their affair & not mine & have gone on till the Sultan had put his name to an *engrossed* Treaty of Peace, which I should have carried about with me for that purpose.

I hope your weather will be more like yesterday than today and that we shall have a fine October.

231. *Shugborough.*[1] *7 Oct. 1829.*

    Cf. *Lorne, pp. 56–62.*

I arrived here the day before yesterday, Littleton having transferred his party to this place on account of some private theatricals holding

---

[2] Gordon, Guilleminot and Muffling, the British, French and Prussian representatives in Constantinople, had urged moderation on the Russian commander in the Balkans. The Treaty of Adrianople was signed on 14 Sept.

[1] Palmerston was visiting Lady Elizabeth Vernon at St Clare.

[1] Viscount Anson's place in Staffordshire.

here, in which Ld Anson and Ld & Ly Belfast performed with tolerable success, and divers other ladies & gentlemen with remarkable want of skill. I go today to Ld Anglesey for a couple of days and thence to Liverpool where I shall take steam for Dublin. It is raining here as usual on alternate days, but yesterday we rode & saw Ingestrie & Tixall. This is not as nice a district as I expected; the places are all in low bottoms with sluggish rivers overflowing on the slightest rain and now of course under water.

So at last peace is made between Russia & Turkey and upon Russia's own terms; I hope & trust that Greece will now be placed upon a proper footing and our Govt will find that they have failed of both their objects, having succeeded neither in preventing the establishment of Greece, nor in protecting the Sultan from the arms of Russia. We shall therefore have lost our influence both with the free, & the despot. This is the fate of those who are unable to pursue a straight course, because their inclination leading one way, & necessity driving the other they are forced into the diagonal.

I had a curious conversation on Saturday evening at the Travellers with Sir Richd Vivian the member for Cornwall;[2] Sir Wm Heathcote had called on me at Bds last week & told me he expected Vivian at Hursley & that he wd be sorry to find me absent from Hampshire, as he knew that Vivian wished to see me. Finding Vivian at dinner at the Travellers I sat down by him & we fell to forthwith to politics & cutlets, & the dialogue ended in his proposing to me to be Leader of the H. of Cs to a Mansfield, Eldon, Newcastle, & Knatchbull Administration.

I began by observing that the Duke seemed to be getting the Tories round again & recovering his strength so as to be able to meet Parliament again without any reinforcements. Vivian said this was quite a mistake, that the Tories were more adverse than ever, that few people knew better than he did what they were about, that the Duke of Wn was tottering more than ever & that even in a fortnight or three weeks a new govt might be formed, that the King had not seen his first minister since some day in August, and was only watching for an opportunity to get rid of him—that at all events Peel could not possibly meet the House again as Leader. He then asked how I felt myself & to what degree bound to Huskisson, whether I could & would take office without him & whether I should be disposed to join such a govt as he had mentioned; that Huskisson frightened the country gentlemen; that I had only pledged myself on foreign politics, & was free about trade & currency; that I should probably feel no difficulty in leading the He of Cns. I said that as to Huskisson &

<hr>

[2] Sir Richard Vyvyan, 8th Bart. In a letter of 13 Mar. 1832 to Littleton, Palmerston called him 'that strange coconut' (Hatherton Papers).

myself we found ourselves from various circumstances acting together, and that we agreed in opinions, but that we were each of us free with respect to the other; that I should have no cause to complain if he accepted office without me, & I considered myself as having a similar freedom with respect to him; that as to my opinions on trade & currency, it had certainly so happened that no occasion or opportunity had arisen for me to express them in Parliament in any detail, but that they were formed, & formed upon some reflection and as far as I could judge were not likely to be altered; & that they were intirely in unison with that system, which though much older than Huskisson was perhaps first carried extensively into practice by him & which had exposed him to such undeserved censure; that consequently I should not be disposed to join any government who intended to retrace the steps which Parliament has taken on these subjects; that as to joining any particular govt all I could say was that I had no personal antipathies but that no man could answer such a question in the abstract & by anticipation, but must first know who the men were who were to be proposed to him as colleagues, & what system of government they intended to pursue.

He went on in the same way & at length said that the question he had for some time been desirous of putting to me, was whether I should have any objection to have my name mentioned to the King as willing to be Secy of State for the Colonies & Leader of the Hs. to such a govt as he had alluded to, saying that I should be a great card to them, and that the King might be more likely to agree to the formation of such a govt if he found that a certain number of persons were willing to become members of it. He had by the way in the commencement of the conversation expressed his opinion that the D. of Wn was a man of most unmeasured ambition, who wants to make all Europe a military camp & to govern upon arbitrary principles; in proof of which he adduced the recent establishment of Polignac in France and the late Police Bill here. My reply to this specific proposition was of course a negative. I said that, I certainly could not wish my name so to be mentioned to the King; that if any proposition was made to me by a govt already formed or in the act of being formed, my answer would be the same as that which I made to the Duke in Jany 1828, first tell me who are your men, and what are to be your measures, & then I shall be able to say whether it would suit me to become your colleague. He then went on to discuss lightly various men, apparently with the view of letting me see indirectly how it was intended that the projected govt was to be formed. Ld Mansfield would of course he said be at the head. Eldon would be a member. Brougham he thought must be got out of the Hs. of Cns as he would be too formidable as an antagonist; and why should he not make an excellent Chancellor; Lyndhurst had been tried & must go. Fitzgerald he said is a quick clever fellow & would be most useful. Did I think he would unite himself with such a Govt. I said I thought he scarcely could or would join a govt formed upon the ruins of that of the Duke & Peel. Young Stanley he praised as a man that should be obtained, & he discussed whether Stanley would require a cabinet office or would take one out of the cabinet. Herries he commended as a man full of most useful knowledge. Huskisson he mentioned in connection with the Chancellorship of the Exchequer. Did I think that he & Herries could or would serve together. I said I really could not guess. Robert Grant would make an admirable Speaker of the House, and Charles Grant (who I suppose is too much identified with free trade for this party) might be made Governor of Jamaica. (This appointment by the way seems to be the Chiltern Hundreds of political men who are to be got out of the way.)[3] Ld Grey was deemed impracticable as a colleague; Falmouth unmanageably obstinate; the Duke of Newcastle lauded generally for his good sense & understanding; and Sir E. Knatchbull pointed out as Secy of State for the Home Department.

My part in all this was chiefly that of listener, or suggester of general remarks for the purpose of leading on the conversation. I said that I should much doubt the success of such a govt as he was sketching out, & thought that no govt would sufficiently carry public opinion with it that did not contain more persons with whom as public men the country was already acquainted; that the King too must have some ostensible reason for changing his Govt, & could not here do as in France, & send word one fine morning to his ministers that he had appointed another set; and that moreover the Govt must be turned out for doing something or for not doing something, & that their successors must be bound to do the reverse of that whether omission or commission for which they were dismissed. This he treated very lightly, saying the King never could be at any greater loss for a reason to turn out his present ministers, than Russia always is for a reason to make war with Turkey—at all events he said that if nothing were done before Parliament met yet that very first day, if the Tories & Whigs & Canningites would only unite in an amendment, the Govt must be beat. When we parted he asked where he should direct to me if he should have occasion to write to me while I was in Ireland, & expressed great pleasure at having had this conversation with me— begged me however to consider it as intirely private between ourselves; that what I had said to him would go no further than himself, & requested that what he had said to me might be confined to me (which I do not consider myself as violating by telling you); and

[3] Canning had offered Jamaica to Palmerston in 1827.

particularly begged me to say nothing about it to *Huskisson*. This I said I could easily undertake, as I had no chance of seeing him for some time. He also during our conversation remarked that the D. of Cumberland was getting round again in public opinion.

All this is curious as showing how busily Cumberland & Eldon are still at work and how much they flatter themselves with success in getting the Duke out, provided they can only hold out to the King the prospect of a decent government. It is plain they have opened their eyes to the utter impossibility of making a purely Tory govt, & that they are now come to the next step, that is to try to mix with a predominance of old fellows saturated with the brine of Toryism, a few young men of the liberal parties, who shall not be able to set up as objections to any course proposed, the assertion (convenient in discussion because it supersedes argument upon questions themselves) that they cannot agree, because it would be inconsistent with their own former pledges. Hence they shrink from Huskisson & Charles Grant, & wish to gag Robert Grant by the Speaker's wig, to get FitzGerald who they think would join any party & embrace any opinions, & tempt me by brilliant offers to forego opinions to which I do not happen to be personally tied by any public declarations. I suspect that foreign affairs are intended for Vivian himself, who in most points agrees with us, & is violently against the Metternich & Apostolical School of which the Duke & Aberdeen are disciples. Stanley they think would be a good decoy for the Whigs.

The probability is that all will end in smoke & nothing be attempted before Parliament meets, but all this shews how much the Duke deceives himself if he really fancies that he is getting back the Tory party. He however must know the real state of things, & it is not impossible that he may himself anticipate his enemies, and try to get to *his* Govt some of the people whom they are reckoning upon for theirs. As far as I individually am concerned it seems to me that my interest as well as inclination leads me to adhere to the party with whom I have been thrown. I consider myself as being free if I chose, because we never have met or consulted or acted in concert as a party, & have upon no one occasion voted as a body; we sit together, but upon almost every question last Session voted different ways. But as to going to the Tory Party even if they really & in good earnest were to propose to me to be their He of Cns Leader, though I should not be quite in the same false position as Peel because he has always concealed his opinions more or less & I have avowed mine, yet still to belong to people you do not think with cannot answer. In fact the only govt which could really answer the wants of the nation at the present moment would be one composed of men known & looked up to; fancy Knatchbull & Vivian Secretaries of State! The Duke has a great hold upon public feelings; *no* other individual perhaps now living has as great a one. Whether this is well or ill founded is nothing to the purpose, but so it is. There is no great public controversy to stand instead of established reputation, and obscure & unknown men even if backed up by the popularity of Cumberland never would stand their ground unless they rested upon principles of govt popular & approved by the intelligent part of the Country; and a Mansfield Govt would of course take the opposite line. I need not I well know enforce upon you the preservation of silence about the contents of this letter but pray let me have any observations that occur to you upon reading it. I should perhaps explain that Vivian & I have had frequent communications on political subjects, foreign & domestic & that while I was in the Cabinet I took him by Dudley's leave to the Foreign Office to read over a mass of papers about the war between Russia & Persia, & so far succeeded in altering his opinions upon that event as to lead him to give up an intention he had formed of giving notice of a motion about it; so that our habits of personal intercourse naturally led to a more confidential communication on his part than the distance between Cornwall & Hampshire might have suggested.

Adieu direct to me in Stanhope Street from whence my letters will always follow me; or rather direct to me at Post Office Dublin which will save time.[4]

232. *Hotel de Rivoli, Paris.*[1] *4 Dec. 1829.*

   Add. MSS.

Here is a pretty cargo for you, but these are answers to letters that ought never to have come here, so I shall not have to send you such a batch again. I have sent a general report of all things to William, to whom I refer you.[2]

---

[4] Palmerston had previously sent a detailed account of this conversation to Lady Cowper on 3 Oct., but it is incomplete. In a second letter of 10 Oct., reporting on his country house visits just before he embarked from Liverpool for Dublin, he commented briefly on his conversation with Vyvyan: 'I was determined to say nothing to him that should check the flow of confidential communications with which he was honouring me, but what a notion that a man should leave a set of clever gentleman-like men with whom he finds himself acting, in order to join the noodles of Boodles, and become leader of the lame and the blind.' (B.P.W.; see also B. T. Bradfield, 'Sir Richard Vyvyan and the Fall of Wellington's Government', University of Birmingham *Historical Journal*, xi, 1968, pp. 141–56.)

[1] Palmerston had returned from Ireland on 10 Nov. and embarked at Dover for Calais on 27 Nov.

[2] See Bulwer & Ashley, i. 347–53.

233. *Paris. 9 Dec. 1829.*

   Bulwer & Ashley, i. 353–6; MS. not found.

Palmerston reports on French politics.

234. *Hotel de Rivoli [Paris]. 11 Dec. 1829.*

   Add. MSS.

Will you have the goodness to have these letters sent to their destination, giving your frank to that for the Reverend James.[1]

Samway[2] will bring to you a small book which I wish you would direct to me here, & then send to the Foreign Office to come by the Ambassador's Bag.

There is no further news here about the Ministry. But the King is gone for a few days to Compiègne where by the bye he contrived in shooting to slip & tumble & strain his leg (these little incidents are historical facts in these countries), and the ministers are all gone to their respective country seats. 'Il est si fraix à present et si doux l'air de la campagne', says sneeringly one of the Opposition papers. I believe two negotiations are going on, one by Polignac to try to form a government of moderate royalists of which he should be the head, & excluding on the one hand Bourmont as too violent, and on the other Courvoisier, Haussez & Chabrol as too liberal, but this will not succeed for want of any elements out of which to make it. The other is carrying on by Roy to try to make a govt of liberals retaining if they will agree to do so Polignac individually as a peace-maker with the King. In the mean time all tongues seem now untied & even some of the Noailles, the great courtiers, plainly say that it matters little who is minister as long as Charles is King; for that till the King will yield to public opinion, & adapt himself to the times which Charles will not do, no ministry can act in such a way as to carry with them the confidence of the people. However Charles is beat, & the only matter in doubt is the time when he shall surrender the keys. Some think he will capitulate forthwith, some that affairs will go on as they are till the Chambers meet. My own opinion is that the discord which prevails in the Cabinet itself makes this last course impossible. The convalescence of Nicholas is a great thing for all Europe. I have heard & from a channel which I place confidence in, though not from Pozzo di Borgho that recently Nicholas has communicated to this Govt his anxious desire to see maintained those constitutional institutions which were established under the auspices of his brother Alexander.

It seems that soon after the installation of the present government here, the several Courts of Europe were sounded, in order to ascertain

---

[1] Not identified.
[2] Samways had succeeded Harrison as butler in Stanhope St in 1824.

with what an eye they [*?would*] see an attempt on the part of Charles to get rid of, or essentially to regalize the present constitution. England & Austria of course were delighted at the idea, and indeed it was not without some hopes, at least on the part of Metternich, that such might be the march of events, that such efforts were made to get rid of the last & bring in the present ministry. The declaration of Russia has vexed & discomposed some people here. I heard two days ago a strong confirmation of what I before reported about the disposition of the troops. A friend of mine was talking to an officer of rank in the *Garde Royale, the* corps if any upon which the King ought to be able to rely. This officer, after saying that the men were almost all liberal & the officers many of them so too, that if orders were given to fire on the people he could not undertake to say whether they would be obeyed, said that besides the officers & men there was a third class who were much more *prononcés* in their opinions & who were liberal to a man & these were the non-commissioned officers. So much for any chance of carrying a *coup d'état*; upon the power of doing which the only hope of this Ministry rested.

We hear in this place that our Duke in Downing Street strongly condemns Polignac for getting rid of La Bourdonnaye. I hope this is not true, as it would be a proof to [*sic*] too great ignorance of the state of things here, or of too perverse a folly.

[*PS.*] It is freezing hard & we have quite January weather.

235. *Paris. 25 Dec.* [*1829*].
     Add. MSS.

I send you a last cargo, as I shall start from hence on Monday. I generally send back to my War Office correspondents their post-humous applications, but to spare these poor devils the postage I forward them to you. The cold increases & the snow continues. There is no news, all things remain as they are. Some of the libel prosecutions have failed, & the Govt is damaged by the speeches as well as by the issue of the trials.

Thank you for your letters & I am really delighted to hear such satisfactory accounts of Stephen.

236. *Broadlands. 15 Jan. 1830.*

I am sorry to hear from Fanny that you doubt about coming here, in consequence of a fresh cold; pray come by all means cold or no cold; be assured that it will do you much good to make the run, and if we do not cure your cold in a week I will engage to take it off your hands.

We will put you into one of the great arm chairs in the saloon by the fire side & the [*?then*] roast the cold out of you in four & twenty hours.

We have continued frost but no great degree of cold. The thermometer has seldom even at night been below 20; and generally only a few degrees below freezing.

237. *Stanhope St. 3 Feb. 1830.*

   Add. MSS.

This weather is really *too* cold for country excursions by night; but when it grows somewhat milder, I shall be delighted to dine with you.

How can your friend Mr Corbett[1] be such a ninny as to fancy that the Duke would ask me, or that I should accept.

238. *Broadlands. 22 April 1830.*

   Add. MSS.

Many thanks for your bulletins. I fear the case looks as bad as possible, and with our prospects for the future, it is a great misfortune. Who would have thought some years ago, that the continued existence of the then Prince of Wales would have been of great importance to the public good! This reflection however inspires one with hope for the future, and we may find William a better & steadier sovereign than we expect.

I should guess that he would make no change in his chief minister, though he might wish to mix up other members with him in the Administration. That might make a difficulty on the part of the D. of Wn, but as he is resolved to be minister as long as his health allows, he would readily throw overboard his lumber & draught his crew if the ship could not be kept in commission without it. The jumble however would not be easily worked out.

Our weather latterly has been rather cold, & inclined to rain, but on the whole very enjoyable. I shall probably return on Saturday and will dine with you on Wednesday if I am not engaged, which I believe I am not, but cannot undertake to answer for till I have looked at my card rack.

[1] Not identified.

239. *Cambridge. 5 July 1830.*

> *Add. MSS.*

We cannot make out here whether there is to be a contest or not.[1] The ultra Tory & anti Catholic Party want one excessively, but they see little chance of success, and can find no good candidate. Lowther is talked of today; Beckett had not been heard of here; French the Master of Jesus went to town on Saturday & was to return this evening, & he was to see if he could find a good candidate on communication with Lyndhurst. I think there will be no contest; but if there is I feel confident of success. Cavendish is not quite so strong, as some people have taken umbrage at his name being found in some small O'Connel minorities & they magnify the matter & accuse him of radicalism; on the other hand a Trinity inceptor today said he could not promise me his vote because he believed I was adverse to *election by ballot,* which he made a *sine quâ non.* I have been very well received by all but the old anti Catholic few, whose feelings are unchanged & treat the question as if it was still pending, & you may rely upon it this feeling will be found prevalent in many parts, & will act unfavourably to the Govt. Goulburn never could have faced it, & if he had come would have met with many a rebuff. I return tomorrow evng for the division on Grant's motion.[2]

240. *St John's. 1 Aug. 1830.*

> *Add. MSS.; cf. Airlie, i. 172–4.*[1]

Palmerston reports his unopposed re-election in Cambridge and welcomes the revolution in France.

[1] James Abercromby had written to Carlisle on 4 June 1830: 'I have heard of an opposition at Cambridge. Palmerston I suppose would be the person run at, but that does not much diminish the evil of a struggle.' (C.H.P. 2/13.) The other sitting member was a Whig, William Cavendish (afterwards 7th Duke of Devonshire), who had gained the seat at a by-election in June 1829 following Tindal's appointment as Chief Justice of Common Pleas.

[2] Robert Grant's motion to settle the regency question was supported by only 93 votes with 247 against.

[1] 'Sinner Browning' in Lady Airlie's version (i. 173, line 5) should read 'Sinner Brown's'. There were at the time among the fellows of Trinity both a John Brown and a George Adam Browne. According to Wright, i. 56, they were distinguished by the nicknames 'Saint' and 'Sinner'. Presumably the 'Sinner' was George Adam Browne, a political ally of Palmerston's at the time of this letter.

241. *Broadlands. 8 Sept. 1830.*

    Add. MSS.

I return you the inclosed with a memorandum[1] of what I should say to the Treasy if I were now Secy at War.

Thank Elizabeth for her note, & tell her that William at my request asked George Bowles[2] to come down here, before we left London, but I will write to him that there may be no mistake.

We find partridges very scarce, but hope to meet with more when the barley is more completely cut.

We have had Matou Shivitz for three days & Shee for one; we are going today to Baring Wall's for a day & the Flemings come to us Friday, & then we shall go with them for a day to Binstead.[3]

The harvest has been very fine & well got in. We were received with all the honors of war, a triple royal salute from a battery of 3 pounders lately purchased by the innkeeper at Romsey for use on great occasions, ringing of bells, and a concert of the burgher band with the local militia instruments who came & proved how strangely it was possible to metamorphose 'O' Jenny will thee gang with me'.

Our weather has been fine. We dined one day at Stanley's who has all the grandeur of an M.P. and one day at Bourne's where we met Huskisson who staid a day there on his way to Liverpool looking well & grown stout.[4] Russia cannot keep the line she has begun with, about France though the events there & in Belgium will sorely alarm her about her own provinces & about Poland. The latter country especially is likely to take advantage of any favourable opportunity to regain something more like independence.

242. *Broadlands. 12 Oct. 1830.*

    Add. MSS.

I am off for Brighton, Dieppe being the shortest way, & no steamer leaving Southampton till Saturday. I shall embark tomorrow at eight.

---

[1] Lacking.

[2] William Bowles's brother, a distinguished soldier.

[3] Count André Joseph Matuscevitz (*ob.* 1842) was attached to the Russian Embassy in London, 1829–35. Charles Baring Wall (1795–1853) was a grandson of Sir Francis Baring, 1st Bart, and another Hampshire neighbour. Binstead Lodge was another place of the Flemings', at Ryde.

[4] William Sturges Bourne's seat was Testwood House, near Southampton. Nothing, unfortunately, is known about what was said or agreed at this meeting, though Anglesey, who met the Canningites at Cowes, reported them 'all ripe for mischief & full of fight'. A letter Huskisson addressed to Palmerston immediately afterwards discussed in detail the results of the General Elections and made plans for them to meet at Stapleton after Huskisson's ill-fated visit to Liverpool. (Anglesey to Littleton, 1 Sept., Hatherton Papers; Huskisson to Palmerston, 3 Sept., B.P., G.C./HU no. 119.)

I shall be much obliged to you if you will send my letters as you promised, by the Foreign Office.[1]

[*PS.*] I believe the packets must be at the Foreign Office by four o'clock, or soon after to go by the courier of the day.

243. *To Mrs Sulivan. Dieppe. Thursday, 14* [*Oct. 1830*].

I arrived here yesterday at half past 7, after what is called a remarkably good passage, with a good deal of tossing and a cold east wind. I embarked at eight having reached Brighton by about 3 in the morning.

The custom house ceremonies with regard to my carriage made it impossible for me to go on last night.

My companions in the steam boat were the Prince & Pss de Leon, who had been over to Lulworth for a fortnight. Charles it seems is going to Edinburgh to live at Holyrood House. How curious that he should return there to end his days after so different a position.

244. *To Mrs Sulivan. Hotel de la Tamise, Rue de Rivoli* [*Paris*]. *16* [*& 18*] *Oct. 1830.*

I arrived here yesterday morning at 9 o'clock having made a tolerably quick journey from Dieppe by Rouen, which latter town by the bye has made immense progress since I was there before, a good few years ago. I found a very good apartment at the first hotel I drove to, & so here I am again very comfortably established. It would be absurd to give any fixed opinion upon the state of things in France after the first four & twenty hours one has been in Paris. But nothing that I have yet heard leads me to entertain any considerable apprehension of further convulsions. At the same time there are many uncomfortable circumstances in the present position of affairs. The public mind is deeply excited about the trial of the late ministers. Some awkward measures of the Government & the Chambers about Mr Tracy's proposed law for the abolition of death in cases of political

---

[1] Palmerston had come up to London to see Clive on 6 Oct. about an approach to join Wellington's Government. They met again on the morning of Sunday, 10 Oct., but Palmerston did not, as he afterwards stated in his 'Autobiographical Sketch' (Bulwer & Ashley, i. 382), 'to cut the matter short ... set off immediately for Paris'. Rather, he returned to Broadlands for a couple of days and before setting off for Paris gave full details of his travel plans to Clive so that the Duke could make further contact or even recall him. (Clive to Wellington, 10 Oct.; I am grateful to the late Earl of Powis for providing this information.)

offences, coining, burning buildings not inhabited, & infanticide, raised a notion that a Party juggle was going on to defeat the ends of justice and save the ex-ministers by a trick.[1] This produced a ferment two days ago in the Fg St Antoine, or rather a demonstration of feeling on the part of the populace, which the Govt understood, & it was yesterday announced *officially* in all the *workshops* of Paris, that the further consideration of that law was to be postponed till 1831.

This will I daresay be called in England a proof of weakness; it is so in one sense, because it is a confession of a well known fact, that the present Govt which was created by the popular will cannot stand *against* the popular will; but that is the necessary result of circumstances. But it was a wise measure, and perhaps the most favourable to the accused, since it tends to allay the ferment for the present, & give time for calmer feelings to spring up. The trial begins early in Novr but may last all December through, & possibly to Jany. I believe it may be said that *all* the middle & lower classes of Paris from the first rate shopkeepers downwards anxiously desire the execution of the ministers. The King, the Govt, the Peers, & the gentlemen & ladies in the Red Book of course have opposite feelings. The question will be whether a sentence of imprisonment for life, forfeiture of all property & deprivation of all honours & privileges, will satisfy the public resentment. I am inclined to think it will, and that this will be the sentence. But then it must not be discussed now, otherwise it would be cried down by anticipation. The best thing for the culprits is that every body should seem to expect their death, & exhaust their vengence in words. If the Peers go gravely to work, & shew no favour in the mode of conducting the trial, probably the people will acquiesce in their sentence. But the only force which could protect the prisoners from popular outrage is the National Guards, and in *that case*, though I believe in that *alone*, they would offer no resistance to anything the mob might attempt. Mad. de F[*lahault*] told me she was urging the other day to a shopkeeper all the arguments which are in everybody's mouth in favour of mercy in this case. The man folded his arms & said calmly, 'Madam, if you had seen three of your neighbours lying stiff before your door, if you had seen two of your children shot dead before your eyes, you would be of a different opinion; and would think that the severest punishment was justly due to the authors of these outrages'.

There is much commercial distress all over the Country, part of which existed before July, but much of which has been created by the stoppage of all transactions in consequence of the revolution. Bills

[1] Destutt de Tracy was attempting to ensure that Polignac and the other former ministers of Charles X were not executed.

which came in from foreign parts during the crisis were not paid, people all hoarding & not chusing to part with their money; credit was suspended, & orders for the manufacture of commodities for a time ceased, from the uncertainty whether there would be any purchasers. All people still continue to limit & contract their transactions from similar reasons, so that there is a stagnation of trade & of production. Added to this the harvest has been deficient, and the revenue as might have been expected has very much fallen off. All this keeps the Country in a feverish state, & these causes cannot at once cease, but must continue to operate for some months to come. Then the violence of conflicting parties seizes hold of every topic of irritation to serve their several purposes. The ultra Royalists here, like our Brunswickers, have turned radicals from spite, & wish to subvert the fabric in which they are no longer allowed to rule, & their papers are more revolutionary than even the Republican ones. The Republican Party which is not large, and the ultra liberal which is very large, and which contains all the *unpromoted* newspaper editors, indulge of course in free & general strictures on everything done by the Govt, right or wrong, & these attacks have more effect here where a free press is a late creation, than with us who have been used to it from our constitutional cradle; and on the other hand also, the ministers being many of them men who have hitherto been themselves only critics, and have but just become authors, give by their inexperience in action, rather more handle to attack than they would do if they had served their full apprenticeship; some changes may perhaps take place among them, but they will be only changes of *men* & not of institutions. The King seems fully to understand his position. He is abused by many for weakness, & yielding to everybody & upon all occasions, but he appears to me to know that if the tree does not bend to the wind, while the roots have as yet not struck in to the earth, it will probably be laid prostrate. Lafayette said to him the other day at one of his great levées, 'do you know Sir I have found a man who is a better Republican even than either you or me.' 'Aye,' said the King, 'I should like much to know who that can be.' 'Why no other than the Duke of Orleans.' 'Oh!' said the King, 'I suspect you are quite right there.'

All these things satisfy the public mind. For the lower classes who bore the brunt of the battle begin to ask themselves & others, what they have *gained* by the revolution, forgetting that their *gain* has been all they have not *lost*; & that the fight was defensive & not offensive. But every month gives strength & solidity to the system, and if they can get well over the winter, which they probably will, they will *do*. Lafitte who seems satisfied with his speakership, for the present at least and not to be ambitious of personal responsibility, says that the long nights & bad weather will be the best allies of the Govt. In Ire-

land those things told the other way, but the Parisians like fighting
as well as haymaking while the sun shines. The National Guard are
the great security however; they are all, at least the officers, deeply
interested in the maintenance of order, and maintain it they will.
There are sixty thousand of them in Paris, who are to be reviewed
on Sunday week; I shall probably be tempted to stay to see them.
The Chambers have adjourned or at least are doing nothing. They
are waiting for 140 new elections to fill up vacancies by resignation
or acceptance of office. The choice of new members will be a test of
public opinion; but it probably will be good. There seems no disposition for war; unless driven to it in self defence. If peace continues,
order will be maintained; if war arises, it must become national, popular feeling must be appealed to & excited, and further convulsions
would follow. This it is which makes them all so careless about
Belgium; they know that any meddling there would involve them in
war, & just now, war is what they most wish to avoid. Besides they
are not anxious to see a republican model government set up at their
door, the example would do no good here, and I verily believe the
French Govt would give any aid they could towards any settlement
of Belgium which should place the sovereignty in the hands of the
Prince of Orange. A shrewd person observed to me yesterday, when
your own house is on fire you are more likely to think of putting out
the flames than of setting fire to your next door neighbour's.

I fear that our Duke has something to answer for as to the unsuccessful attack on Brussells. I hear that when applied to by the Dutch King
for military aid he said, 'we can give none, but why do you apply
to us, have you no troops of your own, can't you trust your Dutchmen,
& if you can, why don't you make use of them.' This is merely hearsay,
but it comes from a pretty good quarter, & likely to know something
about the matter. Nicholas continues to require all his Russians to
come home & they say, has given Pozzo a rap on the knuckles for
being too much overjoyed at the *success* of the *successful* party; one
should have thought a diplomatist safe so far. The Russian recognition
is however known to be on the road. Northern Italy is swarming with
Germans, & if Austria has nothing else to do but to keep the Italians
quiet, she will do that effectually. The Spanish revolution has missed
fire, & it seems doubtful whether it will go off with a second priming.
They have not yet got to use the French detonator. As to any external
traces of the revolution there are hardly any, except a prettier flag
waving over the Tuileries. The favourite *pièce* at the Vaudeville, is
the 3 days of July, in which an Englishman figures away, not to be
quizzed, but to be applauded & admired.

Adieu. This is all I have as yet picked up, & as I give no names,
I care not who reads.

[*PS.*]   Monday [*18 Oct.*]
I finish this today. I went yesterday to Versailles to see 15 thousand
National Guards reviewed by the King, an interesting sight & a
beautiful day—indeed the French climate has redeemed itself by its
fineness. All is going on well in the main—but attempts are made
to excite popular feeling agst the ex-ministers, & there were some cries
in the Palais Royal last night. This is at present the weak point of
the Govt. They are bent upon saving Polignac & Co. & the lower
& middle classes are determined to wreak vengeance upon them.

245. *Paris. 20 Oct. 1830.*

   Add. MSS.

Your letter of the 12 inst reached me the day before yesterday here.
I should say on the whole that your first intention was the best, that
is to say, setting out of the question the financial consideration, of
which I cannot judge, not knowing what difference of expence would
follow the entering Stephen as fellow commoner instead of as pensioner. I think the higher entry would throw him into better society,
& give him greater facilities in making acquaintances which you
would wish him to form; as to study I should not think it could make
any material difference; there are idle men in one class as well as
another, & if Stephen has not in himself the energy required, to break
through the little temptations to indolence which beset people everywhere it does not signify what gown he carries on his back; but if
he has that energy (which I am convinced he has), he will not the
less exert it for being placed as you thought of placing him. I should
say the danger lay more in the likelihood of expensive habits than
of neglect of study. But in his case, there would be no fear upon that
score either.[1]
   Things are going on here *so-so-ish.* The resentment against the ex-
ministers has been seized hold of by the agitators as a lever by which
to raise up troubles, but it will not do any material mischief. People
have collected in the Palais Royal crying for punishment & a party
went off to Vincennes the night before last to ask the Governor for
his prisoners. The King has been repeating some speeches which he
made yesterday morning to the National Guard. The Guard may be
relied upon to keep Paris quiet. They are mostly shopkeepers & others
to whom disturbance is ruin. I went last night at about 12 to see what
was doing in the Palais Royal, but the streets were all quiet. The Govt
however had expected a row. There were about 1000 men or more,

---

[1] Stephen Henry Sulivan had been admitted pensioner at St John's in Jan. 1830
and Duckett Scholar in Nov. (*Alumni Cantab.*)

line & guards mixed, bivouacking in the first court of the Palais Royal, & strong detachments of guards patrolling the streets but nothing took place, except the arrest of three or four people who were seized by *inhabitants* & delivered over to the guard. This excitement cannot last & must exhaust itself before the trial comes on. It is a pity the Chambers are not sitting, for though they have not here that influence on public opinion which Parliament exercises in England, still they would probably take the public mind somewhat out of the hands of the newspapers, which now exercise uncontrouled sway; and as the Govt promote to office every editor who becomes dangerously factious, you may conceive that uno avulso non deficit alter.[2] There will probably be a change in the Ministry, Broglie, Guizot, & Louis will go out. Louis is the Bexley of Paris & voted a twaddle. Broglie & Guizot are political swimmers, who have learnt their art to perfection on the dining table, but are bothered at finding themselves for the first time in running water.

But I still see no ground for serious uneasiness, because there is no real public grievance and the bulk of the nation is interested in preserving order.

246. *Paris. 23 Oct.* [*1830*].
   Add. MSS.

Pray send this as soon as you can to my house. Things are going on well here, & the Govt has gained much stability within the last few days. The agitators tried hard to get up a row, but the Govt appealed to the National Guard, who stood well by them & put down the *nigri* in capital style. I have no time for more.

[*PS.*] I leave this on Sunday night & shall be in town on Tuesday night or Wedy morning.

247. *To Mrs Sulivan. Stanhope St. 18 Nov. 1830.*

Most of the Cabinet arrangements are now settled, at least the following are arranged:

First Lord	– – – – – – –	Grey
President of Council	– – – – – – –	Lansdowne
Privy Seal	– – – – – – –	Durham
Duchy of Lancaster	– – – – – – –	Holland
Foreign Secy	– – – – – – –	Palmerston

[2] 'When one is plucked away, another shall not be wanting' (Virgil).

Home   do.   — — — — — — —   Melbourne
Colonial (perhaps)   — — — — — — —   Goderich
India   — — — — — — —   Chas Grant
Chancellor of Exchequer
  & Leader of the Hs. Cns — — — —   Althorp
Admiralty   — — — — — — —   Sr J. Graham.
Chancellor (not settled)
Ordnance   — — — — — — —   D. Richmond
Ld Lieut. Ireland   — — — — — — —   Anglesea
Secy to   do.   — — — — — — —   Stanley
Board of Trade (perhaps) — — — — —   Goderich

The Whigs wish Althorp to lead as likely to keep their Party from straying. Perhaps this may be well; as I have the Foreign Office I do not care.

yrs in haste

[*PS.*] Howick will be Secy at War.[1]
This is all in *strict confidence* as it has not yet been submitted to the King.

248. *Stanhope St. 22 Dec. 1830.*

Bulwer & Ashley, i. 365; MS. not found.

I send you the note you wish for; I have been ever since my appointment like a man who has plumped into a mill-race, scarcely able by all his kicking and plunging to keep his head above water.

249. *Cambridge. 24 April 1831.*

Add. MSS.

If you can send any thing to Littleton do so. We want circulars & lists. The election will be Tuesday week & last probably Wedy & Thursday. St John's gets blacker & blacker—Tatham & Blick

---

[1] This appears to be the only indication that Howick was at one time destined by his father for the War Office at the formation of the Government. The following day Grey suggested Robert Grant for that office, but though both Palmerston and Charles Grant were in favour of his taking it Robert Grant preferred to be Judge Advocate General. Finally, on 25 Nov., Grey wrote: 'This business of the secretary at war, which has plagued me more than any part of the arrangements with which I have been charged, is at last settled. Charles Wynn is to have it.' (Palmerston to Grey, '7 o'clock' [19 Nov.], and C. Grant to Grey, 19 Nov., Grey Papers; Grey to Sandon, 25 Nov., A. Aspinall, 'The Last of the Canningites', *E.H.R.*, 1, 1935, p. 663, n. 2.)

even are against, & I suspect Wood will perhaps not even come & vote.[1]

Some of them mean I hear even to plump for Cavendish rather than vote for me: Trinity however are zealous & cordial. Among the residents, 180 in number, I should be beat. All depends on the country clergy, & how & in what numbers they come up. We all however in my committee talk big & confidently, & say to each other who's afraid. It is too soon however as yet to form an opinion. I shall probably return to town on Tuesday.

[*PS.*] Peel is gouty & cannot come. Goulburn & Cavendish are arrived.

250. *Foreign Office. 28 Feb. 1832.*

    Add. MSS.

It does not seem to me that the functions of the Secry of State can vary with peace & war, more especially as our condition in this respect may change from month to month, & between the time when the annual Establishment is fixed, & the end of the year for which it is fixed. I should say that the Establishment of the army like that of the navy, is a matter which must depend in some degree upon the political relations & prospects of the Country, & that it ought to be considered & determined by the Cabinet before it is submitted to the King. If the Secy at War happens to be a member of the Cabinet, he would of course bring the subject under the consideration of his

---

[1] There were three Tatham brothers who had been students of St John's: Ralph, who had been Stephen Sulivan's tutor and was now president of the college; Thomas; and William, another fellow. In 1826 all three had voted for Palmerston. But in 1831 Ralph and Thomas both voted for his opponents. William, on the other hand, had plumped for Palmerston in 1826 and seems to have compromised in 1831 by not voting at all. Probably, therefore, he was the Tatham who appears among the members of Palmerston's 1831 election committee. The list (preserved in B.P.W.) is long and impressive. The other Johnians were Professor Henslow (as chairman), Dr John Haviland (Regius Professor of Medicine) and John Birkett. In addition there were Martin Davy (the Master) and William Henry Hanson from Caius, George Leapingwell and John Tinkler from Corpus, Marmaduke Ramsay and William Hustler from Jesus, John Croft and Edward John Ash from Christ's, Richard Dawes from Downing, John Lodge from Magdalene, Professor William Smyth from Peterhouse, and Professor Adam Sedgwick, James Alexander Barnes, G. A. Browne, William Ralph Payne, Joseph Romilly and Richard Wellesley Rothman from Trinity. Palmerston was right about Wood, who did not vote at all, but Blick compromised by giving one vote to Palmerston and one to William Yates Peel. Palmerston also incurred considerable expenditure. From his accounts it would appear that Henry Elliot, who presumably took care of things in London, received £706. 3s. 0d. in cash, while another £40. 0s. 10d. went to someone called Talbot for messengers. In Cambridge Professor Henslow received £400, of which £10. 17s. 3d. was unspent. In spite of all these efforts the sitting members were decisively defeated by Peel and Henry Goulburn, Palmerston coming last of all.

colleagues; if the Secy at War is not in the Cabinet I should say that the Colonial Secretary of State is the officer who ought to do so, both because he is more peculiarly responsible for the colonies & cognizant of their wants, & because in the event of war, he would be charged with the conduct of our military operations. But the Colonial Secretary ought certainly to discuss the Establishment previously, with the Secy at War, whether he receives the plan of it, from the Secy at War, or from the Commr in Chief.

As to the taking of the King's pleasure with respect to the amount of the Establishment that ought certainly not to be done by the Commander in Chief, who is answerable for the good government of the army but not for the amount of its Establishment.

My impression is that the Establishments for the various army services have not been countersigned by the Secretary at War, but by a Secretary of State; and if so, it would rather seem that it is the Secy of State who takes the King's pleasure upon these matters; but the only doubt can lie between the Secy of State & the Secry at War.

It was found some time ago by the Cabinet that Ld Hill had conceived himself to have taken the King's pleasure upon the Establishment for this year, and it was settled that Goderich should do so again, as if nothing had been done by Ld Hill, & that Ld Hill should be told that it was not his province. The new move of Goderich's therefore was not as you suppose the result of a stratagem of the Horse Guards, but a measure of controul upon that office.[1]

251. *Foreign Office. 17 Aug. 1832.*

Add. MSS.

The deed is done & Stephen is already on the list of this Office; the sooner he presents himself to Backhouse the better.[1]

[1] Hobhouse had taken over the War Office at the beginning of Feb. determined, not only to mitigate corporal punishment in the Army, but also to carry out numerous economies. Encouraged by Althorp's cooperation, he thought he was pressing for reductions already agreed by the Cabinet. But Lord Hill, the C.-in-C., did all he could to frustrate Hobhouse's plans and Goderich, too, had complained that his authority as Secretary of State was also being ignored. (*Broughton*, iv. 183–6.)

[1] Sulivan had written, probably on 19 July 1832 though it appears to read 1831 (B.P., G.C./SU no. 21), to say that his son looked to diplomacy as a career and that he might as well gain experience as finish his academic career. 'His indifferent success in mathematics', Sulivan explained in passing, 'is no proof of idleness; his other attainments shew a fair capacity.' John Backhouse (1784–1845) was permanent undersecretary at the Foreign Office.

252. *Stanhope St. 14 Nov. 1832.*

Add. MSS.

Thank you for your work; and I am very glad to hear you are making such progress in improving your health as well as the public departments.

I can see no reason why you should not send your pamphlet to any members of the Govt.[1]

[1] Hobhouse had decided that if he made no progress with his reductions and reforms, then he would either have to force a drastic reform of army administration or resign. Eventually, in Jan. 1833, he agreed with the Chancellor of the Exchequer, Althorp, on a plan to subordinate the C.-in-C. to the Secretary at War. When Palmerston had seen it he wrote to Althorp: 'I most entirely concur in the expediency of the arrangement proposed to be established by your minute; it is the only way of putting the government & management of our military affairs upon their proper footing.' Althorp had given Hobhouse the impression that his proposals were 'to be finally determined on by Palmerston'. But when Grey heard of it he quickly disabused the Secretary at War. It was an 'opinion' he had wanted from Palmerston, he said, and not his 'assent'. Subsequently Grey asked Hobhouse to consult together with John Russell and the Duke of Richmond and on 20 Mar. they produced a scheme for the C.-in-C. to take over the purely military functions of the Master General of the Ordnance and for a new Financial Board, headed by a Cabinet minister, to take over all the civil functions of the War Office, Ordnance, Pay Office etc. Their report was submitted to the King the same day but any action on it was deferred, partly because of the opposition of the Master General and partly because of other political crises which resulted before the end of Mar. in Hobhouse leaving the War Office for the Irish Secretaryship.

Hobhouse was succeeded at the War Office by Edward Ellice. Grey was doubly glad about the change. One of its advantages, he told Sir Herbert Taylor, was that he could avoid any change regarding corporal punishment in the Mutiny Bill. Another was that he would be able 'to postpone all changes ... connected with the administration of the Army till they can be maturely & carefully considered'. Taylor reported the King in turn to be well pleased since he considered Hobhouse 'to have been hampered by former ... pledges ... and to have yielded too much to the influence & advice of subordinates, whose feelings & proceedings have been jealous of & hostile to the military branches of the service'. A further letter from Grey led Taylor to write the following day: 'I am glad also that you have put Ellice on his guard against Mr Sulivan, who, though a kind-hearted man, an amiable member of society and an excellent father and husband, has unfortunately imbibed a feeling of hostility & jealousy towards the military departments and authorities which is greatly to be lamented as being injurious to the public service.' (*Broughton*, iv. 262–95; Hobhouse's Journal, 4 and 7 Jan. 1833, Broughton Papers, Add. MS. 56557; Palmerston to Althorp, 13 Feb. 1833, Ellice Papers; Richmond to Althorp, 11 Nov. 1833, Goodwood Papers; Grey to Taylor, 28 and 29 Mar., and Taylor to Grey, 29 and 30 Mar. 1833, Grey Papers, RA.)

However distasteful Sulivan may have been to the Horse Guards, he was in the matter of the consolidation of Army Departments sometimes misrepresented. His printed pamphlet, marked simply no. 2 and dated Oct. 1832 (Add. MSS. 59782–3), indeed argued that the Horse Guards should be confined to 'purely military' matters and not interfere in financial affairs, while the Secretary at War, having 'at present ... either too much or too little' responsibility, should be either abolished or raised to the position of Secretary of State. However, he was wholly opposed to the creation of any sort of military board. In addition, when called upon to give his evidence before a subsequent Royal Commission in 1834, he agreed with all the leading military men in condemning extensive consolidation as being too much for any departmental head to supervise and the notion of a board as being too loose and inefficient (*Parliamentary Papers*, 1837, xxxiv, Pt I, 'Report from Commissioners appointed to inquire into the Practicability and Expediency of Consolidating the different Departments connected with the Civil Administration of the Army', pp. 177–8).

253. *Stanhope St. 20 Nov. 1832.*

Add. MSS.

Many thanks for your kind note about Hants.[1] I think I am on pretty sure grounds. I would not declare till the whole Division had been nearly canvassed, & the enclosed is the return sent to me, & upon which I issued my advertisement.

There is always a possibility that people may not attend but still, there is also a chance that out of the 1244 who vote for Fleming, more than 93 may give a second vote to me. I think therefore that I stand as well as any body can do in a thing by its nature precarious.

---

[1] Following his defeat at Cambridge Palmerston had been found another seat by the Treasury at Bletchingley. But either through a misunderstanding or, as he thought, a trick, Palmerston had discovered in Mar. 1832 that Bletchingley was a much more expensive seat than he could afford. Having paid £800 for it in 1831, he refused to pay a similar sum the following year and compromised on £500 to cover the period up to the General Election following the passage of the Reform Act. In any case Bletchingley was disfranchised by that Act and so Palmerston searched actively during the summer of 1832 for an alternative parliamentary seat. At first he had hoped to revive his attempt upon Cambridge University. But a visit in Commencement Week and correspondence with James Wood had convinced him by the middle of Aug. that it was hopeless. Fortunately he had already had other approaches, including Cambridge Town, South Hampshire, Tower Hamlets, Lambeth and Falmouth and Penryn; later Southwark and Windsor were also mentioned. Of these Falmouth and Penryn was his favourite, probably because it was so far away that he believed he would not be bothered so much by the constituents. But a preliminary canvass by his brother (who was on leave from Naples) revealed that he could rely only on a minority of votes and that, Reform Act or no, the electors of Penryn expected £5 each for theirs and the electors of Falmouth the restoration by the Government of their iniquitous packet privileges.

Consequently, while he kept the pot boiling in the West Country, he also entertained an alternative approach from Lambeth, adding from exploratory canvasses there a sum of £205 to the £452. 14s. 11d. he had spent on Falmouth and Penryn. Other offers were turned away with the reply that he was already 'pledged'; but these pledges, apparently, were conditional upon a satisfactory preliminary canvass and a limited financial commitment on his part. This was still the situation when, in Sept., a group of South Hampshire 'reformers' also approached him to stand, together with Sir George Staunton, against his old friend and neighbour, John Willis Fleming. About the same time Sloane Stanley approached him with a view to his standing as a sort of 'conservative' candidate with Fleming and against Staunton. This second approach was clearly out of the question, but since neither Lambeth nor Penryn in the end quite met his conditions, Palmerston evidently agreed to stand for South Hampshire. He did not do so, however, until after he had received a firm undertaking that he would not be called upon to pay more than £1,000 in expenses and a favourable report of a preliminary canvass of the whole constituency. He also insisted that he should not be asked to canvass in person, since he was so busy in the Foreign Office, but appear only on polling day. On 3 Oct. he was told that a canvas had secured him promises from just over 1,000 out of the 2,500–3,000 who were expected to register. This did not satisfy him. But on 24 Oct. he was told that out of 3,200 registered voters nearly half (1,455) were promised to him, and that although this was less than Fleming's (1,753), it was more than Staunton's (1,437) and likely to be increased by 119 who would transfer from Fleming to Palmerston and assure him of election. So on 10 Nov. he formally accepted. (Palmerston's accounts and election papers in B.P.W.; Grey to Palmerston and Palmerston to Grey, 1 Nov. 1832, Grey Papers.)

I am glad to hear you are going out of town. I *wish* very much that you would resolve to do so *immediately*. After keeping a week in bed & suffering a great deal of pain it is quite impossible that you can be fit to launch again at once into all the harrassing squabbles which beset you in your office; and knowing as I do your anxious & susceptible temperament I am quite sure that if you do not withdraw for a little while into better air and a quieter element you will get yourself into bad health for the rest of the winter.

Are the matters in dispute worth this sacrifice on your part? and a sacrifice too which deeply affects so many others?

Be advised. Take care of your health in the first place; make that your first object, and office arrangements your second; and if the consequence should be that you do not carry all your points, what then? at least you preserve that health which is in every point of view, of much more importance.

[*PS.*] Of course my Hants Return is private & confidential.

[*Enclosure:*]   20 Nov. 1832

Palmerston
  Plumpers   57
  P. & S.   1374
  P. & F.   93
                    ——
                                  1524
Staunton
  Plumpers   61
  S. & P.   1374
  S. & F.   27
                    ——
                                  1462
Fleming
  according to
    Wm Stanley 10th Novr   1244

Total registered _____ 3112

Plumpers P.   57 ⎫
  do Staunton   61 ⎪
P. & S.   1374 ⎬   2736
Fleming plumpers   ⎪
  or split with   ⎪
  P. & S.   1244 ⎭
                                    ——
                        remains   376

of whom are reported

neuter	43 ⎫		
	⎬	163	
against Fleming	120 ⎭		

remains 213

Suppose the whole 213 to vote singly for Fleming he would
have – – – – –   1244
                                              213
                                              ‾‾‾‾
                                              1457

which would still be below 1524
but suppose any portion of the 163 to vote for P. the majority would
be increased.

254. *Foreign Office. 28 Nov. 1832.*
      Add. MSS.

You will like to see this last return from Hampshire which is equi-
valent to 4 by honors & the odd trick.

[*Enclosure:*]   26 Nov. 1832

total registered – – – – – – –		3114
plumpers P.	56	
Palm. & Staunton	1419	
Palm. & Flemg	137	
total Palm.	1612	
plumpers Staunton	59	
P. & S.	1419	
S. & F.	34	
total Staunton	1512	
plumpers P.	56 ⎫	
do S.	59	
P. & S.	1419 ⎬	1708
neuter	52	
against F.	122 ⎭	

remains for Fleming   1406[1]

---

[1] The result of the poll, on 18 and 19 Dec., was: Palmerston, 1,628; Staunton, 1,532;
Fleming, 1,279. In addition to his £1,000, Palmerston incurred a mere £6. 19s. 6d.
on hotel expenses in Southampton and gave £100 to the poor in lieu of a chairing.

255. *Woburn.*[1] *27 Nov. 1833.*

   Add. MSS.

It is very difficult to form an opinion upon so general a statement of a case, as that which your letter contains & therefore I may be wrong in that which I am disposed to give. But as a general rule I should say that one ought not to assume offence without having good reason to suppose that it is intended; and that one ought not to make a stand upon a personal matter unless one feels pretty confident of being able to make indifferent persons not only understand the point at issue but incline to think one right. The proceeding as you describe it is certainly not considerate, nor courteous; but still it does not follow that it was intended to give offence; and at all events the point is a narrow one.[2]

I should therefore recommend your not complaining, or at least if you do so, I would suggest your doing it as a simple matter of official routine, without shewing any personal feeling.

A Commission is going to be appointed, consisting of John Russell, Kempt, Ellis, ye D. of Richmond and one or two more to take the Duke's plan of consolidation into consideration, & to make a report upon it before Parliament meets.[3]

[*PS.*] I shall be in town again tomorrow.

256. *Foreign Office. 29 Nov. 1833.*

   Add. MSS.

Return me this as soon as you have read it, and pray consider it as strictly confidential. The Commission about to be appointed will have to report on this plan.[1]

---

[1] Palmerston, with about half the Cabinet, was spending three days shooting with the Duke of Bedford (Palmerston to William Temple, 3 Dec., Bulwer & Ashley, ii. 176–7).

[2] Sulivan's specific complaint is not known, but see no. 301.

[3] In spite of Ellice's taking over the War Office, Richmond had persisted with his plan for army consolidation and on 11 Nov. had re-presented his project, with the modification of keeping one place on the proposed Board for an officer in place of the Master-General. The Cabinet had recommended on 23 Nov. and the King accepted on 25 Nov. a Royal Commission of Inquiry consisting of those named by Palmerston and Maj.-Gen. Sir Robert L. Dundas.

[1] Presumably Richmond's revised plan of 11 Nov.

257. *Stanhope St. 13 June 1834.*

   Add. MSS.

I received yesterday your letter of the 4th from which I see you were in a considerable fuss, as might well have been expected, about events here.[1] You will by this time have heard the results and you will have seen that the vacancies caused by retirements have been filled up in such a way as to alter as little as possible the outward character of the Govt. The losses we have sustained are great, and particularly so to me individually. I have lost colleagues with whom I was most intimate, & with whom in general I fully and intirely agreed. I deeply regret their retirement, and though I could not share their opinions on the particular point on which the difference arose I must always bear testimony to the perfect honor & good faith with which they acted on that as on every other occasion. I did all I could up to the very last moment, to prevent their resignation, and if they had delayed it till the next day, my belief is that it would not have been necessary, as I think we should have carried the previous question.

It is most unfortunate in my view of the matter, that they should have entertained so strong an opinion on such a point. They had agreed to reduce ten Irish bishops; to take away so much per cent from the revenue of every Irish clergyman of a parish; to suspend filling up vacant livings if service had not been performed in them for 3 years previous to 1833; but they could not consent to the principle that if upon inquiry it should turn out that the revenues of the Irish Church in the aggregate are more than is required for the spiritual wants of Ireland, the surplus shall be appled to moral & religious purposes different from those to which it is at present allotted. I certainly cannot nail myself to such an opinion as this of theirs, but as they entertain it, they are perfectly right to act upon it.

You will see that the administration as now filled up, is conservative, but reforming; the radicals have been excluded, but the new members are men attached to the principle of improvement. The Peers will not give us any trouble this Session; what they may attempt next year is another thing, but that is some way off, and enough for the year are the events thereof. Our Session will scarcely be over before the very last days of July and I should not be surprised if we borrowed a day or two from August. I think it was the duty of the remaining members of the Govt to hold together, & to try to reconstruct the administration. If Ld Grey had given up, what could have happened? a Tory Govt & a Dissolution of Parliament? Even with a Dissolution

---

[1] Sulivan was on holiday abroad when Graham, Richmond, Ripon and Stanley resigned from the Government.

a Tory Govt would not have stood. But Peel might have formed an administration by uniting with the seceders? He may do this next year, but *now* it would have been hardly possible for them to have joined him. They would have been accused of breaking up the Grey Govt for the purpose of uniting with the Tories. But was Durham to come in, with Tennyson[2] & who can tell who? That surely is not an administration for which it would have been wise to make way. There was nothing then left for the remaining members of the Cabinet but to remain, and to look out for the best substitutes they could find, for those who had left them.

I hope to hear better accounts of Lizzy; and that your water drinking has been productive of benefit. But a man who is accustomed to drink such pailfuls cannot expect to find any effect from the moderate drafts which men of ordinary capacity are in the habit of taking.

258. *11 Nov. 1834.*

Add. MSS.

Private & Confidential

Gordon of the India Board is to be Secry at War. Do not mention this till you hear it from others.[1]

259. *Stanhope St. 15 Nov. 1834.*

There is a paid attachéship vacant at the Hague and at Brussels; would you like me to appoint Stephen to either.[1] The salary would be £250. The Hague is the one which on the whole would suit the

---

[2] Charles Tennyson D'Eyncourt (1784–1861).

[1] Edward Ellice had indicated to Melbourne that he was determined to vacate the War Office. Since Ellice had taken a very different line both about Army consolidation and corporal punishment after Grey had ceased to be his chief, Melbourne wrote on 11 Oct.: 'You have been the instrument of getting us into the difficulty about the Army, & you ought to see us through it.' But Ellice had replied on 17 Oct. refusing to reconsider and adding: 'But pray don't appoint a gentleman equally qualified for this situation with Sir Geo Shee for the management of your diplomatic relations with the North of Europe.' (Ellice Papers.) Shee had just been nominated by Palmerston as minister in Berlin, and this was generally considered a 'job' and an outrage. Robert Gordon (1786–1864), though not destined for the Cabinet like his predecessor, was defended by Melbourne as 'a good man of business, very firm, efficient in the House of Commons & popular with the House' (Melbourne to Brougham, 6 and 7 Nov. 1834, Brougham Papers). Macaulay, who had served with Gordon on the Board of Control, had called him in 1832 'a fat, ugly, spiteful, snarling, sneering, old rascal of a slave-driver' (T. Pinney, ed., *The Letters of Thomas Babington Macaulay*, ii, 1974, p. 139). Sulivan was saved from having Gordon as his chief by the dismissal of Melbourne's Government on 14 Nov.

[1] Stephen Sulivan had been appointed Palmerston's précis-writer at the Foreign Office on 16 Nov. 1832 and promoted to private secretary on 3 May 1833.

best, as there is young Crampton at Brussels who has a claim to the attachéship there; and I think the Hague would be a better place for Stephen than Brussells, which swarms with rum English.[2] I really can hardly say whether it would be best for Stephen to go thither or to remain where he is; but you & he must decide.

260. *Stanhope St. Sunday, 16 Nov. [1834].*

We are to give up the Seals tomorrow at ½ past two. I thought the Duke had his list ready, but I did not give him credit for having his troops actually on the ground ready to relieve guard so immediately.

Send me to-day the Bishop's recommendation of Mr Berry for Leghorn & I will do the thing.[1]

261. *Foreign Office. Sunday, 9 p.m. [16 Nov. 1834].*

I will appoint Stephen to the Hague according to the decision which you & he have made. But how old is young Blackburn and is he *fit* for a clerkship in this office. Fit I mean as to attainments & instruction. It will not do to appoint a schoolboy here; he would be of no use in the office, and would not be able to take care of himself.[1]

[*PS.*] I will write to Leghorn tonight about Mr Berry.

262. *Foreign Office. 16 Nov. [1834].*

If young Blackburn is within reach send him to Stanhope Street by eleven o'clock tomorrow morning that I may see him.[1]

[2] On 24 July 1835 Palmerston wrote to Shee, who had asked for the Brussels legation: 'The quantity of English scamps who infest Brussels render it far from an agreeable post for the English minister.' Lord William Russell, he explained the next day, had already turned it down on account of the number of British half-pay officers who 'haunted' that capital and would therefore have made it an expensive burden on the British Minister's hospitality. (Shee Papers.) What may have been of still more importance for young Sulivan was that the then chargé in Brussels was reputedly a pederast (Bulwer to Durham, 2 Mar. 1836, Lambton Papers; *cf.* Georgiana Blakiston, *Lord William Russell and his Wife*, 1972, pp. 333 and 454).

[1] The Rev. William Windsor Berry had been family tutor with the Sulivans. Palmerston subsequently obtained further preferment for him.

[1] John Edward Blackburn, the eldest son of Palmerston's Johnian contemporary, was born in 1818. He was appointed Foreign Office clerk, on 17 Nov. 1834 and was subsequently, in 1836–7, attached to the legation in Naples. He was apparently celebrated in the office for his wit, but suffered from ill-health and was often absent (Sir Henry D. Wolff, *Rambling Recollections*, 1908, i. 63). He retired on pension on 18 Nov. 1851 and died in Paris on 27 Jan. 1855.

[1] 'I have appointed Stephen paid attaché at the Hague; & sent Mr Berry chaplain to Leghorn; I have appointed Blackburn's son clerk in Foreign Office & got Maria Stewart [Dugald Stewart's daughter] a civil list pension of £200 a year', Palmerston wrote to William Temple on 25 Nov. 'So I have wound up my affairs well ...' (B.P., G.C./TE no. 231.)

263. *To Mrs Sulivan. Broadlands. 28 Dec. 1834.*

Thank you for the inclosed which is very satisfactory. I am glad Stephen likes the Hague so much, and I really believe it is the very best place he could have been sent to for his throwing off. I am amused at the kind interest taken by His Nethd Majesty in my good health. He will however be obliged to submit to have me very soon back again in Downing St for as to this Govt lasting 48 hours after the King makes his speech to the new Parliament, I cannot believe it to be possible. Can a Hs. of Commons elected under the present law tolerate such a set of ultra Tories as fill all the offices of Govt? Impossible; it never can be. Shee may or may not have said to Burghersh something like what Stephen has heard, though it is not likely & I should doubt their having met; but nothing that Shee could have said or left unsaid could have led the Duke to send him to Berlin. It would have been an act of egregious silliness in the Duke to send to a foreign mission a person who stood in Shee's situation with respect to the preceding Secy of State, & whatever may be the Duke's faults, want of shrewdness is not one of them.[1]

I continue my active & laborious life.[2] Yesterday I started from hence on horseback for Southampton at a qtr before nine; sailed across to Hythe; canvassed there; returned to Southampton; canvassed there till six; & rode back to dinner here. I have lately enjoyed the luxury of bodily fatigue from exercise out of doors, to which I had been a stranger for four years. I consider myself quite sure, though we shall not know our numbers till Wednesday and I should not be surprized if Staunton came in also. The ultra Tory composition of the Govt and our agitating speeches at eight places, have done us a great deal of good, and I hear that the opinion of the County is becoming more favourable to us every day. Fleming is, as you say, very unpopular individually, and it is quite wonderful how many people he has contrived to make his enemies. He is besides a bad canvasser, stiff and unconciliatory. But then an immense number of the gentry & all the clergy are with him; and you would be surprized at the number of men who have said to us: 'My heart is with you

---

[1] Wellington had cancelled Shee's appointment to Berlin on taking office. Burghersh was a crony of the Duke's and, at this period, on rather bad terms with both Palmerston and Shee about their failure to provide him with what he thought was adequate compensation for expenses he claimed to have incurred during his own diplomatic service (Westmoreland Papers 7. xi, Northampton County Record Office).

[2] Although Palmerston expected the new Peel Government to dissolve Parliament and had accordingly formed a committee to canvass his constituency, he felt so sure of success that he dallied overlong in London. But early in Dec. he heard that he and Staunton would this time be faced by two conservatives, Fleming and Compton. Compton, Palmerston knew, was 'a formidable opponent', and so he hurried off to Hampshire on 2 Dec. for a long and arduous canvass (Lady Holland to Carlisle, 'Fri' [5 Dec. 1834], C.H.P. 2/17).

but I dare not vote for you. I must attend a little to my interests and
I cannot risk the loss of my livelihood by voting for you.' I am very
nearly a convert to ballot; only I fear it would not accomplish its
professed object, because people would be bullied for their promise,
as they are now bullied for their vote. Tomorrow we canvass our way
to Mr Thistlethwayte's near Fareham.[3] The next day we finish the
neighbourhood of Purbrock. Wedy we have a meeting to cast up
accounts of votes & I return here in the evng. Thursday I finish some
votes at Eling which we had not time to call upon when in that neighbourhood the other day; and Friday I must go to town for a day or
two; and I suppose the elections will come on early in the ensuing
week. I have promised Nightingale to be present at his nomination
at Andover.[4]

264. *To Mrs Sulivan. Broadlands. 18 Jan. 1835.*

You will see by the papers that we are beat, and by a great
majority.[1] I never was more annoyed & disappointed in my life. Till
within the last two days I had felt confident of beating Compton;
and I should have done so if all had voted for me who had promised
to do so. But our opponents or at least their supporters, for I acquit
Fleming & Compton, resorted to the most dishonourable means, &
not content with using threats & influence to make unwilling men
promise against us, actually compelled numbers who had promised
for us, to break their promise and vote against us.[2] Among other persons who practised this moral course, is the Revnd Dr Woodcock,[3]

[3] Thomas Thistlethwayte of Southwick Park (1779–1850).
[4] William Edward Nightingale, Florence's father and another Hampshire neighbour,
had been foremost among those who pressed Palmerston to stand for South Hampshire
in 1832. He was defeated in his single attempt to gain a seat for himself at Andover.
[1] The figures at the close of the poll on Saturday, 17 Jan., were: Fleming, 1,765;
Compton, 1,683; Palmerston, 1,515; Staunton, 1,474. It probably did not please Palmerston, either, that he had to pay more for his defeat in 1835 than for his victory
in 1832. The combined statement for 1832 and 1835 he and Staunton subsequently
received from a John W. Drew listed the expenses incurred as:

		£	s.	d.
1832	election expenses	1,690	3	11
	charities	210	0	0
1834	legal fees	11	11	8
1835	election expenses	3,080	4	5
	total	4,992	0	0

Since each candidate had advanced £1,000 on each occasion, and Palmerston had
made an extra donation of £100 in 1832, he received a request in June 1835 for a
further £396 against Staunton's £496. (B.P.W.)
[2] He reckoned there were 114 such 'defaulters' (Palmerston to Russell, 22 Jan.,
R. Russell, ed., *Early Correspondence of Lord John Russell*, 1913, ii. 71).
[3] Henry Woodcock (*ob.* 1840) was Rector of Michelmersh in Hampshire.

who made a man called Fay, break his word to us, & vote for Fleming & Compton. The loss of the election however is chiefly owing to want of due activity on the part of our friends at the time of registration. The Tories succeeded in placing several hundred fresh votes of theirs on the register, & our friends did not put on all who might have been added on our side. Besides this there has been an immense effort made by the landowners, gentry, clergymen, & magistrates in favour of the Tory candidates; & since Rowley's defeat at Portsmouth the Govt has very actively interfered.[4] Our adversaries had a committee sitting in the Dock Yard, a thing never known at any former time. If the electors had been left to follow their own inclinations, or if ballot had been the mode of voting, we should have come in by a decided majority. Then, it was unlucky for us that the price of corn is very low & the farmers much distressed. They are looking for abatements in their rent, & more than usually dependent on their landlords. Fleming too is owner of the great tithes in Romsey Parish, and after last election he made abatement to those who had voted for him but none to those who had voted against him. The result of this contest proves not *re*action in the modern sense of the word, but *action*, & that of the most violent kind. Adieu. I am going to meet Leuchtenberg at Salisbury & to dine with him there.[5]

265. *Broadlands. 22 Jan. 1835.*

Add. MSS.

Thank you for your kind letter. I am indeed greatly provoked & annoyed at my defeat, and the more so, as it might have been prevented by a little timely activity on the part of my supporters here at the period of registration. No exertion however has been omitted by any of us since the change of Govt. But the combination of Tory influence & efforts has been prodigious; and it was much assisted by the temporary distress of the farmers in these parts owing to the low price of wheat. They are all in arrear; unable to pay; & looking for abatements. The influence of landlords & tithe lords over such men

[4] After the election in 1832, Fleming had in his 'parting address' attributed his defeat to 'the very unfair & unhandsome coalition of his opponents, backed by the unconstitutional influence of government'. The dockyard vote, however, was very small—Palmerston estimated it in 1834 at only 125—and it had also split. Even without his share, apparently, the agricultural vote would have been enough to ensure victory for Palmerston. However, the old charges were renewed in the 1834–5 election. (Press clippings of Dec. 1832 and Nov. 1834–Jan. 1835 in Staunton's journal, Perkins Library, Duke University; correspondence between Palmerston and Compton, Feb. 1835, B.P.W.) Sir George Rowley had been only narrowly defeated for the second seat at Portsmouth.
[5] The Duke of Leuchtenberg was on his way to marry the young Queen of Portugal. He died soon after, on 28 Mar.

must be paramount. The squire & the parson never had such a pull before. As to my friends who have opposed me, I really feel no resentment whatever against them. The contest was a great political struggle & those who carried it on tooth & nail without indulging in acrimonious personalities, only did their duty according to their opinions. It was not a matter with which private friendship had any thing further to do than to make people oppose one like gentlemen. My very particular friend Sloane Stanley however is an exception to this, & I cannot forgive him for his offensive attack upon my personal character as a public man on the day of nomination. I told him so yesterday when he called here; he expressed much regret & offered to write me a letter to be shewn to my friends. I thanked him but begged him to leave bad alone. The only thing that can be said in his excuse is that he is a regular ass.

I rather think I shall go to town tomorrow or next day for a day or two to make inquiries as to possible vacancies; though nothing can of course be done till 14 days after Parliament meets.

[*PS.*] I know I could register several hundred good votes, which I shall infallibly do next July, but of this say nothing.

266. *Stanhope St. 1 Feb. 1835.*

Add. MSS.

I meant to have driven down to you today, but have been kept at home all day by a succession of visitors. I go tomorrow to Panshanger, & return on Wednesday, but merely to pass through town in my way to Portsmouth where I am to attend a Reform Dinner on Thursday. I fear therefore I have no chance of being able to dine with you.

Pray let me know how Harry is going on, I hope he is getting better.[1] Have you heard from Stephen.

267. *Stanhope St. 16 April 1835.*

Add. MSS.

I have heard nothing more from Melbourne; & can tell you nothing.[1] I have no doubt that Ellice has been undermining but I believe

---

[1] Henry Sulivan had had a complete nervous breakdown following an unsuccessful attempt to gain a fellowship at Christ Church (Palmerston to William Temple, 1 Aug. 1835, B.P., G.C./TE no. 238).

[1] Attempts to remove Palmerston from the Foreign Office and to transfer him to

also that Grey allowed himself to be worked upon by Pozzo. No man is a hero to his valet de chambre, and it is sometimes mortifying to see the weaknesses which close inspection discloses, in men who are the best of their day—but so it always was, & so it always must be.

[*PS.*] I have reason to believe however that the F.O. will be offered me; & moreover that John Russell himself had really no wish to have it but the reverse.[2]

268. *Stanhope St. 9 June 1835.*

    Add. MSS.

I shall not fail to recollect the wishes which you have expressed in favour of Mr Curtis, but consulships are seldom vacant, and I have an excessively numerous list of candidates, among whom there are many persons with strong claims, so that I fear I should only be misleading Mr Curtis if I were to induce him to suppose that I can see at present any prospect of an opportunity which could enable me to give him an appointment.[1]

269. *To Mrs Sulivan. 27 Jan. 1836.*

Thank you for your letter & its inclosure which I return. I am glad to hear tolerable accounts of you all and as the weather now means to improve I hope to hear still better. I am as you suppose overwhelmed with business. The constant struggle of a Minr of F.O. being to cram two hours work into one hours time; & never able to finish one thing before he is tugged & dragged to begin another.

Affairs however look well at home & abroad. The Corporation

---

another department of State (almost certainly the Colonial Office) had been wrecked, first by the refusal of Grey to take the Foreign Office and secondly by Palmerston's refusal in an interview with Melbourne on 14 April to take another office if anyone but Grey were appointed in his old one. Melbourne, who had not particularly wanted to form a government and did not believe he could succeed if Palmerston were not a member of it, had subsequently written to Palmerston on 15 April plainly indicating that Palmerston would probably be offered the Foreign Office after all. (Sir Charles Webster, *The Foreign Policy of Palmerston 1830–1841*, 2 vols., 1951, i. 419–21 and ii. 838–41.)

  [2] The possibility of John Russell succeeding Palmerston had been rumoured for some time and it seemed certain that Melbourne did suggest it to him (Howick's Diary, 10 April, Grey Papers). But according to John Allen, it was known at Holland House by 14 April that Russell preferred the Home Office (Allen's Diary, Add. MS. 52205 I).

  [1] There are several letters in the S.P. from John Curtis (1791–1862), the entomologist.

Elections have fixed us for the present in office & have dashed to the ground the Tory hopes.

270. *Stanhope St. 27 Mar. 1836.*

Howard says in a letter of the 12th: 'Stephen Sulivan is so much better that you will have the advantage of his hand for my despatch of this day. He has got over his attack extremely well. The first symptoms of fever were very severe, but [*?precautions*] having been taken in time, the disease was subdued at the outset. I have not seen him yet as I keep as clear from chance of infection as possible, having a young family about me, but Dr Martin tells me that he shall allow him to go out again in 3 or 4 days if the weather is fine.'[1]

[*PS.*] The despatches of the 12th *are* written again by Stephen.

271. *Stanhope St. 18 May 1836.*
        Add. MSS.

I cannot say how sorry I am for the distressing account you have received from poor Blackburn. She will be the greatest loss to him, to her children, & her friends.[1]
I send you two supplementary notes for Mr Birch.[2]

272. *Stanhope St. 29 July 1836.*
        Add. MSS.

Pelham who brings in this Bill tells me that the words under lined in [*the*] first page were put in by him at the request of Blamire, Aglionby & some other North Country members with a view to make the Bill more applicable to their part of the Country; and he drew my attention to clause 42. The Bill is going through its stages in order to be passed this Session. Let me know whether you think any words necessary & what, that I may see if I can get them put in.[1]

[1] Charles Augustus Ellis, 6th Lord Howard de Walden (1799–1868), was British Minister in Lisbon. Stephen Sulivan, who had been transferred there in 1835, had fallen victim to smallpox (Palmerston to Shee, 25 Mar. 1836, Shee Papers).
[1] Palmerston's old flame, Mrs Blackburn, had died at St Helena on her way back from Mauritius (Palmerston to William Temple, 1 June, B.P., G.C./TE no. 246).
[2] Not identified.
[1] The Enclosure Act of 1836 contained the first recognition that it might be desirable, on the grounds of public good, to prevent some enclosures and, specifically, any within ten miles of London and other towns. Charles Anderson Worsley Pelham (1809–62)

273. *Stanhope St. 3 Aug. 1836.*

    Add. MSS.

I put the following clause into the Inclosure Act on its third reading last night:

    Provided always & be it further enacted that nothing in this Act contained shall authorize the Inclosure of any open or common fields or of any open or common meadows or pastures situate and being within ten miles of the City of London.

This will I think cover you completely. Pelham made no objection, and other members thought the clause an improvement. The Bill has passed our House. We must see that the Lords do not play any tricks with the Bill. We rather expected to have turned 30 in our majority, but we knew we could not go beyond 35. Shiel made one of his best speeches.[1]

274. *Broadlands. 29 Dec. 1836.*

Your travellers are arrived safe & sound, but I very much regret that you have not come with them—could you not run down for a couple of days at least, before we return to town?

275. *Foreign Office. 1 Feb. 1837.*

    Add. MSS.

I have recd your note about Stephen. If he is not to come to England he had better stay where he is; he cannot go to a better climate and the warm baths of Caldas which will be available in the spring are excellent for rheumatism.

    I sent Howick's paper back on Monday, having read it as I came up from Brighton the day before. I do not think it would do to propose creating a new Secy of State. The Hs. of Commons would object, & the Whigs could not do it, having at the end of the war proposed to abolish the Colonial Secy, & hand the Colonies over to Home Office. Such a plan might give facilities in the department but would meet with insurmountable difficulties elsewhere. You have an old & recognized officer, keep him, & give him whatever duties you like;

---

was M.P. for North Lincolnshire; William Blamire (1790–1862) was M.P. for East Cumberland; Henry Aglionby Aglionby (1790–1854) was M.P. for Cockermouth.

    [1] R. L. Sheil had spoken the previous night on the Lords' amendments to the Irish Tithes Bill (3 *Hansard*, xxxv. 828–38).

his authority & importance will depend on his powers & not on his name. Besides the change now proposed is not of sufficient magnitude to justify such an alteration.[1] Machiavel says if you want to alter things easily, preserve names; if you want to preserve things, alter names. I will look to the other points when we go over the report.

276. *Foreign Office. 2 Feb. 1837.*

My note was an answer to yours about Stephen. I have had no application from him for leave of absence. I do not know much about the expences of living at Lisbon, but I should think the sum you mention, would be quite sufficient.

277. *Broadlands. 28 Oct. 1837.*

    Add. MSS.

I had desired, before I left town that the exchange between Stephen & Jerningham should be gazetted, and if it was not in yesterday's *Gazette* it will no doubt be in Tuesday's.[1]

I am greeted on my arrival here with rain, but I have always plenty to do within doors.

[1] Richmond's project, like Hobhouse's previously, had run into considerable difficulties in 1833–4, for Grey still hesitated to offend Windsor and, Richmond suspected, was unwilling for Ellice to lose his place through any sort of army consolidation. Althorp, at the Exchequer (Richmond to Stanley, 19 Dec. 1833, Goodwood Papers). for the head of his Financial Board of the Army and that Ellice should replace him, Althorp, at the Exchequer (Richard to Stanley, 19 Dec. 1833, Goodwood Papers). But nothing had been settled and Richmond's work was first 'suspended' by his resignation from the Government and then 'terminated' by Melbourne's dismissal (Melbourne to the King, 17 Nov. 1835, Melbourne Papers, RA). In Dec. 1835 a new Commission was appointed, consisting of Howick, Palmerston, Russell, Spring-Rice, Hobhouse and Strafford. This Commission's report, on 21 Feb. 1837, abandoned Richmond's scheme for a Board and recommended instead that the Secretary at War take over virtually all the civil and financial administration of the Army and that he should consequently always be a member of the Cabinet. (*Parliamentary Papers*, 1837, xxxiv, Pt I.) But Melbourne, too, would not grasp the nettle and no major change occurred until after Palmerston had become Prime Minister.

[1] According to his mother, Stephen Sulivan, as well as being ill there, very much disliked Lisbon (Mrs Sulivan to William Temple, 9 Dec. 1835, B.P.W.). But Palmerston was reluctant to move him again so soon. Instead he promoted him Secretary of Legation in 1836. 'It is a jump', he wrote; 'but as the vacancy happens while he is there, & he has been doing the duty for more than a year, and it is well to make hay while the sun shines, & not to leave one's own kin to the tender mercies of Tory successors I did the deed.' (Palmerston to William Temple, 1 Nov. 1836, B.P., G.C./TE no. 252.) However, when Stephen eventually came home on leave, Palmerston agreed to move him (Palmerston to William Temple, 4 Aug. 1837, B.P., G.C./TE no. 262). George Sulyarde Stafford-Jerningham was appointed to Lisbon and Sulivan to Turin, 1 Nov. 1837.

278. *Stanhope St. 22 Dec. 1837.*

  Add. MSS.

I still hope to get down to Broadlands for ten days or a fortnight though I shall not now be able to go till the middle of next week.

I expect nobody there but the Bowleses and you & yours. I hope you will be able to come if it is only for a week. It would do both you & Lizzy good, & no harm to the rest.[1]

[*PS.*] Unless the War Office is much changed since I was there, both the Secry at Wr & his Deputy might well be away for a week or ten days at Christmas.

279. *Broadlands. 1 Sept. 1839.*

  Add. MSS.

I have recd the inclosed. I have been unable sooner to answer your letter about Mr Larpent, consul at Antwerp. But I did not decide his case without full consideration. He behaved very ill, and ought to have been intirely dismissed; but I have moved him to Riga, as a mitigated punishment.[1] He chose to marry a Ward of Chancery after he had been officially and in his capacity of consul applied to by the solicitor of the family to warn him not to do so; and there was not the slightest excuse for his violation of the law, and contempt of the Court of Chancery, because the young lady came to him in her own name, and within 3 months after he had received the letter from the solicitor, warning him not to assist & countenance the marriage. I referred the papers to the Queen's Advocate who pronounced Mr Larpent's conduct to be perfectly unjustifiable.

The chaplain who co-operated with him has also been removed.[2]

I have frequently before had reason to find fault with him. He is a vain conceited self-sufficient man, with no great regard for fixed rules of conduct.

My Tiverton expedition answered extremely well; and I found my constituents pleased at my having come to them.[3] I shall be in town again Monday or Tuesday, & Wednesday I go to Windsor to meet King Leopold.

---

[1] Mrs Sulivan had died suddenly early in the morning of 13 Nov.

[1] John James Larpent (1783–1860), 7th Baron de Hochepied of the Kingdom of Hungary, however, retired on a pension on 1 Oct. 1839. He was succeeded in Antwerp by a relative of Palmerston's mother, Godschall Johnson.

[2] Samuel Locke had been chaplain in Antwerp since 1823.

[3] Palmerston had secured a seat in Tiverton in the summer of 1835 and been re-elected at the General Election of 1837. The next General Election was in the summer of 1841; but Palmerston was expected to attend as steward at the races every year.

280. *Broadlands. 3 Sept. 1839.*

Add. MSS.

I forgot to return you the inclosed. The account given in it of the transaction to which it refers is very inaccurate. The upshot of the case is that Mr Larpent, a servant of the Crown, gives his official aid to marry a Ward in Chancery knowing her to be such, and having been warned by the solicitor in the case not to do so; his aid & presence moreover being necessary for the marriage, & his refusal to assist being sufficient to have prevented it. The consul at Rotterdam under similar circumstances very properly refused to marry the parties, and they went off to Antwerp to find Mr Locke the chaplain & Mr Larpent the consul.

I have been here two days in incessant rain; but William went out shooting for an hour this afternoon & killed 4 brace. I go to town tomorrow morning, and to Windsor on Wedy to meet Leopold, & I shall have to stay there as long as he does.

281. *Windsor. 10 Sept. 1839.*

Add. MSS.

I have been unable sooner to answer your letter of the other day. I am very much obliged to you for the little packet you sent me; which is to me of the greatest possible value; and I am much gratified by what you have done at Romsey. Melbourne means to offer the War Office with the Cabinet to Macaulay who is I believe abroad; but before he does so, he has thought it right to consult Lansdowne who is at Ems or Baden. Nothing will therefore be decided yet awhile. This is of course intirely in confidence.

282. *Windsor. 15 Sept. 1839.*

Add. MSS.

Pray thank Mr Palmer for the letter about China.[1] I had seen it in the *Times*. There is much in it deserving of attention but we must wait for further accounts of what has happened before we can finally make up our minds what to do. It is lucky for those who like occupation that one question starts up as soon as another is settled and thus Turkey & China take the place of Belgium & Spain. It is lucky also in the other way that while new questions spring up, some of the old ones are disposed of.

I shall remain here some few days longer.

[1] *The Times* of 11 Sept. had printed a letter on the opium trade, addressed to John Horsley Palmer by 'One Long Resident in China'.

283. *Windsor. 24 Sept. 1839.*

    Add. MSS.

Macaulay accepts the War Office, but his appointment is not to be announced just yet. You will like him very much.

284. *Windsor. 31 Oct. 1839.*

    Add. MSS.

The arrangement with the Govt of Portugal to which the inclosed letter related has not taken place, & you may let the letter continue to rest where it has done till you hear again officially from the Foreign Office.[1]

I have already spoken to Murray about Harry, & have written to Wm Bathurst. I should much fear however from what Murray said to me that Harry's chance of success is not great.[2]

It is as you say a long time since we have met, and I am *very* sorry for it; but I shall soon be in town again & stationary, and we shall then have more frequent meetings.

My stay here has been good for health, and in a political point of view useful both to me personally & to the Government; but it is not very favourable for business, because with every exertion I can make I am barely able to keep pace with the current business of the day, & cannot possibly find time to dispose of many matters which got into arrear during the Session. I was obliged to start off for Tiverton the very night of the day Parliament was prorogued, & had to come down here two days after I returned from Tiverton to town; and there are so many hours of the 24, over which one has no command here, that one's business somewhat suffers. The business of my department is one which cannot be neglected for a single day; it consists in dealing with events which will not wait the leizure of the English Secy of State; if you deal with them timely, you may direct them, if you let them go by they drag you down. The life of a Secy of State for Forn affrs is that of a tight rope dancer in a theatre; if his mind is not constantly intent upon every step he makes, he will surely get a fall, and never get up again. However our affairs have gone pretty prosperously, & success has been the reward of labour.

---

[1] This probably referred to a plan to write off some claims against Portugal in return for the cession of Goa.

[2] George Murray was Bishop of Rochester and Dean of Worcester; William Bathurst, afterwards 5th Earl Bathurst, was Clerk of the House of Commons. Henry Sulivan appears not to have become a deacon until 1841 and a priest the following year. In 1841 he appears in the Clergy List as Thomas Garnier's curate at Bishopstoke, Southampton.

I have long wanted an opportunity of mentioning to you a private affair concerning myself, from which I confidently expect much future comfort & happiness. I am going to be married to the Dr Lady Cowper but as nothing is so disagreeable as the congratulatory state, I wish you particularly to say nothing about it at present to any body, but William & Bowles, the only two persons to whom I have said a syllable on the subject. It will probably be, about the end of November or beginning of December, after the cabinet meetings are over; most likely not till the second week in December; and it will not be declared till a short time before it takes place. This change in my domestic condition will at all events render my house more useful to your girls.

285. *Stanhope St. 10 Dec. 1839.*

Add. MSS.

I asked Bowles as I did you. He said he would come back if I very much wished it, but that he had not yet sufficiently recovered his calmness to be able to be present without much pain. I of course said that I would not for the world press him.[1]

I hope you and yours will be able to come because otherwise I shall have only William. There will be very few persons present; probably Melbourne, Ld & Ly Cowper, Ly Fanny Cowper, and one of the sons who is in town. It will not be till Monday.[2]

286. *Stanhope St. 11 Dec. 1839.*

Add. MSS.

Where is Mrs Fortescue that I may write to her. Do you know Maria Stewart's direction?

287. *Stanhope St. 13 Dec. 1839.*

I have taken the liberty of giving your name to Lumley[1] as one of the trustees of my marriage settlement, William being the other,

[1] Palmerston's elder sister, Mrs Bowles, had died on 13 Nov. 1838.

[2] Palmerston and the Dowager Lady Cowper were married at St George's, Hanover Square, on 16 Dec. Palmerston had written to his brother on 11 Sept.: 'The wedding will be as simple & unostentatious as possible, & will be unattended with the numerous presents and other things which do very well for two young persons but are unsuitable for people of a certain time of life.' (B.P., G.C./TE no. 275.) But Lady Cowper's children were embarrassed by the marriage and wished not even to attend the ceremony.

[1] R. W. Lumley, a member of the firm of Oddie, Forster & Lumley, now handled Palmerston's legal affairs in London.

and I hope you will not disavow me. It is a mere matter of form, and will not involve any trouble; though I well know that this would not be a consideration with you. I will let you know tomorrow or next day the hour fixed upon.

288. *Stanhope St. 14 Dec. 1839.*
   Add. MSS.

The persons who will be present on the ladies' side will be, as I told you before Ld & Ly Cowper, Ly Fanny, Ld Melbourne, and the two sons. The Ashleys wished to come, but as they are at St Giles's in Dorsetshire, Ly C. thought it not worth while to give them the trouble of so long a journey. Do as you like about your girls; of course I shall be better pleased if they come. It will be at half past nine on Monday, as we have a long drive to Broadlands, & wish not to arrive there very late. Perhaps you had better call here as you go by.

289. *Broadlands. 22 Dec. 1839.*

Thank you a thousand times for your kind & affectionate letter. The ceremony of last Monday did indeed from associated recollections fill the mind with feelings most various and conflicting, and I could not, any more than you, trust myself to say anything for fear of touching chords which would vibrate painfully to us both. Your kind wishes for my happiness are realized and will I am sure continue to be so. I wish very very much that you and yours could come down to us; for I want you to be well acquainted with my partner, and a few days in a country house are better for this purpose than many months in London.

We remain here all this week & possibly till Monday next; would it be possible to tempt you down during that time?

290. *Broadlands. 8 Sept. 1840.*
   Add. MSS.

I am sorry I did not see you yesterday but I had given directions to let nobody in, and as I have a new porter he probably did not know that you were an exception to such directions. I came up to town yesterday morning from Windsor and after working a few hours in London came down here to dinner. Such are the facilities which railways afford for business as well as pleasure. I fear my stay here cannot be long as I expect to be summoned back to town any day for the exchange of the ratifications of our treaty. As to war I never expected it, from the first, and my opinion is confirmed by every day's information & events. France has no just cause for war; she has no interest in making war. On the contrary she would have nothing to gain and much to lose by war; among other things so to be lost Louis Philippe knows he must reckon his crown. Therefore I was sure from the outset of the discussion that France would scold and complain and bully, but would not make war; we on the other hand have not the slightest intention of making war against France, and therefore the peace will be kept.

I am sorry to hear such an indifferent account of yourself but I hope that country air and comparative quiet may set you right again. I will certainly give Stephen leave for the winter months to go to Naples for his health. It is not an easy matter indeed it is impossible to make changes of posts at one's will, & for the convenience of particular individuals and without any vacancy and vacancies happen seldom, and rarely at the places where he wants them.[1] We are here quite by ourselves for in the extreme uncertainty in which I am as to my movements and being liable to be called up from day to day we have been unable to ask any body but the place is in great beauty. We met Harry in Southampton the other day as we were going to Cowes to deposit Ly Fanny with the Ashleys in our way to Tiverton; I thought him looking well.

291. *Broadlands. 23 Dec. 1840.*

Here we are I trust for ten days or a fortnight. I was very sorry again to miss seeing you when you called the other day. Is there any chance of our seeing you and your girls here while we stay here? We should be very glad if you could come. It is an immense while now since I have seen you.

---

[1] Stephen Sulivan had been moved from Turin to Munich in May 1839. Presumably his health was still suffering and his uncle had determined to move him again as soon as he could. In the meantime, instead of giving him leave, Palmerston seized on a dispute with the Two Sicilies to send him to Naples as a special commissioner, jointly with Sir Woodbine Parish, to liquidate claims arising out of the sulphur monopoly. Palmerston wrote to his brother in 1841 asking how Stephen was and whether he could 'walk with tolerable ease', and suggesting that he take 'Indian baths' during the summer. The appointment lasted from 17 Nov. 1840 till 29 Dec. 1841, by which time Palmerston was out of office. He would have liked to promote Stephen before he went, Palmerston wrote, but had no chance of doing so. So Stephen returned to Munich. (Palmerston to Shee, 17 Aug. 1840, Shee Papers, and to William Temple, 25 May and 17 Aug. 1841, B.P., G.C./TE nos. 292 and 293.)

292. *Carlton Terrace.*[1] *17 May 1841.*

Add. MSS.

I will let you know tomorrow if there is a likelihood of an immediate change, but if you do not hear from me in the course of the day you may conclude that at least during the present week things will remain as they are.[2] If you wish to go out of town I should advise you to do so at once; send me your direction & I will give you timely notice of any thing which would render your return expedient. I think the debates on the two resolutions[3] will continue during the rest of the week.

293. *Powis Castle. 22 Nov. 1841.*

Add. MSS.

Here we are arrived after a very prosperous visit to Ireland,[1] and a tour round North Wales; not quite so prosperous as far as weather goes. I find Powis very well & in high force. We had a very boisterous passage over to Ireland, & some bad weather for a few days afterwards; but from that time till the day before we embarked the weather was fine. I found my works & improvements in Sligo going on well, and promising a satisfactory result. The condition of the people visibly improved, & the district wearing a more civilized appearance. My harbour is nearly finished & will now answer its purpose, which it did not do before.

We saw much of the De Greys on our return to Dublin where we remained a week.[2] They both seem to like their position, and will I think be personally popular. It remains to be seen whether politically, he will be able to steer the middle course which he has chalked out for himself, or whether by attempting it, he will not cool the zeal of his friends without effectually conciliating his opponents. I greatly doubt the possibility of a Tory Ld Lt pursuing with success this neutral line. But if on the other hand he throws himself into the arms of the

---

[1] The Palmerstons had rented Lord Caledon's house, no. 5 Carlton House Terrace, as more suitable than that in Stanhope St for Lady Palmerston's renewed career as political hostess. Subsequently they moved, first to no. 3 in the same terrace, then to no. 4 Carlton Gardens, and finally, in 1855, to no. 94 Piccadilly.

[2] In a year of rapidly declining fortunes Melbourne's Cabinet had been deeply divided whether to resign or to dissolve. Melbourne was opposed to either course; Palmerston strongly in favour of a dissolution.

[3] On the sugar duties.

[1] This was Palmerston's first visit to Ireland since 1829, though Bowles had made an inspection for him in 1835.

[2] Goderich's elder brother had assumed the style of Earl de Grey in 1833. He had become Lord Lieutenant of Ireland in Sept. 1841. His elder daughter was married to Lady Palmerston's eldest son, the 6th Earl Cowper.

Orange men, he will then raise a storm from the other party which he will find it hard to weather. On the whole I should say that the most striking feature in the present state of Ireland is the lull of party conflict, but though party animosity is certainly moderated, it is not extinct; & the two sides are only waiting to see what line the Govt & the Ld Lt will take. We have had frost & snow for our picturesque tour. We went to see the waterfall at Powerscourt in one of the heaviest snow storms I ever was out in, and the Welsh Hills have been white as glaciers ever since we landed. This rather improves the scenery by giving it an Alpine character.

How are you in health? Have you kept free from cold in all this changeable weather. Let me know. We are going to pay a few visits in Staffordshire & shall be in town in about ten days. I must say I have much enjoyed my holydays and have no wish to shorten their duration for some time to come; but I chuckle at the labour which I know Aberdeen must be going through.

[*PS.*] Our party consists of the Smythe Owens, Fredc Cornewall and Ly Caroline.[3]

294. *Brocket. 4 Nov. 1842.*
Add. MSS.

I received your letter here some days ago, and since that time we have taken advantage of railway facilities to run down to Broadlands & back again. Melbourne is very much better, and is recovering rapidly, but as he cannot yet receive company, the society of his family is a resource & amusement to him, and Ly P. therefore is naturally desirous of being here for some little time longer. I was sorry to find by your letter that you had no favourable change to report to me.[1] While that remains the case I will not bore you by asking you to write to me; but shall be much obliged to you if you will let me know whenever you may have any alteration to report.

I suppose George Bowles is arrived as I hear the Guards landed last week.

Income Tax is producing much discontent everywhere and many poor people who have a little sum in the Funds prefer submitting to

---

[3] Edward William Smythe-Owen of Condover (1793–1863) was married to a sister of Mrs Blackburn; Frederick Hamilton Cornewall of Delbury (1791–1845) was the son of the late Bishop of Worcester and a distant connection of Powis's; Lady Caroline was Powis's elder daughter.

[1] Palmerston had reported to William Temple on 12 Aug. that Henry Sulivan was 'going on well but his progress is slow, & attended with many alternations of relapse' (B.P., G.C./TE no. 302).

the deduction from their dividends rather than incur the trouble of proving that their whole income is under 150, or rather than disclose to their country neighbours the exact amount of their little hoard in the Funds.

But all these things & agricultural complaints to boot may make Peel more unpopular & weaker, but will not give us a majority for a long time to come either in Parliament or on the hustings.

295. *Brocket. 27 Nov. 1842.*
    Add. MSS.

I received your very welcome letter of the 24th just as we were leaving Broadlands and I had not time to write to you during the one day we staid in London. I am truly delighted at the good account you sent me, and earnestly hope it will be followed up by a continuance of amendment.

I have never ceased to hope for a favourable turn, & have always felt sanguine as to the prospect of a complete recovery.

We have found Melbourne very much better than he was even when we left him last week. His progress have [*sic*] been steady & rapid; and he now walks and drives every day.

These Asiatic triumphs are indeed gratifying to us of the late Govt because they shew that our policy was right and that there was far less difficulty in carrying [*it*] out than our opponents chose to represent.

As to the present Govt, to them these successes are just so much bread to a starving man. They will relieve the Govt from embarrassments of all kinds. Our manufacturers will get employment, our merchants will find a market and Goulburn will find money.

If any man had ventured ten years ago to predict that we should compel the Emperor of China to sign a treaty in terms dictated to him by a British plenipotentiary, he would have been voted insane.

We shall stay here about a fortnight & then I hope to get to Broadlands for the short remnant of the recess.

296. *Brocket. 4 Dec. 1842.*

I am delighted at receiving your good account of yesterday, which is as satisfactory as could possibly be expected. Of course so severe an illness must for some little time to come leave traces in its effects; but those effects will gradually disappear when their cause has ceased to act, and I confidently hope that the recovery will be complete.

I am sorry to hear what you say of Stephen, but I think that if he had had any serious relapse you would have heard of it from some of the persons about him.

I am much grieved at poor Montgomery's fate; it will be a great distress to all the Pembroke family but what a curious accident.[1]

The marriage of George Elliot's daughter will be a great comfort to all her family; the connection is everything they could wish, both nationally & professionally.[2]

Melbourne is going on as well as possible, & improves every day. He walks in his grounds every morning, & then drives out in his carriage. He will soon be equal to having other people in his house, & we shall then return to Broadlands.

297. *Carlton Terrace. 11 Feb. 1843.*

Thank you for your note and for the good account, for such I consider it, of Harry. Of course after so severe an illness you must expect the recovery to be slow, and sometimes interrupted; but as he has made so great a degree of progress there seems good ground for hoping that his recovery will be complete. Whenever you come to town I shall hope to see you.

Our Session will be active; there are many questions to be discussed which will give rise to much debate but I see nothing before us that is likely at all to affect the majority of the Govt, nor will that be shaken till the next General Election. Then, perhaps the balance of parties in the Hs. of Cns may be a good deal altered.

In the meantime the present Govt are lowering the position of England in regard to foreign nations, as fast as they can and they are in this respect doing great & serious mischief. Aberdeen is I hear in a bad state of health; the best thing he could do for himself and the Country, would be to retire, & let Stanley take the Foreign Office. He is the fittest man in the present Cabinet, for that office; & notwithstanding some faults would probably do the business tolerably well. At all events with more spirit than poor Aberdeen.

Ellenborough must be recalled. India is not safe in his hands. What with him in the East, & Ashburton in the West the present Govt have been unlucky in their choice of agents.

Give my best love to your girls, & remember me kindly to Harry.

[1] The Rev. George Augustus Montgomery, Rector of Bishopstone, South Wiltshire, had been killed on 1 Dec. by falling masonry when inspecting the progress of a new church being built near the Pembrokes' home at Wilton House (*Hampshire Advertiser & Saturday Guardian*, 10 Dec. 1842). Presumably, he was an illegitimate connection of the Pembrokes (T. Lever, *The Herberts of Wilton*, 1967, pp. 169–72).
[2] The eldest daughter of Adm. Sir George Elliot, the 2nd Earl of Minto's younger brother, married in Feb. 1843 the 8th Earl of Northesk.

298. *Carlton Terrace. 1 Mar. 1843.*

I hope your invalid continues to improve, and that you have no fresh invalid on your sick list. I want your opinion on the following confidential matter. Easthope the proprietor of the *Morning Chronicle* has just lost by resignation in consequence of illness one of his principal writers for his paper, a man of the name of Fox.[1] He is anxious to supply his place by some person not only intelligent & capable of writing forcibly & well, and liberal in opinions, but intirely honorable and trustworthy; and he asked me whether I happened to know any person that I thought likely to suit his purpose. The only person that occurs to me as at all likely to be fit for that sort of thing is Flower Ellis; but I have lost sight of him for some time, and I do not know how he is at present occupied & engaged, nor whether it is likely that he would undertake such an occupation; and moreover I am not quite sure whether he has that sort of facility in correct writing that would enable him easily to do what would be required of him.

I fancy that what would be wanted would be two or three leading articles in the course of each week, upon matters of interest of the day, and for that he would of course receive some yearly emolument. The duty would not interfere with any professional pursuits, & the pay might be worth having. Of course I do not mean you to make any communication to Flower Ellis, at present, but let me know what you think of him with reference to such a proposal if it were to be made to him.

299. *Carlton Terrace. 10 April 1843.*

As you say, there is nothing to be done but to wait for Stephen's answer and he will probably say that he is ready to set out in a short time for Munich. But from what Mellish says in his note it seems clear to me that in a few days the Foreign Office will hear from Ld Erskine that he either has returned or is about to return to Munich.

It is evident that having heard of Ly Erskine's danger he set off to go to her without waiting for leave, and of course he will not return to Munich, whatever application he may afterwards make from thence for leave, but finding on his arrival there the instructions about the affairs of Greece, he will no doubt execute them himself. I think therefore that you need be under no apprehension that the execution of that duty will fall upon Stephen. Erskine having gone away without leave must necessarily return to his post at the earliest possible

[1] William Johnson Fox (1786–1864), journalist, unitarian preacher and subsequently M.P. for Oldham.

moment & arriving there will find & act upon the instructions in question.[1]

[*PS.*] Ly P. desires me to say that she takes it very ill that you did not come to her party. She thought you either in the country or at Broom House; but she begs that you will consider yourself & yours as always not only invited but much wished for, at any party she may ever give. The only use of a card in your case is to inform you of the fact that she is at home & if that information reaches you by other means, she expects you to act upon it.

300. *Carlton Terrace. 31 Aug. 1843.*

Thank you very much for your kind note. It is indeed a heartbreaking event; never were two young people more happy nor more likely to contribute for many years to come, to the happiness of each other and of all who belonged to them.

I never saw a young person for whom upon so short an acquaintance I felt so strong an interest; she was so natural, so simple minded, so full of affection, and with so much good sense. Ly Palmerston is deeply afflicted for her own loss, as well as for that of William Cowper. This calamity & that of poor Charles Howard are sad afflictions.[1]

We are going to Broadlands either Saturday or Monday most likely the latter day. Wm Cowper will probably come down to us there.

[*PS.*] If we stay till Monday I will ride down to you Sunday afternoon.

301. *Melbourne. 8 Oct. 1843.*
        Add. MSS.

Your letter of the 5th has followed me here, and has only reached me this morning.[1] It seems to me that an answer to your question

---

[1] The Foreign Secretary had given Stephen Sulivan official leave of absence in April 1842 and renewed it in July and Dec., saying on the last occasion that there was no need for him to hurry back to Munich (Aberdeen to Laurence Sulivan, 7 April, 22 July and 12 Dec. 1842, S.P.). The Minister in Munich, Lord Erskine, had left his post to attend his dying wife. Richard Charles Mellish was the senior clerk in the F.O. in charge of German affairs. Sulivan had returned to his post by 17 June 1843 when he took over as chargé d'affaires from Erskine.

[1] The first wife of William Cowper, Lady Palmerston's second son, had died on 28 Aug., little more than two months after her marriage. The wife of Charles Howard, a younger son of the 6th Earl of Carlisle, had died on 26 Aug., little more than a year after her marriage.

[1] Sulivan's letter of the 5th is lacking, but from that he wrote on 9 Oct. (B.P., G.C./ SU no. 27) it is clear that he had complained again to Palmerston about his chief,

is to be looked for in an inquiry what is the nature of the office of Deputy Secy at War in relation to the Secy at War, and to the establishment of the War Office. Now I conceive the Deputy Secy at War to be in all respects the double & locum tenens of his Cheif [*sic*], as well as the principal organ of that Chief. I apprehend that when the Chief is present, the Deputy as second in command gives out to the office & the persons out of the office with whom the office has to deal, such orders of the chief, as the chief may not think it necessary, or may not be accustomed to issue himself; but though in strictness perhaps all communications between the chief & the rest of the establishment ought to pass through the Deputy, yet for the convenience of business, & for the fuller information of the Secy at War, this rule must in practise be constantly departed from. When however the Secy at War is absent I apprehend that the Deputy stands in all respects in the place of the chief, and can do almost all things for the chief, not excepting the taking the pleasure of the Sovereign.

Now how do these data, if correct, bear upon Hardinge's new rule? Why as long as the Secy at War is present the rule seems needless

Sir Henry Hardinge, afterwards 1st Viscount Hardinge of Lahore. As long ago as 10 Nov. 1828, less than six months after Hardinge had succeeded Palmerston in the War Office, Sulivan had written to his brother-in-law to complain of the 'daily disagreements' arising from the habits of his new chief (B.P., G.C./SU no. 19). Hardinge, he suspected, thought the office was top heavy and had taken to dealing directly with Sulivan's juniors, especially Brown and Lukin but even lower down. 'I need not tell you', Sulivan wrote, 'that I have been very long obnoxious to Lukin's branch of the office.' In any case, he went on, to be treated as a 'non-entity' made him 'heartily sick' and very willing to quit. But he was not prepared to leave the War Office under any sort of cloud and he was still there when Hardinge left in July 1830. Hardinge's parting tribute to his Deputy's 'very able superintendence' of the office and the 'implicit confidence' it had earned him was, perhaps, an invitation to Sulivan also to leave without loss of honour (Hardinge to [?Treasury], 16 July 1830, P.R.O., W.O. 4/724). Sulivan probably expected to fare better with his friends back in office and whatever his experience may have been during the brief tenure of Sir Henry Parnell, he certainly seems to have got on very well with Hobhouse. But with Edward Ellice Sulivan's position in the office again deteriorated and in less than a year under his new chief he was again complaining about some slur upon his status. Quite what it was about is far from clear, but the *bête noire* among his colleagues he named to Palmerston in a letter of 28 Feb. 1834 (B.P., G.C./SU no. 22) was now not Lukin, who was ill and near his end, but the Chief Examiner, Edward Marshall. Edward Marshall, who died at the age of ninety about 1869, had been one of those clerks with whom Hardinge liked to do business direct, and Hardinge had taken care as he left the office in 1830 to have him succeed Brown as Chief Examiner. According to his 'Account' of Jan. 1851, Sulivan had also incurred Marshall's animosity by checking a large increase of clerks in the Chief Examiner's department. Whatever Palmerston may have advised— and it does not seem to have been entirely uncritical of his friend—Sulivan stayed on under Ellice and under the still more difficult Howick. But as the second Melbourne Government drew towards its close, and Sulivan no doubt realised Hardinge might soon be back, he wrote again to Palmerston to say that he would long ago have resigned but for his duty to his children and that if the Government cared 'to buy me out with something requiring little trouble' before the new Minister was installed, he was to be had 'very cheap' (4 Aug. 1841, B.P., G.C./SU no. 26). But evidently not cheap enough, for Oct. 1843 found him still in the War Office and once again the slighted victim of Hardinge's preference for Marshall.

and inapplicable. When the Secy at War is present, the Deputy ought to issue no directions except with the previous sanction of the Secy at War, either specially given, or implied by former instructions; and therefore to say that in such case the Deputy is not to issue directions about any particular branch of business, without consulting the Chief Examiner of Army accounts, is in fact a restriction upon the Secy at War himself; and only amounts to this, that the Secy at War declares that he will not decide upon any question connected with accounts which may be submitted to him by the Deputy, without having at the same time before him the report thereupon of the person superintending the Department of Accounts. Now the manner & occasion of making this declaration may be objectionable or offensive; but the rule itself, as a rule for the Secy at War's own guidance, does not seem a bad one; and indeed is so natural a course of proceeding that one can hardly understand how it should now for the first time come into question. Of course however like all such rules, its rigid observance in each particular case must vary with the nature & importance of each case.

Then as to occasions when the Secy at War is absent, and when the Deputy stands precisely in his place. One should say with regard to such cases, that if the Secy at War can without impropriety towards the Deputy, resolve that when he himself is present he will make no decision, & give no new orders as to accounts without having before him the report of the Chief Examiner upon the question, it must be equally competent for the Secy at War to request his Deputy to act on such matters in his absence in the same manner in which he himself makes it a rule to act when he himself is present; and not to give any such orders without such previous report. I do not therefore see in the rule itself anything derogatory to the Deputy Secy at War, nor anything different from what I should say was the proper & natural course of official proceeding; supposing always that the rule to consult the Chief Examiner does not mean that the Chief Examiner's opinion is to be conclusive. It would no doubt be perfectly competent for the Secy at War to resolve in his own mind that he would be guided by the opinion of one officer on his establishment rather than by that of another, and he might chuse to prefer the opinion of the inferior officer to that of the superior; and as the Secy at War is after all the individual upon whom the responsibility for what is done, must fall, the Deputy could not with reason complain of his adopting the opinion most in unison with his own. But such a determination so to be guided might be announced in a manner offensive to the Deputy & calculated to lower him in the eyes of the office, and of that, if it were so, the Deputy would have good right to complain.

The conclusion therefore to which I come is that the substance of

Hardinge's rule is not a matter of which you can complain; and it must depend upon the manner & occasion of it whether it is worth your while to remonstrate. I write this in a great hurry for your letter arrived just before we were going to church, and the post goes out at a little after two.

302. *Carlton Terrace. 10 Oct. 1843.*

> *Add. MSS.*

I received your letter this morning as I was leaving Chatsworth. From what you say, Hardinge's opinion as to consulting Marshall does not seem to have been given adversely, inasmuch as it was given in a case in which you had consulted him.

I can quite enter into your feelings about Marshall as an individual, for though a clever man, he is one of the most unpleasant to deal with, that I have often met with; frequently wrongheaded, and in such cases particularly pertinacious.[1] But I should think that Hardinge must be as much aware of this as we are; and what you call consulting Marshall, I presume means, referring matters to him for any suggestion or observations he may have to make upon them before you or Hardinge decide; and that practise is I think in cases of that kind often very convenient. As to the feelings of the man referred to, being hurt by his suggestions not being adopted that is his affair; if he is a sensible man he may profit by experience in that respect. It was very much the practise in the Foreign Office to refer matters which admitted of being so referred, to the clerks at the head of departments.

I was sorry to hear at Chatsworth an indifferent account of Backhouse's state of mind from persons who had met him in Italy. They state his faculties to be much impaired though his bodily health had improved.[2]

I was glad to see Chatsworth which I had not seen since 1829, since which time it has been greatly embellished. I should conceive it now to be the most magnificent and complete residence that any subject in Europe possesses. But it is too far north or rather too high up in the hills to excite my envy. Art set in motion by money & directed by taste can accomplish almost everything else, but it cannot alter climate.

---

[1] M. Boyd, *Reminiscences of Fifty Years*, 1871, pp. 42–4, relates, from Marshall's side, a clash that supposedly occurred with Palmerston in the War Office which had left behind an undying sense of grievance.

[2] Backhouse had retired from the Foreign Office on account of ill-health in April 1842.

Dan has proved himself not so good a General as the Duke.[3] If Dan had not chosen to call the largest of all his meetings, or rather that which was intended to be so, under the noses of the garrison of Dublin 3,000 men could not well have been brought to preoccupy the ground; and the Govt would probably not have interfered at the eleventh hour to forbid a meeting, if in consequence of that meeting being appointed at some place at a distance from any military station, they would have been unable to bring an overwhelming force to bear upon it. This was a great error in strategy committed by the great Dan, fully as great as that by which Marmont gave an opportunity for the victory of Salamanca.

The shortness of the notice given is certainly open to criticism; it may have been however unavoidable, or it may have been intentional, in order to prevent the Repealers from arming themselves or from having time to deliberate upon their course; but it might have led to collision. These vigorous measures, it will however be said, might have been taken much sooner. Perhaps the Cabinet were not agreed about them sooner. I should say that they are a proof that measures of conciliation for next Session have been agreed to by the Cabinet.

We go to Broadlands Saturday & hope to see you there.

303. *Broadlands. 18 Oct. 1843.*

We should have been delighted to see you and your girls the end of this week but we have just had an invitation to Windsor for Monday next, & to remain there till Wednesday, but if you can come to us on Thursday the 26th we shall be very glad to see you, & hope you will stay as long as you can.

304. *Broadlands. 22 Oct. 1843.*

I am very glad that you can come on Thursday though I regret that you cannot give us a longer visit.

Pattison's victory is a triumph for the Liberals especially considering that some of the Whigs were either for Baring or neutral from personal & family considerations.[1] But the late vigorous measures in Ireland will rally the Tory Party to the Govt, and give Peel much

---

[3] O'Connell had planned to hold a 'monster meeting' in Clontarf on 8 Oct. to agitate for the repeal of the Union, but the meeting was banned the day before and the ground occupied by the military.

[1] James Pattison (1786–1849), who had lost his City of London seat in the General Election of 1841, had regained it in a by-election against Thomas Baring, second son of Sir Thomas Baring, 2nd Bart.

additional strength next Session. I hope he will take advantage of his improved position to propose some measures of conciliation both as to trade & as to Ireland.

305. *Broadlands. 7 Jan. 1844.*

  Add. MSS.

I am very sorry that you cannot send me a better account of Harry, but I did not feel so sanguine as you say the medical men were as to the prospect of so early an improvement; we must hope however that time may bring us a better state of things.[1] I wrote some time ago to Milbanke much to the effect of what you desire, & requesting that when he should arrive at his new post, he would let me know what Stephen was doing. I have no doubt that I shall hear from Milbanke and I will then let you know what he says.[2]

George Bowles left us today for Paultons, whence he goes tomorrow to Savernake.

We too had one night of sharp frost; thermometer down at 19, but it went off again, and does not seem disposed at present to return.

I see the O'Connell jury is likely to have no Repealers on it; if so, the question of conviction will depend on the strength of the evidence, and not on the strength of a juryman's stomach. The best thing that could happen would be a conviction, if the charges shall be fully proved. At all events we are likely to have a lively Session.

306. *Brocket. 28 Jan. 1844.*

  Add. MSS.

I received yesterday the inclosed from Milbanke. It decides the question which you wished me to ask him, by shewing that there has been no change of persons, and that his [*Stephen's*] intentions remain unaltered. I have requested Milbanke to let me know if he at any time learns anything more on this subject.

[1] Henry Sulivan's condition had become so bad that he was placed under restraint in a house specially rented for the purpose. Palmerston feared there was little hope of recovery and in May Laurence Sulivan reported that his son had had to give up his curacy. (Palmerston to William Temple, 5 April, B.P., G.C./TE no. 308; Laurence Sulivan to Fitzherbert, 10 May, Fitzherbert Papers.)

[2] John Ralph Milbanke (1800–68), 8th Bart and Lady Palmerston's cousin, had been appointed as Erskine's successor in Munich. Erskine left Munich on 20 Oct. 1843 and between then and Milbanke's arrival on 24 Dec. Stephen Sulivan acted again as chargé d'affaires. Palmerston reported to William Temple on 4 Oct. (B.P., G.C./TE no. 307) that Sulivan was 'able to go through his duties' and from the following letter (no. 306) it is clear that what was worrying everyone now was Stephen's declared intention of marrying his mistress.

We came hither from Woburn the day before yesterday, & go on to town tomorrow, to be ready for the conflict on Thursday. I imagine however that there will be no amendment moved in our House. John Russell will move none if the speech should not render it necessary to do so; and though Roebuck talks of one yet it is probable that his may end in smoke.[1] The Session however will be a lively one, or rather a some what boring one for the Govt, what with Ireland & what with Corn Laws.

I suppose there is no change in poor Harry's state or I should have heard from you. This is indeed a sad affliction.

307. *Carlton Terrace. 12 Aug. 1844.*

I have seen Mrs Fleming & her daughters and they would be very glad to see you any day that you might call—they dine at four, & drive out in the evening, but before their dinner or after their drive you would be sure to find them at home.

We are just setting off; that is to say tomorrow.

[*PS.*] If you want at any time to write we expect to be at Berlin the last days of this month & the first few days of September, and at Vienna about the 16th or 18th of Sept.[1]

308. *Brussels. 16 Aug. 1844.*

From typescript; MS. not found.

We arrived here safe & sound the night before last thanks to the rapid arrangements for locomotion in the present day. We started from London on Tuesday by the $\frac{1}{2}$ past 3 o'clock train, slept at Dover, started on the steamer, and rather a slow one, at 9 on Wednesday morning, reached Ostend at 3, set off by railway at 4, and were here by a little after 9 in the evening. Yesterday we employed in seeing sights & today we dine at Laeken with the King. We shall go on to Cologne tomorrow or next day by rail, and on the day afterwards we shall be at Ems. There we shall stay a couple of days, & thence we shall cut across the country to Berlin, & so by Dresden & Prague to Vienna.

This is a beautiful town and is increasing every year in extent &

---

[1] The new session of Parliament opened on Thursday, 1 Feb. Both John Russell and Roebuck spoke but neither proposed any amendments.

[1] This was Palmerston's first visit to the Continent since 1830. He kept a detailed diary extending from 13 Aug. to 4 Nov. and this survives in B.P.W. no. 1988. Some short extracts are published in Bulwer & Ashley, iii. 150–6, but the dates are confused.

in population. The Country in general is prosperous both in agriculture & commerce though of course here as elsewhere those who would like to be better off complain, and they who are doing well say little about it. Our weather hitherto has been dull & cloudy with a little rain, but not cold, & not wet enough to interrupt our peregrinations. I still think we shall be home again by the end of October.

We are in the Hotel Bellevue which indeed deserves its name and is so cheerful & pretty that if we had not so long a journey before us we should be tempted to stay here a week.

309. *Wiesbaden. 6 Sept. 1844.*

  Add. MSS.

I take advantage of Dr Phillimore's[1] return to England to send you a few lines from hence where we have lingered longer than we intended, partly to keep the Beauvales company, & partly to take the baths & waters ourselves; I to revenge myself on a little gout that pinched my toe before I left England, & Ly P. to exterminate a slight rheumatism which she caught at the Hampshire Agricultural. On Monday we go for a day to Ld Leveson's place near Worms, & thence by Frankfort to Berlin, where I suppose we shall be in about a week from the time we leave the Levesons. At Berlin we shall stay a few days & then dash down by Dresden & Prague to Vienna. Our weather for the last ten days has been beautiful, & my only regret has been that we have been taking it out at a place where the day is so much cut up by water drinking & bathing. Our hours would suit even you. We get up at six, walk & drink & then breakfast at 9, bathe & then dine at 4, walk after dinner & get to bed soon after ten. I do not know how we shall ever contrive to get back to our English *country* hours. This place is quite an English colony, & our countrymen & women come flocking in every day. Chas Wynn, Phillimore, Dr Nicol, the Clarendons, Ld Gosford, the Pollens, Trench, Wm Bathurst, the Orfords, the Lansdownes, & several others have been here on & off; & for foreigners we have had here & at Ems, Sebastiani, Duchatel & his wife, & Jacqueminot the Commr of the National Guard of Paris, besides Kielmansegge & all the Rothschildt tribe who are now united at Frankfort, where they meet once in 7 years from N.S.E. & W. to settle their affairs. Peace or war is the grand topic of conversation, & as we get here in the reading room most of the English & all the French papers we have plenty of means of discussing the subject. The general opinion is that peace will be maintained. But public opinion does not run high in favour of the ability of our present English Govt.

[1] Probably Joseph Phillimore (1775–1855), Regius Professor of Civil Law in Oxford.

They are universally voted to be a set of geese who know nothing whatever of the manner in which our foreign relations ought to be conducted, and the most contemptuous things which I have heard said of them have come from Parisian authorities. They are represented as wanting in foresight & in timely activity, as being wretchedly ill informed and bigotted to their own prejudices. They treated with ridicule the information given them by France that there would be a revolution in Greece, & thus lost the opportunity of giving to that event the turn which they might have preferred; & when warned last year by France that her disputes with Morocco were growing serious & would lead to consequences they boasted that the Emperor would be entirely swayed by them & that they could answer for his doing whatever they advised him; but when their mediation was accepted they sat for 8 months with their arms folded doing nothing, & allowing matters to come to their present crisis & having had that warning from France they nevertheless proposed to station *one* ship of the line in the Mediterranean. The French seem to have the lowest opinion of Peel's knowledge of foreign affairs and to reckon *Aberdeen* far his superior!—at least in such matters. All these opinions of course are not to be quoted, or they might get back to the people from whom I had them.

Germany seems a magnificent country, rich & productive; and beautiful in scenery. The food of man & beast is certainly more abundant than with us; but then they have not nearly so many mouths to the square mile to be fed. The vintage hereabouts will be bad, but that of Bordeaux has been or will be remarkably fine. Pollen was looking very well & Ly Pollen was in high force. They are gone to stay a month at Frankfort to wait for Mrs Craven's marriage to a French Count who is to be a Duke when some relation dies.[2]

310. *Wiesbaden. 16 Sept. 1844.*

Our visit to this place has not answered as well as might have been for instead of curing the gout I find these waters give it. I was very well when I came but for the last week have had a regular fit of gout first in one foot & then in the other, but I trust to be able to start tomorrow to continue our journey. The delay has been very tiresome, and we are dead sick of the place. Our weather still continues fine, and I hope we shall have it so during the rest of our tour. The Lansdownes go off today, and the Beauvales tomorrow or next day. This is the time of year when the German troops assemble for their

---

[2] Georgiana, widow of George Augustus Craven, younger brother of the 2nd Earl of Craven, married in Oct. 1844 Edmond, afterwards Duc de la Force.

annual exercise, and the Nassau contingent is in the field, six thousand strong infantry & artillery, fine looking troops & destined to form part of the garrison of Mayence in case of a war. Sir A. Woodford[1] & Lansdowne saw them in the field yesterday. Dr Granville is here on his way to England and I have had his assistance for my gout. He says he was always sure that Harry would get well again, but that he will always be obliged to be careful to avoid any great excitement. He says that the immediate cause of the quarrel between Stephen & Middleton was that Middleton came up to Stephen to find fault with him for walking arm in arm with the Italian in the public walk. I hear that Sr Alexr Malet is to succeed Shee at Studtgardt. I own I am not surprized that Aberdeen should remove Shee after the declaration of his marriage. It made necessarily a great awkwardness in regard to English families that the Head of a Mission should have an unpresentable wife, and as Aberdeen had no personal or party feelings to restrain him it was to be expected that he should send somebody else to Studtgardt. I am truly sorry for Shee, not on account of the mission he has lost but on acct of the wife he has taken. It is lamentable that a man who might have held so good a position in society should by such an act of folly sever himself from all his natural connexions.[2]

So our disputes with France are for the present at rest, but while our neighbours continue so restless and we so pluckless, fresh subjects of discussion will not long be wanting. Now the immediate cause of quarrel is over, we seem to be getting ready those ships which, if ready a year ago, might perhaps have prevented the whole thing.

[1] Lt Gen. (afterwards Field Marshal) Sir Alexander Woodford (1782–1870).

[2] Palmerston had found a new diplomatic appointment for Shee as soon as he could after returning to the Foreign Office in 1835. Shee's first wife had died childless in 1832—she had drowned after falling from a boat—and in 1841 Shee declared in Stuttgart that he had remarried and simultaneously produced a daughter already a few years of age. This, of course, caused grave offence in Stuttgart and gave ammunition to Shee's political opponents at home, and in Oct. 1844 he was recalled by Aberdeen. Shee was never employed again and in part blamed Palmerston for neglecting to champion his cause. He claimed in particular that his 'domestic position' was 'perfectly well known' in London at the time of his 1835 appointment. This his patron strongly denied. Palmerston, by the 1840s, had evidently lost patience with Shee and his troubles. When Shee's first wife was drowned in 1832, Palmerston wrote to Lady Cowper: 'The manner of the thing was shocking, but the thing itself is no loss to him.' When he heard of Shee's new marriage in 1841 Palmerston wrote to his brother that he ought rather 'to have pensioned off the Mama, when he brought out and acknowledged the young lady'. When Shee sent him a long 'statement' of complaint in 1846, Palmerston bluntly refuted it and on the same lines as his letter to Sulivan of 1844. Shee, to his credit, accepted Palmerston's rebuke very meekly and, as he said, 'with unshaken attachment'. (Palmerston to Lady Cowper, 5 Oct. 1832, B.P.W.; Palmerston to William Temple, 26–28 Nov. 1841, B.P., G.C./TE no. 294; Shee to Palmerston, 17 and 19 Nov., and Palmerston to Shee, 18 Nov. 1846, Shee Papers.)

311. *Frankfort. 22 Sept. 1844.*

Add. MSS.

We left Wiesbaden on Tuesday last as we had intended, and came on to this place but I found the journey rather brought back my gout, and I have been detained here ever since trying to get intirely quit of it before we proceed further on our journey. Though not a severe attack it has been singularly obstinate, but I think that tomorrow or next day we shall be able to go on. It is a bore to be laid by the foot at any time, but especially when one has allotted a certain number of weeks for travelling a certain number of miles.

We have never lost sight however of English society. Here we have Mr & Ly Mary Stanley & their daughter; Ld Elphinstone, and Orme[1] now paid attaché here & who was unpaid at Munich; a gentlemanlike & agreeable man. The Rothschildt family too are in great force here, & have been excessively civil & attentive. Hitherto the weather has been very fine & though I thought it imprudent to continue my journey I have driven out every day in the very pretty country round this thriving & improving town. The suburbs are full of new well built houses like those in the neighbourhood of London; only built more gaily, and looking more as if calculated for fine weather. The Fair has passed off tolerably well, but the communications between towns & countries are now so easy that much of the business which used to be done at these Fairs, is now done at other times of the year.

We are at the Russian Hotel very well & comfortably lodged. We still mean to go from hence to Berlin, & when once we get under weigh I have no doubt we shall get quickly over the ground. But we shall probably shorten our tour, as we have now lost more than a month by different casualties.

I will write to you again from Berlin.

312. *Berlin. 1 Oct. 1844.*

Add. MSS.

Here we are at last; we got here by easy stages the night before last, having travelled through a very interesting, and in some parts extremely beautiful country, by Fulda, Eisenach, Gotha, Weimar & Leipzig. The country about Eisenach especially is highly picturesque. The road all the way excellent and made with great expence & care, quite in the style of Telford's road through N. Wales to Holyhead. The horses too are strong & well fed, and the postillions have no lack

[1] See no. 321.

of whip, thong or spurs, but in spite of all this one cannot manage to get on faster than about five miles an hour stoppages included throughout the day. From Leipzig here, there is a railway, well constructed & carried across a country which for 140 miles is as flat as the palm of your hand; but the railways here keep the same proportion of slowness to ours, that their posting holds to our posting, and accordingly we were eight hours performing the 140 miles. However this is a wonderful acceleration compared with posting. Leipzig was as full as an ant hill; the Fair was just beginning and the streets were swarming with people & crowded with carts, waggons, bales of goods, packages, boxes, stalls & booths. It is a handsome & very thriving town & looks like high civilization. The whole country from Frankfort to Leipzig is rich & well cultivated; much of it the red sandstone soil like the western counties of England. The crops were fine, but backward in consequence of the coldness & wetness of the summer. The oats just cutting, much oats & barley still standing and even some wheat not yet carried. All these crops however were luxuriant & long in the straw. But the peasantry are ill clad & apparently ill fed. Many men and almost all the women working & walking without shoes & stockings; cows oftener seen than horses ploughing and cart & waggon drawing. What strikes one most is the slowness of all their proceedings, agricultural, domestic, and locomotive—an English population of equal number would draw twice as much out of the soil as these people do. The country is certainly thriving and advancing in civilization, but it would take them a hundred years at least to reach the point at which England is arrived in the arts of life; & what makes a journey through the country, the town & villages particularly interesting, is, that one fancies one sees in many things, what the habits & manners & ways of living in England were a hundred & fifty years ago. But the people are a good people. Honest, quiet, kind hearted, civil, obliging & in their own way industrious. Security of property seems to rest upon universal confidence that nobody will invade it. There is hardly such a thing as a fence of any kind out of doors, & seldom does one find a lock that will fasten, in doors. Manufacturers are extending & doing well, but they have scarcely yet got as far as the difficulty we are dealing with between hand loom & power loom weavers; they are struggling with an earlier difficulty between hand spinners & spinning jennys; and we are told that in Silesia the hand spinners are in the greatest distress and that much misery is expected among them this next winter. Their linen is yielding in third markets to ours; as we can make better looking things at lower prices. Their weavers are all cottagers & thus the merchant who exports has to buy from a great quantity of small manufacturers, & can never be sure of making up a uniform cargo. There is now open a great exhibition of German manufacturers, consisting of every sort of thing that man can want from boats & carriages to pins & needles. It is interesting, & many of the things are good; but I cannot say that it is calculated to inspire any fear for the commercial prosperity of England.

The picture gallery contains a large collection, many of them of great merit; but the peculiarity of the collection is that it consists of specimens of every stage of the art of painting from the earliest to the latest period classified & chronologically arranged; so that you see the whole history of the progress of the art. This makes the collection of great value for study to artists. Berlin has hitherto been too inaccessible to allow any of these things to be generally useful, but now one gets here by railway from Hanover in one day & in a year or two they will begin a railway from Leipzig to the Rhine. We dined yesterday with the King & Queen & were very generously received.

Having lost so much time at Wiesbaden & Frankfort we shall be obliged to give up the southern part of our tour, & to leave Vienna, Munich, Studtgardt etc. for another year. We shall go next week to Dresden, stay a few days there, & then work our way back again to the Rhine & thence home by the latter end of this month. I am afraid I shall thus miss seeing Shee which I shall be very sorry for; but as he is now no longer tied officially to Studtgart we may be more likely to see him in England, though I suppose his permanent residence will be abroad. This is a very handsome town & full of fine public buildings. It has now about 330,000 inhabitants, and is yearly increasing. The country round it is not pretty or interesting, being a sandy flat growing chiefly mossy grass, indifferent crops, and diminutive Scotch firs, but as the latter are meant for firewood they are not wanted to be large.

313. *Dresden. 15 Oct. 1844.*

   Add. MSS.

I have received your letter of the 8th. We arrived here on Friday last the 11th in one day from Berlin by railway, and we start from hence the day after tomorrow; but as the French say *l'appetit vient en mangeant*, & we find ourselves so stout and the weather so good that we mean to push on to Vienna which may be reached in four days travelling from hence, with an additional day to see Prague in the way. As we are so far in Germany it would be a pity not to do our whole tour, though this may throw back our return to England to the second week in November. This place is very interesting. The gallery contains upwards of 1,800 pictures; among which as may be supposed there are good bad & indifferent; the two latter classes of course are the most numerous, but the good are excellent in their respective classes; Italian, Dutch, Flemish & German. But the building is ill-adapted for the purpose; it is a rambling set of rooms in an old palace. The pictures are unmethodically arranged, many hung so high that they cannot be seen, and almost all of them, except a few that are covered with glass, suffering great injury from damp & dirt. The gallery is closed from the end of October to the beginning of May, & there are no means of warming or of keeping it dry during the winter. The pictures in some of the rooms suffer too from over heat in the summer. The Govt want the Chambers to vote money for building a new gallery which would require a hundred thousand pounds & several years; & they will not spend the two or three hundred pounds which would establish a hot water apparatus to save their best pictures from further injury. There is here a collection of carvings, jewels, & curiosities in gold & silver that is like nothing but a description in the Arabian Nights—one is quite bewildered with the magnificence of the display & on coming out one begins to consider diamonds to be as plentiful as pebbles, and pearls as oyster shells. The town itself has little that is remarkable but the country round is pretty. We dined one day with the King at his Palace of Pilnitz about nine miles out of town, a nice palace, & pretty situation. The whole royal family were there, very gracious & agreeable. The King & his brother P. John are highly informed, & the King seems delighted with his visit to England. This is a rich & thriving country; their manufactures & agriculture prosper, and the people are comfortable in general. But even here as elsewhere there are poor, and the manufacturing work-people do not seem to be at all better off than ours in England. They gain about 7 or 8 shillings a week for the support of a whole family; they live chiefly on potatoes, and seldom eat meat or wheaten bread.

The town must be unpleasant in hot weather, as the common sewers run down the middle of each street but a small depth below the surface, and at every twenty or thirty yards there is a wooden covering of iron planks over the sewer instead of a solid arch which, intended to help them to get out the contents of the sewer, succeeds in letting out divers most disagreeable smells. Bradshaw,[1] his wife & daughter are here, as he says for economy. He & the daughter go out, Mrs B. not having yet attained the art of speaking French & knowing no German sits at home as being a less dull occupation than going into an assembly room where she could not communicate an idea if she had such a thing in her head, to any human being.

Our present intention is to go from Vienna to Munich, and from thence to Ratisbon to Nuremberg and so home by the Rhine taking

---

[1] Probably James Bradshaw, M.P. for Coventry. He had married Charles Kean's sister-in-law, Anna Maria Tree.

Studtgardt or not, as our time holds out. If we do not get to Studtgardt perhaps Shee may be able to meet us at Nuremberg for a day. I am very sorry for his recall because I think it is a great loss of comfort and enjoyment to him especially considering the domestic position in which he has placed himself, but I cannot help suspecting that that position & especially his recent declaration may have contributed towards it, as it increased the awkwardness of his position in regard to English families visiting the place. At the same time I must say that with reference to his own private comfort it seems to me that having committed the egregious folly of the marriage, he has done well in declaring it, and in thus simplifying his domestic situation & arrangements. At all events if a man has committed an irreparable piece of folly it is better for his own comfort that he should think that he has done a meritorious act, than that he should suffer all the mortification of a full consciousness of his mistake.

I shall of course see Stephen at Munich & will let you know how I find him.

[*PS.*] We are off tomorrow for Prague.

314. *Dresden. 23 Oct. 1844.*

    Add. MSS.

Our plans are again changed. When we got to Prague on our way to Vienna I found that to undertake so long a journey as round by Vienna & Munich at this time of year & with the cold weather setting in would be too great a fatigue for Ly P. & so we determined to retrace our steps and return straight to England. Accordingly after seeing Prague which is on the whole the most beautiful & striking town I ever was in, we came down the Elbe hither, through the Saxon Swizzerland; scenery which may well vie with the most beautiful part of the Rhine, and in picturesque beauty is perhaps its superior. The steamers are good and I always think that rivers are best seen from their own surface. We stay here tomorrow and then make our way back to Mainz from whence we shall steam down the Rhine to Cologne & compare the Rhine with the Elbe, and so reach London some time between the 2nd & 4th of next month. We have been delighted with our trip into Bohemia & Saxony, and I shall recommend all my friends not to let another summer pass over their heads without visiting Konigstein, the Bastei & Prague; but especially the latter.

315. *Carlton Terrace. 5 Nov. 1844.*

We arrived here yesterday afternoon,[1] and are going tomorrow for a couple of days to Brocket, from whence we return to town, & then go & establish ourselves at Broadlands where we shall hope to see you & your girls whenever it may suit you to come.

How are you all? We had a very cold journey home from Prague, and found no reason to repent our not having gone round by Vienna, Munich & Paris.

Shee writes me word that he is to be at Lockleys about the 11th or 12th.

316. *Broadlands. 30 Nov. 1844.*

Noel was in such a hurry to get subscriptions that he could not wait for my return to England but fired off a letter at me to Studtgardt which Shee sent me after my return.

My answer was very much what yours seems to have been. I said that the inconvenience of Romsey Church is that from its size it is difficult to warm, and to fill with the voice. That to remove the gallery & organ, & throw the western end of the church into one with the body of the building would make the church colder, & diminish the number of sittings within hearing distance & that therefore I thought that part of his proposed alterations would be no improvement & that to say the truth I did not think what he had done near the communion table any improvement. That as to scraping off the whitewash that would certainly add to the beauty of the building, but that I pay a large sum annually for church rates, & am informed that there are substantial repairs still needed; and I should like to know that the church rates had completed those repairs before I subscribed for merely ornamental changes.

In reply I have received the inclosed note from Noel,[1] but I have not yet met him in the church to understand his explanations. They say he has already raised 1,800£ out of the 2,000£. I should doubt it. Certainly the general appearance of the church would be improved by throwing down every partition and laying it all in to one but the temperature would not thereby become more genial nor would Noel's small voice be better heard.

Ly P. I am happy to say has got perfectly well again. The repose,

---

[1] They had arrived in Dover at 6 a.m. the day before and moved on after a mere two hours' rest before breakfast. Palmerston recorded in his diary that his trip had cost in all a little over £500.
[1] Noel to Palmerston, 4 Oct., B.P.W.

interests, and good air of this place have cured her of all the pains & aches which annoyed her during her travels. Then to be sure we are leading a very wholesome life & keeping good country hours. I have been out hunting & had good sport in spite of the occasional frost. I hope we shall get rid of our painters in ten days time & that their smell will go with them.

We had a grand dinner at Paultons for the D. of Cambridge who was as good humoured and foolishly noisy as ever.

We go to town on Monday to go down to Windsor for a day on Tuesday, & return here on Thursday. We have got as we hope a good gardener in exchange for our Methodist preacher but new servants generally do well; remains to be seen the by & by.[2] Ld Malmesbury's correspondence is really very interesting, & shews what an able man he was when in his vigour; but the slipslop of his style of writing is curious in a man who evidently had a highly cultivated mind.[3]

I suppose Shee means to stay in England till the Spring. This is not a time of year to make an unnecessary journey. Beroldingen's[4] letter to him was certainly very flattering because it went beyond the usual & conventional formalities of diplomatic regret.

It seems to me that the ministers are in a mess as to their affairs in general but there is no other party strong enough as yet to take advantage of their blunders & so they will flounder through and barring a little dirt will be none the worse for it.

317. *Broadlands. 7 Dec. 1844.*

We were in town for one day only on some business which required my presence. We did not go to Windsor having been put off on account of the death of the Pss of Gloucester.

We should like very much to have you here at Christmas, & hope you will make your arrangements to come to us at that time; I think Shee will be here also at Christmas. But really it is difficult to imagine that Christmas is not come already. I scarcely ever remember so sharp a frost so early in the winter and with so much appearance of lasting.

We are still limited to Ly P.'s sitting room not having yet been able to expel our workmen.

We have the Ashleys with us for a week in their way to St Giles's.

[2] In 1842 Palmerston had brought in a new gardener called Herenan on trial from Brocket and Panshanger, but he was not a success either in his gardening or in his manner and after sending what Palmerston called 'a controversial letter' of complaint he had been given notice in Mar. 1844 (B.P.W.).

[3] The first edition of the *Diaries and Correspondence of James Harris, 1st Earl of Malmesbury*, 4 vols., edited by his grandson, had just appeared.

[4] Count Joseph von Beroldingen was Würtemberg Minister of Foreign Affairs, 1823–48.

Noel is unwell himself or pretends to be so as an excuse for skipping church, but he has already much lowered the temperature of the building by taking away the large curtain which hung behind the organ.

318. *Broadlands. 8 Jan. 1845.*

Do not come down to us on Saturday because we go that day to Windsor & shall not be here again till Tuesday afternoon. If you want Charlotte or if she wishes to return to her home come for her the Saturday after, but we shall be delighted to keep her here till we come to town, and it will be a real pleasure to Ly P. to have Charlotte with her. We shall be in town on Monday for a night in our way back hither from Windsor.

319. *Brocket. 21 Mar. 1845.*

We came down here yesterday & remain till Tuesday on which day we shall pass through London in our way to Broadlands to remain there till the following Monday when I must return to town.

Would either of your girls like to go down with us on Tuesday. We should be very glad to have either of them, & would take charge of her going down & returning. How is Harry? I shall be glad to hear that he is going on well & has not suffered from returning to his family.

What weather! The lake here is still frozen over in one half of its length, and the remains of the snow continue wherever the sun misses; this house too which when lived in even for a few days, is very warm in the coldest weather, still feels like a building which has been empty for a couple of winter months Melbourne having come down only yesterday.

320. *Broadlands. 26 Oct. 1845.*

You are going down I conclude with your girls to Binstead for the Fleming marriage;[1] I am invited over & shall probably go. We are remaining here till the 10th or 12th when we are going to visit Spencer Cowper in Norfolk.[2] Will you and the Bridesmaids take Broadlands either going to, or returning from Ryde? Pray do if you can.

[1] Mrs Fleming's second son, Thomas James Fleming (1819–90), was married in Nov.
[2] Lady Palmerston's youngest son had inherited Sandringham and a fortune from his father's friend, John Motteux, in 1843.

321. *Carlton Terrace. 29 June 1846.*

Add. MSS.

I have this morning received the inclosed from Harry. Lady Lynd-hurst sent us a message a few days ago by Lady Beauvale to say that they had made or were going to make this offer to Harry, and we have written to thank the Lyndhursts.

The explanation is, that Ly L.'s sister is married to Orme now attaché at Frankfort, for whom of course they want promotion; and as I should have no objection to give him a move, if an opportunity should occur there could be no reason against Harry's accepting this living if it suited him to do so.[1]

322. *Broadlands. 18 Jan. 1848.*

Add. MSS.

I was much concerned this morning at receiving from Bowles a very bad account of poor Powis, and deeply grieved at seeing afterwards in the newspaper the fatal termination of his wound. This is a most afflicting thing for all his friends, but dreadful for his family from the manner in which the accident happened.[1] Our early friends and associates are passing away from us, we must hold fast to the ties that still remain.

323. *Broadlands. 13 Sept. 1848.*

Add. MSS.

I have written on the inclosed[1] that which I understand you to wish, & that which is in accordance with my conception of the matter. The Deputy Secy at War has always as I apprehend been competent to re-ceive & signify the pleasure of the Sovereign in the absence of the Secy of War, just as the Under Secy of State does so in the absence of his chief. But the Secy at War is a single officer, & therefore if he should be abroad as I for instance was more than once while holding

---

[1] Mrs Orme and Lyndhurst's second wife were the daughters of Lewis Goldsmith, a notorious propagandist and spy in both London and Paris. The bargain appears to have been prospective, for it was not completed until 1851–2. Henry Sulivan was now curate at Sonning near Reading and he remained there until he obtained the living of Yoxall from the Lord Chancellor in 1851. Frederick Doveton Orme was pro-moted Secretary of Legation at Copenhagen in Dec. 1852.

[1] The 2nd Earl of Powis died on 17 Jan., having been accidentally shot by one of his sons while pheasant shooting.

[1] This letter is endorsed 'inclosed to Mr Maule 14 Sept. 1848', but I have not been able to trace this enclosure in the Panmure Papers in the Scottish Record Office.

the office the service would come to a stand [*still*] if his Deputy was not competent to perform all the functions of the principal. In the case of a Secy of State each of the three is competent to act for any one of the others, and therefore it can seldom happen that the Under Secy of State can be required to do any material act for his chief when absent. There are however, as I apprehend, certain things which Acts of Parliament require to be done by a Secy of State or by the Secy at War without naming the alternative of the Under Secy or the Depy Secy at War. You do not explain precisely what the new regulation of the court is out of which your question arises but I suppose from what you say that it is one which seeks to place the Depy Secy at War in a different class from the Under Secries of State, & to that supposition I have applied my mem.

Our weather is very fine but cold and Octoberlike; our sprained ankle I am happy to say is nearly well.

[*PS.*] Is there any chance of our seeing you or any of yours?

324. *Broadlands. 7 Sept. 1850.*

    Add. MSS.

I have established ever since I have been in the Foreign Office the system of free church for chaplaincies abroad; and as the resident British subjects pay half the salary I let them chuse their own chaplain subject to my approval and confirmation. Mr Brown therefore must get himself recommended by some congregation abroad if he wishes to be a chaplain to British subjects at a foreign station.

I am sorry to hear that your excursion has not answered as much as you expected. The weather with us has certainly been cold but it has been fine. My register thermometer tells me that last night it was only a few degrees above freezing, but today is brilliant. Can you not come down to us here. It would be the next thing to being at home. We expect no company though we may have somebody dropping in now & then, but you would be as much at your ease as at Fulham and the change of air might do you good, with the greater opportunities of being in the air during the day. I happened to see Parys[1] the other day on an official matter and he told me he was sure that all you require is to get your stomach right. Come with your girls whenever you like, only let us know the day before that your rooms may be ready for you.

---

[1] John Ayrton Paris (1785–1856) was President of the Royal College of Physicians.

325. *Broadlands. 24 Dec. 1851.*

I received last night this very kind & friendly letter from Lord Truro.[1] I have written to him to thank him, & to say that I will take steps to have sent to him the testimonials which he properly requires, and that I shall in the meanwhile keep the presentation paper in my own hands to be returned to him if the testimonials should not prove satisfactory to him. I know I am safe in so doing, & I felt it was due to him.

I think the best thing you can do will be to get the Arch Bishop, the Bishop of London, & the Bishop of Lincoln to write to the Chancellor as to the points mentioned in his letter. You can return me his letter at leizure.

326. *Broadlands. 26 Dec. 1851.*

Add. MSS. and, for the second sheet, S.P.

I have had too much to do in winding up to be able to answer your inquiry sooner. The story however is soon told. On the 3d of this month in talking with Walewsky about what had happened the day before at Paris, I expressed my opinion that the course of events during the preceding period since the meeting of the assembly had placed the assembly & the President in such a state of antagonism that a conflict between them had obviously become inevitable and that it probably was true as asserted, that if the President had not dissolved the Assembly the Assembly would have tried to arrest him, & that it seemed to me to be better for France & for the tranquillity of Europe that the President should prevail over the Assembly than the Assembly over the President because the success of the Assembly who had no good candidate to offer for the government of France would probably lead to civil war.

Walewsky in writing to Thurgot the French Minister for Foreign affairs briefly paraphrased my conversation with him by saying that I intirely approved of what the President had done; which was going somewhat beyond the meaning of what I had said. Normanby had in the meanwhile written to ask whether he should alter his relations with the French Govt in consequence of what had happened, & I told him in a despatch not to do so, nor to do anything which would wear the appearance of any interference in the internal affairs of France.

In reply he said he had stated to Thurgot the direction which he

---

[1] Truro, as Lord Chancellor, was arranging for Henry Sulivan to have the living of Yoxall.

had received, & that Thurgot said the communication was scarcely necessary as he had heard from Walewsky two days before that I intirely approved what the President had done. This report of his brought on a correspondence between John Russell & me. He found fault with me for having expressed any opinion without having first taken the opinion of the Cabinet. I replied by explaining at length what my opinion had been & the grounds on which it rested; & that it had been expressed in one of those unofficial conversations which take place every day between a Secy of State & foreign ministers, & that I had in no way fettered the action of the Government; & that the opinion expressed had been expressed intirely as my own.

This however did not satisfy John Russell & he thereupon repeated the intimation with which he had begun, that he should place the Foreign Office in other hands. He offered me at the same time the Ld Lieutenantcy of Ireland. This I of course declined. The ground of removal from the Foreign Office was alleged indiscretion, which however I do not admit, and which I contend is refuted by the offer of an office for the performance of the duties of which prudence & decorum which he alleged I had violated, cannot be dispensed with. The [*second sheet*] specific ground therefore of my removal is that in conversation with Ct Walewsky when he told me the last news from Paris, I expressed the opinions I have stated above. All these details are for your own information but not to be stated to others at present.

[*PS.*] John Russell's doctrine would make it almost impossible for a Secy of State to have any familiar intercourse with foreign ministers as he could scarcely open his mouth till he had summoned a cabinet & asked what he should say. His position would be like that of a person I knew who being asked one day how he felt & whether he felt better said he could not tell as he had not seen his doctor, but he was coming at four and if his friend would come back at five he would then be able to tell him how he felt and whether he was in less pain that morning.

I meant the Bishop of Lichfield & not of Lincoln.

327. *Carlton Gardens. 24 Feb. 1852.*

    Add. MSS.

The lists which you will see in the newspapers are I believe quite correct. The Ministry is purely Protectionist — no person of any other shade of opinion having joined it. Derby wrote to me on Sunday to ask me to call on him which I did.

He invited me to join him, but as he said that his adherence to or abandonment of protective duties on corn was to depend on the result of the next General Election, that announcement created a preliminary obstacle which rendered all further discussion as to any other points needless. I could not however have joined him even if that objection had been removed, because his Government was not to be formed upon any broad principle of a general union of parties, but he meant me to come in singly, and the office of all others which he had intended to propose to me was that of Chancellor of the Exchequer which is of course departmentally subordinate to the First Lord of the Treasury. His note to me asking me to call on him was extremely civil & courteous and our interview was friendly on both sides. These particulars I mention to you confidentially; the only facts necessary to be known are that I declined his offer to join his Govt, and that the question of Protection made any further discussion impossible. I do not mean to say that I should have been much disposed to join him in any case; but if his Govt had been framed on a comprehensive principle, and Protection had been thrown over board the matter would have required consideration.

As it is I cannot conceive that such a Govt can last, but the House of Cns will probably allow it to try the result of a General Election. I do not see how John Russell can refuse to acquiesce in such a course after having publicly declared that he felt he had lost the confidence of the present House of Commons.

328. *Broadlands. 7 Mar. 1852.*

From typescript; MS. not found.

We have very much enjoyed our bit of country though the weather sunshiny enough has been bitterly cold. My thermometer the night before last was down at 24°. We return to town tomorrow.

I received two days ago an invitation from John Russell to attend his meeting which of course I civilly declined to do.[1] It was natural that he should try to decoy me, but old birds are not caught with chaff. It would never have done for me to have inlisted again under his command is such a way as that.

The Romsey murder trial gives but a bad picture of the morality of this town; but the curates lay it all on the beer shops licensed to

[1] Russell had called a meeting for 11 Mar. to discuss the new Opposition's tactics in Parliament.

'be drunk' on the premises.[2] Carus is going to build a house not on a rock indeed but upon a gravel hill.[3]

329. *Carlton Gardens. 29 April 1852.*

   Add. MSS.

   Rich and John Russell propose an augmentation in the number of enrolled pensioners, as a substitute for the militia.[1] I should like to know what is the number of enrolled pensioners in Great Britain and what the number in Ireland. I observe in the Army Estimates of this year that there are 22,556 out pensioners of Chelsea & Kilmainham at rates not exceeding 10d. a day, of whom 9,760 are at 9d. & 10d., leaving only 12,796 at lower rates. I should like to know what are the present conditions as to length of service or disability which are required as qualifications for the ten penny, nine-penny & lower pensions. I conceive that any man who has a pension higher than 10d. must by age or infirmity be little fit even for home service; and probably the 2,048 ten penny men are not very efficient.

   If this is so, and if the 22,556 pensioners at 10d. & lower rates include all in Ireland as well as in Great Britain, the pensioner list is probably exhausted as a fund for a reserve force for home defence.

   I should like also to know what the bounty for men entering the regular army now is, and what is the term of years for which they engage, and whether they are liable for duty as veterans in case of invasion, for any period of time, after the expiration of the time for which they are engaged to serve in the line.

330. *Lissadil.[1] 16 Aug. 1852.*

   Many thanks for your entertaining letter. I should like much, again to visit the scenes of our early tour; what a crowd of recollections the remembrance of it and of the years that have gone by since, brings to my mind! I can fancy many parts of that Country much altered.[2]

---

[2] The *Hampshire Advertiser* of 6 Mar. 1852 reported the proceedings of a trial for a Romsey murder in which all the principals, including victim, assailants and witnesses, appear to have been drunk.

[3] Noel had been succeeded as Vicar of Romsey in 1851 by the Rev. Canon William Carus but his widow still occupied Abbey House and Carus presumably planned to build a new vicarage (F. H. Suckling, *Around Old Romsey* (reprints from the *Romsey Register*, 1910–16), pp. 59–60).

[1] Henry Rich (1803–69) and Russell had both spoken in the Commons on 23 April against the Government's Militia Bill (3 *Hansard*, cxx. 1042–51 and 1089–1101).

[1] Lissadell was the Sligo place of Sir Robert Gore-Booth, 4th Bart (1805–76).

[2] This perhaps refers to a tour of Wales that Palmerston had made with Sulivan in 1803.

Our excursion hither has been very prosperous & satisfactory barring two days of unwelness of Emily; but she is quite well again and we resume our march tomorrow. I find Ireland much improved since I was here last in 1845, notwithstanding potato failures, & farming and my own estate especially has been very much improved and is in a very satisfactory state. All the townlands have been squared, that is to say the tenants instead of having their holdings in different patches like the patterns in a tailor's book, have had them all consolidated into rectangular parallelograms. Instead of having their houses huddled together in a village half cabins, half dunghills, each man's house is on his own square and instead of each man having to cross some neighbour's land to get at some part of his own—each man's holding borders upon a high road or an accomodation road either in front or in rear. The result has been that cultivation is improved in character & increased in extent and that the numberless quarrels which mutual interference was perpetually creating have intirely ceased. The only drawback is rather an alarming beginning of potato blight, which makes many of the people clamorous for free passage to America. I am sending a small batch, but to send all who want to go would be too expensive.

We are here in a very fine place the very reverse of my adjoining property. Sir R. Gore Booth has about 3,000 acres in his own hands as farm, park, gardens & plantations while I have about fifty in hand, as nursery & pasture. I have about six thousand people living on my estate. He has a comparatively small number. He has a capital large house, I have a small inn. But we have both as beautiful scenery of sea & mountain as can be imagined.

We go today to Mr Cooper at Markray Castle near Sligo,[3] from thence to Dublin, and to Tiverton by the 25th to attend the races there on the following day, a duty to be performed towards constituents, especially so soon after an election.

We think nothing of politics except local questions, and therefore we have ceased to speculate about majorities or minorities, or the duration of ministries. But we hear much of the violent conduct of the priests at the late election. In many places they proposed candidates, and always in violent & often in seditious speeches. They frequently headed armed mobs, sometimes being armed themselves, the object of those mobs being to intimidate or to force electors to vote against their inclinations for the priests' candidates.

[3] Edward Joshua Cooper of Markree Castle (1798–1863), who had married the daughter of Owen Wynne of Hazlewood, was M.P. for Co. Sligo in 1830–41 and 1857–9.

331. *Carlton Gardens. 28 Aug. 1852.*

As you may hear that Emily has been ill I write two lines to say that she is greatly better and going on as well as possible. She was rather unwell on Wednesday morning the day I was engaged to go down to Tiverton and before I started I placed her in the hands of Dr Latham, one of the few medical men left in London at this season.[1] Some hours after I had gone her illness assumed suddenly the form of a severe attack of English cholera which however by Latham's skill and energy was speedily mastered. I got the intelligence of this the next morning & came up immediately by the express, blessing the invention of railways and of electric telegraphs by the latter of which I had received a favourable account. I am happy to say she is going on well, indeed to use Latham's words today 'in all respects as well as possible', and though so severe an attack & the treatment necessary to subdue it must of course leave much weakness behind them, yet the soundness of her constitution and her heavenly temper and angelic sweetness & cheerfulness of mind & disposition have greatly assisted the skill of the physician and the progress she has already made towards recovery is greater than he expected.

It was really providential that I gave up the intention with which we left Dublin, of going to Tiverton without passing through London —such an attack in a bad inn with indifferent or distant medical advice would have been very serious.

As soon as she is well enough to move we shall either go to Bds or for a day to Brocket & we shall then remain quiet till the meeting of Parliament. I hear that is to be, about the middle of November and I should imagine the Session will then really begin, & that there will only be a short adjournment over Christmas. The Govt cannot well meet Parliament without explaining its views & opening its measures, and it cannot do this without at once tendering to Parliament the bills necessary for carrying those measures into execution.

332. *Carlton Gardens. 31 Aug. 1852.*

I am happy to be able to send you a continued good account of Emily who is going on as well as possible, though of course after so severe an attack as she had the return of strength must be a slow and gradual process; but Latham who attends her says he is quite satisfied with the progress that she is making.

[1] Peter Mere Latham (1789–1875).

333. *Broadlands. 28 Sept. 1852.*

　Add. MSS.

Many thanks for your letter. Emily is I am happy to say quite well again and we intend to enjoy the country. We arrived here on Saturday & mean to remain here till Parliament meets. You & yours will be welcome whenever it suits you to come.

Probably Hardinge is on the whole the best person for the command of the army. I should have been puzzled to determine between him & Fitzroy Somerset who is his senior, and as an individual has I think the most practical good sense. But Hardinge will do very well; and I believe Fitzroy is intended to succeed Dalhousie as Govr Genl of India for which he will do extremely well; and it will be a good appointment for him.

I can't say much for Johnny Russell's speech at Perth. It seems to me to have been a stringing together of twaddling common place topics which had no real bearing upon the accusation from which he undertook to defend himself.[1] It does not follow that because it was right to emancipate the Catholics, to set free the Dissenters, to enlarge Municipal Corporations, to enfranchise the great towns and disfranchise the close boroughs, to repeal the corn laws, & to liberalize our commercial system it is *therefore* necessary or right now to make further organic changes in our Constitution; and indeed the prima facie case is the other way. Moreover the charge against Johnny was not that he wanted to deprive the Crown or the House of Lords of any of their lawful prerogatives or powers, but that he meant to overbalance those prerogatives & powers by unduly increasing the strength of the democratic element in the House of Commons.

334. *Carlton Gardens. 24 Dec. 1852.*

　Add. MSS.; cf. Bulwer & Ashley, v. 3–4.

Palmerston reports that as Clarendon is to have the Foreign Office he has, after all, agreed to join Aberdeen's Government as Home Secretary. I should if I had persisted in standing aloof either have been left in a little agreeable political solitude, or I should by the course of events have been thrown into connection with the 310 Derbyites who were looking for me with the same anxiety with which an Italian little state in the middle ages looked for some *condottiero* of good repute who was about to be out of employment. That party would have wished to have me as their leader instead of Disraeli, but though there are many men among them that I should be proud of being connected with, yet I

[1] See S. Walpole, *The Life of Lord John Russell*, 2 vols., 1889, ii. 158, n. 1.

am not ambitious of leading Spooner & Sibthorp, and then besides
the disagreeableness of finding oneself at the head of men with whom
one has for 25 years differed, opposing men with whom one has during
that period agreed, I have not faction enough in me to make a good
opposition leader. *He is glad therefore that he has had second thoughts and
adopted a course that is best both* for the public interest and for my own
comfort.

The Govt will be strong in the ability of the men who compose it,
and though it has not at starting a majority in the House of Commons,
on which it can positively reckon, yet I am inclined to think that we
shall find ourselves well supported and at all events there is a dissolution as a last resource; and a double house tax, as substitute for the
small loaf to be held up against the opposition candidate.

[*PS.*] John Russell & not Clarendon takes the Foreign Office.

335. *Carlton Gardens. 31 Dec. 1852.*
    Cf. *Airlie, ii. 151–3.*[1]
    Palmerston defends his joining Aberdeen. The manuscript continues:

Viewing then the matter either as a question of public duty, in a
crisis of some importance to the Country, or as a question of mere
personal advantage or disadvantage I am quite sure I have done right,
and I have been told so by quantities of people who have no particular
interest in saying so if they do not think it.

As to serving under Aberdeen which was the ground of my objection in the first instance people at large have such short memories
for things which do not directly concern them, that few now recollect
Aberdeen's differences with me on foreign affairs, and few would
understand or acknowledge the validity of that ground for my refusal
to join a Govt composed of men with whom I have been acting for
22 years, & especially when Lansdowne & John Russell & others who
were parties to my foreign policy & had been involved with me in
Aberdeen's censures had waived such an objection. As to John Russell
people in general consider that when I turned him out last year, we
were quits, and that if I had refused to serve with him I should have
been carrying resentment to the pitch of rancour. I believe that if it
was put to the vote by ballot among the Whig Party whether he or I
should be their chief I should have most votes but there he is, and he
cannot be put down, nor put away. People must in this world take
things as they find them, and deal with them as best they can; and
they who think they can have every thing their own way, generally
find that every thing goes the way they wish it not to go.

[1] On p. 153, line 16, for 'one' read 'men'.

336. *To Sulivan's daughters, Mary and Charlotte. Carlton Gardens. 5 Jan. 1853.*

I must write two lines to say how inexpressibly rejoiced I am to get the good account which Bowles brought me this morning.

I trust in God that all will now end well, and that we shall soon see him restored to health. I only heard of his illness last night on my return from Tiverton.[1]

337. *Carlton Gardens. 10 Jan. 1853.*

Thank you for your note. I thought that Ferguson[1] might hit off some quicker way of restoring you to your usual health and Paris would not take amiss a thing which is of every day occurrence. I am glad to hear you are mending & hope to see you soon quite well again.

338. *Carlton Gardens. 31 Jan. 1853.*

Add. MSS.

Many thanks for your kind letter, the contents of which I shall communicate to Emily who went down to Ly Melbourne at Brocket yesterday. I am going thither tomorrow.[1]

The loss is naturally very distressing to Emily who was affectionately and devotedly attached to her brother, with all that warmth of heart which belongs to her. Of course the possibility of such an event must have been suggested by the infirm state in which he had been for the last two or three years. He had moreover enjoyed great health and freedom from illness of any kind for the last year, but his constitution was not strong enough to throw out this last attack of gout, and instead of attacking the extremities it hung about interior parts & thus proved fatal.

Poor Ly Melbourne is in a sad state of affliction and despair.

I am glad to hear that you are getting gradually well, but in this cold weather you are quite right to take every precaution essential to complete recovery.

---

[1] Palmerston had heard that Laurence Sulivan was very ill.

[1] Probably William Fergusson (1808–77), Professor of Surgery at King's College, London.

[1] Emily's brother Frederick, who had succeeded as 3rd and last Viscount Melbourne in 1848, had died on 29 Jan.

339. *Carlton Gardens. 28 Feb. 1853.*

I am delighted to hear that Lizzy has done her duty so well & successfully; pray in due time give her my best congratulations.[1]

340. *Melbourne. 28 Aug. 1853.*

From typescript; MS. not found.

Thanks for your letter but I am sorry to have missed you. I hope however that you may wander southwards & come to us at Broadlands while we are there. We came down here on Tuesday for a stone laying and we shall be in town again on Wednesday for a couple of days.

I expect to find William in town when I get there. I have been hard at work at boxes & have no time to say more.

341. *Carlton Gardens. 19 Dec. 1853.*

Cf. *Bulwer & Ashley, v. 19–20.*

The newspapers have left me nothing to tell you except that the *Times* is a deliberate liar which you knew before. *Palmerston then proceeds to defend his action in resigning against the attacks made upon him in the leader of 16 December,*[1] *and concludes:* All this is of course only for yourself, except as far as it may be already publicly known.

342. *Carlton Gardens. 25 Dec. 1853.*

Bulwer & Ashley, v. 21; MS. not found.

Palmerston reports that he is to remain in the Government.

343. *Broadlands. 11 Jan. 1854.*

Add. MSS.

I am happy to say that William is going on as well as possible and I hope & trust that he will get quite right again. Both Beddome who attends him, and Ferguson whom I consulted give me reason to

---

[1] Mrs Hippisley had given birth the day before to her first child, Emily, who afterwards married the 12th Earl of Carnwath.

[1] Palmerston actually wrote 'impudent untruth' when reverting in his last paragraph to *The Times*'s accusation.

expect that it will be so.[1] Ferguson said that it was merely a sort of rheumatic local attack, and with care would go off. It made me very uneasy at first and was extremely distressing. But Ferguson said that if the attack had been of a serious nature it would have extended beyond the face, which however it never did.

It has been a great constraint upon William because what with the blisters that have been applied behind the ear & which have had good effect, & what with my wish not to produce him before company till all traces of the attack should have disappeared he had been kept a prisoner to his own room upstairs and to mine below; and as he has had to take doses though small ones of calomel he has not been able to go out. I hope however that he will be well enough to go to town with us next week.

As to public affairs they are not so bright looking as could be wished. My belief is (and it is shared even by Colloredo the Austrian,[2] though he is not to be quoted) that if the measures now tardily resolved upon had been taken when I first recommended them six or eight months ago, much of the present difficulty would have been averted. As matters now stand it seems hardly possible that a war between England & France on one side and Russia on the other can be avoided. Such a war however must as far as we are concerned have a very limited range, and must consist chiefly in blows struck by us and received by our adversary. It is however just possible that the Emperor may calculate consequences and may be inclined to be reasonable. Ten days or a fortnight will decide this point.

344. *Grosvenor Square.*[1] *16 Aug. 1854.*

    Add. MSS.

I have this morning recd yours of the 14 and am glad to be able to give you as good an account of all of us as under the afflicting circumstances of the case would be possible.[2] Ly P. and Ly Jocelyn have not suffered in health more than was the inevitable consequence of so sudden & severe a shock, & both are becoming calmer & more composed. The disease though an awful one in its rapidity & violence is not infectious and none of those who attended poor Jocelyn have suffered. Ly J. never left his couch side from first to last. Ly P. & I are

---

[1] Sir William Temple was home on leave; John Reynolds Beddome was a doctor in Romsey.
[2] Count Colloredo was the Austrian Ambassador in London.
[1] The Shaftesburys' London house was at no. 24.
[2] Lady Palmerston's son-in-law, Viscount Jocelyn, had died suddenly of cholera on 12 Aug.

going to Brighton for a couple of days & then afterwards to Broadlands. I am anxious to take her out of town. William came back yesterday from Binstead. Emily has written regularly to the Shaftesburys but if you see them tell them what I say in case any of Emily's letters should have miscarried. The Doctors told Emily yesterday that if there had been any danger or chance of infection the time within which it must have shewn itself was gone by. Ly Jocelyn goes tomorrow to Hyde Hall to stay ten days with Ld & Ly Roden, with her children & then comes to us at Bds. I have engaged a good medical man to go down & stay with her at Hyde Hall during that time to make Emily's mind easy.

345. *4 Feb. 1855.*

Add. MSS.

I expect to hear in the course of the day that John Russell has fasted & in that case it will probably be my turn; with a view to that I should like to know whether you can tell me what Panmure's general state of health is. Some say that he has such long & frequent attacks of gout as to disable him from an office of constant labour.

346. *Downing St. 10 Sept. 1855.*

Add. MSS.

The Russians have evacuated the town of Sebastopol, retiring to the north side of the harbour, setting fire to the town, blowing up their magazines, burning & sinking all their ships; & they asked for a suspension of arms to carry off the remainder of their wounded. These are the consequences of the capture of the Malakoff and the subsequent pressure of our cannonade.

The accounts just arrived by telegraph.

347. *Piccadilly. 22 Oct. 1855.*

I was much grieved to learn what you wrote to me on Monday. I did not know that poor Anna Maria had been seriously ill.[1] Laborious office, and Parliamentary duties cut one off sadly from private intercourse.

My acquaintance with her began even before yours, and dates from our childhood. These losses of early ties make us cling closer to those that remain.

[1] Lady Anna Maria Donkin, the eldest daughter of the 1st Earl of Minto and a close childhood friend of Palmerston's, had died on 18 Oct.

348. *Piccadilly. 3 Feb. 1856.*

Add. MSS.

Here is a letter from William which you may like to see as the last from him.

All things are going well. We are resigned to peace, and prepared for war. My own opinion is that we shall have peace; because Russia is too much exhausted to carry on the war. Her loss of men has been enormous and her battalions nominally 1,000, scarcely muster 500. Her money runs short, and her proprietors are ruined.

349. *Piccadilly. 16 April 1856.*

Add. MSS.

We are all in great affliction at the sudden & unexpected death of Ld Cowper yesterday afternoon at Maidstone. He had been in bad health for some time past, but as a matter of duty as Lord Lieutenant went down yesterday to attend a metting at Maidstone about county affairs. He was seized in Court at three o'clock with violent internal spasms and though attended by good medical men on the spot he sank at half past nine.

Deedes[1] the member for the county brought me an account of his illness in the Hs. of Cns at seven but his account did not seem to imply any thing serious. But a subsequent telegraphic message induced Lady Cowper to set off with Wm Cowper and Dr Ferguson. They could not arrive however till after all was over.

You may well imagine how completely Emily and Ly Cowper have been overwhelmed by such an affliction. I trust however that their health may not be materially impaired.

350. *Piccadilly. 17 May 1856.*

Add. MSS.

Many thanks for your very kind letter which gave me great pleasure.

We came back from Bds yesterday afternoon and after the cabinet today we are going to Brocket where Emily will stay some days.

I must be back in Downing St by ten on Monday to settle the new loan. We are both quite well.

Public affairs are prosperous though we shall have something of a row tomorrow about the stoppage of the Sunday bands. I could not help stopping them though against my own opinion. The Arch Bp of

---

[1] William Deedes (1796–1862) was M.P. for East Kent.

Canterbury represented, and I found we should be beat in the Hse of Cns, so I thought it better to give in with a good grace.

How could you suppose that I was going to propose to John Russell. We are very good friends and he has known ever since I came in that he may go to the Hs. of Peers when he likes, but I have no wish to have either him or Ld Grey as colleagues though I should infinitely prefer Johnny of the two.

351. *Piccadilly. 22 July 1856.*

I am glad to say that William has taken my advice. I wrote to him this day week urging him to do whatever his physician recommended, and especially to leave Naples during the hot weather. My letter must have reached him on Sunday, and yesterday evening Clarendon had a telegram from him asking for leave which was given by telegram last night so that he may be leaving Naples for Castellamare today.

I had a letter from him two days ago about politics but saying nothing about his health.

352. *Piccadilly. 29 July 1856.*

We heard today by telegraph that William left Naples for Marseilles accompanied by his physician. He is coming to England or going to some German baths. I had a long letter from him dated the 21st, the day on which he applied for leave by telegraph saying among other things that he had been advised to go to Germany or to come to England, that he had applied for leave & that if he got it he should wait a week or ten days to see if any instructions came to him to be acted upon. His sailing today was therefore in accordance with his intentions but his taking his physician with him looks as if he was in a state of health that required care and attention. It was however a prudent measure, and makes one feel more easy about his journey than one might otherwise have done.

[*PS.*] I have found his letter and send it you.

353. *Piccadilly. 2 Aug. 1856.*
    Add. MSS.

You will see'by the inclosed that William arrived safe & sound at Paris last night & will be here on Monday. I have taken good rooms for him at an hotel in Dover Street next door to Ashburnham House.

As he left Naples on the 29th and got to Paris on the 1st, performing the journey in four days, he cannot be much amiss.

354. *Piccadilly. 4 Aug. 1856.*

William arrived today, and is lodged at Percy's Hotel in Dover Street next door to Ashburnham House where you would find him between two and four or later if he does not drive out. His Doctor Roskelli has come with him, and is very uneasy as to the state of his health. You will indeed find him looking very ill, & suffering from cough, & the hollow tone of his voice will strike you. I am not without hopes however that it may turn out that the evil is a derangement of liver, and an affection of the mucous membrane and I have great confidence in Ferguson—unluckily I find this evening that he has been summoned down to Poole, & will not be back till tomorrow night or Wednesday morning, but as William has stood his rapid journey from Naples in a temperature varying from 80 to 97, a day's delay cannot make much difference.

When you see him you will of course not let him perceive that you think him looking ill & much altered & you will talk to him about any thing but his own health.

355. *Piccadilly. 9 Aug. 1856.*
      Add. MSS.

This is Ferguson's report of today and I have just left William who certainly seems better—but Ferguson does not expect to be able to form an opinion till he sees more decidedly the effects of his treatment.

I am going to Brocket this afternoon and return on Monday.

356. *Piccadilly. ½ past 9, 24 Aug. 1856.*

It is all over. I was sent for twenty minutes ago but before I could get ready a second message came to say it was over. He was feeble when I left him last night and the servant expressed anxiety as to the night. I did not however expect so early a termination, but as hope had vanished we can only consider it a merciful release from suffering. I am going presently to the hotel. I have not as yet seen any body from thence.

357. *Piccadilly. 25 Aug. 1856.*

I have appointed Burnett (a partner of Nicholl[1] who is himself out of town) to come here on Wednesday at twelve to open the will. Would you come here at that time?

358. *Piccadilly. 1 Sept. 1856.*
   From typescript; MS. not found.

You have made an inquiry whether we are going to put our servants into mourning. This was not done upon three former occasions when Emily lost her two brothers and when this year we lost Ld Cowper, and therefore I have not proposed it to her on the present occasion.

359. *To Sulivan's daughter, Elizabeth. Broadlands. 29 Sept. 1856.*

The arrangement to which your letter relates was I know my poor brother's wish & intention and I was sure you would value it as a proof of the warm affection which he felt for you all.[1]

360. *Piccadilly. 14 Dec. 1856.*

I shall have in the course of this week to pay to your three girls a dividend on their Slate shares. Will you let me know what banker they keep their account with. We are off to Broadlands tomorrow, direct your answer to me there.

I am glad to hear you are benefitting by the mild climate of Torquay.

361. *94 Piccadilly. 20 Jan. 1857.*
   Add. MSS.

Many thanks for your letter. I have had rather a sharp bout with the gout as far as one foot was concerned, & I had to use crutches for some days. I am however nearly right again & am glad it came on before Parliament met. We came to town yesterday & have had a regular London day of rain & gloom. Public affairs look well and I do not hear of any particular threatening for the Session.

---

[1] Frederick J. Nicholl and R. F. Burnett of 18 Carey St.
[1] William Temple had left his shares in the now very profitable Welsh Slate Co. jointly to the Sulivan girls.

Of course there will be plenty of work, and no lack of disposition in some quarters to take advantage of any opportunity to harrass the Govt, but we have the Country with us, and our most difficult foreign questions have been settled or will be so.

362. *94 Piccadilly. 14 Sept. 1857.*

Add. MSS.

You will probably have seen by today's papers the attack made upon Stephen at Lima and the dangerous wounds which he received. I send you copies of the despatches received today at the Foreign Office giving an account of what happened.[1] I much fear from the nature of the wounds that his recovery can scarcely be looked for. It is a sad and distressing affair whatever may have been the cause.

363. *Piccadilly. 14 Sept. 1857.*

Add. MSS.

I send you these papers though they do not add much to what I sent you by messenger this afternoon.[1] It seems that three of the bullets were extracted but the surgeons feared that more must have entered the body and I should apprehend that there there [*sic*] can be little hope of recovery.

The Peruvian despatch sent me by Hammond contained only a repetition of what the other papers stated.

364. *Broadlands. 5 Oct. 1857.*

Add. MSS.

I have received the inclosed from Lima.[1] I conclude that the writer is some respectable English merchant residing there. His impression seems to be that the crime was committed by the Vivanco rebels.

---

[1] The despatch, dated 12 Aug. and marked 'separate' from John Barton, the Vice-Consul in Lima, a copy of which is in Add. MSS. 59782–3, reported that Stephen Sulivan's wound would probably be fatal.

[1] Capt. Charles Barker, H.M.S. *Retribution*, Callao, 12 Aug., and Adm. H. W. Bruce, H.M.S. *Monarch*, Payta, 15 Aug., enclosed in Admiralty to F.O., 14 Sept. 1857, F.O. 61/178, copies of which are also in Add. MSS. 59782–3.

[1] This letter is endorsed: 'This covered the very interesting letter of Mr Fernandez of Lima to Lord Palmerston.' But no such letter has been found either in Add. MSS. 59782–3 or in the F.O. files.

365. *Broadlands. 7 Oct. 1857.*

I send you a letter which I have received from the Queen whom I have thanked in reply.

I believe a watch was sent to Broom House which is intended for Harry as a memorial of poor William to whom it belonged. I had sent it to the maker to be put in order and it had not come back in time to be put into the writing box.

The watch I gave you is a repeater.

Our weather here is like the squares on a chess board alternately black & white—one day beautifully fine, the next like today cloudy and rainy; but the farmers are glad of the watering which the earth required.

366. *94 Piccadilly. 8 June 1858.*

Add. MSS.

I have received from Malmesbury the inclosed copy of a despatch from Lima, which shews that poor Stephen's fate was owing not to any private quarrel but simply to his performance of a public duty.

[*PS.*] You may keep the inclosed.[1]

367. *94 Piccadilly. 21 Nov. 1858.*

Add. MSS.

I got home here at half past one last night and am going down to Broadlands tomorrow & have been unable to get to Broom House today, among other reasons, because I have brought home a cold in my head which I wish to leave behind me in London.

My excursion has in many respects answered extremely well.[1] They were all very civil & courteous, and the visits of English to the Emperor serve as links to maintain and strengthen the English alliance. Our weather was not the most fortunate. I went over to Boulogne in a gale of wind, which however did not signify as it was in the right direction and I was not sick, but out of four days at Compiegne three were rainy, and thus I lost a stag hunt in the old style in the forest, for though we all went out and were expecting

---

[1] John Barton (acting Consul-General, Lima), no. 17, to Malmesbury, 8 April 1858, F.O. 61/180, of which there is a copy in Add. MSS. 59782–3.

[1] Palmerston had just returned with Clarendon from a visit to Napoleon III at Compiègne.

the stag to bolt, he was not at home and a heavy rain drove us all in again. Friday was fine, and we had a great shooting party, killing upwards of 500 head of game. Of English we had the Cowleys, Clarendons, Alfred Paget & his wife, Craven & Ly Mary, & Ld Hertford;[2] but we sat down between 60 & 80 every day to dinner.

I saw Bowles today who said that Harry is under good care, and therefore all we can hope is that this attack may not be of so long duration as the last.

I go down tomorrow to Broadlands, and we are to be at Shrubland[3] on the 30th.

368. *Broadlands. 22 Sept. 1859.*

    Add. MSS.

I am glad to find by your letter that you are returned safe & sound from your wandering & I heard a good account of you from friends who met you on the railway.

We are all well & have the Middletons & George Bowles & some others here.

I am obliged however to go to town tomorrow for cabinet but shall only remain a day and a half in London; and we may hope perhaps to see you & yours here before we return to town towards the end of October.

The country is no doubt pleasanter than London but there are advantages in being in London, and the being there probably saved me from having my head broke by the fall of a large piece of the ceiling of my new sitting room; it is now repairing and I hope will soon be ready for service again.

This China affair is very provoking and the more so because while on the one hand something decisive ought to be done against the Celestial Emperor, on the other hand distances and climate & other physical circumstances make it difficult to trouble him as he deserves.

369. *94 Piccadilly. 6 Dec. 1859.*

I have been prevented by various causes—business, weather, etc. from getting to you.

We hope to be able to go to Broadlands some time next week,

---

[2] The 1st Earl Cowley was Ambassador in Paris; Lord Alfred Paget (1816–88) was his half-brother. William George Craven (1835–1906), a grandson of the 2nd Earl of Craven, had married a daughter of the 4th Earl of Hardwicke.
[3] William Fowle-Middleton's place in Suffolk.

and we hope that you and Charlotte will come and spend your Christmas with us, and stay with us as long as you can.

370. *Broadlands. 1 Jan. 1860.*

    Add. MSS.

I have not heard from you as to when you mean to come here, and I write therefore to say that we shall be full here till Friday, but shall be very glad to see you and your girls on that day. Our stay here will unluckily be shorter than usual as in consequence of the early meeting of Parliament I shall probably have to go to town some time in the week after this next.

I am exceedingly sorry for the difficulty Bowles has got into by the publication of his official correspondence about the *Princess Royal* mutiny, in the *Morning Post*; but there was no help for it.[1]

371. *Broadlands. 30 Sept. 1860.*

    Add. MSS.

I will answer Thornton. People think I have livings to give away every week, while I have scarcely one in a twelvemonth.

We have been deluged but the sun comes to dry us ever & anon, and we have lost no trees by the gales that have blown over us. There is however still some wheat uncut, and much barley that would have been better if it had not been cut. Soaked with rain one day and partially dried by sun and wind the next. On the whole however the harvest is not thought to be a bad one. Our river is brim full, partly by the rains, partly because the Andover Canal is partially dried up and springs & streams that used to fill its bed now are returned to their original owner the Test.

I believe affairs are going on prosperously. Garibaldi is too much surrounded by Mazzini & Co., but I am convinced he means to be true and loyal to Victor Emmanuel. He is foolish enough however to fancy he can drive the French garrison out of Rome, and the Austrians out of Venetia, & he wants to keep his army in his own hands till he has done these things. But the defeat of part of his troops before Capua will probably have taught him that though his army can conquer kingdoms when unresisted it is not capable of facing French or Austrian forces.

Volunteer Reviews are the order of the day, and the Hampshire

---

[1] The *Post* of 28 Dec. 1859 had printed a full account of this affair, which had taken place in Portsmouth Harbour where Bowles was Admiral Superintendent.

Rifles have asked to be reviewed in the park here. That will take me back to our Local Militia campaigns. We are neither of us quite as active as we were in those days, but we may both be thankful for much health and enjoyment of life, and I trust our Rifles will with other things prevent the French from coming here to disturb our tranquility.

Emily desires her kindest remembrances.

372. *94 Piccadilly. 7 Sept. 1861.*

 Add. MSS.

Many thanks for your letter. We came up today from Walmer to meet the Shaftesburys who are expected this evening. Their affliction has been great; the last illness of the poor girl was very painful and full of suffering and the strain upon Lady Shaftesbury's health, nerves and feelings has been most severe.[1] The end had long become a mere question of time, and of more or less suffering and it has at last been a release to all. We hope to persuade them to go back with us to Walmer and to stay there some time.[2] It is quiet and healthy, and free from painful associations.

We shall stay a day or two with them and then go to Broadlands to remain there.

373. *Broadlands. 3 Oct. 1861.*

Many thanks for your letter which I was glad to receive, but you left out an announcement which I am sure you intended to make if you had not been in a hurry when you wrote, and that was to tell us on what day we might expect you here. Pray fill up this gap in your statements. I am in a hurry too so no more at present from

374. *Broadlands. 6 Oct. 1861.*

 Add. MSS.

We were glad to get your letter this morning. I am going on Tuesday on an expedition to see the works at Portsmouth, and if I can manage it, at Portland and we shall be full from Saturday to Tuesday but we should be delighted to see you on Tuesday sennight the 15th and the longer you stay, the better pleased we shall be.

[1] The Shaftesburys' second daughter Mary had died on 3 Sept.
[2] Palmerston had become Warden of the Cinque Ports on 27 Mar.

375. *Broadlands. 26 Jan. 1862.*

Add. MSS.

I am quite well barring a bit of a cold caught the day before yesterday. I am going to town on Thursday for good & all. As to the American affair the merit belongs to the whole Cabinet, but specially to Russell, Lewis, Newcastle and Somerset, for their energy in their several departments. If we had not shewn that we were ready to fight, that low-minded fellow Seward would not have eat the leek as he has done.

376. *94 Piccadilly. 18 Mar. 1862.*

I am very sorry to hear from Shee that you have had a bad fall, for a bad one it must be when you fell upon the hard boards of a floor. Pray let us know how you are; we hope that the bad effects have passed away.

377. *94 Piccadilly. 1 June 1862.*

I have been prevented from riding down to you today by occupations not to be laid aside. I send my groom with this to ask you how Lizzy is going on.

378. *Broadlands. 25 Jan. 1863.*

I am glad the pheasants reached you safely, and much more so that you have been relieved from your two apprehensions. I shall be in town on Tuesday. Ld [?*Ly*] P. will follow in a few days afterwards.

379. *94 Piccadilly. 14 April 1863.*

Add. MSS.

We have lost poor Lewis.[1] It has been an unexpected blow. He was unwell at Harpton in the beginning of the week, on Sunday his liver became greatly congested, the inflammation spread to the lungs and he died yesterday afternoon. It is a great loss privately and politically.

[1] Palmerston's Secretary for War, Sir George Cornewall Lewis, had died on 13 April.

My Scotch expedition answered extremely well; the people of all classes were most kind & cordial to me, and what is better loyal and contented with our institutions and in spite of cotton distress, they were doing pretty well even at Glasgow.

I found a girl whom you must recollect, (though I had forgotten her existence) as little Peggy at Lothian House, grown into an old woman but apparently living comfortably, but full of recollections of that time.[2]

I also managed to get up again to the top of Arthur's Seat, and really without much more difficulty than when I used to start from Lothian House. Edinbr. & Glasgow are much improved & are very handsome towns.

380. *94 Piccadilly. 7 Sept. 1863.*

Add. MSS.

I was right glad to hear the good account which your letter of last week gave me of yourself.

We are going to Broadlands in a couple of days, and we should be very glad if you and yours could bring us into your arrangements. The sooner you could come the better pleased we should be; and the better would be the rural condition in which you would find Broadlands.

I made a run last week to the North Wales slate quarries and found every thing going on in a satisfactory manner. Whether the result of the Frankfort Congress will be equally satisfactory time will shew, but it is not an easy thing to unite bodies which have separate existences they are not inclined to give up, and between which the principle of mutual repulsion is stronger than that of attraction & cohesion.

[2] 'Peggy' had presumably been a servant of Dugald Stewart's at the time Sulivan and Palmerston were students in Edinburgh.

INDEX

Bevelandt, 110
Beverley, John, 40
—, Earls of *see* Percy
Bexley *see* Vansittart
Bicester, 155 n. 2
Bicton, 35 n. 2
Billington, Elizabeth, 29
Bilson-Legge, Henry, 2nd Baron Stawell, 140
Binstead, 241, 295, 309
Birch, Mr, 264
Birkett, John, 249 n. 1
Bishopstoke, 269 n. 2
Bishopstone, 276 n. 1
Bistern, 155
Blackall, Samuel, 55, 79, and n. 3, 82, 83, 84
Blackburn, Edward Berens, 6, 16–17, 54, 160, 258 n. 1, 264
—, Mrs (Elizabeth), 16, 17, 127, 264, 274 n. 3
—, John, 6
—, John Edward, 17, 258
Blackman, John, 120
Blamire, William, 264
Blenheim Palace, 173
Blessington *see* Gardiner
Bletchingley, 252 n. 1
Blick, Charles, 180 n. 1, 182 n. 3, 248–9
Blomfield, Charles James, Bishop of London, 11 n. 41, 298
Blücher, Gen. Gebhard Lebrecht, Prince von, 127, 143
Boehm, Edmund, 44 n. 1
Bohemia, 102, 292
Boileau, Lady Catherine, 184
—, Sir John Peter, 1st Bart, 184
Bolbec, 128
Bolton *see* Orde-Powlett
Bonaparte *see* Joseph *and* Napoleon
Boodles, 236 n. 4
Booth *see* Gore-Booth
Bordeaux, 286
—, Henri, Duc de, 228
Boscawen, Edward, 1st Earl of Falmouth, 234
Botany Bay, 60
Bothwell, 58, 61
Bouchain, 142
Boulogne, 48, 223, 315
Bourke, Count Edmond, 223 n. 1
—, Countess, 223
Bourmont, Louis Auguste Victor, Comte de Ghaisne de, 237

Bourne, William Sturges, 190–3, 197, 199–200, 205, 241
Bouverie, Edward, 83
—, John, 83
—, William Pleydell, Viscount Folkestone (*afterwards* 3rd Earl of Radnor), 100
Bow St, 92
Bowles, Gen. Sir George, 241, 274, 283, 316
—, Adm. of the Fleet Sir William, 27 n. 83, 168, 173 n. 1, 241 n. 2, 267, 270, 296, 306, 316; helps P. in Cambridge, 180 n. 1; inspects P.'s Irish estates, 273 n. 1; marries P.'s sister, 168 n. 3; and *Princess Royal* mutiny, 317
—, Mrs William ('Fanny': *formerly* Frances Temple), 1, 27 n. 83 & 84, 37, 38, 44, 48, 79, 98, 100, 103 n. 1, 104, 110, 118, 119, 121, 131, 132 n. 1, 134, 136, 140, 141, 142, 144, 146, 168, 173 n. 1, 199, 215, 229, 238, 267; courted by Ashburton, 45 n. 2; dies, 270 n. 1; marries, 168 n. 3
Bowood, 200
Bradshaw, Harriet Maria (*afterwards* Langley), 291
—, James, 291
—, Mrs (*formerly* Anna Maria Tree), 291
Braganza, House of, 97
Brand, John, 182, 183 n. 2
Brandsby, 4, 44
Brazil, 11 n. 43, 97
Brecon, 162 n. 1
Breda, 161
Brest, 91
Bright, Henry, 40
Brighton, 23, 176, 219, 230, 241, 242, 265, 309
Brinkburn, 45
Bristol, 40 n. 2
—, Marquesses of *see* Hervey
Broadlands, 2, 4, 11, 18, 28, 38, 58, 86, 103, 110, 113, 118, 119, 130, 131 n. 1, 147, 154, 165, 166, 186, 187, 220, 229, 232, 242, 274, 275, 276, 278, 303, 309, 310, 320; gardener, 294; housekeeper, 104 n. 1; hunting at, 106, 108, 116, 136–7, 140, 148; Huskisson at, 204 n. 1; P.'s honeymoon at, 271; P.'s management and improvements at, 72–3, 92, 108, 117; P.'s mother ill at, 29, 31–2, 33, 35,